STABILITY AND CHANGE IN MODERN PROPERTY LAW

This book examines the English and German version of the *numerus clausus* principle, which holds that there is a closed list of permitted property rights.

It challenges recent views that the principle renders property law inflexible and unable to accommodate social and economic changes. Relying on a novel approach combining property theory and comparative research of English and German law, it argues that the restrictions the principle imposes on the creation of new property types actually does accommodate social changes through a process of 'functional transformation' of the existing property rights.

This is a fascinating, unique study, that makes a rigorous, original contribution to property law theory.

International Studies in the Theory of Private Law: Volume 17

International Studies in the Theory of Private Law

This series of books, edited by a distinguished international team of legal scholars, aims to investigate the normative and theoretical foundations of the law governing relations between citizens. The context for such investigations of private law systems is set by important modern tendencies in systems of governance. The advent of the regulatory state marks the withdrawal of the state from direct control and management of social and economic activity, and the adoption instead of procedural regulation and co-regulatory strategies that promote the use of private law techniques of ordering and self-regulation in social and economic interactions between citizens. The tendency known as globalisation and the corresponding increases in cross-border trade produce the responses of transnational regulation of commerce and private governance regimes, and these new systems of governance challenge the hegemony of traditional national private law systems. Furthermore, these tendencies towards transnational governance regimes compel an interaction between different national legal traditions, with their differences in culture and philosophy as well as their differences based upon variations in market systems, which provokes questions not only about competing policy frameworks but also about nature and adequacy of different kinds of legal reasoning itself.

The series welcomes a diverse range of theoretical approaches in the examination of these issues including approaches using socio-legal methods, economics, critical theory, systems theory, regulation theory, and moral and political theory. With the aim of stimulating an international discussion of these issues, volumes will be published in Germany, France, and the United Kingdom in one of the three languages.

Volumes published with Hart Publishing, Oxford

1. David Campbell, Hugh Collins und John Wightman (eds), *Implicit Dimensions of Contract: Discrete, Relational and Network Contracts* (2003)
2. Christian Joerges, Inger-Johanne Sand and Gunther Teubner (eds), *Transnational Governance and Constitutionalism* (2004)
3. Oren Perez, *Ecological Sensitivity and Global Legal Pluralism: Rethinking the Trade and Environment Debate* (2004)
4. Harm Schepel, *The Constitution of Private Governance* (2004)
5. Nili Cohen and Ewan McKendrick, *Comparative Remedies for Breach of Contract* (2005)
6. Marc Amstutz and Gunther Teubner (eds), *Networks: Legal Issues of Multilateral Co-operation* (2010)

7. Gunther Teubner (edited and with an Introduction by Hugh Collins), *Networks as Connected Contracts* (2010)
8. Christian Joerges and Josef Falke (eds), *Karl Polanyi, Globalisation and the Potential of Law in Transnational Markets* (2011)
9. Poul F Kjaer, Gunther Teubner and Alberto Febbrajo (eds), *The Financial Crisis in Constitutional Perspective: The Dark Side of Functional Differentiation* (2011)
10. Jean Braucher, John Kidwell and William C Whitford (eds), *Revisiting the Contracts Scholarship of Stewart Macaulay: On the Empirical and the Lyrical* (2013)
11. Thomas Dietz, *Global Order Beyond Law: How Information and Communication Technologies Facilitate Relational Contracting in International Trade* (2014)
12. Anna Beckers, *Enforcing Corporate Social Responsibility Codes: On Global Self-Regulation and National Private Law* (2015)
13. Nahel Asfour, *Wrongful Enrichment: A Study in Comparative Law and Culture* (2017)
14. Pablo Marcello Baquero, *Networks of Collaborative Contracts for Innovation* (2020)
15. Christian Joerges, *Conflict and Transformation: Essays on European Law and Policy* (2022)
16. Marcus Moore, *Regulating Boilerplate: Resolving the Issues of Imposition and Unfairness in Standard Form Contracts* (2025)
17. Ernesto Vargas Weil, *Stability and Change in Modern Property Law: A Comparative Approach to the Principle of Numerus Clausus* (2025)

Volumes published in German by Nomos Verlagsgesellschaft, Baden-Baden

1. Peer Zumbansen, *Ordnungsmuster im modern Wohlfahrtsstaat: Lernerfahrungen zwischen Staat, Geseelschaft und Vertrag* (2000)
2. Dan Wielsch, *Freiheit und Funktion: Zur Struktur- und Theoriegeschichte des Rechts der Wirtschaftsgesellschaft* (2001)
3. Marc Amstutz, *Evolutorisches Wirtschaftsrecht: Vorstudien zum Recht und seiner Methode in den Diskurskollisionen der Marktgesellschaft* (2001)
4. Christian Joerges and Gunther Teubner, Gunther (eds), *Rechtsverfassungsrecht: Recht-Fertigungen zwischen Sozialtheorie und Privatrechtsdogmatik* (2003)
5. Gunther Teubner, *Netzwerk als Vertragsverbund: Virtuelle Unternehmen, Franchising, Just in Time in sozialwissenschaftlicher und juristischer Sicht* (2004)
6. Daniel Dédeyan, *Macht durch Zeichen: Rechtsprobleme der Kennzeichnung und Zertifikation* (2004)
7. Dietrich Claus Becker, *Von Namen und Nummern: Kollisionen unverträglicher Rechtsmassen im Interent* (2005)

8. Vagias Karavas, *Digitale Grundrechte: Elemente einer Verfassung des Informationsflusses im Intenet* (2007)
9. Peter Korth, *Dritthaftung von Ratingagenturen* (2009)
10. Cordula Heldt, *Baukooperation und Franchising als multilaterale Sonderverbindung. Vertragsnetzwerke – Parallelschuldverhältnisse – Personengesellschaften* (2010)
11. Jan Lüsing, *Die Pflichten aus culpa in contrahendo und positiver Vertragsverletzung* (§ 241 II BGB): *Über den hybriden Charakter der Schutzpflichten und zur Selbstbindung ohne Vertrag* (2010)
12. Moritz Renner, *Zwingendes transnationales Recht: Elemente einer Wirtschaftsverfassung jenseits des Staates* (2011)
13. Christoph Lüscher, *Zur Konzeptualisierung von Verbrauchervertragsrecht unter besonderer Berücksichtigung des schweizerischen und europäischen Verbrauchervertragsrechts. Eine Untersuchung im Schnittfeld von Vertragsrecht, Systemtheorie und Ökonomie* (2011)
14. Daniel Klösel, *Compliance-Richtlinien. Zum Funktionswandel des Zivilrechts im Gewährleistungsstaat* (2012)
15. Chunyi Qi, *Rechtstransfer in Chinas Produktionsregime? Zur Kontrolle der Allgemeinen Geschäftsbedingungen im deutschen und chinesischen Recht* (2013)

Stability and Change in Modern Property Law

A Comparative Approach to the Principle of Numerus Clausus

Ernesto Vargas Weil

•HART•

OXFORD • LONDON • NEW YORK • NEW DELHI • SYDNEY

HART PUBLISHING

Bloomsbury Publishing Plc

Kemp House, Chawley Park, Cumnor Hill, Oxford, OX2 9PH, UK

1385 Broadway, New York, NY 10018, USA

Bloomsbury Publishing Ireland Limited, 29 Earlsfort Terrace, Dublin 2, D02 AY28, Ireland

HART PUBLISHING, the Hart/Stag logo, BLOOMSBURY and the Diana logo are trademarks of Bloomsbury Publishing Plc

First published in Great Britain 2025

A catalogue record for this book is available from the British Library.

A catalogue record for this book is available from the Library of Congress.

Library of Congress Control Number: 2025936861

ISBN: HB: 978-1-50998-192-2
ePDF: 978-1-50998-194-6
ePub: 978-1-50998-193-9

Typeset by Compuscript Ltd, Shannon

www.bloomsbury.com

For product safety related questions contact productsafety@bloomsbury.com

To find out more about our authors and books visit www.hartpublishing.co.uk. Here you will find extracts, author information, details of forthcoming events and the option to sign up for our newsletters.

Para Stephanie

Preface

ONE OF THE initial experiences of any PhD student is meeting their supervisor. At these encounters you want to come across as someone knowledgeable, who will be capable of making a 'distinct and significant contribution to the subject' of your research. In hindsight, this was probably far from the first impression I gave my own supervisor. During our early meetings at Bentham House, I had to constantly interrupt him to ask (very) basic questions such as what is 'overreaching' or a 'restrictive covenant'. Now that I teach these same concepts to undergrad students, I realise how little I knew about the subject of my own research back then. For readers not familiar with English law, this is equivalent to a football player joining a Champions League team asking the manager what the 'offside rule' is, just before entering the pitch on their first game. Bearing that in mind, I am truly amazed that the central idea of my original PhD proposal remained at the centre of this project and ended up becoming the core of this book.

The roots of this project stretch back a decade to my LLM at New York University (NYU), where I first encountered its core themes: change in property law, comparative law and the principle of *numerus clausus*. Coming from Chile – a jurisdiction where the idea that property rights are strictly limited by the law is taken for granted – I was fascinated by the elaborate conceptual debate this same basic principle had triggered in common law scholarship in recent years. At the time I was a legal practitioner with a strong academic leaning, eager to prove to my sceptical colleagues that theory can shape the law in action. Thus, when I decided to apply for a PhD, it was only natural to pick up on these topics to develop a more general theory about how property law evolves over time.

Several factors were instrumental in turning those initial ideas into this book. The patience and support of my supervisor Professor Ben McFarlane – who, despite my initial 'legal naïveté', always believed in the potential of my project – was decisive. Equally important was the opportunity to teach undergrad students, first at University College London (UCL), and now at Cambridge. The challenge of guiding extremely bright students through the labyrinth of English land law and the arcane concepts of Equity forced me to familiarise myself with topics that are completely alien to my legal tradition, but foundational for the thesis of this book. Waking my dormant (and rusty) German was also key, as it allowed me to access primary sources and navigate the dense pages of the *Kommentare* to the German Civil Code (BGB). Although not a completely painless experience (to say the least!), this also gave me the chance to re-connect with a language I had not extensively used since high school. Finally, a decisive moment for this project was attending a workshop run by Hart in the Spring of 2023. There I met their editorial team, who encouraged me to submit a book proposal and guided me through the process.

This book is the outcome of more than six years of work. Its core stems from my PhD at UCL, much of which was written in a London basement flat throughout the Covid-19 lockdown, supplemented by additional research conducted during my time as Fellow in Law at Selwyn College, Cambridge. The final manuscript was finished in late 2024, largely while commuting back and forth between London and Cambridge. It is no surprise railways feature so prominently in it.

Ernesto Vargas Weil
London, December 2024

Acknowledgements

In writing this book I have acquired several personal and professional debts to family, friends, colleagues and institutions. I don't think I will ever be able to repay them, but I want – at least – to acknowledge them here. My main debt is with my wife, Stephanie Weber, who supported me with patience and love during my PhD and encouraged me to turn its outcome into a book. I also owe a great deal to Ben McFarlane, not only for accepting to supervise my doctorate at University College London (UCL), but also for having the kindness to carry on with me after leaving for Oxford and advising me on drafting the proposal to turn my thesis into a book. Without his guidance this monograph would not have been possible. I also want to express my gratitude to Henry Smith and Ian Willams for examining my PhD *viva* and for the feedback and input they generously provided to me afterwards. In addition, I want to acknowledge my life-long friend Rodrigo Kaufmann for commenting on many of my drafts and supporting me during the process of writing this book. I am also grateful to many people who, at different stages and in varying forms, kindly spent their time discussing my research with me or provided me with material essential for my project, even if some might not remember it. They include Álvaro Anríquez, Bram Akkermans, Cristián Banfi, Ioannis Bazinas, Alexandra Braun, Thomas Bullemore, Rodrigo Campero, Trevor Clark, Lorren Eldridge, Carsten Gerner-Beuerle, Birke Häcker, Martín Juarez, Maria Lee, Yael Lifshitz, Poorna Mysoor, Carlos Nóbrega, Luminita Olteanu, Janet O'Sullivan, Francesco Parisi, Michelle Rencoret, Kenneth Reid, Joe Sampson, Lionel Smith, Thomas Papadogiannis, Konstanze von Schütz and an anonymous reviewer of my book proposal. Finally, I also want to acknowledge UCL, Selwyn College, Cambridge and the Cambridge Faculty of Law for providing me with intellectually stimulating environments and financial support to develop my research, as well as my editors at Hart for encouraging me to send them a proposal and accepting to publish its outcome.

Contents

Abbreviations

ALR	*Allgemeines Landrecht für die Preußischen Staaten*, General State Laws for the Prussian States (Prussia, 1794)
BAG	*Bundesarbeitsgericht*, Federal Court for Labour Law (Germany)
BayObLG	*Bayerisches Oberstes Landesgericht*, Higher Regional Court of Bavaria (Germany)
BGB	*Bürgerliches Gesetzbuch*, Civil Code (Germany, 1900)
BGH	*Bundesgerichtshof*, Federal Court of Justice (Germany)
BVerfG	*Bundesverfassungsgericht*, Federal Constitutional Court (Germany)
BVerfGG	*Bundesverfassungsgerichtsgesetz*, Constitutional Court Act (Germany, 1951; reenacted, 1993)
CPR	Civil Procedure Rules 1998 (England & Wales, 1999)
GG	*Grundgesetz für die Bundesrepublik Deutschland*, Basic Law for the Federal Republic of Germany (1949)
EGBGB	*Einführungsgesetz zum Bürgerlichen Gesetzbuche*, Act for the Introdution of the German Civil Code (Germany, 1900; reenacted, 1994)
EI	*Erster Entwurf zum BGB*, First Draft of the BGB (1888, Germany)
ErbbauRG	*Erbbaurechtsgesetz*, Superficies Right Act (Germany, 2007)
ErbbauVO	*Erbbaurechtsverordnung*, Superficies Right Regulation (Germany, 1919)
HRA 1998	Human Rights Act 1998 (UK)
LPA 1925	Law of Property Act 1925 (England & Wales)
LP(MP)A 1989	Law of Property (Miscellaneous Provisions) Act 1989 (England & Wales)
LRA 1925	Land Registration Act 1925 (England & Wales)

LRA 2002	Land Registration Act 2002 (England & Wales)
IA 1986	Insolvency Act 1986 (UK)
InsO	*Insolvenzordnung*, Insolvency Regulation (Germany, 1999)
MietenWoG Bln	*Gesetz zur Mietenbegrenzung im Wohnungswesen in Berlin*, Rent Control Act for Berlin (Germany, 2020)
Motive	*Motive zu dem Entwürfe eines Bürgerlichen Gesetzbuches für das Deutsche Reich (1888)*, Explanatory notes to the First Draft of the BGB (Germany, 1888)
OLG München	*Oberlandesgericht München*, High Court of Munich (Germany)
RG	*Reichsgerricht*, Imperial Court (Germany)
KG Berlin	*Kammergericht*, Chamber Court of Berlin (Germany)
TierVerbG	*Gesetz zur Verbesserung der Rechtsstellung des Tieres im bürgerlichen Recht*, Act for the improvement of the position of animals in private law (Germany, 1990)
TOLATA 1996	Trusts of Land and Appointment of Trustees Act 1996 (England & Wales)
VG Berlin	*Verwaltungsgericht Berlin*, Berlin Administrative Court
WEG	*Wohnungseigentumsgesetz (Gesetz über das Wohnungseigentum und das Dauerwohnrecht)*, Flat Ownership Act (Germany, 1951; 2007)
WRV	*Weimarer Reichsverfassung*, Weimar Constitution (Germany, 1919)
ZGB	*Zivilgesetzbuch*, Civil Code (German Democratic Republic, 1976)
ZPO	*Zivilprozessordnung*, Civil Procedure Regulation (Germany, 1879; reenacted, 2005)
ZwVbG	*Zweckentfremdungsverbotsgesetz*, Misuse Prohibition Act (Germany, 2013)

List of Figures and Tables

Table of Cases

Australia

England & Wales

Germany

United States of America

Table of Legislation

England and Wales

European Union

France

Germany

United States of America

New Zealand

South Africa

Introduction: The Spell of Property

MODERN PROPERTY LAW has been said to be a '*belle endormie*'.[1] This claim is not without intuitive appeal: in many western jurisdictions, the core of contemporary property law has remained unchanged for more than a century. It is no coincidence that the publication of this book marks the first centenary of the English Law of Property Act 1925 (LPA 1925) and the 125th anniversary of the German Civil Code (*Bürgerliches Gesetzbuch*, BGB). For most of this time, private law scholars have mostly accepted the sleepy state of property law, shifting their attentions to the more dynamic law of obligations. However, worried by the problems of a changing world, some of them have been trying to revive property law once more. To break the spell, they have relied on a number of theories, but nothing seems to have worked. The reason for this is simple: property law is not really sleeping, but rather it is quietly and constantly adapting its old structures to new realities. This monograph explains how this works.

This is a book about property law and legal change. It seeks to answer a theoretical question from a comparative perspective: how can private law systems made of a limited number of seemingly static, rigid and formalistic property forms deal with an ever-changing reality? To answer this question, the book dissects the English and German versions of the principle of '*numerus clausus*' or 'closed list' and explores its impact on the ability of property law to adapt to new circumstances. Its main conclusion is that property law is as little bit like chess: it has a small number of pieces that can only move in strictly limited ways across the board, but by combining them in an intelligent manner, the actions of (good) players can give rise to an almost unlimited number of different games.

The principle of *numerus clausus* is one of the main doctrines that gives modern property law its petrified appearance. According to this principle, the number and content of property rights are strictly limited by the law. This creates two inbuilt sources of rigidity in contemporary legal systems: first, it denies private parties the freedom to create new property forms by contract, and second, it restricts the power of courts to develop the property system. That is

[1] Rémy Libchaber, 'La Recodification Du Droit Des Biens', *Le Code civil 1804–2004: Livre du Bicentenaire* (Dalloz and Litec 2004) 298; Sjef Van Erp, 'From "Classical" to Modern European Property Law?' in National and Kapodistrain University of Athens (ed), *Essays in Honour of Konstantinos D. Kerameus – Festschrift für Konstantinos D. Kerameus*, vol I (Sakkoulas and Bruylant 2009) 1519.

why those seeking to 'wake' property law so frequently argue in favour of relaxing this principle and expanding the list of property rights.

Contrary to these views, this book puts forward the argument that the *numerus clausus* principle provides modern property law with a doctrinal structure that is inherently capable of accommodating new realities without the need of constant reform. Borrowing elements from classical models on legal change in property law, as well as from recent scholarship on property theory, the core of this thesis holds that the restrictions that the *numerus clausus* imposes on the free creation of property rights ensure that property law retains a 'modular design'[2] that preserves the liberty of third parties to 'functionally transform'[3] the object of their property rights in the face of changing circumstances, without the need for constant state intervention. This basic model is supplemented with a number of doctrinal and institutional devices, including the 'forced relocation' of property modules by expropriations, their 'internal re-modularisation' through private law legislation, their 'external re-shaping' by public law regulation, and occasional 'legal scaffolding'[4] by courts.

To advance this view, the book combines elements from different disciplines into a single explanatory model. The most general of these frameworks comes from New Institutional Economics (NIE) and serves to outline the relation of property rights with a changing world. This model also provides the main 'themes' of the book: (i) the structure of property rights; (ii) the role of the state in property law; (iii) the ideology underpinning property law; and (iv) the impact of technological change on property law. The second framework comes from Anglo-American property theory. It consists in the distinction between two different and distinctive third-party effects of property rights: (i) their ability to bind successors in title ('successor liability') and (ii) their ability to bind pure strangers ('trespassory liability').[5] This distinction – also known to German scholarship[6] – provides the main analytical tool to explain how the *numerus clausus* ensures the 'functional transformability' of property rights by limiting their free delineation by private parties and courts. Finally, a loose version of the functional method of comparative law serves to structure the content of the different chapters and provide real-life examples that show how the 'functional transformation' of property rights works in practice.

The roadmap of the book has the following structure: chapter one accounts for the gaps and limitations of our current understanding on how property law evolves over time and presents the approach taken by the book to this problem.

[2] Borrowing from Henry E Smith, 'Property as the Law of Things' (2012) 125 *Harv L Rev* 1691.

[3] Using a concept from Karl Renner, *The Institutions of Private Law and their Social Functions* (Agnes Schwarzschild tr, Routledge and Kegan Paul 1976).

[4] The term comes from Alan Watson, *Society and Legal Change* (Temple UP 2001) 87, 91, 122.

[5] James Penner, 'Duty and Liability in Respect of Funds' in John Lowry and Mistelis Loukas (eds), *Commercial Law: Perspectives and Practice* (LexisNexis Butterworths 2006) 215.

[6] eg Heinz Hübner and Joachim Riegner, *Sachenrecht* (Translatia 1948) 7; Hermann Eichler, *Institutionen Des Sachenrechts*, vol 1 (Duncker & Humblot 1954) 6–7.

Chapter two looks at the English and German concepts of a property right, introducing the distinction between 'successor' and 'trespassory' liability. Chapter three accounts for the black-letter rules and practical applications that make up the German and English versions of the principle of *numerus clausus*. Chapter four addresses the 'institutional aspect' of the *numerus clausus*, that is, its effects on the distribution of law-making competences between legislators and courts. Chapter five discusses the function and justification of the principle of *numerus clausus*, arguing that this doctrine seeks not only to standardise property rights, but also to standardise them *in a precise manner*, namely, according to a modular design that preserves individual freedom to functionally transform the property. Chapters six and seven test this view through a contextual analysis of some leading English and German cases. The former addresses cases of trespassory liability, while the latter develops on successor lability. Chapter eight answers the question that motivates the book by presenting all the elements developed in the previous chapters in a framework informed by the contemporary 'form and substance' debate. Chapter nine briefly discusses the implications of the findings of this book for the future of the *numerus clausus* and for property law more generally.

1

Legal Change in Property Law

I. THE PARADOX OF PROPERTY LAW

IN A FREQUENTLY quoted passage, the American judge Benjamin Cardozo stated that the 'existing rules and principles can give us our present location, our bearings, our latitude and longitude. The inn that shelters us for the night is not the journey's end. The law, like the traveller, must be ready for the morrow. It must have a principle of growth'.[1] Common wisdom assumes that this requires the law to be flexible and in constant reform.[2] However, there is one area at the core of most modern legal systems that does not appear to live up to this maxim: across jurisdictions, contemporary property law is frequently described as static, rigid, formalistic and, above everything else, obsessed with certainty.[3]

Despite this, modern property systems seem to be largely capable of accommodating the demands created by a vast array of social, economic and technological changes, without undergoing noticeable transformations. How is this paradox possible? One conceivable answer is that there is no real paradox: either the description of property law as static and rigid is false or, conversely, it is accurate, and property law is failing to keep in step with social change. Another option is to embrace the paradox and defeat common wisdom by explaining how contemporary property systems *can* deal with changing social needs, while retaining their stability.

This book is an attempt to contribute to the solution of this paradox through the second path. It does so by addressing a legal doctrine that is central to the reputed rigidity of property law: the *numerus clausus* principle of property rights. To achieve this end, the book answers a narrow question from a broad perspective: how do English and German property law, two systems made of a limited number of standardised property types, accommodate social, economic and technological changes? This narrow focus allows for an ambitious approach that combines a rich contextual account of the English and German versions of the *numerus clausus* principle, with an interdisciplinary understanding of its interactions with changing realities.

[1] Benjamin N Cardozo, *The Growth of the Law* (Yale UP 1924) 19–20.
[2] eg see Raymond Wacks, *Law: A Very Short Introduction* (2nd edn, OUP 2015) 118.
[3] See section II.

Following this path, the book shows how two leading property systems subject to a *numerus clausus* principle[4] accommodate new social and economic realities without undergoing structural change, through a process of 'functional transformation' driven by individual freedom. Building on this, the book concludes that the *numerus clausus* principle enables modern English and German property law to deal with new realities by ensuring that they keep an 'internal' or 'doctrinal' structure that is inherently capable of accommodating external change without the need of constant reform.

The topic of this book is a relevant matter. Due to its decisive impact on social and economic development, property law – broadly understood as an arrangement for allocating scarce resources – is a constitutive element of any society.[5] The creation of new property rights and the modification of the existing ones are normally major social events that entail the potential of reshaping the fabric of society.[6] Therefore, both stagnation and change in property can be the source of potentially extreme and violent disagreement.[7] Understanding how a field of law so frequently described as static and rigid interacts with a changing external world is of paramount importance, not only for legal scholarship, but also for other social sciences and policy making.

The primary function of any property system is solving the aforementioned 'allocation problem' in a peaceful and predictable manner.[8] Experience has shown once and again that social, economic and technological developments always bring new challenges to this problem.[9] What makes law 'modern' is the acknowledgment that the rules and principles that solve such problem are not static, but a dynamic social reality that can be shaped to achieve different outcomes.[10] Thus, if modern property law hopes to succeed in fulfilling its most basic allocative function, it must have a way – a principle of growth – to guide these changes. However, what *is* and what *should be* the 'animating',[11] 'organisational'[12] or 'guiding'[13] principle of property law is highly contested,

[4] Although this is disputed in England. On this, see ch 3, section III.

[5] Ernst Nordtveit, 'The Changing Role of Property Rights: An Introduction' in Ernst Nordtveit (ed), *The Changing Role of Property Law: Rights, Values and Concepts* (Edward Elgar 2023) 1–3.

[6] Hanoch Dagan, *A Liberal Theory of Property Law* (CUP 2021) 158.

[7] eg, property has been said to be 'theft'. Famously, Pierre-Joseph Proudhon, *What Is Property? An Inquiry into the Principle of Right and of Government* (University of Virginia Library; NetLibrary 1996) 38.

[8] Jeremy Waldron, *The Right to Private Property* (OUP 1988) 31–32.

[9] Alexander Peukert, *Güterzuordnung als Rechtsprinzip* (Mohr Siebeck 2008) 1–2.

[10] Marietta Auer, *Der Privatrechtliche Diskurs der Moderne* (Mohr Siebeck 2014) 6, 12.

[11] Dagan (n 6) 2, 104–05, 120.

[12] Jill Robbie, 'Moving Beyond Boundaries in the Pursuit of Sustainable Property Law' in Bram Akkermans and Gijs van Dijck (eds), *Sustainability and Private Law* (Eleven International Publishers 2019) 59; Bram Akkermans, *Sustainable Property Law: Reckoning, Resilience, and Reform* (Eleven International Publishers 2022) 12.

[13] Richard Epstein, 'The Plasticity of Property: Legal Transitions between Property Regimes for Different Resources' in Ernst Nordtveit (ed), *The Changing Role of Property Law: Rights, Values and Concepts* (Edward Elgar 2023) 17.

and different views lead to different approaches as to how property law should deal with external change.

In the Anglo-American context, these positions have been schematically placed in two opposite camps: that of 'progressive' and 'information' theorists.[14] The former normally build on values such as the promotion of 'human flourishing',[15] 'personal autonomy'[16] or 'sustainability'.[17] They accept significant contextual decision-making, typically arguing in favour of relaxing the effects of the *numerus clausus* principle and expanding the list of property rights.[18] In contrast, 'information theorists' focus on aggregate efficiency. They are normally concerned with the control of the informational externalities that property rights impose on third parties, tending to be more cautious about expanding the list of property rights. In consequence, they prioritise rule-based enforcement of the owner's 'right to exclude' and are normally supportive of the *numerus clausus* principle and the legislative monopoly it entails.[19] Some of them identify the animating principle of property law (although not labelling it as such) with the idea of 'modularity'; that is, with a system made of individual units that can be efficiently combined in a variety forms, thanks to a design that contains complexity within 'modules' with limited external interfaces.[20]

In Germany, the animating principle of property law is normally equated with individual self-determination, as a manifestation of a more general commitment of private law to individual autonomy. However, unlike Anglo-American progressive approaches, in this view 'autonomy' is understood as absence of external interference. In turn, this principle finds its limit in the social duties that the German Constitution (*Grundgesetz*, GG) imposes on ownership and the general concretisation of its order of values.[21] However, the nature of the interaction of both forces is subject to discussion. In the traditionally dominant view, contemporary German private law – including property law – is viewed

[14] Jane Baron, 'The Contested Commitments of Property' (2010) 61 *Hastings LJ* 917; Rachael Walsh, *Property Rights and Social Justice: Progressive Property in Action* (CUP 2021) 2–3.

[15] Gregory Alexander and others, 'A Statement of Progressive Property' (2009) 94 *Cornell L Rev* 743.

[16] Dagan (n 6) 2, 104–05, 120.

[17] Robbie (n 12); Akkermans, *Sustainable Property Law* (n 12) 12.

[18] In the context of continental Europe, eg Akkermans, *Sustainable Property Law* (n 12) 15, 20–22. In the common law context, Dagan (n 6) 110–12.

[19] Especially, Thomas W Merrill and Henry E Smith, 'Optimal Standardization in the Law of Property: The Numerus Clausus Principle' (2000) 110 *Yale LJ* 1.

[20] Henry E Smith, 'Property as the Law of Things' (2012) 125 *Harv L Rev* 1691; Henry E Smith, 'Economics of Property Law' in Francesco Parisi (ed), *The Oxford Handbook of Law and Economics: Volume 2: Private Law and Commercial Law* (OUP 2017).

[21] Heinrich Honsell, 'Einleitung Zum BGB' in Dagmar Kaiser and Markus Stoffels (eds), *J. Staudingers Kommentar zum Bürgerlichen Gesetzbuch mit Einführungsgestetz und Nebengesetzen: Eckpfeiler Des Zivilrechts* (6th edn, Sellier & de Gruyter 2018) 13–14, 66–87; Fabian Klinck, 'Sachenrecht' in Dagmar Kaiser and Markus Stoffels (eds), *J. Staudingers Kommentar zum Bürgerlichen Gesetzbuch mit Einführungsgestetz und Nebengesetzen. Eckpfeiler Des Zivilrechts* (6th edn, Sellier & de Gruyter 2018) 1322–32; Fritz Baur, Jürgen Baur and Rolf Stürner, *Sachenrecht* (18th edn, Beck 2009) 1. For discussion, see ch 2, section II.B and ch 8, sections III and IV.

as underpinned by a normative shift from a 'formal' ethic of liberty towards a 'material' ethic of social responsibility, traceable to the early twentieth century.[22] However, this view has recently by subject to criticism by authors who, using property law as leading example, argue that private law is not explained by such a normative shift, but by an 'immanent tension' between enlightened individualism and illiberal counterforces that gives rise to a dialectic process.[23] Different to what happens in the Anglo-American discussion, none of these accounts make a strong normative claim about the *numerus clausus*. However, both share the view that the *numerus clausus* is a product of enlightened (classic) liberal property law that has, to some extent, been superseded by contemporary needs.

This book contradicts the absolute terms of the Anglo-American dichotomy, as well as the German 'normative shift' and 'dialectic' models. Instead, it advances an understanding of the *numerus clausus* principle that shows that modern property systems are 'animated' by a principle-based protection of individual autonomy, that combines some elements put forward by Anglo-American progressive theorists and German enlightened liberalism. However, this book shows that this 'organisational principle' actually leads contemporary property systems to adopt 'modular designs', as those proposed by information theorists. In this view, the *numerus clausus* promotes both individual autonomy and allocative efficiency by ensuring that property law maintains a carefully designed internal structure that allows the 'functional transformation'[24] of property rights over time, displacing most concerns of progressive theorists to public law and politics.[25]

This view runs against some common intuitions. As shown in this chapter, from a legal perspective, the static and rigid aura of property law stems from two sources. On the one hand, as a result of following a principle of *numerus clausus*, modern property systems leave very limited room for their adaptation through judicial creativity and party autonomy. In England, the LPA 1925 provides for a closed list of legal estates and interests and limits the permissible equitable interests to those existing before the coming into force of the Act.[26] In a similar fashion, in Germany, the Explanatory Notes of the First Draft of the BGB (*Motive*) explicitly hold that new types of property rights can only

[22] This view is generally attributed to legal historian Franz Wieacker and reflected in standard German textbooks. See Franz Wieacker, *Privatrechtsgeschichte der Neuzeit unter besonderer Berücksichtigung der deutschen Entwicklung* (3rd edn, Vandenhoeck & Ruprecht 2016); Karl Larenz and Manfred Wolf, *Allgemeiner Teil Des Bürgerlichen Rechts* (9th edn, Beck 2004) 29–37. For discussion, see ch 8.

[23] Especially, Auer (n 10). This view has now also reached new versions of leading textbooks, eg Jörg Neuner, *Allgemeiner Teil Des Bürgerlichen Rechts* (13th edn, Beck 2023) 94–117.

[24] Borrowing from Karl Renner's terminology. See n 31 and accompanying text.

[25] In the framework of this book, this includes the 'forced relocation' and 'regulatory re-shaping' of the existing property modules by the state, and the supply of new property rights by 'legislative re-modularisation'. For an overview, see ch 8, sections III and IV.

[26] LPA 1925, ss 1 and 4(1).

be created by legislation.[27] On the other hand, property law also seems to be highly resilient to pressures for legislative change. In England, the basic structure of modern land law – the LPA 1925 – has just turned 100 years old, while its terminology and structure evoke the feudal language of a far more distant past. In Germany, the core of property law – Book 3 of the BGB – has remained essentially untouched since 1900 and its conceptual roots can easily be traced to the pre-existing system of Roman law.[28]

Legal history warns us not to be misled by legal systems that appear to be stable and immutable: the law is in constant flux, although the rate of change varies from time to time as epochs of stagnation alternate with periods of rapid evolution.[29] Contemporary property regimes are probably less static and rigid than they appear at first sight, although the patterns of evolution might be harder to perceive than in other areas of private law. For example, Alan Watson argued that English land law survived over centuries with minor modification thanks to the use of a variety of 'legal scaffoldings' that hid the divergence between legal rules and social needs at the cost of adding complexity to the operation of the system.[30] Similarly, in the context of continental property law, Karl Renner maintained that the ownership rules of modern civil codes, originally developed to encompass the household as a unity of production and consumption, went through a radical 'functional transformation' (ie, a transformation in how they were *used* by private parties), as part of the development of modern capitalist societies, while the black letter rules contained in codes remained unchanged.[31]

Accounting for this process in contemporary legal systems is an open question.[32] In general, the 'patterns of legal change' are inadequately understood by legal scholarship and, as consequence, remain little studied and undertheorised.[33] In this context, the existing accounts of the evolutionary patterns of contemporary property law seem especially incomplete. Scholarship tends to focus on very abstract issues (eg history of ideas[34]), specific developments (eg transitional processes[35] or the role of expropriations[36]), extinct legal systems (eg legal history[37]) or systematising the law as it is at the present

[27] *Motive* 1–3.

[28] See ch 2, sections II and III.

[29] RC van Caenegem, *An Historical Introduction to Private Law* (CUP 1992) 181–82.

[30] Alan Watson, *Society and Legal Change* (Temple UP 2001) 47–58, 87–97, 122, 131–32.

[31] Karl Renner, *The Institutions of Private Law and their Social Functions* (Agnes Schwarzschild tr, Routledge and Kegan Paul 1976).

[32] See Epstein, 'The Plasticity of Property' (n 13) 15, 17.

[33] Paul Mitchell, 'Patterns of Legal Change' (2012) 65 *Current Legal Problems* 177, 177.

[34] eg Auer (n 10); Anna Di Robilant, *The Making of Modern Property Law: Reinventing Roman Law in Europe and Its Peripheries* (CUP 2023).

[35] eg Amnon Lehavi, 'Land Law in the Age of Globalization and Land Grabbing' in Michele Graziadei and Lionel Smith (eds), *Comparative Property Law: Global Perspectives* (Edward Elgar 2017) 295–97.

[36] eg Dagan (n 6) 210–42.

[37] eg John Baker, *Introduction to English Legal History* (5th edn, OUP 2019) 241–337; Wieacker (n 22); van Caenegem (n 29).

(eg doctrinal accounts[38]). Other legal disciplines that could offer useful analytical tools to account for legal change in this field, including comparative law, sociology of law, and law and economics, have traditionally not been very interested in property law.[39] In contrast, starting with the seminal work of Harold Demsetz,[40] the evolution of property rights has attracted a great deal of attention in New Institutional Economics (NIE). However, due to their very nature, these approaches have not been specially concerned with the concrete doctrinal forms that property rights adopt in practice. Hence, even if it might seem clear that modern property law can somehow adapt to new realties, we do not know *how* it does so.

Over the last years, a growing number of studies have highlighted the need of providing more attention to the impact of the passage of time in property law[41] and the challenges that new social and economic realities pose to existing property rights.[42] As a consequence, the interface of property law with external change has been thematised in a variety of contexts that, however, remain fragmented and isolated. This book puts forward the argument that the ability of comparative law to bring different legal and extra-legal disciplines together and shed light on the 'living problems that lurk behind [the] technical facades [of the law]'[43] can provide a novel framework to analyse this material and thus advance towards finding a solution for the paradox of property law.[44] The outcome is a new version of Renner's 'functional transformation', underpinned by contemporary property theory and comparative research.

II. THE STATIC AURA OF PROPERTY LAW

A. Technocratic Conservatism

Change in private law is a topic on the rise.[45] For example, the Obligations VIII conference held in 2016 had 'Revolution and Evolution in Private Law' as its central topic. Summarising the papers presented, Sarah Worthington suggested

[38] See Martin Dixon, 'A Doctrinal Approach to Property Law Scholarship: Who Cares and Why?' in Susan Bright and Sarah Blandy (eds), *Researching Property Law* (Palgrave 2016) 6.

[39] See section II.

[40] Harold Demsetz, 'Toward a Theory of Property Rights' (1967) 57 *Am Econ Rev* 347.

[41] See Sarah Blandy, Susan Bright and Sarah Nield, 'The Dynamics of Enduring Property Relationships in Land' (2018) 81 *MLR* 85, 88; Sjef van Erp, 'Comparative Property Law' in Mathias Reimann and Reinhard Zimmermann (eds), *The Oxford Handbook of Comparative Law* (2nd edn, OUP 2019) 1050–53, 1056; Peukert (n 9) 1–7; Dagan (n 6) 210; Epstein, 'The Plasticity of Property' (n 13) 17.

[42] eg Nordtveit (n 5) 1; Akkermans, *Sustainable Property Law* (n 12); Epstein, 'The Plasticity of Property' (n 13) 15.

[43] Konrad Zweigert and Hein Kötz, *An Introduction to Comparative Law* (Tony Weir tr, 3rd edn, OUP 1998) 4.

[44] See section IV.

[45] See nn 41 and 42.

that legal change in private law has three essential components: creative lawyers who push the boundaries of the law with new arguments, judges sympathetic to such claims who are willing to develop inventive responses to them, and imaginative scholars who can depict these developments in newly conceived frameworks.[46] On a common view, property law seems to lack all these elements: according to recent comparative research, across jurisdictions, property law is immersed in a mentality of 'technocratic conservatism' that tends to preserve the *status quo* and accepts changes only when they become unavoidable.[47] As highlighted in the Introduction to this book, using the eloquent words of a French scholar, property law has even been said to have entered a stage of '*belle endormie*'.[48]

In England, this image seems nowhere more apparent than in land law. In the whole history of English law, few reforms (if any) have been so often proposed and failed as reforms to simplify the transfer of land. Despite having been seen as a defective system by the commissioners of the 1829–33 period, significant progress in this field was only achieved by the end of the nineteenth century and was not consolidated until the LRA 1925.[49] Similar cases can also be found in contemporary England. In the early 2000s the Law Commission described the law of escheat as 'indefensible' and in need of 'fundamental reform', and expressed its desire to review feudal land law. However, in 2011 the reform of feudal law was left out the programme of the Law Commission, following the argument that greater public benefit would result from other projects.[50] More recently, the many proposals of the Law Commission to introduce positive covenants[51] have not led to legislative reform.

English courts do not seem generally more eager to innovate. For example, in *Prudential Assurance Co Ltd v London Residuary Body*, one of the leading cases on the English law of leases, the House of Lords refused to change the rule requiring leases to be subject to a certain term from the outset – despite holding it to be an 'ancient and technical' rule that produces a 'bizarre outcome' and has no 'satisfactory rationale' nor 'useful purpose' – as any judicial change

[46] Sarah Worthington, 'Revolution and Evolution in Private Law' in Sarah Worthington, Andrew Robertson and Graham Virgo (eds), *Revolution and Evolution in Private Law* (Hart 2018) 4.

[47] van Erp, 'Comparative Property Law' (n 41) 1037.

[48] Rémy Libchaber, 'La Recodification Du Droit Des Biens', *Le Code civil 1804–2004: Livre du Bicentenaire* (Dalloz and Litec 2004) 298; Sjef van Erp, 'From "Classical" to Modern European Property Law?' in National and Kapodistrain University of Athens (ed), *Essays in Honour of Konstantinos D. Kerameus – Festschrift für Konstantinos D. Kerameus*, vol I (Sakkoulas and Bruylant 2009) 1519.

[49] AH Manchester, *A Modern Legal History of England and Wales, 1750–1950* (Butterworth 1980) 303, 306, 310, 326. On change in English land law, also see Watson, *Society and Legal Change* (n 30) 47–60.

[50] Ian Williams, 'The Certainty of Term Requirement in Leases: Nothing Lasts Forever' (2015) 74 *CLJ* 592, 606–07, especially at fn 86.

[51] Law Commission, *Making Land Work: Easements, Covenants and Profits à Prendre* (Law Com No 327, 2011). On this proposal, Elizabeth Cooke, *Land Law* (2nd edn, OUP 2012) 236–42.

'might upset long established titles'.[52] In turn, when courts have departed from the rigid doctrines of property law to satisfy practical outcomes,[53] scholars have also criticised them for incurring in 'remedialism'.[54] Even when Parliament has created new property types to deal with new social problems, practising lawyers frequently prefer to stick to the old property forms they already know, as revealed by the negligible practical relevance of the commonhold, which was introduced in 2002.[55] This situation is in strong contrast with the English law of obligations. In modern times, contract law is said to have experienced the rise, fall and revival of freedom of contracts,[56] and some of its fundamental dogmas have been wiped-out by case law[57] and legislation;[58] while tort law[59] and unjust enrichment[60] have also experienced similar paradigm shifts.

Despite having a different structure, German private law reveals a surprisingly similar picture. Descriptions of property law as static, rigid or conservative are ubiquitous in mainstream doctrine,[61] especially when compared to the law of obligations.[62] According to one of these accounts, the core structure of property law is a closed system based on a set of principles that have remained unchanged since the entering into force of the BGB in 1900.[63] Enactment of new property rules is rare and the interpretation of the existing ones is highly conservative, as the central questions of property law have been mostly settled for many years. Accordingly, the scope of the topics covered by judicial decisions of higher tribunals is narrow, there is little space for new solutions and questions presented by case law and the opinions of scholars change rarely and slowly.[64] Indeed,

[52] *Prudential Assurance Co Ltd v London Residuary Body* [1992] 3 WLR 279, 287.

[53] eg *Manchester Airport plc v Dutton and others* [2000] QB 1333, CA, discussed in ch 6, section II.B.

[54] eg William Swadling, 'Opening the Numerus Clausus' (2000) 116 *LQR* 354, criticising the majority opinion in *Dutton*.

[55] See Lu Xu, 'Commonhold Developments in Practice' in Warren Barr (ed), *Modern Studies in Property Law*, vol 8 (Hart 2015) 332, 334–35; Law Commission, *Reinvigorating Commonhold: The Alternative to Leasehold Ownership* (Law Com No 394, 2020).

[56] PS Atiyah, *The Rise and Fall of Freedom of Contract* (Clarendon Press 2003) 571–680.

[57] eg *Central London Property Trust Ltd v High Trees House Ltd* [1947] KB 130, on promissory estoppel.

[58] eg Contracts (Rights of Third Parties) Act 1999, on privity of contracts.

[59] eg *Donoghue v Stevenson* [1932] AC 562 and *Robinson v CC West Yorkshire Police* [2018] UKSC 4, on duty of care.

[60] eg *Lipkin Gorman v Karpnale Ltd* [1991] 2 AC 548, on mistaken payment of money.

[61] eg Christian Grüneber, 'Einleitung', *Palandt: Bürgerlicher Gesetzbuch mit Nebengesetzten* (80th edn, Beck 2021) 4; Honsell (n 21) 19; Reinhard Gaier, 'Einleitung Zum Sachenrecht' in Franz Jürgen Säcker and others (eds), *Münchner Kommentar zum BGB* (7th edn, Beck 2017) [24]; Friedrich Quack, *Münchener Kommentar zum Bürgerlichen Gesetzbuch. Sachenrecht*, vol 6 (Friedrich Quack ed, 3rd edn, Beck 1997) 17.

[62] eg Jan Wilhelm, *Sachenrecht* (5th edn, De Gruyter 2016) 5; Manfred Wolf, 'Beständigkeit und Wandel im Sachenrecht' [1987] *NJW* 2647, 2647.

[63] Hans Hermann Seiler, 'Einleitung Zum Sachenrecht' in Elmar Bund and others (eds), *J. von Staudingers Kommentar zum Bürgerlichen Gesetzbuch mit Einführungsgesetz und Nebengesetzen* (Sellier & de Gruyter 2007) 38.

[64] Quack (n 61) 17–18.

German property law has even been mocked as 'millimetre law'.[65] German scholars seem also frequently hostile to reforms.[66] For example, a leading *Kommentar* to the BGB attributes the infrequent changes in property law to the high quality of the BGB, openly criticising subsequent legislation that departs from its basic principles for not measuring up to such quality.[67] It is tempting to attribute this static image to the codified nature of German private law, but this would be a mistake. Parts of the BGB dealing with family and succession law have been subject to heavy transformations since the 1950s,[68] while the 2002 Act for the Modernisation of the Law of Obligations[69] brought into the code several matters covered by special statutes, as well as some paradigm-shifting doctrines developed *praeter legem* by courts over the previous 100 years.[70]

B. The Place of the *Numerus Clausus*

The aura of property law as a petrified part of modern legal systems seems to result from three linked but different approaches. At a purely descriptive level, its static nature has been attributed to some features inherent to the structure of property law. For example, sociology of law has pointed to the historically great effort involved in the reform of property systems and the lack of incentive for legislative bodies to incur the political costs of engaging in such reforms.[71] Economic analysis has formalised a similar idea, arguing that the inertia of property law is explained by its network effects and path dependence. First, property rights are subject to path dependence due to the high fixed costs involved in setting up the system. Second, property systems are subject to 'network effects', meaning that they become more valuable the more people use them (like the internet or phones), which implies that they become harder to change the more they expand. Thus, once a particular *style* of property rights is established by organised actors capable of overcoming collective action problems and paying the initial fixed costs, and the use of this system grows over time, the style of the system becomes increasingly hard to change. In the common law such style comes from the introduction of the feudal system in England after the Norman conquest, while in the civil law it comes from Roman law, as received and systematised by the nineteenth century civil codes of France and Germany.[72]

[65] Rolf Stürner, 'Dienstbarkeit Heute' (1994) 194 AcP 265, 265.
[66] Seiler (n 63) 38.
[67] Quack (n 61) 18.
[68] Larenz and Wolf (n 22) 39–41; Neuner (n 23) 90–91.
[69] *Gesetz zur Modernisierung des Schuldrechtrechts vom 26 November 2001* (BGBl I 2001 S 3138).
[70] For example, the enactment of the doctrine of the fall of the basis of the transaction in § 313 BGB. On this topic, Larenz and Wolf (n 22) 42; Reinhard Zimmermann, *The New German Law of Obligations: Historical and Comparative Perspectives* (OUP 2005) 1–4, 30–34.
[71] Notably, Watson, *Society and Legal Change* (n 30) 115, 118, 131–32.
[72] Yun-chien Chang and Henry Smith, 'An Economic Analysis of Civil versus Common Law Property' (2012) 88 *Notre Dame L Rev* 1; Yun-chien Chang and Henry E Smith, 'Structure and Style

This logic is replicated on a more granular level. For example, once the current land registration book was introduced in Germany, structural reform of this system has been said to be no longer feasible in practice.[73]

The second approach is essentially normative. It holds that the strong commitment of property law with keeping social peace[74] and creating legal certainty[75] has led it to become a rather petrified legal field. As shown in chapter two, across jurisdictions, the most characteristic doctrinal feature of property rights is their ability to impose duties or liabilities on third parties. Because property rights affect people that have not agreed to be bound by them, it is frequently held that such rights need to be subject to a high level of certainty and predictability.[76] This view is reinforced by policy arguments that stress that property rights must be stable in order to provide owners with expectations that allow them to plan, invest and develop information about the relevant asset.[77] In England, this is well reflected in a relatively recent opinion by Lord Millet stating that 'property rights are determined by fixed rules and settled principles. They are not discretionary. They do not depend upon ideas of what is "fair, just and reasonable". Such concepts which in reality mask decisions of legal policy have no place in property'.[78] Thus, to a large extent, property law is not only perceived as static, but also as an area of law that *ought to be* static in order to achieve social peace and economic efficiency. To meet this end, civilian and common law scholars alike tend to assume that property law must be highly rigid, technical, detailed and largely mandatory in character, leaving little space for private autonomy.[79] As a result, in both England[80] and Germany[81] scholars highlight that the 'boring' nature of property should be seen as a compliment, as it reflects its capability to solve extremely relevant social disputes in a dispassionate form. If this is true, the success of property law in channelling this tension cannot be explained by chance: there must be a guiding principle that explains how property systems are organised in both static and dynamic terms.[82] This book seeks to uncover this principle.

in Comparative Property Law' in Theodore Eisenberg and Giovanni B Ramello (eds), *Comparative Law and Economics* (Edward Elgar 2016).

[73] Honsell (n 21) 19.

[74] eg Ugo Mattei, *Basic Principles of Property Law: A Comparative Legal and Economic Introduction* (Greenwood 2000) 30.

[75] eg van Erp, 'Comparative Property Law' (n 41) 1032.

[76] eg J Michael Milo, 'Property and Real Rights' in Jan M Smits (ed), *Elgar Encyclopedia of Comparative Law* (2nd edn, Edward Elgar 2012) 726; van Erp, 'Comparative Property Law' (n 41) 1032; Smith, 'Economics of Property Law' (n 20) 170; Epstein, 'The Plasticity of Property' (n 13) 17; Christian von Bar, *The Foundations of Property Law* (OUP 2023) 69–70, 76.

[77] Smith, 'Economics of Property Law' (n 20) 150. In this same line, AM Honoré, 'Rights of Exclusion and Immunities Against Divesting' (1959) 34 *Tul L Rev* 453, 468; Dixon (n 38) 7.

[78] *Foskett v McKeown* [2001] 1 AC 102, 127.

[79] van Erp, 'Comparative Property Law' (n 41) 1032; Milo (n 76) 726. For a different view, Dagan (n 6).

[80] eg Ben McFarlane, *The Structure of Property Law* (Hart 2008) 4.

[81] eg Quack (n 61) 18.

[82] Epstein, 'The Plasticity of Property' (n 13) 17.

To achieve this, the core of this book focuses on a third approach: the legal doctrine most modern property systems are said to rely upon to provide third parties with predictability and clarity regarding the property interests that might affect them, namely, the principle of *numerus clausus* of property rights.[83] Across jurisdictions, this doctrine is the most recurrent explanation for the rigid and static nature of property law.[84] Under this principle, as discussed extensively in chapter three, the number and content of property rights are limited by the law, and only rights that conform to such pre-existing list are enforced as property rights by courts. In this way, the principle of *numerus clausus* creates two in-built sources of rigidity in modern property systems: first, it denies private parties the freedom to create new property forms by contract; and, second, it restricts the power of courts to develop the property system.[85] This is said to create a self-evident pressure on modern legal systems:[86] the lower the number of property rights, the greater the need for reforms;[87] the lower the number of available options, the less autonomy parties enjoy.[88] In turn, as examined in chapter four, by limiting courts to enforcing an existing list of recognised property interests, at least formally, the principle places the whole authority to adapt property law to new realities within the competence sphere of legislators,[89] who for various reasons, have not always been regarded as especially interested in developing private law.[90] As a consequence the *numerus clausus* has come under increasing pressure in several jurisdictions,[91] with scholars working in a variety of contexts arguing in favour of making the principle more flexible, for example, by adopting a

[83] See Bar (n 76) 69–70, 76; Peter Birks, 'Five Keys to Land Law' in Susan Bright and John Dewar (eds), *Land Law: Themes and Perspectives* (OUP 1998) 475.

[84] This link has been suggested countless times over the last decades in a variety of forms and contexts. From a comparative perspective, Milo (n 76) 726; van Erp, 'Comparative Property Law' (n 41) 1042–44; Bram Akkermans, 'The Numerus Clausus of Property Rights' in Michele Graziadei and Lionel Smith (eds), *Comparative Property Law: Global Perspectives* (Edward Elgar 2017) 100–01, 115–17; Michael Weir, 'Pushing the Envelope of Proprietary Interests: The Nadir of the Numerus Clausus Principle?' (2015) 39 *Melbourne U L Rev* 651. In property theory, Dagan (n 6) 9, 110–11. In English law, Worthington (n 46) 5; Chris Bevan, 'The Doctrine of Benefit and Burden: Reforming the Law of Covenants and the Numerus Clausus "Problem"' (2018) 77 *CLJ* 72, 90. In German law, Larenz and Wolf (n 22) 252–53; Wilhelm (n 62) 10–11; Peukert (n 9) 7–13; with less clarity, Neuner (n 23) 245.

[85] Merrill and Smith, 'Optimal Standardization in the Law of Property' (n 19) 58; McFarlane, 'The Numerus Clausus Principle and Covenants Relating to Land' in Susan Bright (ed), *Modern Studies in Property Law*, vol 6 (Hart 2011) 309; Akkermans, 'The Numerus Clausus of Property Rights' (n 84) 102.

[86] eg Birks (n 83) 475.

[87] Christian von Bar, 'The Numerus Clausus of Property Rights: A European Principle?' in Louise Gullifer and Stefan Vogenauer (eds), *English and European Perspectives on Contract and Commercial Law: Essays in Honour of Hugh Beale* (Hart 2014) 454; Bar (n 76) 78–79.

[88] Dagan (n 6) ch 4.

[89] Merrill and Smith, "Optimal Standardization in the Law of Property' (n 19) 58.

[90] Alan Watson, 'From Legal Transplants to Legal Formants' (1995) 43 *Am J Comp L* 469, 469; Watson, *Society and Legal Change* (n 30) 115–18, 133.

[91] Bar (n 76) 70; Birks (n 83) 475.

'*numerus quasi-clausus*',[92] having an '*ex post numerus clausus*',[93] providing for a 'residual category' that allows parties to create new property rights,[94] or even, getting rid of the restrictions on the free delineation of property rights altogether.[95] This book argues against these views by showing how the *numerus clausus* allows property law to adapt to new realities in practice.

C. Pressure for Change

As shown in this book, the previous account of property law as static and rigid is only a half-truth. As acknowledged in a variety of contexts, property law is continually interacting with changing social and economic circumstances,[96] with practising and academic lawyers putting constant pressure on the conceptual categories of property law to evolve.[97] It is tempting to see these developments as part of socio-political events that are alien to the core of the well-established domestic property systems of the West, typically transitional processes (eg ex-Soviet states, China, South Africa),[98] or as confined to narrow problems that do not shake the edifice of domestic property law, like the recognition of property rights in a limited number of new objects (eg human body parts, pecuniary claims, public law licences, digital assets),[99] or EU law.[100] However, this is only the tip of the iceberg. Across jurisdictions, new challenges, spanning from climate change to market integration, have been said to make a change of mentality in this field not only imminent, but also unavoidable.[101]

This trend is putting pressure on the core of contemporary property system. For example, in the common law tradition, proponents of a 'liberal theory of

[92] Sjef van Erp, 'A Numerus Quasi-Clausus of Property Rights as a Constitutive Element of a Future European Property Law' (2003) 7 *Electronic J Comp Law*.

[93] Bram Akkermans, *The Principle of Numerus Clausus in European Property Law* (Intersentia 2008).

[94] Dagan (n 6) 110–12; Hanoch Dagan and Irit Samet, 'Express Trust: The Dark Horse of the Liberal Property Regime', *Philosophical Foundations of the Law of Express Trusts* (OUP 2023) 148–49.

[95] Richard A Epstein, 'Why Restrain Alienation?' (1985) 85 *Colum L Rev* 970; Richard A Epstein, 'Notice and Freedom of Contract in the Law of Servitudes' (1981) 55 *S Cal L Rev* 1353.

[96] For modern examples in England, although prior to the 1950s, William Cornish and others, *Law and Society in England 1750–1950* (2nd edn, Hart 2019) 168–93; for Germany, Werner Schubert, 'Die Diskussion über eine Reform des Rechts der Mobiliarsicherheiten in der Späten Kaiserzeit und in der Weimarer Zeit' (1990) 107 *ZRG Germ Abt* 132; for America, Epstein, 'The Plasticity of Property' (n 13). For a current example regarding the use of servitudes to create 'conservation easements' in Germany and England, Inga Racinska and Siim Vahtrus, 'The Use of Conservation Easements in the European Union' (NABU Bundesverband 2018) 60, 99.

[97] JE Penner, *The Idea of Property in Law* (OUP 1997) 35.

[98] eg Lehavi (n 35) 295–97.

[99] eg Sabrina Praduroux, 'Objects of Property: Old and New' in Michele Graziadei and Lionel Smith (eds), *Comparative Property Law: Global Perspectives* (Edward Elgar 2017) 57–67.

[100] eg Akkermans, 'The Numerus Clausus of Property Rights' (n 84) 116.

[101] van Erp, 'A Numerus Quasi-Clausus of Property Rights as a Constitutive Element of a Future European Property Law' (n 92) 1037.

property' and other similar views call for more forms of collective ownership in contexts such as housing and the workplace,[102] while in continental Europe, progressive scholars concerned with climate change and inequality argue for new forms of 'resilient' property underpinned by a paradigm-shift away from welfare maximisation and towards sustainability.[103] However, proposals for reform are not limited to progressive streams. For example, some information theorists have recently suggested that relaxing the constrains that many legal systems impose on the creation of future interest could help aging societies to deal with challenges brought about by the demographic transition.[104]

In line with these views, this book shows that even a superficial approach to English and German domestic property law reveals constant activity aiming to keep property law in step with society. Despite being described as 'without doubt the greatest single monument of legal wisdom, industry and ingenuity which a statute book can display',[105] the scheme established by the 1922–25 English land law legislation has experienced a number of relevant reforms impacting areas such as the family home,[106] formalities,[107] trusts of land[108] and registration,[109] while, in a number of cases, English courts have taken flexible and innovative approaches to achieve doctrinal outcomes that better fit new social realties.[110] German property law has also been impacted by a variety of legal reforms, most of which have taken place outside Book 3 of the BGB. These include legislation providing for new types of property rights in land[111] and excluding animals from being objects of property (see § 90a BGB).[112] Modern case law has also reshaped the property concepts of the BGB 'from outside'. On the one hand, civil courts have developed new legal interests that strongly resemble property rights,[113] while, on the other, the BVerfG has re-interpreted the BGB's concept of ownership in light of the social duties the GG imposes on property rights

[102] eg Dagan (n 6) 84–87, 107–10.

[103] eg Akkermans, *Sustainable Property Law* (n 12) 21–22.

[104] Yun-chien Chang, *Property Law: Comparative, Empirical and Economic Analyses* (CUP 2023) 96.

[105] Manchester (n 49) 324–25, quoting RE Megarry and HWR Wade, *The Law of Real Property* (4th edn) at 1157.

[106] Matrimonial Homes Act 1967.

[107] Law of Property (Miscellaneous Provisions) Act 1989 (LP(MP)A 1989).

[108] Trusts of Land and Appointment of Trustees Act 1996 (TOLATA 1996).

[109] Land Registration Act 2002 (LRA 2002).

[110] For example, the development of the common intention constructive trust since the 1970s, see Cooke (n 51) 87–96. Closer to the argument of this book, see the development of 'recreational easements' discussed in ch 3, section III.C and ch 7, section II.A.

[111] See Superficies Right Regulation (*Erbbaurechtsverordnung*, ErbbauVO), Superficies Right Act (*Erbbaurechtsgesetz*, ErbbauRG), WEG and §1192 (1a) BGB.

[112] Introduced by the Act for the improvement of the position of animals in private law (*Gesetz zur Verbesserung der Rechtsstellung des Tieres im bürgerlichen Recht*, TierVerbG).

[113] Especially, *Sicherheitstum* (security ownership) and *Antwartschaftsrecht des Käufer* (anticipation right of buyers). For discussion, ch 3, section II and ch 7, section III.

(*Sozialpflichtigkeit des Eigentums*),[114] facilitating new environmental, artistic and animal protection legislation.[115]

This overview leaves a conflicting image of legal change in property law. On the one hand, property law is recurringly described as rigid and static; but, on the other, there is also plenty of evidence of constant developments in this field. Solving the paradox of legal change in property law requires placing both strands in a single conceptual framework that can account for stability and change in property law at once. As shown in the next section, for different reasons, the existing theories dealing with the evolutionary patterns of property law are not able to do this.

III. SEARCHING FOR EVOLUTIONARY PATTERNS

A. Existing Models

To a relevant extent, the insufficient understanding of the dynamic dimensions of property law can be explained by the rigid aura of this field. In contrast to the law of obligations, which is perceived as a dynamic area of private law, property law is frequently regarded as far less exciting.[116] However, different disciplines also have other reasons for having neglected this topic. Doctrinal analysis is primarily devoted to providing a systematic understanding of the law as it is in a given place and time,[117] making it inherently committed to explain property law from a static perspective. By contrast, legal history tends to focus on historical legal systems and its structural change over much longer time spans;[118] and when historical arguments are made in actual legal disputes, they are frequently used to justify property law as it currently is,[119] not to explain how it changes.[120] In turn, in the realm of Anglo-American property theory, progressive approaches tend to be theories *for* legal change rather than *of* legal change,[121] while information theorist have an abstract style that is normally detached from social and economic contingency. In a similar vein, theories recently advanced in German

[114] Especially with the 1981 'Wet Gravel Case' (*Nassauskiesungsbeschluss*), BVerfGE 58, 300. In general, Seiler (n 63) 49–50. For details, ch 2, section II.B.

[115] Quack (n 61) 3, 19. The same with protected tenancies, see ch 8.

[116] van Erp, 'Comparative Property Law' (n 41) 1033. Also see nn 80 and 81 and accompanying text.

[117] Dixon (n 38) 6.

[118] For example, see Baker (n 37) 241–337; Wieacker (n 22); van Caenegem (n 29). However, there are also efforts of legal historians to explain the general patterns of legal change, eg Mitchell (n 33).

[119] Alfred L Brophy, 'Doing Things with Legal History: Historical Analysis in Property Law' in Markus D Dubber and Christopher Tomlins (eds), *The Oxford Handbook of Legal History* (OUP 2018) 924, 925–32, 940–41. Although historic arguments are occasionally used to achieve change, eg see *Berrisford v Mexfield Housing Co-operative Ltd* [2011] UKSC 52, [2012] 1 AC 955.

[120] See Mitchell (n 13) 177–78.

[121] Borrowing wording from Lorna Fox O'Mahony and Marc Roark, *Squatting and the State: Resilient Property in an Age of Crisis* (CUP 2022) 8.

private law[122] are rooted in an abstract dialectic worldview that is hard to pin down and extrapolate to other contexts and, in any case, are subject to criticism of its own. Finally, sociology of law has been mostly interested in the opposite direction of influence: how the law can change society – assuming as obvious that legal change reflects wider social developments.[123] In this context, despite their analytical value, the few attempts to account for the impact of social and economic change in property law from a systematic perspective seem outdated: Watson's interpretation ends with the English land law reform of 1922–25 and explicitly excludes continental codifications and other contemporary efforts to rationalise the law;[124] while Renner's book,[125] originally written in 1904 and updated in 1929, has a classic Marxist framework that leads him to concentrate on how property rights were used in the development of a capitalist economy during the nineteenth century. More recent approaches to the interaction of property law and society, although valuable, tend to be limited to specific problems (eg, squatting in the residential context),[126] and do not really offer a new encompassing conceptual framework.[127]

A notable effect of the relatively scarce theoretical interest in property law is that comparative law and law and economics, which are for some[128] the two most relevant attempts to understand the law developed during the twentieth century, mainly focused on tort and contract law and, until recently, remained, in comparison, uninterested in property law.[129] This has deprived this field of some key insights on the dynamic nature of contemporary legal systems, including the theories of efficient evolution of the common law,[130] legal transplants[131] and legal formants.[132] However, there are deeper reasons explaining the underdeveloped status of property law in both fields. In comparative

[122] Especially, Auer (n 10).

[123] Roger Cotterrell, *The Sociology of Law: An Introduction* (2nd edn, OUP 1992) 45, 49. A notable exception to this, although not dealing with private law, is Philippe Nonet and Philip Selznick, *Law and Society in Transition: Toward Responsive Law* (2nd edn, Transaction Publishers 2001), discussed in ch 4, section IV.B, ch 5, section IV.B and ch 8, section IV.A.

[124] Watson, *Society and Legal Change* (n 30) 48, 55, 136. The last edition of William Cornish's book does not leave us much further, as it ends in 1950, see Cornish and others (n 96).

[125] Renner (n 31).

[126] See Fox O'Mahony and Roark (n 121) 6, 9, 146–47.

[127] See n 150 and accompanying text.

[128] Ugo Mattei, 'Efficiency in Legal Transplants: An Essay in Comparative Law and Economics' (1994) 14 *Int Rev Law and Econ* 3, 18.

[129] For comparative law, van Erp (n 41) 1032–33, 1036–37; for law and economics, Smith, 'Economics of Property Law' (n 20) 149, 153.

[130] Paul H Rubin (ed), *The Evolution of Efficient Common Law* (Edward Elgar 2007); Richard A Posner, *Economic Analysis of Law* (7th edn, Aspen 2007) 249–73.

[131] Alan Watson, *Legal Transplants: An Approach to Comparative Law* (2nd edn, University of Georgia Press 1993).

[132] Rodolfo Sacco, 'Legal Formants: A Dynamic Approach to Comparative Law (Installment I of II)' (1991) 39 *Am J Comp L* 1; Rodolfo Sacco, 'Legal Formants: A Dynamic Approach to Comparative Law (Installment II of II)' (1991) 39 *Am J Comp L* 343; Watson, 'From Legal Transplants to Legal Formants' (n 90).

law this is frequently explained by the difficulty in reconciling the highly national and technical rules of domestic property systems,[133] that is, by a methodological limitation. By contrast, the relative lack of interest of law and economics has been attributed to conventional price theory and standard economics assuming property rights as fixed when carrying out their analysis of tort and contract law.[134]

Considering the relevance that economic analysis had in triggering the contemporary approach to the *numerus clausus*,[135] it is relevant to account for its bias in more detail. The most common explanation for the tendency of law and economics to see property rights as static is that Ronald Coase's foundational work for the movement[136] has been normally interpreted as disregarding the importance of the allocation and delineation of property rights or as assuming them as fixed and well-defined entitlements that are a precondition of his model.[137] This has been argued to be the result of the powerful but also simplified way in which Coase's conclusions are normally presented: as a theorem with corollaries.[138] The 'Coase Theorem'[139] has been presented in different forms.[140] Its central idea is that, in a world with zero transaction costs, people will always reach a wealth-maximising result through contracting, *regardless of the legal assignment of property rights*.[141] Accordingly, the standard approach of law and economics sees the foundation of property rights in a theory of bargain, which is more concerned with contractual problems than with property law. In this account, the role of property law in 'the real world' is reduced to: (i) 'lubricating' bargaining by establishing simple, clear and certain property interests; and (ii) initially allocating the property interests to whoever values them the most, in order to avoid unnecessary transactions.[142] As a result, the primary concern of traditional economic analysis of law regarding property rights is their clarity and stability, not their evolution and change,[143] evidencing an inherent bias towards seeing property rights as static.

[133] van Erp (n 41) 1032–1033; Milo (n 76) 726–727.

[134] Thomas W Merrill, 'Introduction: The Demsetz Thesis and the Evolution of Property Rights' (2002) 31 *J Legal Stud* 331, 331.

[135] See ch 3, section III and ch 5, section II.

[136] Ronald Coase, 'The Problem of Social Cost' (1960) 3 *J Law and Econ* 1.

[137] Brian Lee and Henry Smith, 'The Nature of Coasean Property' (2012) 59 *Intl Rev of Economics* 145, 147–49.

[138] Thomas W Merrill and Henry E Smith, 'Making Coasean Property More Coasean' (2011) 54 *J Law and Economics* 77, 93–95.

[139] First framed as such by George J Stigler, *The Theory of Price* (3rd edn, Macmillan NY; Collier-Macmillan 1966) 113.

[140] Robert Cooter and Thomas Ulen, *Law & Economics* (6th edn, Pearson 2012) 81.

[141] Merrill and Smith, 'Making Coasean Property More Coasean' (n 138) 93; Lee and Smith (n 137) 148; Cooter and Ulen (n 140) 85.

[142] eg Cooter and Ulen (n 140) 74, 85, 88–90, 92–93.

[143] On this, also see ch 5, section II.A.

B. New Institutional Economics as Starting Point

By contrast, since its origin in the 1970s, NIE has been very interested in property rights and their evolution.[144] The point of departure of this process was the work of Demsetz, who picked up the problem laid down by Coase but, instead of looking to contracts, focused on the role of property rights in dealing with externalities.[145] In a path-breaking article he argued that 'property rights develop to internalize externalities when the gains of internalization become larger than the cost of internalization'.[146] The idea behind his thesis is that the primary function of property rights is internalising (ie allocating) benefits and harms in a world of positive transaction costs. Hence, the evolution of property rights can be explained by the emergence of new beneficial and harmful effects that need to be internalised; that is, the emergence of new externalities, which are ultimately triggered by events such as technological changes or the opening of new markets. He explains this through the process by which the native inhabitants of the Labrador Peninsula moved from an open access to a private property system in land to avoid overexploitation, after they started hunting for commercial purpose with the arrival of the French.[147]

Despite its persuasiveness, Demestz's model does not say much about a few matters that are critical to understand the evolution of property law in practice, including (i) the process by which a society moves from one property system to another,[148] (ii) the concrete form that the emergent property rights might take,[149] and, most importantly for this book, (iii) the manner in which private property systems already in operation accommodate social and economic changes. Recent scholarship on the transition between property regimes has shed some light on the two first phenomena in the American context.[150] However, such research does not advance a general conceptual theory on how private property systems that are already 'up and running' deal with change and its findings cannot be directly extrapolated outside the American context.

Filling these gaps requires moving from the existing abstract approaches to the evolution of property rights to concrete research on how real-world property interests are used to serve new purposes and re-shaped over time in different jurisdictions. Relevant advance in this direction has recently been made in at least two contexts. In the US, Henry Smith has shown that property law has an internal architecture made of 'modular' blocks that can be combined in different forms to serve an almost infinite number of purposes,[151] while in Germany,

[144] Smith, 'Economics of Property Law' (n 20) 159.
[145] Merrill and Smith, 'Making Coasean Property More Coasean' (n 138) 78.
[146] Demsetz (n 40) 350.
[147] ibid 350–53.
[148] Merrill (n 134) 333, 336.
[149] ibid 333, 335–36.
[150] eg Epstein, 'The Plasticity of Property' (n 13).
[151] See Smith, 'Property as the Law of Things' (n 20); Smith, 'Economics of Property Law' (n 20).

Marietta Auer has developed a 'dialectic model' that accounts for change in property law as a process of 'non-linear evolution' underpinned by the 'immanent contradictions' of modern property law.[152] However, more research on the concrete operation of actual property rights is needed to assess *whether* and *how* these models work in practice. In line with this, this book emphasise not only *what* outcomes property law achieves, but *how* this happens.[153] In other words, it seeks to move from functional to conceptual aspects of legal institutions.[154] The next section expands on this approach.

IV. THE APPROACH OF THIS BOOK

A. Basic Elements

Over the last years, a number of relevant advances regarding the patterns of legal change in property law have been made in a variety of contexts, including domestic property doctrine, property theory and comparative law. However, for different reasons, none of these approaches provides an encompassing view of this phenomena. On the one hand, English[155] and German[156] doctrinal scholarship offers some enlightening research linking property doctrine to changing social circumstances, but its findings are very context-specific and are not placed into larger conceptual frameworks that account for their general patterns. On the other hand, general models tend to be too abstract. For example, recent theories developed in Germany focus on how the history of ideas has shaped the concept of ownership over time,[157] but do not offer an answer as to how contemporary property law interfaces with changes in the material world. Similarly, American property law scholars have developed a strong conceptual framework on this problem in the form of the 'modular theory', but with insufficient engagement with actual doctrine and tangible practical events.[158]

A core aspiration of this book is developing a new version of the modular theory, enriched by English and German doctrine. The starting point of this model

[152] Auer (n 10).

[153] Borrowing from Ben McFarlane, 'The Trust and its Civilian Analogues' in Lionel Smith (ed), *The Worlds of the Trust* (CUP 2013) 512.

[154] Borrowing from Merrill and Smith, 'Making Coasean Property More Coasean' (n 138) 78, 100.

[155] eg Blandy, Bright and Nield (n 41); Kelvin FK Low, 'Certainty of Terms and Leases: Curiouser and Curiouser' (2012) 75 MLR 401; Susan Pascoe, 'Re-Evaluating Recreational Easements – New Norms for the Twenty-First Century?' in Ben McFarlane and Sinéad Agnew (eds), *Modern Studies in Property Law*, vol 10 (Hart 2019); Bevan (n 84).

[156] eg Hermann Amann, 'Grunddienstbarkeiten im Wandel der Zeit und von Verjährung Bedroht – Zugleich Anmerkungen zu den Urteilen des BGH v. 18. 7. 2014 – V ZR 151/13 Und v. 22. 10. 2010 – V ZR 43/10' [2015] DNotz 164; Peukert (n 9); Wolf (n 62); Valesca Maria Molinari, *Die Tradition Staatlicher Interventionen in den Mietwohnungsmarkt* (Mohr Siebeck 2021).

[157] eg Auer (n 10).

[158] Smith has argued that property theory suffers a kind of reductionism that confines it to the 'stratosphere of abstraction'. Henry E Smith, 'Emergent Property' in James Penner and Henry Smith (eds), *Philosophical Foundations of Property Law* (OUP 2013) 320.

is a strong intuition from everyday life: 'well-advised citizens can, at some cost, almost always obtain results denied to them by one legal device using another'.[159] Thus, according to Thomas Merrill and Henry Smith, private parties can normally achieve their idiosyncratic goals by more or less complex combinations of the standardised building blocks of property law, a feature they call the 'generative power of the system'.[160] In Smith's more refined view, this provides property law with a 'modular structure' that allows private parties to combine them in many different forms to achieve an almost infinite variety of practical purposes.[161] According to the model advanced in this book, this 'modularity' is what permits Renner's 'functional transformation' of property rights, by ensuring that owners retain sufficient exclusionary powers to 'set the agenda' for the thing.[162]

Smith's 'modular theory' provides a simple and powerful model to explain how a property system made of a limited number of rigid interests can accommodate new realities without undergoing apparent change. However, because this model is framed in the highly abstract style of American law and economics,[163] it also has a limited ability to explain how property law interfaces with changing realities in practice, especially outside the American context. Due to the importance it gives to the 'law in action',[164] comparative law is in an excellent position to provide this missing input,[165] including actual cases of 'functional transformation'. The timing could not be better. Over the last years, the European harmonisation and unification efforts have triggered a vivid interest in the dynamic aspects of property law among comparative scholars.[166] This discussion has placed vast parts of the domestic property laws of Europe in a comparative perspective[167] and the *numerus clausus* principle has been one of its main concerns.[168]

[159] Bernard Rudden, 'Economic Theory v. Property Law: The Numerus Clausus Problem' in John Eekelaar and John Bell (eds), *Oxford Essays in Jurisprudence. Third Series* (Clarendon 1987) 239.

[160] Merrill and Smith, 'Optimal Standardization in the Law of Property' (n 19) 36.

[161] Smith, 'Property as the Law of Things' (n 20) 1692, 1701, 1707–08.

[162] Borrowing from Larissa Katz's view of 'property as an office'. Larissa Katz, 'Exclusion and Exclusivity in Property Law' (2008) 58 *U Toronto LJ* 275; Larissa Katz, 'The Regulative Function of Property Rights' (2011) 8 *Econ Journal Watch*; Larissa Katz, 'Property's Sovereignty' (2017) 18 *Theo Inq L* 299.

[163] Although Smith would probably place his work as part of 'New Private Law'. See ch 5, section I.

[164] See Zweigert and Kötz (n 43) 11, 38; Florian Wagner-von Papp, 'Comparative Law & Economics and the Egg-Laying Wool-Milk Sow' (2014) 9 *J Comp L* 137, 155; Florian Faust, 'Comparative Law and Economic Analysis of Law' in Mathias Reimann and Reinhard Zimmermann (eds), *The Oxford Handbook of Comparative Law* (2nd edn, OUP 2019) 837–38.

[165] I expanded on this in Ernesto Vargas Weil, 'Map and Territory in Comparative Law & Economics' (2022) 11 *Global J Comp L* 1.

[166] van Erp (n 41) 1034.

[167] eg Sjef Van Erp and Bram Akkermans (eds), *Cases, Materials and Text on Property Law* (Hart 2012); Bar (n 76).

[168] Especially, Akkermans, *The Principle of Numerus Clausus in European Property Law* (n 93). Also van Erp, 'A Numerus Quasi-Clausus of Property Rights as a Constitutive Element of a Future European Property Law' (n 92); Peter Sparkes, 'Certainty of Property: Numerus Clausus or the Rule with No Name?' (2012) 20 *Euro Rev Priv L* 769; Bar (n 87).

However, the approach taken by this book has advantages that go far beyond providing 'raw material' to test an abstract model. First, its comparative approach allows to assess the modular theory through the eyes of legal systems that have not been subject to the pervasive influence of the American law and economics movement,[169] especially the 'historic rationality' of English law and the 'doctrinal' or 'systematic' exegesis of German law.[170] In this manner the book achieves a conceptual cross-fertilisation between the civilian and common law traditions that, on the one hand, enables English doctrine to learn from German conceptualism and, on the other, allows German doctrine to benefit from the more casuistic and pragmatic style of English law. Finally, the emphasis (good) comparative law puts on understanding the function of legal institutions within the context of the wider social fabric of society[171] provides this book with the 'interdisciplinary links' to incorporate dynamic elements from other legal and extra-legal disciplines into its analysis of property law.

The main challenge of this approach is bringing all this material into a coherent framework. This is not helped by the 'chronic methodological weakness' of comparative law[172] and the intrinsic difficulties to pursuing comparative research in property law.[173] The strategy followed by this book to overcome these pitfalls is based on modesty:[174] besides dealing with a narrowly defined problem (see section I above), it (primarily) focuses on property rights in land. There are good reasons for this that cannot be explained in detail here,[175] including its historically central role in property law[176] and economic production.[177] Maybe

[169] Richard A Posner, 'The Future of the Law and Economics Movement in Europe' (1997) 17 *Int Rev Law and Econ* 3, 5; Kristoffel Grechenig and Martin Gelter, 'The Transatlantic Divergence in Legal Thought: American Law and Economics vs. German Doctrinalism' (2008) 1 *Hastings Int'l and Comp L Rev* 295, 298; Wagner-von Papp (n 164) 141–44.

[170] On the style of English and German legal thinking, Wagner-von Papp (n 164) 141; Otto Kahn-Freund, 'Introduction' in Karl Renner, *The Institutions of Private Law and their Social Functions* (Routledge & Kegan Paul 1949) 12–14.

[171] Zweigert and Kötz (n 43) 11, 38; Mary Ann Glendon, Paolo Carozza and Colin Picker, *Comparative Legal Traditions: Text, Materials and Cases on Western Law* (3rd edn, West Academic Press 2006) 16; Ralf Michaels, 'The Functional Method of Comparative Law' in Mathias Reimann and Reinhard Zimmermann (eds), *The Oxford Handbook of Comparative Law* (2nd edn, OUP 2019) 369; Geoffrey Samuel, *An Introduction to Comparative Law Theory and Method* (Hart 2014) 5.

[172] See Mathias Reimann, 'The Progress and Failure of Comparative Law in the Second Half of the Twentieth Century' (2002) 50 *Am J Comp L* 671, 685–86, 688–89; Ralf Michaels, 'Im Westen nichts Neues? 100 Jahre Pariser Kongreß für Rechtsvergleichung – Gedanken anläßlich einer Jubiläumskonferenz in New Orleans' (2002) 66 *Rabels Z* 97, 111, 114; Michaels (n 171) 346.

[173] Mattei (n 74) 21; Milo (n 76) 727; van Erp (n 41) 1032. See ch 2 for discussion.

[174] On 'modesty' in this context, Uwe Kischel, *Comparative Law* (Andrew Hammel tr, OUP 2019) 31–34.

[175] For these reasons, Waldron (n 8) 33–37; Dixon (n 38) 7; Larissa Katz, 'Corporate Shares as Shares' in Ben McFarlane and Sinéad Agnew (eds), *Modern Studies in Property Law*, vol 10 (Hart 2019) 109–11.

[176] Cooke (n 51) 6–7; McFarlane, *The Structure of Property Law* (n 80) 6–12; Baur, Baur and Stürner (n 21) 9, 167–68.

[177] Paul A Samuelson and William D Nordhaus, *Economics* (19th edn, McGraw-Hill 2010) 9, 267–69, 503.

more important, land has some inherent characteristics, like its limited supply,[178] uniqueness and durability,[179] that make temporality issues in land law extremely pressing.[180] However, this decision also responds to practical concerns: the status of the *numerus clausus* in England is far more certain in land law than in any other context.[181]

From the perspective of the Theory of Legal Families,[182] choosing England and Germany can be justified in the fact that these jurisdictions have traditionally been seen as the heads and most representative members of the common law and the Germanic civil law families.[183] Furthermore, in both jurisdictions the *numerus clausus* has a well-established position in private law doctrine,[184] ensuring that there will be meaningful domestic material to compare. Third, both jurisdictions have been at the centre of the comparative research done in the context of European unification and harmonisation efforts,[185] also providing a comparative body of literature to engage with. Nonetheless, due to the relevance that law and economics had in triggering the contemporary interest in the *numerus clausus* and the strong ties between American and English property theory, this book will also permanently engage with American scholarship.

Finally, to avoid biases inherent to comparative research, the book accesses the laws of England and Germany afresh, mainly relying on domestic primary and secondary sources available to native students, scholars and practitioners.[186] To place this material in the relevant external context, the book primarily relies on interdisciplinary approaches like law and economics, legal history and law and society, but also borrows directly from a number of extra-legal disciplines, including economic history, NIE, philosophy, urbanism and policy making.

B. A New Conceptual Framework

To structure this large number of disconnected elements into a coherent conceptual model, the book follows an original approach that combines frameworks coming from NIE, Anglo-American property theory and comparative law.

[178] ibid 269, 270.

[179] McFarlane, *The Structure of Property Law* (n 80) 7–8.

[180] Richard A Epstein, 'Past and Future: The Temporal Dimension in the Law of Property' (1986) 64 *WashU LQ* 667, 669.

[181] See ch 3, section III.

[182] On this, Zweigert and Kötz (n 43) 64–73.

[183] ibid 132–275.

[184] See ch 3, sections II and III.

[185] See ch 2, section I and ch 3, section I.

[186] For the BGB I am using the translation by Neil Mussett, revised and updated by Samson Übersetzungen GmbH, Dr Carmen v Schöning, available at www.gesetze-im-internet.de/englisch_bgb/englisch_bgb.html#p3489; and for the GG the translation used is by Christian Tomuschat, David P Currie, Donald P Kommers and Raymond Kerr, in cooperation with the Language Service of the German Bundestag, available at www.gesetze-im-internet.de/englisch_gg/#:~:text=Basic%20Law%20for%20the%20Federal%20Republic%20of%20Germany.

The most general of these frameworks comes from Douglass North's 'Institutional Theory' and serves to structure the topics of the book. According to this theory,[187] explaining economic performance in history requires, among other things, complementing the basic neoclassical economic model (the same used by mainstream law and economics) with a 'theory of institutions' made of three basic building blocks: a theory of property rights, a theory of the state and a theory of ideology. In this view, 'property rights' are understood as human-created devices that reduce transaction costs and organise exchange, thereby setting the basic personal and group incentives of the economic system. In turn, property rights are created and enforced by 'the state', which is therefore ultimately responsible for the functioning of the property system. Finally, the costs of maintaining and enforcing the property system derive from the world-view or 'ideology' that exists in the relevant community in a given moment. Technological change alters the relative terms of exchange, impacting how property rights are perceived by the community (ie the 'ideology'), which in turn puts pressure on how the state delineates and enforces property rights. Following this framework, chapter two (on the concept of a property right) and chapter three (on the *numerus clausus*) explore the legal features of 'property rights' in England and Germany. Chapter four discusses the role of 'the state' in the operation of the *numerus clausus*. Chapter five addresses the 'ideology' of the *numerus clausus* principle, by asking about its function and justification. Chapters six and seven present some case studies that discuss how property law accommodated some specific 'technological changes'. Chapter eight brings all these institutional elements together into one single model, and chapter nine discusses some implications for the institutional design of property law.

The second framework comes from Anglo-American property theory – more precisely, from James Penner's distinction between two different and distinctive third-party effects of property rights: their ability to bind successors in title ('successor liability') and their ability to bind strangers *in general* ('trespassory liability').[188] As shown in chapter two, although largely unexplored, this distinction has recently gained popularity in English scholarship[189] and is also known to German doctrine.[190] This analytical device will be instrumental in identifying the justification of the *numerus clausus* (chapter five) and distinguishing how it

[187] Douglass C North, *Structure and Change in Economic History* (WW Norton 1981) 3–4, 7–8, 11–12, 17–18, 49–53.

[188] James Penner, 'Duty and Liability in Respect of Funds' in John Lowry and Mistelis Loukas (eds), *Commercial Law: Perspectives and Practice* (LexisNexis Butterworths 2006) 215.

[189] eg see Ben McFarlane and Robert Stevens, 'The Nature of Equitable Property' (2010) 4 *J Eq* 1; William Swadling, 'Property: General Principles' in Andrew Burrows (ed), *English Private Law* (3rd edn, OUP 2013) 180; Simon Douglas and Ben McFarlane, 'Defining Property Rights' in James Penner and Henry Smith (eds), *Philosophical Foundations of Property Law* (OUP 2013) 240, 241.

[190] eg Heinz Hübner and Joachim Riegner, *Sachenrecht* (Translatia 1948) 7; Hermann Eichler, *Institutionen Des Sachenrechts*, vol 1 (Duncker & Humblot 1954) 6–7.

protects the general public (chapter six) and successors in title (chapter seven), in practice.

Finally, a loose version of the functional method of comparative law serves to structure the content of the different chapters. Each has separate sections on English and German law that account for the relevant legal features of each system in their own terms, placing them into their wider social, economic and ideological context. In England many of these connections are apparent due to the inclination of its doctrine to approach the law by the contextual analysis of cases. By contrast, in Germany, the abstract style of its doctrine tends to obscure these links: with good reason, Rudolf von Jhering ironically described the style of German doctrine, as a 'heaven of concepts'.[191] However, by the same token German law offers systematic conceptual approaches that are not equally visible in England.

Building on these three frameworks, the book discusses how several developments, spanning from the Industrial Revolution to the growing value of sports and leisure in contemporary societies, interface with property law. This demands a final caveat: this is a book about property law theory and doctrine, not about legal history. Although many of the examples it relies upon are historical, in the sense that they come from a more or less distant past, all of them relate to doctrines and principles that are still valid or relevant to contemporary English and German law. This will become apparent in the next chapter, as history still provides the leading analytical framework to explain the divergence between civilian and common law property systems.[192] As said by Judge Holmes more than 100 years ago, 'a page of history is worth a volume of logic'.[193]

[191] Rudolf von Jhering, *Scherz und Ernst in der Jurisprudenz* (Breitkopf und Härtel 1884) 274–333.
[192] See Van Erp and Akkermans (n 167) 53–55.
[193] *New York Trust Co v Eisner*, 256 US 345 (1921), 349.

2

The Concept of a Property Right

THE PRINCIPLE OF *numerus clausus* applies to 'property rights', that is, to one of the three basic building blocks of the 'institutional theory' that underpins this book. Considering the well-known divergence between civilian and common law property systems, it cannot simply be assumed that such 'property rights' are conceptually the same in England and Germany.[1] Thus, prior to comparing the doctrine of *numerus clausus* in both jurisdictions, this chapter will establish to what extent the objects of this principle are actually comparable. In doing this, it will not aim to find a *concept* of a property right that cuts through domestic definitions, but to account for the way its different *conceptions*[2] are understood within each legal system. To do so, this chapter starts by placing itself within a strand searching for a 'conceptual' approach to comparative property law (section I). Then, it analyses afresh how property rights are understood in Germany (section II) and England (section III). It ends presenting a new comparative view on the conceptual nature of property rights and the impact of constitutional law on it (section IV).

A first conclusion of this chapter is that, although English and German law share a basic understanding of property rights as entitlements enforceable against third parties, each system tends to focus on different third-party effects. English law approaches property rights from the perspective of their effects on successors in title, while German law concentrates on their effects on third parties 'in general', including trespassers and successors. This first conclusion serves to introduce one of the main conceptual tools used in this book to assess the functioning of the *numerus clausus*, namely the distinction between 'successor' and 'trespassory' liability.

A second conclusion of this chapter is that the conception of a property right that underpins the *numerus clausus* has never been intended to work in isolation but in tandem with other forms of state action outside its scope. Even at the height of classical liberalism, governments had the power to relocate the modules of property law by expropriations; and, during the twentieth century, modern states progressively developed the powers to re-shape the modules of

[1] See Bram Akkermans, 'The Numerus Clausus of Property Rights' in Michele Graziadei and Lionel Smith (eds), *Comparative Property Law: Global Perspectives* (Edward Elgar 2017) 102.

[2] Using Waldron's terms. Jeremy Waldron, *The Right to Private Property* (OUP 1988) 31, 38–39, 41.

property rights 'from outside' via regulation. Both forms of state action are not affected by the principle of *numerus clausus* and partially explain how systems subject to a close list of property rights adapt to new realities without altering that list.

I. TOWARDS A CONCEPTUAL-COMPARATIVE APPROACH

Property law has traditionally been the least explored area of comparative private law.[3] The main explanation for this are the well-known doctrinal differences of property law across jurisdictions.[4] However, over the last two decades, this field has been on the rise,[5] dramatically increasing our knowledge regarding the differences, similarities and relations between the property laws of different jurisdictions, especially across the civil-common law divide.[6]

The most basic finding of this literature is that property law is one of the most divergent areas of private law. Traditionally, comparative law saw the divergence of the central concepts of civilian and common law property law as so entrenched that any convergence would be impossible.[7] Indeed, even the most basic terms of the different national property systems frequently do not even have equivalents in other languages.[8] In one recent view, the crucial point of this divide is that civilian and common law property law have 'different ontologies' that are so deep that continental lawyers are normally not able to grasp the feudally-influenced terminology of the English LPA 1925, while a common lawyer might be baffled by the absence of 'estates' in civil codes.[9]

[3] Sjef van Erp, 'Comparative Property Law' in Mathias Reimann and Reinhard Zimmermann (eds), *The Oxford Handbook of Comparative Law* (2nd edn, OUP 2019) 1032; Jan Smits, *The Making of European Private Law* (Intersentia 2002) 245. Although this is less valid for the trust; for example, see Hein Kötz, *Trust und Treuhand. Eine Rechtsvergleichende Darstellung des Anglo-Amerikanischen Trust und Funktionsverwandter Institute des Deutschen Rechts* (Vandenhoeck & Ruprecht 1963).

[4] J Michael Milo, 'Property and Real Rights' in Jan M Smits (ed), *Elgar Encyclopedia of Comparative Law* (2nd edn, Edward Elgar 2012) 727; van Erp (n 3) 1032.

[5] Michele Graziadei and Lionel Smith, 'Preface' in Michele Graziadei and Lionel Smith (eds), *Comparative Property Law: Global Perspectives* (Edward Elgar 2017) x; van Erp (n 3) 1034, 1036.

[6] eg see Ugo Mattei, *Basic Principles of Property Law: A Comparative Legal and Economic Introduction* (Greenwood 2000); Sjef Van Erp and Bram Akkermans (eds), *Cases, Materials and Text on Property Law* (Hart 2012); Michele Graziadei and Lionel Smith (eds), *Comparative Property Law: Global Perspectives* (Edward Elgar 2017); Yaël Emerich, *Droit Commun Des Biens: Perspective Transsystémique* (Éditions Yvon Blais 2017); Christian von Bar, *The Foundations of Property Law* (OUP 2023); Yun-chien Chang, *Property Law: Comparative, Empirical and Economic Analyses* (CUP 2023).

[7] van Erp (n 3) 1032–33. For some bold statements see Milo (n 4) 727; Peter Sparkes, 'Certainty of Property: Numerus Clausus or the Rule with No Name?' (2012) 20 *Euro Rev Priv L* 769, 771.

[8] Paul Matthews, 'The Compatibility of the Trust with the Civil Law Notion of Property' in Lionel Smith (ed), *The Worlds of the Trust* (CUP 2013) 314, 317–19.

[9] Michele Graziadei, 'The Structure of Property Ownership and the Common Law/Civil Law Divide' in Michele Graziadei and Lionel Smith (eds), *Comparative Property Law: Global Perspectives* (Edward Elgar 2017) 72, 74–75. In a similar line, Uwe Kischel, *Comparative Law* (Andrew Hammel tr, OUP 2019) 305.

The dominant explanation for this divergence is the different genealogy of civilian and common law property law:[10] modern civilian property systems developed from the abolition of feudal law, the reception of Roman law and the emergence of national codifications; while English property law developed autonomously, without substantial reception of Roman law, with an important position given to feudal law and resting on case law, without systematic codification.[11] Frequently, these explanations add further elements that account for the persistence of the divide over time. Doctrinal approaches highlight the impact of the *lex rei sitae* conflict rule,[12] this is, the private international law rule holding that the applicable law in the case of a dispute as to property rights is that of where the object is situated,[13] while comparative law and economics has stressed that the high cost involved in modifying property systems once they are already 'up and running' creates a path-dependence that preserves the divergence over time.[14]

Consistent with this, comparative scholarship normally finds the core differences of civilian and common law property law in the historical development of a handful of central legal institutions in one tradition that are absent in the other. First, the reliance of civil codes on a well-defined unitary notion of ownership which does not exist in the common law.[15] Second, the common law theory of estates has no place in civilian systems.[16] Third, civil and common law property systems are seen as taking opposite positions regarding the relationship between ownership and possession.[17] Finally, in common law systems, Equity has been said to create a *duplex ordo* of property rights that does not exist in civilian countries.[18] In this context, trusts are often seen as creating the most salient difference between both traditions, because they seem to create 'parallel' legal and equitable property rights over a single asset, which is at odds with the civilian 'taboo'[19] of the indivisible nature of unitary ownership.[20]

[10] Graziadei (n 9) 76, 84; Yun-chien Chang and Henry Smith, 'An Economic Analysis of Civil versus Common Law Property' (2012) 88 *Notre Dame L Rev* 1.

[11] Smits (n 3) 74–94; Milo (n 4) 727.

[12] eg Milo (n 4) 726; Smits (n 3) 246; van Erp (n 3) 1032, 1045; Kischel (n 9) 305–06.

[13] eg Rome I Regulation, art 4(1)(c).

[14] eg Ugo Mattei, *Comparative Law and Economics* (University of Michigan Press 1997); Mattei, *Basic Principles of Property Law* (n 6) 20-21; Chang and Smith 'An Economic Analysis of Civil versus Common Law Property' (n 10); Yun-chien Chang and Henry E Smith, 'Structure and Style in Comparative Property Law' in Theodore Eisenberg and Giovanni B Ramello (eds), *Comparative Law and Economics* (Edward Elgar 2016).

[15] van Erp (n 3) 1047; Graziadei (n 9) 73–76, 81, 84; Kischel (n 9) 305–06; H Patrick Glenn, *Legal Traditions of the World* (5th edn, OUP 2014) 149; Bar (n 6) 29–30.

[16] van Erp (n 3) 1045; Kischel (n 9) 307; Graziadei (n 9) 73–76, 84.

[17] James Gordley, *Foundations of Private Law* (OUP 2006) 50–52; Van Erp and Akkermans (n 6) 36; Bar (n 6) 28.

[18] Milo (n 4) 727, 728; van Erp (n 3) 1047.

[19] Henry Hansmann and Ugo Mattei, 'The Function of Trust Law: A Comparative Legal and Economic Analysis' (1998) 73 *NYU L Rev* 434, 441, 442.

[20] See van Erp (n 3) 1047; Smits (n 3) 262; Kischel (n 9) 312; Bar (n 6) 61–65.

However, the times of watertight separation between both traditions are gone for good.[21] Despite their doctrinal differences, civil and common law property systems are inspired by the same basic market and private ownership ideology,[22] while their practical operation leads to similar outcomes.[23] Even at a doctrinal level, there is some convergence. Civilian property systems are becoming more flexible and giving more importance to case law, while common law property law is becoming more systematic and widely statutory,[24] and transplants between both traditions are not as infrequent as in the past, especially in relation to trusts.[25] Finally, the property laws of both traditions face similar new challenges, especially due to the impact of constitutional law, human rights, sustainability and new technologies.[26]

Despite this convergent trends, comparative property law remains underdeveloped.[27] One key gap is the meagre comparative research done on conceptual aspects of property law.[28] Despite some recent progress,[29] this is apparent in the scarcity of comparative research done on the very concept of a 'property right'. In this regard, general works normally offer a few important, but still superficial findings. First, property rights are universally characterised and differentiated from obligations by their enforceability against third parties, an idea frequently condensed in the Latin terms '*erga omnes*'[30] or '*in rem*'.[31] Second, the scope of such effects is defined differently in civilian and common law jurisdictions. While in the former, third-party effects of property rights are characterised as 'absolute', meaning that they bind everyone, in the latter, third-party effects are defined by their effect on specific groups of third parties, which is normally attributed to the doctrine of relativity of title.[32] Third, in the common law, the central notion of property law (at least for land) is that of an 'estate', which is defined by the temporal extension of the holder's prerogative, while the cornerstone of civilian property systems is 'ownership', which is defined by the prerogative of its holder over the thing, not by its duration.[33] Finally, the division of legal and equitable ownership allowed by the common

[21] Graziadei (n 9) 71.
[22] van Erp (n 3) 1032; Bar (n 6) 23.
[23] Milo (n 4) 726, 727; Mattei, *Basic Principles of Property Law* (n 6) 18–21. See eg Hansmann and Mattei (n 19) 438, 479.
[24] Milo (n 4) 727; van Erp (n 3) 1038.
[25] See Francois Barriere, 'The Security Fiducie in French Law' in Lionel Smith (ed), *The Worlds of the Trust* (CUP 2013); Bar (n 6) 66.
[26] Milo (n 4) 727; van Erp (n 3) 1036.
[27] van Erp (n 3) 1036; Graziadei and Smith, 'Preface' (n 5) x.
[28] Graziadei and Smith, 'Preface' (n 5) xi.
[29] Graziadei (n 9) 78.
[30] eg Milo (n 4) 726; van Erp (n 3) 1048; Bar (n 6) 32.
[31] eg EU Regulation No 1215/2012 on jurisdiction and the recognition and enforcement of judgments in civil and commercial matter (recast), art 24(1).
[32] eg van Erp (n 3) 1047.
[33] Graziadei (n 9) 77.

law trust is said to blur the clear distinction between property and obligations found in civilian systems.[34]

The overall picture is that, across jurisdictions, where someone has a right in connection to a thing (however it is defined) that is binding on everyone else, then they have a 'property right'.[35] However, what happens beyond that core case is far less clear. As a result, comparative property law has recently been said to be in need of moving from 'formulaic pronouncements' towards 'conceptual' approaches that bring different national understandings regarding the encoding of property rights into a common conversation.[36] The following two sections set the basis for such an approach by offering a new perspective on the German and English concepts of a property right. This will be instrumental in establishing (i) which rights are subject to a principle of *numerus clausus* in each jurisdiction, as well as (ii) which forms of state interventions in property law are affected by it.

II. GERMANY: BETWEEN SAVIGNY AND THE BASIC LAW

In German law, the concept of a property right can be addressed from three different perspectives: (i) their position in the private law system; (ii) the constitutional concept of ownership; and (iii) the specific list property rights contained in the BGB. This section will look at each in turn.

A. Property Rights as Part of Private Law

In Germany, property rights are conceptualised as 'absolute rights in things', that is, as one type of a larger category of 'absolute rights', which includes other rights that are also enforceable against everyone else, such as 'personality rights'.[37] Thus, in German law, 'absoluteness' is not privative to property rights, but a general concept of private law.

Having a proper understanding of the 'absolute' nature of German property rights requires placing them within its larger systems of private law (*Privatrecht*). This is not possible without understanding that, in civilian systems, 'civil law' has a meaning that is alien to Anglo-American private law.[38] As in other civilian

[34] eg Milo (n 4) 728; van Erp (n 3) 1047.

[35] See Bar (n 6) 2, 4–5, 33.

[36] Graziadei (n 9) 72, 94–95.

[37] Fritz Baur, Jürgen Baur and Rolf Stürner, *Sachenrecht* (18th edn, Beck 2009) 6; Fabian Klinck, 'Sachenrecht' in Dagmar Kaiser and Markus Stoffels (eds), *J. Staudingers Kommentar zum Bürgerlichen Gesetzbuch mit Einführungsgestetz und Nebengesetzen: Eckpfeiler des Zivilrechts* (6th edn, Sellier & de Gruyter 2018) 1271; Sebastian Herrler and Hartmut Wiecke, 'Sachenrecht', *Palandt: Bürgerlicher Gesetzbuch mit Nebengesetzten* (80th edn, Beck 2021) 1535.

[38] See Kischel (n 9) 359.

jurisdictions, in Germany, 'civil law' (*Bürgerliches Recht*), means 'general and common private law'.[39] This 'civil law' forms a basic sub-system that provides the foundations of all private law, as its special parts build upon its principles and it always remains applicable as a default rule.[40]

German 'civil law' is codified in the 1900 BGB.[41] Its style is highly technical, abstract and precise, and its contents are organised following the system of the nineteenth century Pandectist School (*Pandektensystem*).[42] Accordingly, the BGB has general and special parts, the former containing abstract concepts, definitions and rules that apply to more than one specific part.[43] In this structure, despite having its core regulation in Book 3, property rights are also regulated in the General Part (*Allgemeiner Teil*)[44] as one case of the broader category of 'private law relations' (*Privatrechtsverhältnisse*),[45] while some specific property rights are developed in a limited number of statutes outside the BGB,[46] most notably the 1951 Flat Ownership Act (*Wohnungseigentumsgesetz*, WEG), which provides for special form of ownership in flats (flat ownership).[47]

The concept of 'private law relation' provides the first key to the German idea of a property right. It is the central concept of German private law,[48] as it applies to contracts, property, torts and restitution. In textbooks it is not infrequently said that these relations connect people either to other people or to things.[49] However, this is not completely accurate. Properly understood, private law relations are always relations between people. In the case of 'rights in things' these relations to things are enforceable against all others.[50] Hence, authors who speak of property rights as 'relations to things' are quick to add that, in these cases, a relation to a person will emerge as soon someone unlawfully interferes in the relation of the person with the thing.[51]

[39] Hans Brox and Wolf-Dietrich Walker, *Allgemeiner Teil des BGB* (36th edn, Vahlen 2012) 11 (my translation).

[40] Jörg Neuner, *Allgemeiner Teil Des Bürgerlichen Rechts* (13th edn, Beck 2023) 67.

[41] ibid.

[42] Heinrich Honsell, 'Einleitung Zum BGB' in Dagmar Kaiser and Markus Stoffels (eds), *J. Staudingers Kommentar zum Bürgerlichen Gesetzbuch mit Einführungsgestetz und Nebengesetzen: Eckpfeiler Des Zivilrechts* (6th edn, Sellier & de Gruyter 2018) 14. For a brief account on the Pandectist School in English, see Konrad Zweigert and Hein Kötz, *An Introduction to Comparative Law* (Tony Weir tr, 3rd edn, OUP 1998) 138–41.

[43] Neuner (n 40) 73–74; Brox and Walker (n 39) 24.

[44] Especially, §§ 90–103 BGB. Klinck (n 37) 1271; Jan Wilhelm, *Sachenrecht* (5th edn, De Gruyter 2016) 4.

[45] See Brox and Walker (n 39) 265–346; Karl Larenz and Manfred Wolf, *Allgemeiner Teil des Bürgerlichen Rechts* (9th edn, Beck 2004) 225–348.

[46] Baur, Baur and Stürner (n 37) 8.

[47] For details, see ch 7, section III.B.

[48] Larenz and Wolf (n 45) 225.

[49] eg Brox and Walker (n 39) 265.

[50] Neuner (n 40) 223.

[51] eg Brox and Walker (n 39) 265. Explaining this, see Neuner (n 40) 223.

Private law relations have two main elements: subjective rights (*subjektive Rechte*) and legal duties (*rechtliche Pflichten*).[52] Subjective rights are said to be the key element of the relation. Definitions found in textbooks vary, but generally refer to a power provided by the law to the 'will' of a person for her self-determination, stressing that the purpose of subjective rights is to provide individuals with a sphere of personal freedom.[53] Thus, following Friedrich Carl von Savigny's ideas,[54] contemporary textbooks describe private law relations as governed by the 'will' of the person, frequently connecting this to Kantian and Hegelian ideas of self-determination.[55] Nowadays, this tends to pass unnoticed as an obvious feature of German private law. However, the emphasis on 'the will' is an outcome of a massive ideological shift experienced by Western private law during the early nineteenth century. This shift consisted in replacing traditional justifications of private law based in Aristotelian concepts of commutative and distributive justice with the modern concept of 'free will'.[56] Following this new paradigm, German scholars following in the steps of Savigny attempted to perfect modern property law by giving it a coherent structure, logically and normatively organised around one central idea: the freedom of the owner's will.[57] Accordingly, German doctrine still sees property law as ultimately underpinned by the recognition of private ownership as the free use of patrimony.[58]

Depending on the object of the right and the circle of people affected by its correlative duties, private law relations take different specific forms. From the perspective of their content, property rights are dominion rights (*Herrschaftsrechte*) that give an absolute and direct power over physical things. These property rights come in two basic forms: ownership (*Eigentum*) and limited property rights (*beschränkte dingliche Rechte*). The first is an encompassing and time-unlimited right over a tangible thing (§§ 903 and 90 BGB); while the second are conceived as fragmentations of ownership, being always limited as to their content and, normally, also their duration. From the perspective of the duty bearers, property rights, like all other dominion rights,[59] are 'absolute', that is, they are good against everyone.[60] Putting this together, the core of absolute rights is frequently described by contemporary authors as a

[52] Brox and Walker (n 39) 265; Larenz and Wolf (n 45) 231–35.

[53] Larenz and Wolf (n 45) 239–42; Brox and Walker (n 39) 268–69.

[54] Friedrich Carl von Savigny, *System des Heutigen Römischen Rechts*, vol 1 (Veit & Comp 1840) 331–32.

[55] eg Larenz and Wolf (n 45) 21–22, 240–42.

[56] Gordley (n 17) 14–16. The content and relevance of this connection is explored in ch 5, section III.

[57] Anna Di Robilant, *The Making of Modern Property Law: Reinventing Roman Law in Europe and its Peripheries* (CUP 2023) 167, 188–89.

[58] eg Baur, Baur and Stürner (n 37) 1.

[59] ie personality rights and intangible property rights.

[60] Neuner (n 40) 235–37; Brox and Walker (n 39) 269–71.

'freedom space' that is legally protected by imposing on all others a generic duty to keep off.[61] The first mention of the principle of *numerus clausus* in German textbooks normally arises in this context: absolute rights are limited in number and content because they must be easy to determine for everyone.[62]

B. The Impact of Constitutional Law

The understanding of property rights discussed above reflects the political ideas that inspired the German civil code. The BGB was the product of the classical liberalism that became dominant in Germany during the nineteenth century.[63] By the middle of the century, the economic doctrine of the Manchester School, which favoured free markets and no state intervention, had become very influential.[64] In this view, the law was expected to provide individual citizens with extensive freedom to conduct their business without external intervention, either from other citizens or the state.[65] Hence, and despite criticism pointing to the lack of social awareness of the First Draft of the BGB (*Erster Entwurf zum BGB*, EI),[66] the BGB was designed to be the core of a private law system underpinned by the individualistic ideas of freedom of contract and free ownership, which, at the time, were seen as instrumental in the development of Germany's modern industrial market economy.[67]

However, this conception of property rights never existed in isolation. At least since the work of Grotius in the seventeenth century,[68] the principle that the Sovereign can take private property rights for good reasons (paying compensation) has been a settled feature of civilian and common law legal doctrine.[69] As a consequence, both the French 1789 Declaration of the Rights of Man and the Citizen and the Fifth Amendment to the United States Constitution work on the assumption that, in case of public necessity, the state can deprive citizens of their

[61] For all, Neuner (n 40) 223; Larenz and Wolf (n 45) 228. In a similar vein, arguing that property rights operate in (i) a positive sense, giving rise to a right to possess, use and dispose of the thing and (ii) a negative sense, empowering its holder to remove what stands in the way of exercising this right, Bar (n 6) 13.

[62] eg Neuner (n 40) 245.

[63] ibid 105; Brox and Walker (n 39) 17. For a summary in English, see Di Robilant (n 57) 167–203.

[64] Honsell (n 42) 4.

[65] See ibid 7; Larenz and Wolf (n 45) 30.

[66] Especially, Otto Gierke, *Die Soziale Aufgabe des Privatrechts* (Springer 1899).

[67] Honsell (n 42) 10–11, 13–14; Larenz and Wolf (n 45) 30–31; Brox and Walker (n 39) 15, 17.

[68] Mathias Schmoeckel, 'Omnia Sunt Regis: Vom Allgemeinen Eigentum des Königes zur Enteignung des Bürger. Ein Überblick zur Geschichte der Enteignung bis Zum 18. Jahrhundert', *Die Enteignung. Historische, vergleichende und politische Perspectiven auf ein Rechtsinstitut* (Springer 2017) 16–17.

[69] JW Harris, *Property and Justice* (OUP 1996) 95; Tom Allen, *Property and The Human Rights Act 1998* (Hart 2005) 7.

property rights.[70] Indeed, in 1810, Napoleon had already issued the first modern expropriation act.[71]

In what is now Germany, following Grotius, the 1794 General State Laws for the Prussian States (*Allgemeines Landrecht für die Preußischen Staaten*, ALR) provided for the 'compulsory purchase' of land for building public roads, canals, streambeds, military infrastructure, etc. Later on, during the early nineteenth century and following the Napoleonic model, the power of the state to take property was re-conceptualised as 'expropriation' (*Enteignung*) by the constitutions of the German States. The acts that made this power operative in the different States aimed to facilitate the construction of infrastructure such as streets, roads, railways, dams and cemeteries.[72] This had not changed substantively by the time of the enactment of the BGB. Aside from some specific provisions for the expropriation of land by railways companies, the 1871 Constitution of the German Empire did not alter this situation, leaving the protection of fundamental rights and expropriations to the individual States that made up the new country.[73] Thus, as in France and the US, the starting point of the German constitutional concept of ownership was that of private law.[74] In this view, private property was seen as the base for the self-responsible development of individuals in economic life and a cornerstone for the expansion of trade and industry.[75]

Over the twentieth century this understanding of ownership was reshaped by constitutional developments underpinned by a very different ideology.[76] This process had been quietly put in motion during the second half of the nineteenth century as legislatures slowly started tightening the limits of ownership to address negative externalities brought about by economic and technological change.[77] However, this only became conspicuous with the inclusion of a provision acknowledging the social duties of ownership (*Sozialpflichtigkeit des Eigentums*) in the Constitution of the Weimar Republic (*Weimarer Reichsverfassung*, WRV),[78] which later found its way into Art 14(2) GG.[79] It is widely acknowledged that the doctrine developed by the Federal Constitutional Court (*Bundesverfassungsgericht*, BVerfG) based on this provision radically

[70] See Waldron (n 2) 16–18; Richard A Epstein, *Takings: Private Property and the Power of Eminent Domain* (Harvard UP 1985) 22–25, 29.

[71] Schmoeckel (n 68) 4.

[72] Foroud Shiravini, 'Entwicklung des Enteignungsrechts vom Frühen 19. Jahrhundert bis zur Weimarer Reichsverfassung', *Die Enteignung: Historische, vergleichende und politische Perspectiven auf ein Rechtsinstitut* (Springer 2017) 28–29.

[73] ibid 40.

[74] Peter Badura, 'Eigentum' in Ernst Benda, Werner Maihofer and Hans-Jochen Vogel (eds), *Handbuch des Verfassungsrecht der Bundesrepublik Deutschland* (2nd edn, De Gruyter 1994) 330.

[75] Shiravini (n 72) 26.

[76] See KD Ewing, 'Economic Rights' in Michel Rosenfeld and András Sajó (eds), *The Oxford Handbook of Comparative Constitutional Law* (OUP 2012); Shiravini (n 72) 42–47.

[77] Di Robilant (n 57) 224–25.

[78] Art 153(3) WRV.

[79] Baur, Baur and Stürner (n 37) 1.

departed from the private law understanding of property rights,[80] especially regarding ownership in land.[81] This view was consolidated in the 1981 *Gravel Pit Case* (*Nassauskiesungsbeschluss*),[82] in which the BVerfG declared that the concept of ownership protected by the GG must derive from itself and that its content cannot be established on the basis of infra-constitutional private law concepts.[83] By following this approach, the BVerfG departed from private law doctrine, which sees ownership as a natural right with an essential content, favouring an understanding that sees ownership simply as an institution to be delineated by the legislator within the limitations set forth by the GG.[84] This re-interpretation of ownership relativised some traditional principles governing property law, facilitating public law limitations of property rights, in fields such as environmental, artistic and animal protection.[85] In the context of housing, for example, in 2016 the Berlin Administrative Court (*Verwaltungsgericht* (VG) Berlin) declared the constitutionality[86] of an act that put heavy regulatory constraints on the power of owners to use a residential space for holiday, commercial or professional purposes or to make renovations that affect its ability to serve as a dwelling.[87] However, following the BVerfG, the expansion of regulation does not deny that the constitutional protection of the right to private property is ultimately justified by its ability to provide a patrimonial space of freedom for the development of an autonomous life.[88]

When analysing the implications of these developments, German scholarship normally holds that there is a constitutional and a private law concept of ownership, each serving different purposes.[89] The main difference between both is that the former is wider than that the latter, encompassing almost any patrimonial interest, regardless of whether it counts as a property right from the perspective of private law, including, for example, non-disposable rights such as social security rights.[90] This divergence is explained by the different functions of each concept within the broader legal system. The private law concept

[80] Friedrich Quack, *Münchener Kommentar Zum Bürgerlichen Gesetzbuch. Sachenrecht*, vol 6 (Friedrich Quack ed, 3rd edn, Beck 1997) 18.

[81] Larenz and Wolf (n 45) 33; Reinhard Gaier, 'Einleitung Zum Sachenrecht' in Franz Jürgen Säcker and others (eds), *Münchner Kommentar zum BGB* (7th edn, Beck 2017) [26].

[82] BVerfGE 58, 300.

[83] On this, Christian Bumke and Andreas Voßkuhle, *German Constitutional Law: Introduction, Cases, and Principles* (Andrew Hammel tr, OUP 2019) 274–75.

[84] Quack (n 80) 3, 19; Gaier (n 81) [26].

[85] Quack (n 80) 3, 19; Gaier (n 81) [26].

[86] VG Berlin, Urt, v 8.6.2016 – 6 K 103.16.

[87] 2013 *Zweckentfremdungsverbotsgesetz* (ZwVbG). On this and other recent housing policies in Germany, see Valesca Maria Molinari, *Die Tradition Staatlicher Interventionen in den Mietwohnungsmarkt* (Mohr Siebeck 2021) 62–66.

[88] See BVerfGE 50, 290, 339.

[89] Dieter Schwab and Martin Löhnig, *Einführung in das Zivilrecht* (20th edn, CF Müller 2016) 26–27; Wilhelm (n 44) 142–46.

[90] See Ulrich Hösch, *Eigentum und Freiheit. Ein Beitrag zur Inhaltlichen Bestimmung der Gewahrleistung des Eigentums durch Art. 14 Abs. 1 Satz 1 GG* (Mohr Siebeck 2000) 27–31.

is part of a relatively static body of rules that aims to peacefully solve conflicts regarding the allocation of resources between individuals[91] that is too narrow to deal with wider political and economic dimensions involved in the allocation of resources in a modern society. This task is assumed by constitutional property law, which aims to articulate the general and the individual interest in the allocation of wealth.[92] A good example of this is the case line leading to the recognition of the right of tenants as a form of ownership under Art 14(1) GG.[93] After avoiding making a decision on the matter for a long time, in 1993 the BVerfG declared that this provision protects both the ownership of lessors and the right to possession of lessees[94] (recall that in civilian systems the rights of lessors are not 'property rights'[95]). Among other things, the court argued that, considering that a high proportion of the German population relies on leases to cover their dwellings needs,[96] the right to possession of tenants is as significant and worthy of protection as that of owners.[97]

Current developments, triggered by a housing crisis in Berlin, might expand the impact of the GG in property law, beyond expropriations and regulation. This new challenge comes from Art 15 GG, a 'constitutional fossil', that has so far lived a 'shadowy existence'.[98] This provision allows the 'socialisation'[99] (*Vergesellschaftung*) of certain forms of property, including land, for the purpose being transferred to public ownership or other forms of public enterprise. Its origin is in the 'Bonn Settlements' arrived by the middle and working-class political parties at the genesis of the German Federal Republic (GFR). However, the provision lost practical importance in the late 1950s, once the German Social Democratic Party (SPD) abandoned its prior policies seeking to socialise productive assets. As a result, until now, Art 15 GG has never been applied.[100]

This might change, thanks to a popular bill[101] put forward in the Senate of Berlin by the initiative '*Deutsche Wohnen & Co enteignen*'[102] after a successful referendum held in 2021.[103] This movement seeks to pass legislation to

[91] Quack (n 80) 18.
[92] Badura (n 74) 329.
[93] For details, see ch 8, section III.D.
[94] BVerfGE 89, 1.
[95] See section III.
[96] On this, see ch 7, section III.B.
[97] On this, see Molinari (n 87) 83.
[98] Alexander Kloth, 'Der Kleine Unbekannte – Art. 15 GG: Die Sozialisierungsermächtigung des Grundgesetzes im Lichte der Berliner Enteignungsinitiative' (2022) 2 *BRZ* 86, 86–87.
[99] The official English translation is 'nationalisation', but 'socialisation' seems more accurate.
[100] Kloth (n 98) 87.
[101] *Volksentscheid über einen Beschluss zur Erarbeitung eines Gesetzentwurfs durch den Senat zur Vergesellschaftung der Wohnungsbestände großer Wohnungsunternehmen.*
[102] See their website: dwenteignen.de.
[103] Expertenkommission zum Volksentscheid Vergesellschaftung großer Wohnungsunternehmen, 'Abschlussbericht' (June 2023) [1], https://content.dwenteignen.de/uploads/abschlussbericht_vergesellschaftung_grosser_wohnungsunternehmen_230627_36052a6b90.pdf, accessed 13 November 2024.

'socialise' more than 240,000 flats owned by big real estate companies, which rent them out to individuals. In that context, the Senate called for a commission of experts to assess the constitutionality of the bill. In 2023 the commission concluded that Art 15 GG gave the City of Berlin competence to 'socialise' the flats. According to the majority of the commission, the proportionality principle does not impede the socialisation of the flats, either because it is not applicable or because its standard could be satisfied. In any case, there was agreement among the majority that proportionality, in the context of Art 15 GG, works in a different way than for Art 14 GG. In this view, socialisation is only possible when there is no other less burdensome option to achieve the required public goal. The majority also agreed that the affected parties would be entitled to compensation, but that its amount is not subject to the same logic as Art 14 GG, implying that it could be less than market value.[104] Whether this bill will be enacted and, eventually, challenged at the BVerfG, remains to be seen, but its existence alone suggests that, in Germany, constitutional law could have an even more decisive impact in adapting property rights to new realities in the future.

C. Ownership as Gateway to Property Law

Despite acknowledging the impact of constitutional law on property rights, German scholarship normally addresses property law relying on pure private law concepts.[105] Because it builds on the concept of a 'private law relation' coming from the General Part, when accounting for the structure of property law, doctrine is not concerned with the concept of 'a property right', but with specific 'property rights', especially ownership.[106] Indeed, the original version of BGB does not even use the term 'property right' (*dingliches Recht*).[107] Its direct source is the *Motive* where it is used to contrast them with 'personal rights' (*obligatorishe Rechte*).[108] Accordingly, property law textbooks[109] and *Kommentare*[110] normally do not expand on the concept of a property right and, at most, stress its absolute nature to highlight its difference with contractual obligations, as in the most common example of relative rights. This lack of emphasis on the conceptual nature of property rights can be attributed to the way the German property system is built: ownership is the encompassing property right over a thing. All other (limited) property rights are understood as

[104] See ibid [36]–[43].

[105] eg Marina Wellenhofer, *Sachenrecht* (34th edn, Beck 2019) 1–16.

[106] See the structure of the leading textbook, Baur, Baur and Stürner (n 37).

[107] Since 2010, it has been used in §§ 197 and 198 BGB.

[108] Hans Hermann Seiler, 'Einleitung Zum Sachenrecht' in Elmar Bund and others (eds), *J. von Staudingers Kommentar zum Bürgerlichen Gesetzbuch mit Einführungsgesetz und Nebengesetzen* (Sellier & de Gruyter 2007) 18.

[109] eg Wilhelm (n 44) 3; Wellenhofer (n 105) 2.

[110] eg Klinck (n 37) 1271; Gaier (n 81) [4]; Seiler (n 108) 18–20.

fragmentations of it. Hence, 'ownership' and not 'property right' is the main doctrinal gateway to German property law.[111]

Nonetheless, the concept of a property right is still essential in order to place property law within the broader system of private law, especially to separate it from the law of obligations. Savigny argued for a universal and clear-cut division between property law and the law of obligations, underpinned by the idea that each of these 'legal relations' apply to completely different real-life objects: the object of property rights is the 'unfree' nature (this is, 'things'); while the object of obligations are individual people.[112] Following Savigny, Reinhold Johow, the drafter of the property section of the EI, understood this strict separation as 'essentially correct' and as a 'pure analytical deduction' resulting from the essence of these legal relations, presenting property law in the *Motive* as an autonomous part of private law (Book 3), completely separate from the law of obligations (Book 2).[113] As shown in chapter three (section II) and chapter five (section III) this had a decisive impact on the German understanding of the principle of *numerus clausus*.

In practice, this strict conceptual division between property and personal rights is softened by some borderline cases in which obligations receive protection against certain third parties,[114] a phenomenon German doctrine calls 'reification of obligations' (*Verdinglichung obligatorischer Rechte*).[115] From a comparative perspective, the most prominent case are leases in land.[116] Despite leases being understood as mere contracts that only give rise to personal rights, the lessee can enforce her rights against the lessor's successors in title, effectively converting her position into a *status*.[117] In Germany, this is coined in the formula 'sales do not break leases' (§ 566 BGB), and has led contemporary commentators to argue that leases have 'some proprietary elements',[118] especially in the

[111] Marietta Auer, *Der Privatrechtliche Diskurs Der Moderne* (Mohr Siebeck 2014) 95. For an example, see Wellenhofer (n 105) 1–27.

[112] Savigny (n 54) 334–45, 367–79, although this division seems to have been more nuanced. On this, see Di Robilant (n 57) 191.

[113] Wolfgang Wiegand, 'Die Entwicklung des Sachenrechts im Verhältnis zum Schuldrecht' (1990) 1/2 AcP 112, 112–15; Wolfgang Wiegand, 'Numerus Clausus der Dingliche Rechte: Zur Entstehung und Bedeutung eines Zentralen Zivilrechtlichen Dogmas' in Gerhard Köbler (ed), *Karl Kroeschell zum 60: Geburtstag dargelegt von Freunden, Schülern und Kollegen*, vol 60 (Verlag Peter Lang 1987) 632–33; Wolfgang Wiegand, 'Funktion und Systematische Stellung des Sachenrechts im BGB' in Michael Martinek and Patrick L Sellier (eds), *J. von Staudingers Kommentar zum Bürgerlichen Gesetzbuch mit Eiführungsgesetz und Nebengesetzen. 100 Jahre BGB – 100 Jahre Staudinger* (Sellier & de Gruyter 1999) 108–10 (my translation).

[114] Wilhelm (n 44) 50–56.

[115] Gerhard Dulckeit, *Die Verdinglichung Obligatorischer Rechte* (Mohr 1951).

[116] The other prominent example is the *Treuhand*, Auer (n 111) 112–13. Discussed in detail in ch 3, section II.C.

[117] See van Erp (n 3) 1041.

[118] Baur, Baur and Stürner (n 37) 393; Volker Emmerich, 'Miete' in Dagmar Kaiser and Markus Stoffels (eds), *J. Staudingers Kommentar zum Bürgerlichen Gesetzbuch mit Einführungsgestetz und Nebengesetzen: Eckpfeiler Des Zivilrechts* (6th edn, Sellier & de Gruyter 2018) 566–67.

residential context.[119] Nonetheless, from a doctrinal perspective, leases are not conceptually explained as giving rise to proprietary rights, but rather to obligations with third party effects.[120] As a result, some contemporary authors have argued that property rights have a core and a periphery, surrounded by purely personal rights. The core is made of property rights in tangible things, which are characterised as absolute, transferable, inheritable, protected in insolvency and fully subject to property law principles, including the *numerus clausus*. The periphery is comprised by a sliding scale from property to personal right, including 'proprietarised' obligations that only possess some of the elements of core property rights.[121] As discussed in chapters six and seven, these borderline cases point to some unexplored similarities between English and German private law that are key to understanding how the *numerus clausus* impacts private law.

III. ENGLAND: BETWEEN PRAGMATISM AND CONCEPTUALISM

Conceptualising property rights in England is less straightforward than in Germany. One the one hand, in contrast to German law, English property law is not systematically built from first principles, but evolved over time. On the other, the traditionally uncertain position of the right to private property in the UK constitution adds further difficulties in establishing the conceptual boundaries of property right in England. Thus, it should not come as a surprise that the English approach to property law has even been described as openly 'anti-conceptualist'.[122]

Identifying the concept of a property right in English law requires working in an inductive manner. This subsection will do this by (i) accounting for the fragmentary nature of English property law; (ii) discussing the idea of 'rights *in rem*' as its unifying principle; and (iii) exploring the influence of the 'bundle of rights' picture developed by Anglo-American private law theory.

A. The Fragmentation of English Property Law

English property law lacks the systematic structure that codification has given to modern German property law. Not even land law, which was subject to major legislative reforms during the twentieth century to make it simpler, constitutes a self-contained body of law, as its understating requires previous knowledge of property principles and vocabulary, and the simultaneous understanding of a

[119] Emmerich (n 118) 956.
[120] eg ibid 982.
[121] Auer (n 111) 111–13.
[122] eg Matthews (n 8) 313.

variety of legislation. Thus, even if the interplay of statutory law and case law may amount to a coherent system, it can hardly be described in simple terms.[123]

The complexity of English property law is increased by the lack of unity of its contents and the variety of its sources. On the one hand, it governs three separate domains which are usually not treated together: land law, personal property and trusts. On the other, as with the rest of English private law, relevant elements of it derive from Equity. The latter has made a significant contribution to property law, but has also increased its complexity by adding a longer list of 'equitable property rights' that behave differently to legal property rights.[124]

From a comparative perspective, a first source of complexity in accounting for the common law concept of a property right is the doctrine of relativity of title. However, its content and conceptual implications are rarely explained.[125] Even if terms such as 'possessory title' are not used in a stable and consistent way by commentators,[126] at least in English law, the doctrine can be sketched in general terms by the 'finders-keepers rule'. In principle, when someone finds a chattel lost on someone else's land, the finder has a better title to it than the owner of the land and can assert such right against the landowner and all others, except the original owner,[127] who in turn has a limited period to assert her right:[128] the title of the finder is relatively better than any one who comes into possession after the finder, but that of the original owner is relatively better than the finder's.

The doctrine also applies to land: the older possessor of land has a title that is relatively stronger than the one of more recent possessors, subject to the statute of limitations. However, there is some debate as to what extent registration has affected its relevance. On the one hand, successive registration systems enacted in England since the nineteenth century have progressively eroded the importance of the doctrine: under the current law, legal title is conclusively vested in the registered proprietor (LRA 2002, s 58), while the limitation period for registered titles has been abolished (LRA 2002, s 96).[129] However, the LRA 2002 does not expressly abrogate the doctrine of relativity of title and several of its provisions operate assuming that the existence of a registered title does not necessarily preclude other titles or interests in the same land, which may exist outside the register.[130]

[123] FH Lawson and Bernard Rudden, *The Law of Property* (3rd edn, OUP 2002) 11, 19–20.

[124] William Swadling, 'Property: General Principles' in Andrew Burrows (ed), *English Private Law* (3rd edn, OUP 2013) 174, 180.

[125] A notable exception is Bar (n 6) 27–28, 49–54.

[126] Luke Rostill, *Possession, Relative Title, and Ownership in English Law* (OUP 2021) 25.

[127] *Hannah v Peel* [1945] 1 KB 509, *Parker v British Airways Board* [1982] QB 1004, CA.

[128] See Limitation Act 1980, s 3(1).

[129] Elizabeth Cooke, *Land Law* (2nd edn, OUP 2012) 243–45, 250–54. Cooke does not mention LRA 2002, s 58 but it is necessary for a full account of her argument.

[130] Amy Goymour and Robin Hickey, 'The Continuing Relevance of Relativity of Title Under the Land Registration Act 2002' in Amy Goymour, Stephen Watterson and Martin Dixon (eds), *New*

A second difficulty arises from the theory of estates. In contrast to German law, in common law systems, individuals do not technically own land (the thing), but *estates* in land (rights over the thing).[131] This doctrine used to accept a variety of complex entitlements,[132] but at least in England, the 1922–25 legislation simplified the system, leaving the fee simple and the leasehold as the only available legal estates (LPA 1925, s 1(1)). From an historical perspective, the fee simple reflects the (now mostly nominal)[133] relation of the estate holder with the Crown (theoretically, the 'owner'), while the leasehold corresponds to that of the tenant with the landlord.[134] However, from a contemporary doctrinal and functional perspective, their central difference lies in their temporal dimension:[135] while the fee simple is an indefinite estate in land, the leasehold *must* have a limited duration.[136]

This does not mean that 'ownership' is absent from English land law,[137] but its place is more that of an 'incident' to legal estates: whoever has a large indefinite set of use privileges and control powers over land – leaseholder or freeholder – is seen as 'owning the land' at that moment.[138] In England, the very notion of 'land for a time'[139] implies that estates are about ownership.[140] In turn, estates can be subject to a series of legal property interests (LPA 1925, s 1(2)), that do not confer 'ownership' in land (eg easements).

Equity adds a third layer of complexity, by providing for a longer list of 'equitable property rights' that behave differently to legal property rights: except for restrictive covenants, these rights (at least in principle) are only binding upon a limited category of third parties, namely (certain) successors in title. However, equitable property rights do not form a homogenous category, as they cluster together rights that mirror legal property rights (eg equitable leases and easements), beneficial rights under a trust, and 'other equitable property rights'.[141] In this context, the trust – 'equity's greatest contribution to the law of property'[142] – is the most important source of complexity.

Perspectives on Land Registration: Contemporary Problems and Solutions (Bloomsbury 2018); Rostill (n 107) 96–97.

[131] Harris (n 69) 68–69; Susan Bright, 'Of Estates and Interest: A Tale of Ownership and Property Rights' in Susan Bright and John Dewar (eds), *Land Law: Themes and Perspectives* (OUP 1998) 530.

[132] See AH Manchester, *A Modern Legal History of England and Wales, 1750–1950* (Butterworth 1980) 302.

[133] In exceptional circumstances, land can still escheat to the Crown, see Ian Williams, 'The Certainty of Term Requirement in Leases: Nothing Lasts Forever' (2015) 74 *CLJ* 592, 599–600.

[134] Cooke (n 129) 15.

[135] Bright (n 131) 130.

[136] *Street v Mountford* [1985] AC 809; *Prudential Assurance v London Residuary Body* [1992] 2 AC 386, [1992] 3 WLR 279. This does not imply that freeholds are necessarily forever, as they can escheat (ie return to the Crown). Williams (n 133).

[137] For discussion, see Rostill (n 126) 166–68.

[138] Harris (n 69) 68–74.

[139] *Walsingham's Case* (1573) 2 Plowden 547, 555.

[140] See Bright (n 131) 530.

[141] Swadling (n 124) 174, 180–81. For discussion, see ch 6, section II and ch 7, section II.

[142] Lawson and Rudden (n 123) 86.

A good starting point to understand trusts is that, in common law jurisdictions, property rights not only can be held outright (for the benefit of the holder), but 'in trust' for another person.[143] This structure is invariably explained by its historical origins in the English court of Chancery,[144] which cannot be summarised here.[145] However, the outline of English property law cannot be sketched without mentioning how the trust impacts the position of the holder of the right (the trustee), the person (or people) for whose benefit it is held (the beneficiary/beneficiaries) and different third parties. The trustee, sometimes misleadingly called the 'legal owner', is the holder of the right and, as such, can manage and sell the property. However, because the trustee holds the property right for the benefit of the beneficiary, misleadingly called 'beneficial' or 'equitable owner', the trustee cannot treat the property as her own: if the trustee neglects or destroys the property, she breaches the trust, becoming liable to the beneficiary.[146] A point frequently missed by civilian lawyers is that it is of the essence of trusts that placing a right under them does not alter its nature: the trustee remains the owner *vis a vis* third parties and thus is (normally) the only one entitled to exercise the rights associated with the trust property.[147]

The trust is credited with providing private parties with flexible elements to structure their dealings.[148] Its main practical effect is facilitating the transfer of property by allowing trustees to deal with it *as if* they held all the rights in it, regardless of their beneficial or legal nature.[149] Only in limited circumstances can beneficiaries enforce their equitable interest directly against third parties. First, if the trustee transfers the property without authority under the trust, the general position is that the beneficiary might recover the property from third parties, unless the later acquired the property in good faith, for value and without notice; and, second, in case of insolvency of the trustee, the beneficiary can enforce her 'equitable property rights' directly against the creditors of the trustee.[150]

[143] Swadling (n 124) 210; Lawson and Rudden (n 123) 86.

[144] See Ben McFarlane, 'Equity' in Andrew S Gold and others (eds), *The Oxford Handbook of New Private Law* (OUP 2021) 549.

[145] For a summary, see Jeffrey Hackney, *Understanding Equity and Trusts* (Fontana Press 1987) 21–28.

[146] Lawson and Rudden (n 123) 86, 87.

[147] Matthews (n 8) 316–17. For an example, see *Re Brockbank* [1948] Ch 206, [1948] 1 All ER 287.

[148] eg McFarlane, 'Equity' (n 144) 548–49; Hanoch Dagan and Irit Samet, 'Express Trust: The Dark Horse of the Liberal Property Regime', *Philosophical Foundations of the Law of Express Trusts* (OUP 2023) 151–53, 156.

[149] eg see TOLATA 1996, s 6(1).

[150] Swadling (n 124) 213–14. In some cases, the assets do not vest in the trustee's bankrupt estate by statute (eg IA 1986, s 283(3)(a)), but even in the absence of such an express provision, the assets are not available to the creditors of the trustee (see *Carter Holt Harvey v Commonwealth of Australia* [2019] HCA 20 [26]–[27] (Kiefel CJ, Keane and Edelman JJ). For another unusual situation, see discussion on *Shell UK Ltd and others v Total UK Ltd and others* [2010] EWCA Civ 180, [2011] QB 86 in ch 6, section II.B.

Building on this, the 'orthodox approach'[151] holds that the rights of the beneficiary of a trust are proprietary because they possess the two most characteristic 'incidents' of these types of rights: first, while they exist, they can (eventually) be enforced against third parties who receive the trust property or come into contact with it and, second, in case of insolvency of the trustee, they give the beneficiary priority to access the trust property. Thus, in this view, even if the right of the beneficiary of a trust does not bind *everyone*, this is sufficient to conclude that such rights are proprietary in nature.[152]

In English land law, this scheme is widely affected by statutory law. At the height of the 'free trade campaign' for the reform of land law, the Settled Land Act 1882 introduced a statutory 'overreaching' system that, in the case of sales, facilitates the transferring of the interest of the beneficiaries from the land to its proceeds, allowing the purchaser to ignore most beneficial interests in it.[153] The 1925 legislation kept this mechanism, making it applicable to registered and unregistered land. This allows buyers to take free from most beneficial interests in land, as long as the transaction meets certain requirements as to the payment of capital (see LPA 1925, s 27).[154] Thus, even if Equity might 'split' ownership in certain regards, from the perspective of third parties, modern trust law essentially does the opposite: it concentrates the powers of disposition in one (or few) owners, who can easily pass an unincumbered title to a third party. That is why contemporary English authors have seen an important continuity in the position of (legal) owners and trustees *vis a vis* third parties, which is consistent with the idea that trusts do not fragment the trustee's rights, but rather keep them in an undivided package, encumbering it with duties towards beneficiaries.[155]

B. Property Rights as Rights *in Rem*

The previous description does not offer much clarity as to the conceptual nature of property rights in England. Nonetheless, across all this doctrinal complexity, as in civilian systems, '[t]he hallmark of a property right is its ability to bind strangers to its creation', and – as in Germany – the *numerus clausus* principle is normally first mentioned in this context, as a means to tell which rights have the ability to produce these third-party effects.[156] Thus, as in German law, English

[151] Patrick Parkinson, 'Reconceptualising the Express Trust' (2002) 61 *CLJ* 657, 657, describing this approach.

[152] eg Charlie Webb and Tim Akkouh, *Trusts Law* (5th edn, Palgrave 2017) 22–24.

[153] William Cornish and others, *Law and Society in England 1750–1950* (2nd edn, Hart 2019) 171, 176–77.

[154] Swadling (n 124) 271.

[155] eg Ben McFarlane, 'Trusts, Property, and Rights' in Simone Degeling, Jessica Hudson and Irit Samet (eds), *Philosophical Foundations of the Law of Express Trusts* (OUP 2023) 50, 52–53, 60.

[156] Swadling (n 124) 174–75.

scholarship essentially understands property as 'rights *in rem*',[157] a similarity already pointed out by AM Honoré in the 1950s.[158]

However, from a comparative perspective, it has been argued that, due to the doctrine of relativity of title and the impact of trusts, common law property rights do not possess the same 'absolute' nature of civilian real rights. In this view, the defining feature of common law property rights is not their general impact on the rest of the world, but their effect *vis a vis* specific third parties that have not contracted with the holder of the interest.[159] This view is confirmed in *Akers v Samba Financial Group*,[160] where the UK Supreme Court denied the claim of the liquidators of a company seeking to set aside a transfer to a third party of certain shares held by a trustee for the benefit of the company, with Lord Sumption stating that

> an equitable interest possesses the essential hallmark of any right in rem, namely that it is good against a third party into whose hands the property or its traceable proceeds may have come, subject to the rules of equity for the protection of bona fide purchasers for value without notice.[161]

Following *Akers*, one way of understating the third-party effects of property rights in English law is that property rights do not need to be absolute to bind third parties. Accordingly, from a doctrinal perspective, property rights are frequently characterised in English scholarship by opposing them to personal rights and showing how the first bind third parties where the latter fail to do so, typically, comparing the effect of lease and licence on future owners of land.[162] This view is confirmed by the aforementioned circumstance that equitable property rights are said to be proprietary in nature, despite (normally) only being able to bind successors in title.[163]

However, reducing the conceptual nature of property rights to their ability of binding successors in title would be inaccurate. In common law jurisdictions, at least legal property rights also have third-party effects that resemble the 'absolute' nature of civilian real rights. This is not obvious at first sight, because such effects are not immediately associated with property law, which concentrates on solving conflicting claims over the same assets. In contrast to civilian systems, which primarily defend owners from attack by strangers by actions that are seen

157 eg Peter Birks, 'Five Keys to Land Law' in Susan Bright and John Dewar (eds), *Land Law: Themes and Perspectives* (OUP 1998) 472–73.

158 AM Honoré, 'Rights of Exclusion and Immunities Against Divesting' (1959) 34 *Tul L Rev* 453, 453.

159 van Erp (n 3) 1047; Bernard Rudden, 'Economic Theory v. Property Law: The Numerus Clausus Problem' in John Eekelaar and John Bell (eds), *Oxford Essays in Jurisprudence: Third Series* (Clarendon 1987) 239.

160 *Akers v Samba Financial Group* [2017] UKSC 6, [2017] AC 424.

161 ibid [82].

162 eg Bright (n 131) 529; Ben McFarlane, Nicholas Hopkins and Sarah Nield, *Land Law: Text, Cases and Materials* (5th edn, OUP 2021) 151–53, 195–96.

163 eg Swadling (n 124) 180.

as specific to property law, such as a *vindicatio*,[164] in common law systems, this protection comes from tort law, typically, through negligence, trespass, nuisance (for land), and conversion (for goods).[165] These torts, are regularly only available for those holding property rights, not mere personal rights. For example, in *Hunter and others v Canary Wharf*,[166] the House of Lords only granted damages against nuisance resulting from the construction of the Canary Wharf Tower in East London to plaintiffs holding property rights in land, rejecting the claims of those who only had licences.[167] The availability of protection via tort law for, at least, legal property rights, shows that having an absolute effect is also a feature of English property rights, although it has been said that an audience needs to be 'reminded' of this.[168]

The latter creates a conceptual challenge for equitable property rights, which, in general, do not afford direct tort claims to its holder. In England, this has recently led some scholars to argue that equitable property rights – including rights of beneficiaries of a trust – should be seen as third type of rights, known as 'persistent rights'.[169] In this view, also advanced in comparative law,[170] equitable rights should not be understood as rights against things nor rights against persons, but as 'rights against rights': when B has a right against the right of A, *prima facie*, anyone who acquires A's right may come under a duty to B.[171] Using the words of the High Court of Australia,[172] equitable property rights are better described not as interests that are 'carved out of a legal estate but impressed upon it'.[173] From this perspective, Lord Sumption's argument in *Akers* misses that the third-party effects of beneficial rights in a trust are essentially different from those of legal property rights.[174] This can have relevant implications for the *numerus clausus*: does it mean that 'persistent rights' are not subject to this principle and can be freely created by parties? This question will be answered

[164] See ch 6, section I.

[165] Peter Cane, *Key Ideas in Tort Law* (Hart 2017) 7–31; Peter Birks, 'Personal Property: Proprietary Rights and Remedies' (2000) 11 *King's LJ* 1, 6–11; Simon Douglas, *Liability for Wrongful Interferences with Chattels* (Hart 2011) 1.

[166] *Hunter and others v Canary Wharf* [1997] AC 665, HL.

[167] Negligence operates in a similar manner. See *Cattle v Stockton Waterworks Co* [1975] LR 10 QB 453.

[168] Ben McFarlane, 'Keppell v Bailey (1834); Hill v Tupper (1863): The Numerus Clausus and the Common Law' in Nigel Gravells (ed), *Landmark Cases in Land Law* (Hart 2013) 2.

[169] See Ben McFarlane, *The Structure of Property Law* (Hart 2008) 23–25; Ben McFarlane, 'Equity, Obligations and Third Parties' (2008) 2008 *Sing J Legal Stud* 308; Ben McFarlane and Robert Stevens, 'The Nature of Equitable Property' (2010) 4 *J Eq* 1.

[170] Lionel D Smith, 'Trust and Patrimony' (2008) 38 *Rev Gen Dr* 379, 392.

[171] McFarlane and Stevens (n 169) 1.

[172] See Simon Douglas and Ben McFarlane, 'Defining Property Rights' in James Penner and Henry Smith (eds), *Philosophical Foundations of Property Law* (OUP 2013) 240–41.

[173] Per Brennan J, *DKLR Holding Co (No 2) Pty Ltd v Commissioner of Stamp Duties* (1982) 149 *CLR* 431, 474.

[174] Ben McFarlane and Simon Douglas, 'Property, Analogy and Variety' (2022) 42 *OJLS* 161, 20–22, 25–26.

in chapter three, section III and its implications will be discussed in chapter six, section II and chapter seven, section II.

C. Bundle of Rights or Right to Exclude?

A different conceptual approach to common law property rights emerges from a key theoretical debate that has been going on in Anglo-American scholarship since the beginning of the twentieth century. This discussion was originally triggered by political forces not that different from those leading to enshrining the social function of ownership in the Weimar Constitution. Similar to the strand later followed by continental codifications,[175] at the height of English liberal thought,[176] Blackstone described the 'right of property' as the 'sole and despotic dominion which one man claims and exercises over external things of the world, in total exclusion of the right of any other individual in the universe'.[177] However, as in Germany, this concept of a property right had long been accompanied by the existence of a public power to expropriate such rights.[178] Indeed, Blackstone himself acknowledged that freemen can be divested from their property by public power, subject to certain proceedings and guarantees.[179]

In practice, at the time England was developing the core of its modern property law, compulsory purchases were already playing a decisive role in transforming Britain from an agricultural to an urban industrial economy. From the mid eighteenth century, industry, transport and urban development imposed new demands on land. In this context, compulsory purchases facilitated by interventionist governments were instrumental in setting new ventures in motion, like building roads, canals, railways and, later on, clearing slums. Since the late eighteenth century, Parliament had even vested canal[180] and railways companies[181] with power to compulsory purchase land, allowing them to build modern infrastructure without having to face holdouts.[182] This power is still constantly exercised in contemporary UK.[183]

[175] Thomas C Grey, 'The Disintegration of Property' (1980) 22 *Nomos* 69, 73.
[176] See Cornish and others (n 153) 65, 67.
[177] William Blackstone, *Commentaries on the Laws of England. Book II: Of the Rights of Things* (Wilfrid Prest ed, OUP 2016) [2].
[178] Allen, *Property and The Human Rights Act 1998* (n 69) 8–9.
[179] William Blackstone, *Commentaries on the Laws of England. Book I: Of the Rights of Persons* (Wilfrid Prest ed, OUP 2016) [135].
[180] eg Monmouthshire Canal Act 1792.
[181] Land Consolidations Act 1845.
[182] On compulsory purchases during this period, Cornish and others (n 153) 155–56; Brian A'Hearn, 'The British Industrial Revolution in a European Mirror' in Roderick Floud, Jane Humphries and Paul Johnson (eds), *The Cambridge Economic History of Modern Britain*, vol I 1700–1870 (CUP 2014) 36–37.
[183] See Land Compensation Act 1961.

However, over the following two centuries, this system based on conceptually well-defined entitlements over things, especially land, that could exceptionally be taken by the state for good reasons, collapsed under the pervasive influence of the metaphor of the 'bundle of rights'.[184] In the prevailing view,[185] the metaphor is presented as a combination of Wesley Hohfeld's analysis of jural relations in terms of 'opposites' and 'correlatives'[186] and Honoré's incidents of ownership.[187] One of Hohfeld's central aims was to make clear that rights *in rem* are not rights against things. In his view, this misunderstanding results from confusing a physical relation (with the asset) with a jural relation between people. Since law regulates relations with other human beings, in order to be clear and direct, all jural relations must be predicated by reference to them. *In rem* or 'multital' rights are characterised by Hohfeld as one of a large number of very similar rights availing against different people of the same class. For example, if A owns and occupies land, a large number of people (not necessarily all) are under a duty to A to keep off the land: A's claim-right against B that B keep off the land is a multital right as it is one of a large number of very similar rights that A also has against, for example, C, D, E etc. The key to this idea is that the right against each of these third parties is a distinct right, turning the traditional understanding of a 'property right' into a collection of discrete legal relations available against specific members of a group.[188]

The early development of the bundle metaphor is closely linked to the progressive agenda of the American Legal Realist movement of the early twentieth century and its aim to facilitate the use of regulation for social policies.[189] Under the takings clause of the American Constitution (Fifth Amendment), individuals only have a right to compensation for loss when they are deprived of their property by the state.[190] The key implication of the bundle picture is that it is always possible to subtract rights from the bundle via regulation and still refer to property as 'a bundle of rights'.[191] During the New Deal era, the bundle of rights idea was embodied in the Restatement of Property 1936, but the approach truly prospered with the law and economics movement after

[184] Grey (n 175) 74, 81.

[185] JE Penner, 'The Bundle of Rights Picture of Property' (1996) 43 *UCLA L Rev* 711, 712, 724–38.

[186] Wesley Newcomb Hohfeld, 'Some Fundamental Legal Conceptions as Applied in Judicial Reasoning' (1913) 23 *Yale LJ* 16, 31, 32; Wesley Newcomb Hohfeld, 'Fundamental Legal Conceptions as Applied in Judicial Reasoning' (1917) 26 *Yale LJ* 710, 722–23.

[187] AM Honoré, 'Ownership' in AG Guest (ed), *Oxford Essays on Jurisprudence* (Clarendon Press 1961).

[188] Hohfeld, 'Fundamental Legal Conceptions as Applied in Judicial Reasoning' (n 186) 718–21.

[189] Grey (n 175) 81; Thomas W Merrill and Henry E Smith, 'Making Coasean Property More Coasean' (2011) 54 *JL & Econ* 77, 82; Henry E Smith, 'Property as the Law of Things' (2012) 125 *Harv L Rev* 1691, 1697; Henry E Smith, 'Introduction' in Kenneth Ayotte and Henry E Smith (eds), *Research Handbook on the Economics of Property Law* (Edward Elgar 2012) 1.

[190] Tom Allen, 'The Right to Property' in Tom Ginsburg and Rosalind Dixon (eds), *Comparative Constitutional Law* (Edward Elgar 2012) 507.

[191] Thomas W Merrill and Henry E Smith, *Property: Principles and Policies* (Foundation Press 2007) 16.

the 1970s[192] (although without its original progressive agenda[193]), until becoming the prevailing understanding of property in mainstream Anglo-American legal philosophy.[194]

In this process, the bundle picture also reached English doctrine.[195] However, considering the radical difference between the American and the British constitutions,[196] and the scarcer influence of legal realism and law and economics in English legal thought,[197] the place of the bundle picture in England needs to be assessed carefully. The UK is an 'extreme outsider' among modern liberal democracies, as it does not have a constitutional court in the American or German sense. This makes the idea that an act passed by Parliament could be abrogated by a court alien to the English legal tradition.[198]

Moreover, until recently, England lacked anything equivalent to the strong Takings Clause of the American Constitution. Even if, since the Middle Ages, the right to private property has formed part of the fundamental law of the Kingdom, its enforceability by courts has historically been limited. Beyond the principle that compulsory acquisitions of property are normally subject to compensation, until very recently, the restrictions on this parliamentary power remained unclear and there was no real scientific development of the principle.[199] The right to private property only achieved a clear constitutional status in England with the entering in force of the Human Rights Act 1998 (HRA 1998),[200] but its impact in English property law remains limited.[201] In consequence, the reception of the bundle picture in England seems better explained by its conceptual appeal, the wish of English scholarship to engage with its American counterpart[202] and its use by some influential progressive scholars.[203]

Since the end of the twentieth century the bundle picture has been subject to a sustained attack.[204] The main argument against it is that it has no

[192] Henry E Smith, 'Economics of Property Law' in Francesco Parisi (ed), *The Oxford Handbook of Law and Economics: Volume 2: Private Law and Commercial Law* (OUP 2017) 152.

[193] See Ron Harris, 'The History and Historical Stance of Law and Economics' in Markus D Dubber and Christopher Tomlins (eds), *The Oxford Handbook of Legal History* (OUP 2018) 29–31.

[194] Penner (n 185) 712.

[195] eg, see Cooke (n 129) 3.

[196] See Kischel (n 9) 338, 342.

[197] See PS Atiyah and RS Summers, *Form and Substance in Anglo-American Law* (Clarendon Press 1987) 116–17, 134, 141–42; Zweigert and Kötz (n 42) 245–49; Florian Wagner-von Papp, 'Comparative Law & Economics and the Egg-Laying Wool-Milk Sow' (2014) 9 *J Comp L* 137, 141; Kischel (n 9) 347–48.

[198] Kischel (n 9) 339–40.

[199] Allen, *Property and The Human Rights Act 1998* (n 69) 8–9.

[200] See First Protocol, Art 1.

[201] See McFarlane, Hopkins and Nield (n 162) 147–48; Rachael Walsh, 'Stability and Predictability in English Property Law – the Impact of Article 8 of the European Convention on Human Rights Reassessed' (2015) 131 *LQR* 585, 600–03.

[202] eg Douglas and McFarlane (n 172).

[203] eg Kevin Gray, 'Property in Thin Air' (1991) 50 *CLJ* 252, 252, 259.

[204] Robert C Ellickson, 'Two Cheers for the Bundle-of-Sticks Metaphor, Three Cheers for Merrill and Smith' (2011) 8 *Econ Journal Watch* 215, 218–19; Douglas and McFarlane (n 172) 219.

explanatory power as it reduces property to a malleable device used to serve contingent policy concerns. In this view, property rights are better understood in terms of a duty of non-interference. The concept is made of two elements: first, a property right understood as a 'right to exclude' and, second, a notion of 'thinghood', which characterises the object of the property right. Once they are combined, the 'thing' mediates between the owner's right to exclude and the correlative duty of all others to keep of it.[205] In this manner, the right to exclude others from the thing and the right to use it 'are opposite sides of the same coin', with the former shaping the understanding of property, and the latter justifying it.[206] This idea is the base of an extensive theoretical account that justifies understanding property rights as 'rights in things'. In this view, thinghood is essential to the concept of a property right, because communicating the duty not to interfere with *a thing* to an anonymous public has much lower costs than communicating different duties not to interfere with *uses* of such thing.[207]

Over the last decades, the understanding of property rights by reference to different aspects of exclusion has become pervasive in common law property theory[208] and has been closely related to the growing interest of Anglo-American property theory in the *numerus clausus* principle.[209] However, there is an odd disconnection in this approach: although it defines property rights by their ability to exclude an indefinite number of third parties from the use of a thing, typically through tort law,[210] its actual examples almost always involve conflicts between holder of rights and successors in title,[211] echoing the tendency of English doctrine to associate the 'basic structure' of property rights with successor liability.[212]

IV. THE CONCEPT OF A PROPERTY RIGHT AND ITS IMPACT ON LEGAL CHANGE

As usual in comparative law, the level of similarity of the English and German concepts of a property right is a matter of perspective. At a very general level,

[205] Penner, 'The Bundle of Rights Picture of Property' (n 185) 714, 817.

[206] JE Penner, *The Idea of Property in Law* (OUP 1997) 71. For an updated version, JE Penner, *Property Rights: A Re-Examination* (OUP 2020).

[207] See Thomas W Merrill and Henry E Smith, 'What Happened to Property Law in Economics?' (2001) 111 *Yale LJ* 357; Thomas W Merrill and Henry E Smith, 'The Property/Contract Interface' (2001) 101 *Colum L Rev* 773.

[208] eg see Douglas and McFarlane (n 172) 243; Larissa Katz, 'Exclusion and Exclusivity in Property Law' (2008) 58 *U Toronto LJ* 275.

[209] See Thomas W Merrill and Henry E Smith, 'Optimal Standardization in the Law of Property: The Numerus Clausus Principle' (2000) 110 *Yale LJ* 1; Merrill and Smith, 'What Happened to Property Law in Economics?' (n 207) 359, 385–88.

[210] eg Penner, *Property Rights* (n 206) 16.

[211] eg Smith, 'Property as the Law of Things' (n 189).

[212] eg McFarlane, *The Structure of Property Law* (n 169) 59–62.

both concepts are ultimately defined by their ability to bind third parties and their protection against state action. However, at a doctrinal level, they evidence significant differences. This final section focuses on those conceptual elements that are relevant to understand the operation of the *numerus clausus* of property rights and its interaction with changing social and economic realities: (a) the impact of public law on property law; (b) 'thinghood' of property rights; and (c) the distinction between successor and trespassory liability.

A. Forced 'Relocation' and Public 'Reshaping' of Property Rights

A first phenomenon identified by this chapter is that a relevant part of the ability of property rights to adapt to a changing world comes from two features outside private law: the forced 'relocation' of property rights by expropriations and their external 'reshaping' by public law regulation. This shows that, contrary to common views arguing that constitutions seek to rigidise property systems to keep social peace,[213] they also infuse them with a dose of flexibility that allows political power to react to new realities without creating massive disruption.

Property rights, as understood in modern private law, have never existed in the vacuum. Since times pre-dating the development of contemporary property systems, in both England and Germany, proprietary entitlements have been subject to the state's power of eminent domain. The constitutional regulation of this power evolved very differently in both jurisdictions. However, it seems clear that, at the time England and Germany were developing their modern property law, expropriations were seen as an essential part of a broader legal framework that placed individual economic self-responsibility and the promotion of trade and industry at its centre. Today, this power still infuses modern property law with a relevant dose of flexibility, allowing the state to forcefully 'relocate' the modules of property when this is needed to address new realities.

However, what ought to be the scope of this power remains disputed, at least in the theoretical debate. Neither efficiency-based nor progressive approaches controvert the convenience of this 'external corrector' to private allocation of property rights by consent. However, both views strongly disagree on the justification of this power. Efficiency arguments typically justify expropriations in the need of solving hold-out problems created by monopoly position over assets essential for projects that would create massive social benefits.[214] Because in these cases there is no market for the relevant asset that ensures its efficient consensual re-allocation, the state (or someone acting on its behalf) is vested with the power to 'take' or 'expropriate' the relevant entitlement, subject to

[213] eg Mattei, *Basic Principles of Property Law* (n 6) 30.

[214] eg Hans-Bernard Schäfer and Klaus Ott, *The Economic Analysis of Civil Law* (2nd edn, Elgar 2022) 511–12.

a duty of paying an objectively determined value.[215] In other words, these are cases in which the right to exclude cannot relocate the modules of property by itself, calling for direct state action over property law to face a new reality.[216]

The relevance of this power in enabling property law to deal with new realities should not be underestimated. For example, contrary to traditional views attributing England's early industrialisation to the existence of stable and secure property rights,[217] at least for land, this must be relativised: the power of compulsory purchases was instrumental in enabling England to develop roads, canals, railways and improve urban living conditions, and the same can be said for Germany. Thus, it should not come as surprise that the sound economic logic of this rule has been put forward to explain why legal systems from very different traditions converged towards the same basic model of expropriations.[218]

In contrast, progressive views justify the power of the state to impose non-consented transfers of property rights in a matter of political legitimacy: for property law to remain justified, it is essential that that the state retains the power to periodically re-examine and change the property system in order to balance the tensions between the rights of owner and no-owners.[219] The relevant implication would be that the state could expropriate property rights, not only to efficiently solve holdout problems, but also to advance broader redistributive goals. Considering that, in practice, the dominant view across jurisdictions is that compensation must reflect the market value of the expropriated asset,[220] this does not seem to be descriptively accurate. However, initiatives such as the one advanced by *Deutsche Wohnen & Co enteignen* to 'socialise' flats owned by real estate companies in Berlin could well be rationalised under this argument. To what extent these policies are feasible in practice[221] and whether they are the best way to achieve redistributive outcomes[222] are different questions.

The type of public law regulation developed during the twentieth century added a second institutional mechanism to adapt property law to new realities.

[215] Guido Calabresi and A Douglas Melamed, 'Property Rules, Liability Rules, and Inalienability: One View of the Cathedral' (1972) 85 *Harv L Rev* 1089, 1092.

[216] Richard Epstein, 'The Plasticity of Property: Legal Transitions between Property Regimes for Different Resources' in Ernst Nordtveit (ed), *The Changing Role of Property Law: Rights, Values and Concepts* (Edward Elgar 2023) 32.

[217] Especially, Douglass C North and Barry R Weingast, 'Constitutions and Commitment: The Evolution of Institutions Governing Public Choice in Seventeenth-Century England' (1989) 49 *J Econ History* 803.

[218] See Ugo Mattei, 'Efficiency in Legal Transplants: An Essay in Comparative Law and Economics' (1994) 14 *Int Rev Law and Econ* 3, 5–7.

[219] For example, Hanoch Dagan, *A Liberal Theory of Property Law* (CUP 2021) 210–12.

[220] Even where constitutions do not explicitly provide for full compensation (like Germany), in practice this seems to be the norm. André van der Walt and Rachael Walsh, 'Comparative Constitutional Property Law' in Michele Graziadei and Lionel Smith (eds), *Comparative Property Law: Global Perspectives* (Edward Elgar 2017) 212; Allen, 'The Right to Property' (n 190) 515.

[221] On the difficulties associated with change in property law, see ch 1, sections I, II and ch 3, section IV.

[222] There is an argument holding that redistribution is better achieved through fiscal policy, this is, by taxation and public spending. Savigny himself was of this view, Di Robilant (n 57) 190.

However, its impact is not equally visible across jurisdictions. The bundle picture put forward by American legal realists in the early twentieth century to advance social policies has a clear functional equivalent in Germany, but its doctrinal content is not found in private law. The political context leading to the enactment of the BGB and the strong allegiance of its drafters to the Pandectist tradition, meant that the demands for 'a drop of socialist oil'[223] did not influence the code. However, with the rise of the Weimar Republic, a functionally equivalent idea developed at the constitutional level in the form of the 'social function of ownership'. This constitutional arrangement has allowed German law to deal directly with the problems created by the need for state action over property rights, without the need of developing a new private law concept of a property right.

In the US, this phenomenon was mirrored by the rise of the doctrine of regulatory takings in the 1920s.[224] The story of the later development of this doctrine is complex and cannot be summarised here, but it is worth noting that the 'bundle metaphor' played an important role in it.[225] This development seems to have been absent in English property law, due to the unique supremacy of the British Parliament and (probably) the strong political expectation that the state would not take property without compensation making it unnecessary. Hence, the rise of the regulatory state in Britain seems to have left no direct tangible marks in the English concept of a property right, other than the importation of the bundle metaphor from the US. A manifestation of this is that, despite acknowledging its importance, the impact of public law is normally explicitly excluded from English property law textbooks.[226]

This shows how the effect of public regulation on property rights was channelled through different institutional arrangements in Germany, the US and the UK. In England and Germany the constitutional framework seems to have allowed regulation to operate very much in parallel to property law doctrine, with no point of contact with the concept of a property rights nor the *numerus clausus* doctrine, creating a certain illusion that nineteenth century property law has passed essentially unaltered into the twenty-first century. However, this impression is not entirely true. As apparent from the developments discussed later in this book,[227] the social and economic concerns that underpinned the rise of the regulatory state during the twentieth century had a relevant impact in English and German property law, especially in connection to housing problems. Some of these social forces have even altered the *numerus clausus* of English and German property law.

[223] Gierke (n 66).

[224] See *Pennsylvania Coal v Mahon*, 260 US 393 (1922).

[225] eg *Andrus v Allard*, 444 US 51 (1979); *Loretto v Teleprompter Manhattan CATV Corp*, 458 US 419 (1982).

[226] eg McFarlane, Hopkins and Nield (n 162) 4–5.

[227] See ch 6, section II; ch 7, sections II and III; and ch 8, sections III and IV.

B. Thinghood of Property Rights

At the level of private law, the Anglo-American picture of the 'bundle of rights' that highlights that rights *in rem* are *not* rights over things seems at odds with the BGB's explicit understanding of property rights as rights in (tangible) things. Nonetheless, if the English and German concepts of a property right are considered within their broader theoretical framework, this difference disappears: in both systems, property rights are ultimately understood as relations between people made of correlative active and passive elements that are mediated through things.

The centrality of 'thinghood' in structuring the concept of a property right in both systems is underpinned by a deeper shared rationality: the role of the interest in using the thing as a justification for the right to exclude. In German law, this is generally implied in the role that Kantian self-determination has in the justification of private law relations, which in the case of property law is supplemented by the Hegelian argument that sees ownership as essential to secure an external sphere for the unfolding of personal freedom.[228] By contrast, in the common law, on the one hand, the adoption of the 'will theory' during the nineteenth century was not primarily underpinned by Kantian and Hegelian philosophical ideas,[229] but by Pothier's Will Theory, loosely based on the natural law tradition;[230] while, on the other, the importance of the interest in using the thing that is the object of the right was later blurred by the rise of the bundle picture. However, the centrality of 'things' resurfaced in Anglo-American property theory after James Penner argued that the right to exclude is justified by the interest of owners in using the thing and was later fuelled by Thomas Merrill and Henry Smith's argument regarding the role of thinghood in reducing information costs in the operation of the property system. In German law, this link with information costs of communicating the *erga omnes* nature of property rights also exists, although it is not directly tied to the thing as carrier of information, but rather to the strict separation between rights against persons and rights over things. In this view, because rights in things affect everyone, their number and content must be standardised by the law, to allow everyone to easily know their duties.

The path of this convergence is surprising. In Germany, where the rise of the regulatory state did not significantly impact property law doctrine, this concept is based on a theoretical framework that seems to be frozen in 1900; while in the common law, after a one-hundred-year long debate pushed by different utilitarian approaches, the concept of a property right seems to be reaching the same point where it has been in Germany since the dawn of the twentieth century.

228 GWF Hegel, *Grundlinien Der Philosophie Des Rechts* (Meiner 2009) 66–69. On this, see ch 5, section III.A.

229 Gordley (n 17) 15.

230 David Ibbetson, *A Historical Introduction to the Law of Obligations* (OUP 2001) 220–21.

Does this mean that the Anglo-American debate has been useless? Not at all. By reaching a similar concept by a different and accidental path, Anglo-American property scholarship has developed a sophisticated analytical framework to conceptualise property rights, including Hohfeldian analysis, the distinction between trespassory and successor liability, the role of things in communicating the right to exclude, and the 'rights against rights' theory. These elements will be central when fleshing out the justification of the *numerus clausus*[231] and assessing its practical impact.[232]

C. Successor and Trespassory Liability

Finally, as previously argued by comparative lawyers, a main difference between the English and German concepts of a property right is the scope of their third-party effects. While in Germany property rights are understood as 'absolute' rights, in England their third-party effects are typically described by reference to specific groups of individuals. In comparative law this has normally been attributed to the doctrine of relativity of title. However, the impact of this doctrine is more apparent than real. Not only has it lost importance due to land registration, but, once it is understood in conjunction with limitations, its practical operation is not too different from the manner in which civilian jurisdictions deal with similar problems. For example, in German law, the buyer of a thing not subject to registration might acquire (absolute) ownership over it upon conveyance, regardless of the validity of the sale (§ 929 BGB). However, in cases where the sale is void but the transfer is valid, the original owner has an action ultimately based on unjust enrichment law (*Bereicherungrechts*) to recover the thing (§ 812 BGB), which will also be limited by time (*Verjährung*, §195 BGB). The practical outcome is that the buyer (new owner) will be able to assert her right over the thing against all but the original owner, who will be able to recover the thing, as long the original owner's claim is not barred by the lapse of time. This not very different from how adverse possession works in unregistered land in England.[233]

The enduring difference between the German 'absolute' conception of property rights and the more 'relative' notion prevailing in England is better explained by the tendency of each system to focus on different third-party effects to characterise property rights. In both England and Germany property rights have two distinct third-party effects: when A grants a property right in a thing to B, then B enjoys protection against, first, third parties who interfere with the thing (X) and, second, third parties who later acquire other property

[231] See ch 5, section IV.
[232] See chs 6, 7 and 8.
[233] For adverse possession in England, see Martin Dixon, *Modern Land Law* (12th edn, Routledge 2021) 499–98.

rights in the same thing from A (C). In the context of Anglo-American law, Penner has called them, respectively, 'trespassory' and 'successor' liability[234] (see Figure 1) and, in German law, authors as Hübner and Riegnar[235] and Eichler[236] called the first effect '*Ausschliessungsbefugnis*' (exclusion right) or '*Drittschutz*' (protection against third parties) and, the second, '*Sukzessionsschutz*' (protection against successors).

Figure 1 Successor and trespassory liability

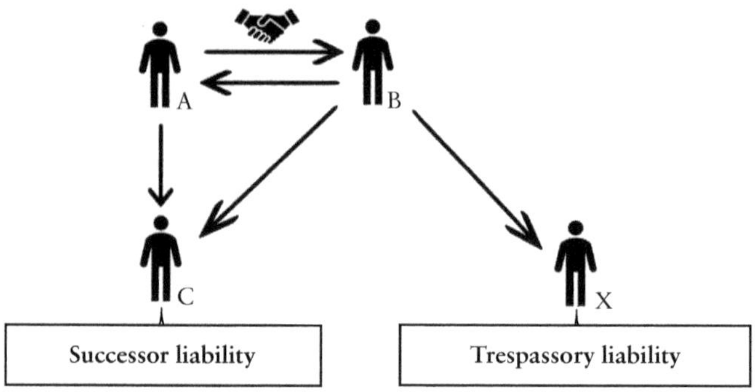

However, each system approaches property rights from a different perspective. German doctrine emphasises the trespassory effects of property rights, as apparent in the central role that the recovery of possession and the protection against physical interference by third parties has in delineating the protection of ownership, while successor liability is seen as a self-evident consequence of this absolute effect. By contrast, as exemplified by Lord Sumption's judgment in *Akers*,[237] in English law, the existence of property rights that only affect successors in title, especially the rights of beneficiaries of trusts, make successor liability the implicit paradigm of the third-party effects of property rights.[238] Indeed, English scholars tend to see successor liability as the source of the 'the basic tension of property law',[239] somehow downplaying the relevance of trespassory liability or displacing it to tort law.

German law also provides for certain rights that might only bind successors in title but not strangers, most notably, the rights of lessees. However, these 'intermediate figures' are not labelled as property rights. This creates a relevant

[234] James Penner, 'Duty and Liability in Respect of Funds' in John Lowry and Mistelis Loukas (eds), *Commercial Law: Perspectives and Practice* (LexisNexis Butterworths 2006) 215.
[235] Heinz Hübner and Joachim Riegner, *Sachenrecht* (Translatia 1948) 7.
[236] Hermann Eichler, *Institutionen Des Sachenrechts*, vol 1 (Duncker & Humblot 1954) 6–7.
[237] See section III.B.
[238] Honoré, 'Rights of Exclusion and Immunities Against Divesting' (n 158).
[239] See McFarlane, *The Structure of Property Law* (n 169) 5–6.

classificatory problem that will resurface in chapter three when discussing the scope of the *numerus clausus* principle in Germany, opening the door to assessing these intermediate cases under the 'rights against rights' theory.[240] A central implication, almost completely overlooked until now in comparative analysis, is that an assessment of the impact of the *numerus clausus* in property law needs to distinguish between trespassory and successor liability.[241]

The previous analysis is not enough to account for the impact of trusts in the comparative analysis of the concept of a property right. This topic has been widely thematised by scholars looking for its functional equivalent in civilian jurisdictions.[242] However, the image of trusts as creating a 'split' or 'double' ownership has been so pervasive that two other aspects of it have been neglected: first, the ability of the beneficiary's rights to bind third parties is very limited; and, second, trusts not only serve to separate ownership, but also to concentrate the power of disposition of the whole asset in one hand *vis a vis* third parties.

The first phenomenon is not unknown to civilian systems, where obligations underpinned by a proprietary aim, typically a relation between seller and buyer, might be enforced against successors in title[243] and creditors,[244] in manners that have been said to resemble the trust.[245] The second shows a striking functional and ideological similarity between two institutions that are normally seen as at the heart of the civil-common law divide: trusts and unitary ownership. The practical development of the trust and the emergence of unitary ownership during the nineteenth century seem to have been driven by the same policy decision of concentrating the powers of alienation on a single hand in order to create modern land markets.[246] Consistent with this view, English scholarship has highlighted the continuity in the position of legal owners and trustees.[247] As a result, the difference between civilian and common law systems seems to be technical rather than ideological: while the former opted to protect third parties acquiring things by limiting the availability of rights running with the asset, the latter protected them by reinforcing mechanisms that allowed buyers to easily acquire free from equitable rights, like overreaching.[248]

[240] As attempted with the French *propter rem* obligations. See Remus Valsan, 'Rights against Rights and Real Obligations' in Lionel Smith (ed), *The Worlds of the Trust* (CUP 2013) 503–11.

[241] As recently argued by Ben McFarlane for English law. Ben McFarlane, 'The Numerus Clausus Principle and Covenants Relating to Land' in Susan Bright (ed), *Modern Studies in Property Law*, vol 6 (Hart 2011) 311.

[242] eg Hansmann and Mattei (n 19); Stefan Grundmann, 'Trust and Treuhand at the End of the 20th Century – Key Problems and Shift of Interests' (1999) 47 *Am J Comp L* 401; Smith, 'Trust and Patrimony' (n 170); Matthews (n 8).

[243] See § 833 BGB and the judicially developed protection of the buyer's interest under a retention of title clause. Wellenhofer (n 105) 165–68, 270–85.

[244] For example, the protection of the judicially developed 'security ownership' in insolvency cases (§ 771 ZPO and §§ 47 and 51(1) InsO). Wilhelm (n 44) 12.

[245] See ch 3, section II.C.

[246] Graziadei (n 9) 81–82, 87.

[247] eg McFarlane, 'Trusts, Property, and Rights' (n 155) 50, 52–53, 60.

[248] On the compatibility of the trust with civil law ownership, see Matthews (n 8).

Finally, the ability of property rights to bind third parties also points to the main doctrinal reason why property law needs to be stable. Different from contractual rights, the creation and modification of a single property right might have vast and enduring effects over an indefinite number of people, including successors in title and pure strangers (trespassers). Even if this might seem obvious, its relevance can hardly be overstated. Across civilian and common law jurisdictions, the enforcement of property rights against third parties explains much of the doctrinal structure of property law. However, in England, binding successors in title seems to be enough to elevate a right to the status of a property right, while that is not the case for Germany. That is why a full understanding of the *numerus clausus* principle requires a more sophisticated approach to the distinction between successor and trespassory liability. The next chapter will continue on this path by accounting for the way the *numerus clausus* principle is understood in England and Germany.

3

The Numerus Clausus *Principle*

THIS BOOK AIMS to explain how private law systems subject to a *numerus clausus* of property rights deal with new circumstances. To this end, this chapter develops on the basic doctrinal elements needed to understand the German and English versions of this principle and its practical operation. This is by no means a novel endeavour. In recent years, the comparative dimension of the *numerus clausus* has been one of the most debated topics in this field. However, this chapter approaches the subject with goals and perspectives that are novel. First, it does not primarily aim to find out to what extent both versions of the principle are equivalent, but to understand them in their own terms and in connection to legal change. Second, it takes a narrower and more conceptual view, focusing almost exclusively on English and German law. Third, different to most comparative scholarship in this field, which has been carried out by civilian lawyers, it incorporates some sophisticated elements of the recent English discussion on the nature of equitable property rights discussed in chapter two.

The chapter starts by briefly accounting for the place of the *numerus clausus* in comparative property law (section I). Then, it develops on the doctrinal elements of the German (section II) and English (section III) versions of the principle and its actual application by courts. Finally, it presents some concluding remarks (section IV). Its first conclusion is that both Germany and England follow a *numerus clausus* principle that limits the creation of new property rights by private parties and courts. However, the 'attitude' to the principle in each jurisdiction is different: German doctrine seems overconfident about it, tending to ignore or downplay the conceptual challenges that borderline figures pose to it, while English doctrine is oversceptical, especially due to the liberty enjoyned by settlors of express trusts to create 'equitable property rights'. This diverging attitude is largely explained by the different concept of a property right prevailing in each jurisdiction described in chapter two: while the narrow German concept of a property right pushes cases that are difficult to square with the *numerus clausus* to the law of obligations, the expansive concept of a property right prevailing in England obscures the fact that trusts have very limited effects on third parties. The main implication of this is that both systems have a 'grey zone' made of 'intermediate rights' with limited third-party effects, where the *numerus clausus* has an uncertain application. The importance of this for the practical operation of the *numerus clausus* is discussed in detail in chapter seven.

The second conclusion is that the list of property rights of both jurisdictions is ideologically, functionally and institutionally similar, but technically different. In both cases the list (i) is the product of nineteenth century classic liberalism, (ii) provides for rights that give similar prerogatives to their holders, and (iii) is mainly controlled by statutory law. However, most of the specific rights contained in the list are quite different. To a large extent, this is an outcome of the different political paths each country followed at the time: while England developed its modern list of property rights over an extremely long period through extensive compromise between divergent interest groups that required practitioners to come-up with elaborate but pragmatic solutions to phase out old property rights, in Germany the *numerus clausus* was developed by academics and imposed over a relatively short time by elites with shared political agendas. A key implication of this is that the *numerus clausus* principle makes the development of property law heavily dependent on legislative bodies and, therefore, on politics; a topic that will resurface in chapters four and eight.

A third conclusion of this chapter is that the failure of legislative bodies to react in a timely manner to pressing social and economic problems sometimes encounters judges who are willing to deviate from the *numerus clausus* to address new realities through 'legal scaffolding'. The implication is that part of the pressure that new realities impose on the *numerus clausus* is simply released by courts that do not always strictly obey the principle. However, courts are extremely reluctant to acknowledge that they are breaching the *numerus clausus* or creating new property types, making these developments hard to identify and conceptualise. The justification for this scaffolding is discussed in chapter five and its implications are developed in chapter eight.

I. THE *NUMERUS CLAUSUS* IN COMPARATIVE LAW

In comparative legal scholarship, the *numerus clausus* of property rights has recently been suggested as one of the most promising lines of research to bring the different national ontologies of property law described in chapter two into conversation with each other.[1] However, the interest in this principle did not emerge in this field, but in a puzzle presented by economic thinking to property law, first addressed in the Anglo-American context.[2] Since then, this principle

[1] eg Michele Graziadei, 'The Structure of Property Ownership and the Common Law/Civil Law Divide' in Michele Graziadei and Lionel Smith (eds), *Comparative Property Law: Global Perspectives* (Edward Elgar 2017) 78; Peter Sparkes, 'Certainty of Property: Numerus Clausus or the Rule with No Name?' (2012) 20 *Euro Rev Priv L* 769, 711.

[2] Especially, Bernard Rudden, 'Economic Theory v. Property Law: The Numerus Clausus Problem' in John Eekelaar and John Bell (eds), *Oxford Essays in Jurisprudence: Third Series* (Clarendon 1987)

gained prominence in common law theory[3] and doctrine,[4] and was then matched with growing comparative research, especially in continental Europe.[5] The latter has been led by the so-called 'Dutch School',[6] mostly covering the law of France, Germany, England and the Netherlands,[7] and has debunked previous conceptions seeing the *numerus clausus* as an exclusively civilian phenomenon.[8] As a consequence, the *numerus clausus* is nowadays a well-established topic in comparative property law.[9]

The main finding of this literature is that, in almost all modern legal systems, the number and content of property rights are limited by the law.[10] Hence, only legal interests that conform to one of a closed number of standardised forms are enforced as property rights by courts.[11] This is said to be a central difference with the law of contracts, which does not know inherent restrictions to the legally enforceable interests than can be created by private parties.[12] However, the status of the *numerus clausus* across jurisdictions varies.[13] Most civilian systems, especially Germany, have long been conscious of this phenomenon, formally

239; Thomas W Merrill and Henry E Smith, 'Optimal Standardization in the Law of Property: The Numerus Clausus Principle' (2000) 110 *Yale LJ* 1. For discussion, see ch 5, section II.

[3] eg Henry Hansmann and Reinier Kraakman, 'Property, Contract, and Verification: The Numerus Clausus Problem and the Divisibility of Rights' (2002) 31 *J Legal Stud* 373; Anna Di Robilant, 'Property and Democratic Deliberation: The "Numerus Clausus" Principle and Democratic Experimentalism in Property Law' (2014) 62 *Am J Comp L* 367.

[4] eg Ben McFarlane, 'Keppell v Bailey (1834); Hill v Tupper (1863): The Numerus Clausus and the Common Law' in Nigel Gravells (ed), *Landmark Cases in Land Law* (Hart 2013); Chris Bevan, 'The Doctrine of Benefit and Burden: Reforming the Law of Covenants and the Numerus Clausus "Problem"' (2018) 77 *CLJ* 72.

[5] eg Sjef van Erp, 'A Numerus Quasi-Clausus of Property Rights as a Constitutive Element of a Future European Property Law' (2003) 7 *Electronic J Comp Law*; Bram Akkermans, *The Principle of Numerus Clausus in European Property Law* (Intersentia 2008); Christian von Bar, 'The Numerus Clausus of Property Rights: A European Principle?' in Louise Gullifer and Stefan Vogenauer (eds), *English and European Perspectives on Contract and Commercial Law: Essays in Honour of Hugh Beale* (Hart 2014).

[6] Sparkes (n 1) 772.

[7] Especially, Akkermans, *The Principle of Numerus Clausus in European Property Law* (n 5).

[8] On these prior conceptions, James Gordley, *Foundations of Private Law* (OUP 2006) 49.

[9] See Jan Smits, *The Making of European Private Law* (Intersentia 2002) 249–54; Sjef van Erp, 'Comparative Property Law' in Mathias Reimann and Reinhard Zimmermann (eds), *The Oxford Handbook of Comparative Law* (2nd edn, OUP 2019) 1049–53; J Michael Milo, 'Property and Real Rights' in Jan M Smits (ed), *Elgar Encyclopedia of Comparative Law* (2nd edn, Edward Elgar 2012) 733–40; Bram Akkermans, 'The Numerus Clausus of Property Rights' in Michele Graziadei and Lionel Smith (eds), *Comparative Property Law: Global Perspectives* (Edward Elgar 2017); Christian von Bar, *The Foundations of Property Law* (OUP 2023) 67–92.

[10] Rudden (n 2) 241–43, 260; Merrill and Smith (n 2) 68; Bar, 'The Numerus Clausus of Property Rights' (n 5) 442; Akkermans, 'The Numerus Clausus of Property Rights' (n 9) 100.

[11] Merrill and Smith (n 2) 3; Ben McFarlane, 'The Numerus Clausus Principle and Covenants Relating to Land' in Susan Bright (ed), *Modern Studies in Property Law*, vol 6 (Hart 2011) 308.

[12] Merrill and Smith (n 2) 3; Akkermans, 'The Numerus Clausus of Property Rights' (n 9) 100; Bar, *The Foundations of Property Law* (n 9) 67.

[13] Bar, 'The Numerus Clausus of Property Rights' (n 5) 454; Akkermans, 'The Numerus Clausus of Property Rights' (n 9) 105. For a global overview, see Yun-chien Chang, *Property Law: Comparative, Empirical and Economic Analyses* (CUP 2023) 64–65. For a European overview, see Bar, *The Foundations of Property Law* (n 9) 70–92.

embodying it in the *numerus clausus* principle of property law.[14] However to what extent they *actually* follow the principle is a different story. For example, the *numerus clausus* has been reported as relatively weak in France, where courts enforce it as loose 'principle', while in Germany it is applied as a stringent 'rule'.[15] Nonetheless, even German courts have been reported to occasionally step in to remedy some harsh effects of the strict application of the principle by enforcing rights outside the *numerus clausus* that, at the least, strongly resemble property rights, typically an 'anticipation right of the buyer' (*Antwartschaftsrecht*) and 'ownership for security purposes' (*Sicherheitseigentum*).[16] Overall, the most salient conclusion of this literature is that the civilian version of the *numerus clausus* principle does not imply that private parties are deprived of all freedom to delineate property rights nor that the list of property forms is permanently closed.[17]

By contrast, the *numerus clausus* principle has historically received little attention in the common law tradition.[18] For a long time, no formal name was attached to the principle,[19] making it also hard to identify.[20] Nonetheless, thanks to the interest taken in it by some American scholars,[21] the *numerus clausus* has also been addressed as such in common law scholarship over the last 25 years,[22] adding an interesting policy aspect to the more doctrinally oriented civilian legal systems.[23] In England, the principle is normally linked to developments in the nineteenth century common law and the enactment of the LPA 1925,[24] while the emergence of the restrictive covenant is normally seen as the paradigm of the judicial creation of property rights.[25] The status of the principle in America has been less studied from a comparative perspective. In domestic scholarship, the American version of the principle has been held to be better explained as a matter of judicial self-restraint[26] and comparative research has

[14] Milo (n 9) 734; van Erp (n 9) 1042; Merrill and Smith (n 2) 4; Bar, *The Foundations of Property Law* (n 9) 72.

[15] Akkermans (n 9) 105–06; Bar, 'The Numerus Clausus of Property Rights' (n 5) 444–45.

[16] See van Erp (n 9) 1038, 1042; Milo (n 9) 737, 740; Akkermans, 'The Numerus Clausus of Property Rights' (n 9) 103–04; Bar, *The Foundations of Property Law* (n 9) 79–80; Akkermans, *The Principle of Numerus Clausus in European Property Law* (n 5) 186–89.

[17] eg van Erp (n 9) 1042–45.

[18] Merrill and Smith (n 2) 4–5; Hansmann and Kraakman (n 3) 373–74.

[19] Merrill and Smith (n 2) 69.

[20] Milo (n 9) 734.

[21] Especially, Merrill and Smith (n 2).

[22] Milo (n 9) 734.

[23] van Erp (n 9) 1050.

[24] eg William Swadling, 'Property: General Principles' in Andrew Burrows (ed), *English Private Law* (3rd edn, OUP 2013) 175–76; Ben McFarlane, Nicholas Hopkins and Sarah Nield, *Land Law: Text, Cases and Materials* (5th edn, OUP 2021) 150–71; van Erp (n 9) 1050; Sjef Van Erp and Bram Akkermans (eds), *Cases, Materials and Text on Property Law* (Hart 2012) 101.

[25] eg Akkermans, 'The Numerus Clausus of Property Rights' (n 9) 101; McFarlane, 'The Numerus Clausus Principle and Covenants Relating to Land' (n 11).

[26] Merrill and Smith (n 2) 9.

adopted this conclusion.[27] Consistent with this, comparative research highlights that the tendency in common law jurisdictions is towards growing awareness and formal recognition of the principle, while in civilian systems the trend is to test its flexibility.[28]

To what extent the civilian and common law versions of the principle are comparable is open to discussion. In England, some commentators have been sceptical about the enthusiasm with which some common law lawyers have assumed the existence of the principle in their own tradition.[29] These authors have approached the findings of the Dutch School in a critical light, arguing that it fails to realise that some key elements of English property law are inconsistent with the civilian idea of *numerus clausus*, including the varying meaning of 'property' in English law, the way in which the LPA 1925 restricts equitable rights in land, and the operation of trusts and overreaching. In this view, the convergence identified by the Dutch School exists only at a very abstract level, namely, in the broad idea that the law imposes some limits on the property rights parties can create, but that this 'rule with no name' is applied differently in both traditions.[30] This English scepticism must be taken seriously, as comparative literature evidences some obscurity regarding the authorities that support the principle and its scope, especially in connection to equitable property rights.[31]

From the perspective of this book, a further problem is that the existing research offers no encompassing conceptual framework regarding the impact of the *numerus clausus* in the process of legal change in property law. On the one hand, even if comparative literature frequently has an implicit or explicit focus on proposing how to develop property law in the context of the unification and harmonisation of European private law,[32] it lacks an elaborated conceptual framework to account for such developments, as it devotes most of its effort to extensive reviews of national doctrine and case law, typically in an historical

[27] eg see Milo (n 9) 734.

[28] ibid 735.

[29] eg Malcolm Merry, 'Landmark Cases in Land Law (Review)' (2013) 5 *Conv* 455, 455–56.

[30] Sparkes (n 1) 772-773, 788–91, 799, 803, 804. On trust and overreaching, ch 2, section III and ch 6, section II.

[31] For example, Milo takes no clear standing as to the whether the principle applies to equitable property rights, see Milo (n 9) 734. Akkermans finds the sources of the principle in the nineteenth century common law and does not exclude equitable rights from its scope, but his references to case law are imprecise and does not account for the role of LPA 1925, see Akkermans (n 9) 101. By contrast, van Erp links the principle to LPA 1925, s 1 but fails to realise that this provision only applies to legal property rights, making no reference to LPA 1925, s 4, see van Erp (n 9) 1050. Finally, von Bar argues that there is no closed catalogue of equitable property rights, but also fails to discuss LPA 1925, s 4. Furthermore, relying on literature that pre-dates the 'discovery' of the *numerus clausus* in England, he argues that Equity is still of 'fertile age', see Bar, 'The Numerus Clausus of Property Rights' (n 5) 448, 450. Contrast this with mainstream contemporary doctrine holding that, at least for property right in land, 'equity may indeed be past the age of child-bearing', Swadling (n 24) 182.

[32] See Akkermans, *The Principle of Numerus Clausus in European Property Law* (n 5) 489–564; Akkermans, 'The Numerus Clausus of Property Rights' (n 9) 116–18; Sparkes (n 1) 804.

perspective.[33] On the other, the research done in the style of law and economics, whilst offering some remarkable theoretical approaches, tends to be highly dependent on the American context and pays insufficient attention to contextual elements alien to economic analysis. All this points to the need of achieving a better understanding of the *numerus clausus*, before analysing its impact on the ability of property law to deal with new realities. The following two sections do this by discussing the doctrinal aspects of the German and English versions of the principle in more detail.

II. GERMANY: THE *NUMERUS CLAUSUS* AS DOGMA

A. A Foundational Principle

Comparative lawyers agree that the principle of *numerus clausus* lies at the heart of most civilian property systems, but also emphasise that it is expressed differently across jurisdictions.[34] In Germany, this doctrine forms part of a wider group of well and long-established principles governing the law of property and are said to provide this field with a distinct theoretical foundation within the general system of the BGB.[35] The importance of the *numerus clausus* in this context can hardly be overstated: this doctrine is frequently described as a 'corner stone'[36] or 'central dogma'[37] of German private law and as the only principle that is truly unique to property law.[38]

The existence and basic content of this principle is accepted with almost no discussion in German case law and scholarship.[39] According to its mainstream account, it holds that the law provides for a closed number of property rights from

[33] Even if comparative research reports the law and economics discussion, it does not really engage with it, nor use its framework, eg see Akkermans, 'The Numerus Clausus of Property Rights' (n 9) 108–11; van Erp (n 9) 1049–50.

[34] eg van Erp (n 9) 1042; Van Erp and Akkermans (n 24) 112; Bar, 'The Numerus Clausus of Property Rights' (n 5). Also see nn 13–15 and accompanying text.

[35] Jan Wilhelm, *Sachenrecht* (5th edn, De Gruyter 2016) 9–10; Fritz Baur, Jürgen Baur and Rolf Stürner, *Sachenrecht* (18th edn, Beck 2009) 35–41; Marina Wellenhofer, *Sachenrecht* (34th edn, Beck 2019) 27; Hans Hermann Seiler, 'Einleitung zum Sachenrecht' in Elmar Bund and others (eds), *J. von Staudingers Kommentar zum Bürgerlichen Gesetzbuch mit Einführungsgesetz und Nebengesetzen* (Sellier & de Gruyter 2007) 6–7, 23–35; Reinhard Gaier, 'Einleitung zum Sachenrecht' in Franz Jürgen Säcker and others (eds), *Münchner Kommentar zum BGB* (7th edn, Beck 2017) [9]–[23].

[36] Holger Fleischer, 'Der Numerus Clausus der Sachenrechte im Spiegel der RechtsÖkonomie' in Thomas Eger and others (eds), *Internationalisierung des Rechts und seine ökonomische Analyse: Festschrift für Hans-Bernd Schäfer zum 65. Geburtstag* (Gabler Verlag 2008) 226.

[37] Wolfgang Wiegand, 'Numerus Clausus der Dingliche Rechte: Zur Entstehung und Bedeutung eines Zentralen Zivilrechtlichen Dogmas' in Gerhard Köbler (ed), *Karl Kroeschell zum 60. Geburtstag dargelegt von Freunden, Schülern und Kollegen*, vol 60 (Verlag Peter Lang 1987).

[38] Wilhelm (n 35) 10.

[39] Fleischer (n 36) 126.

which private parties cannot deviate.[40] German scholarship frequently further explains the principle by distinguishing between the twin concepts of mandatory types (*Typenzwang*) and mandatory content (*Typenfixirung*). According to the first, parties are not allowed to create new property forms; pursuant to the second, parties cannot alter the content of the allowed forms beyond their legal boundaries.[41] The principle is well expressed in case law by a frequently cited 1967 ruling of the Higher Regional Court of Bavaria (*Bayerisches Oberstes Landesgericht*, BayObLG) which states that

> in the field of property law, the BGB follows the foundational principle of the closed list of property rights. This principle holds that the number and types of property rights are strictly determined by legislation and that their content is mandatorily prescribed …[42]

and has been upheld in many other cases.[43]

Despite its importance, the principle of *numerus clausus* is not explicitly acknowledged by the black letter rules of the BGB.[44] However, its existence seems so deeply entrenched in German legal culture[45] that many commentaries and textbooks introduce the principle without aiming to ground it in any formal authority.[46] When formal legal grounding is provided, it relies either in the systematic interpretation of some rules of the code or in the explicit text of the *Motive*. The systematic argument, normally credited to Philipp von Heck,[47] essentially holds that the wording used by the code when authorising the creation of limited property rights (specially § 1018 BGB) implies that these are also the *only* possible such rights.[48] The second argument, especially explored by Wolfgang Wiegand,[49] relies on a section of the *Motive* discussing the place of property law within the broader framework of the BGB. After justifying the

[40] Gaier (n 35) [9]; Seiler (n 35) 24; Wilhelm (n 35) 10; Wellenhofer (n 35) 27; Fabian Klinck, 'Sachenrecht' in Dagmar Kaiser and Markus Stoffels (eds), *J. Staudingers Kommentar zum Bürgerlichen Gesetzbuch mit Einführungsgestetz und Nebengesetzen: Eckpfeiler des Zivilrechts* (6th edn, Sellier & de Gruyter 2018) 1274.

[41] Seiler (n 35) 23; Baur, Baur and Stürner (n 35) 3; Gaier (n 35) [11]; Sebastian Herrler and Hartmut Wiecke, 'Sachenrecht', *Palandt: Bürgerlicher Gesetzbuch mit Nebengesetzten* (80th edn, Beck 2021) 1535. In English, see Bar, *The Foundations of Property Law* (n 9) 70–73.

[42] BayObLG, 3.2.1967. NJW 1967, 1373, 1374 (my translation).

[43] eg KG DNoZ 2006, 470, 471.

[44] Seiler (n 35) 24. The coining of the term is normally attributed to Philipp von Heck, *Grundriss des Sachenrechts* (Mohr 1930) [22]–[23].

[45] Wiegand, 'Numerus Clausus der Dingliche Rechte' (n 37) 623.

[46] eg Gaier (n 35) [11]; Wellenhofer (n 35) 27–28; Herrler and Wiecke (n 41) 1535.

[47] von Heck (n 44).

[48] Seiler (n 35) 24; Wilhelm (n 35) 10.

[49] Wiegand, 'Numerus Clausus der Dingliche Rechte' (n 37); Wolfgang Wiegand, 'Die Entwicklung des Sachenrechts im Verhältnis zum Schuldrecht' (1990) 1/2 AcP 112; Wolfgang Wiegand, 'Funktion und Systematische Stellung des Sachenrechts im BGB' in Michael Martinek and Patrick L Sellier (eds), *J. von Staudingers Kommentar zum Bürgerlichen Gesetzbuch mit Eifübrungsgesetz und Nebengesetzen. 100 Jahre BGB – 100 Jahre Staudinger* (Sellier & de Gruyter 1999).

need for a self-sufficient system of property law,[50] the *Motive* explicitly states that

> [t]herefore, it cannot be open to the parties to attribute proprietary nature to a right over a thing according to their wishes. The principle of freedom of contract, which governs the law of obligations, does not apply to property law. Here the reverse principle applies: the parties can only create the property rights authorized by legislation. The number of real rights is therefore necessarily closed.[51]

A remarkable effect of the unchallenged position the *numerus clausus* principle enjoys in Germany is that some of its key aspects remain undertheorised. For example, the scope of the *numerus clausus* is rarely discussed. Scholarship seems to content itself with simply assuming that it applies to formally defined 'property rights' (absolute rights in things),[52] without problematising the systematic position of 'intermediate rights' that, despite being formally conceptualised as a personal right, can still bind successors in title, such as the rights of lessees.[53] Recent theoretical accounts have made efforts to rationalise these cases as part of a *continuum* between 'core' property rights that have all the marks of an *in rem* right and a 'periphery' made of a sliding scale of property to personal rights, but these approaches also acknowledge that this is hard to square with the principle of *numerus clausus*.[54] The prevailing view seems to be that having a limited 'grey zone' of 'intermediate figures' does not undermine the *numerus clausus* principle.[55] The implications of this will be discussed in section IV below and in chapter seven.

B. The List as Rational System

In Germany, the core of the modern list of property rights is still found in the 1900 BGB. Therefore, the basic configuration of the German *numerus clausus* must be seen as part of a wider project to rationalise and unify German private law. This process was driven by political, economic and intellectual trends that came together during the second half of the nineteenth century. These forces still carry weight today, as the list has not been subject to radical transformation.

By the beginning of the nineteenth century, the German States were mostly traditional agricultural societies,[56] which had feudal landholding as one of their

[50] On this, ch 2, section II and ch 5, section III.
[51] *Motive*, Vol III, 3 (my translation).
[52] eg Jörg Neuner, *Allgemeiner Teil des Bürgerlichen Rechts* (13th edn, Beck 2023) 245.
[53] § 566 BGB. See ch 2, section II.C.
[54] eg Marietta Auer, *Der Privatrechtliche Diskurs der Moderne* (Mohr Siebeck 2014) 114–18.
[55] eg Bar, *The Foundations of Property Law* (n 9) 11.
[56] James Brophy, 'The End of the Economic Old Order: The Great Transition, 1750–1860' in Helmut Walser Smith (ed), *The Oxford Handbook of Modern German History* (OUP 2011) 170–74.

cornerstones.[57] These structures relied on a plethora of different and partially overlapping legal regimes, spanning from local customs and Roman law, to the Prussian ALR and French *Code Civil*.[58] Many of the natural law codes, like the ALR, still admitted the fragmentation of ownership in *dominum utile* (that of the feudal lord) and *dominum directum* (that of the vassal)[59] and did not clearly separate contracts from property.[60] In this scheme, property rights were far more flexible than contracts, providing ample freedom for the creation of traditional rights in land that had the ability to bind third parties.[61]

Early attempts to reform this system following in the steps of the French Revolution were squashed by traditional land-owning aristocracies.[62] However, as Germany transitioned from an agricultural to an industrial economy,[63] modern ideas of free trade associated to the Manchester School became dominant,[64] while democratic political movements drastically expanded the franchise, increasing the political power of middle classes.[65] At the same time, in legal scholarship, the reformist agenda of the early nineteenth century was adopted by moderate but influential Roman law professors, giving the project of re-designing the property system along the lines of Roman law and Kantian-inspired ideas of autonomy a 'scientific' and 'apolitical' aura that made it more palatable to traditional elites.[66] After the 1871 unification, these converging trends gained enough political *momentum* to trigger a radical legal reform: in 1873, a liberal majority managed to pass a reform to give the new *Reichstag* legal competence in land law, family law and succession (*Lex Miquel-Lasker*), setting in motion a process that would crystalise in the enactment of the 1900 BGB.[67] The process counted with the support of Bismarck's conservative government and then, after he fell out with the liberals, it continued with a new conservative majority.[68]

The drafters of the BGB were tasked with preparing a draft inspired by the ideas of freedom of contract, free property and conservative family values that reflected a political consensus between the liberal industrial bourgeoise and the

[57] Anna Di Robilant, *The Making of Modern Property Law: Reinventing Roman Law in Europe and its Peripheries* (CUP 2023) 169.

[58] Heinrich Honsell, 'Einleitung zum BGB' in Dagmar Kaiser and Markus Stoffels (eds), *J. Staudingers Kommentar zum Bürgerlichen Gesetzbuch mit Einführungsgestetz und Nebengesetzen: Eckpfeiler des Zivilrechts* (6th edn, Sellier & de Gruyter 2018) 6; Neuner (n 52) 85. For details, see Franz Wieacker, *A History of Private Law in Europe with Particular Reference to Germany* (Tony Weir tr, Clarendon 1995) 259–69.

[59] Akkermans, *The Principle of Numerus Clausus in European Property Law* (n 5) 171–74.

[60] Wiegand, 'Funktion und Systematische Stellung des Sachenrechts im BGB' (n 49) 108.

[61] Wiegand, 'Die Entwicklung des Sachenrechts im Verhältnis zum Schuldrecht' (n 49) 131.

[62] Di Robilant (n 57) 170–77.

[63] Cornelius Torp, 'The Great Transformation: German Economy and Society, 1850–1914' in Helmut Walser Smith (ed), *The Oxford Handbook of Modern German History* (OUP 2011) 336–37.

[64] Honsell (n 58) 4. For discussion, see ch 5, section III.A.

[65] See Siegfried Weichlein, 'Nation State, Conflict Resolution, and Culture War' in Helmut Walser Smith (ed), *The Oxford Handbook of Modern German History* (OUP 2011) 293–97.

[66] Di Robilant (n 57) 178–79, 188–89.

[67] Honsell (n 58) 2–3; Wieacker (n 58) 371; Neuner (n 52) 85–86.

[68] On this process, Honsell (n 58) 3; Weichlein (n 65) 296.

conservative landowning aristocracies.[69] The different working groups were dominated by liberal law professors educated in the Roman-inspired Pandectist tradition, who imposed their views over those wanting to follow traditional Germanic law. The outcome was a highly systematic and abstract code, said to have been written by professors addressing learned judges, often criticised at the time for being detached from reality and lacking social awareness.[70] Its final draft was approved in 1896 with the support of conservatives and liberals (now politically much closer);[71] while the social democrats (SPD), who had become the largest party in the *Reichstag* in 1894, voted against it, as they saw it as insufficiently progressive.[72]

In property law, the drafters of the BGB were committed to abolishing all institutions of the *ancien régime* and introducing a principle of 'free ownership'. This implied dissolving countless old ties between landlords and farmers that were mediated through property rights in land and limiting the creation of new ones.[73] The key element of this system was a new 'abstract' and 'absolute' formulation of ownership that aimed to put an end to fragmentation by concentrating all the ownership powers in one right holder.[74] In this view, property rights in a thing owned by someone else are seen as exceptional burdens that need to be justified, not as fragmentations or splits of ownership.[75] This settled a long-standing discussion as to what right should count as proprietary.[76] For example, in the law of servitudes, the drafters of the property section consciously moved away from the pre-existing ALR, which allowed the 'proprietarisation' (*Verdinglichung*) of practically any personal right, instead favouring a Roman-inspired system, which only admitted a closed list of standardised servitudes.[77] This design aimed to avoid the creation of pre-modern agrarian proprietary structures that imposed heavy duties running with land.[78] Upon the entering into force of the BGB, the pre-existing rights that did not fit this system were phased out by the act that introduced the code.[79] The outcome was the list of property rights still visible in the BGB: a core made of ownership (*Eigentum*), supplemented by 'limited property rights' (*beschränkte dingliche Rechte*), including rights to make a limited use of a thing owned by someone else

[69] Honsell (n 58) 5, 7; RC van Caenegem, *An Historical Introduction to Private Law* (CUP 1992) 157; Wieacker (n 58) 380–82.

[70] For details see van Caenegem (n 69) 155–57; Wieacker (n 58) 372–75; Honsell (n 58) 8–12; Neuner (n 52) 85–86.

[71] Weichlein (n 65) 297.

[72] On this process, Honsell (n 58) 3; Weichlein (n 65) 296.

[73] Honsell (n 58) 8, 12, 15.

[74] For an intellectual history of these ideas prior to the BGB, Di Robilant (n 57) 167–203.

[75] Wiegand, 'Numerus Clausus der Dingliche Rechte' (n 37) 629; Wiegand, 'Funktion und Systematische Stellung des Sachenrechts im BGB' (n 49) 112.

[76] Wiegand, 'Numerus Clausus der Dingliche Rechte' (n 37) 630.

[77] Rolf Stürner, 'Dienstbarkeit Heute' (1994) 194 AcP 265, 276.

[78] Baur, Baur and Stürner (n 35) 429. Discussed in more detail in ch 7, section III.A.

[79] See §184 and following EGBGB. These rules are now mostly purposeless, see Neuner (n 52) 81.

(*Nutzungrechte*), like servitude and usufruct; security rights that make a thing liable to pay a certain debt (*Sicherungsrechte*), like hypothecs and pledges; and, arguably, acquisition rights (*Erwerbrechte*).[80]

Despite the richness of the forms of property available, the BGB soon came under pressure to extend its original list of property rights to face new realities.[81] In accordance with the principle of *numerus clausus*, much of this pressure was relived through the legislative improvement of property rights contained in the code and the enactment of new property types in special legislation.[82] The most salient cases involve reforms to home ownership, namely the expansion of *superficies* rights in 1919[83] and the creation of flat ownership in 1951.[84]

Under the general rules of the BGB, buildings are normally part and parcel of the land (§ 94(1) BGB) and cannot be subject to separate ownership (§ 93 BGB). The only exception contained in the original text of the code was a weak *superficies* right, which provided for the creation of separate property rights over a building (former §§1012 to 1017 BGB). However, the drafters of the BGB saw such a right as unimportant and did not regulate it thoroughly. After the First World War, this regulation proved inadequate to overcome the increasing housing problems resulting from insufficient access to land, triggering the enactment of special legislation that delineated this right in reliable terms in order to, among others, facilitate its use as a collateral.[85]

In a similar fashion, the BGB did not provide for the creation of separate ownership rights in different parts of a same building (§§ 94, 946 BGB). Once again, faced with a massive post-war housing crisis, in 1951 the first Bundestag passed legislation allowing parties to combine joint ownership over land (*Miteigentum*), with special separate ownership over flats in such buildings (*Sondereigentum*) and providing extensive regulation for the management of the common property.[86] As discussed in chapter seven, section III, this reform was a cornerstone of the policies that ended the post-war housing crisis in Germany,[87] but it is not perceived as a radical breach with the ownership model of the BGB.

The only radical transformation of the *numerus clausus* contained in the BGB was short-lived. In 1976 the German Democratic Republic (GDR) abolished the BGB and replaced it with the *Zivilgesetzbuch* (ZGB). The ZGB provided for new property types, underpinned by a very different political ideology that sought to give 'the working-class power' to 'control and plan economic production' 'through a socialist state' (see § 6 ZGB). These new property types

[80] See Baur, Baur and Stürner (n 35) 31; Herrler and Wiecke (n 41) 1535.

[81] See Seiler (n 35) 26, 38–39; Gaier (n 35) [24]; Wilhelm (n 35) 4; Karl Larenz and Manfred Wolf, *Allgemeiner Teil des Bürgerlichen Rechts* (9th edn, Beck 2004) 43.

[82] For a summary in English, see Bar, *The Foundations of Property Law* (n 9) 79.

[83] ErbbauVO, now ErbbauRG. A *superficies* right is proprietary right to build and maintain a building on land owned by someone else.

[84] WEG.

[85] Siegfried Räfle, *Erbbaurechtsverordnung* (De Gruyter 1986) 1–3.

[86] Wellenhofer (n 35) 20–26.

[87] Stefan Kofner, *Wohnungsmarkt und Wohnungswirtschaft* (Oldenburg Verlag 2004) 157–58.

included socialist ownership (*Sozialistisches Eigentum*), which provided for forms of collective and personal ownership (§§ 18–24 ZGB).[88] A key aspect of this ideology was withdrawing dwelling space (*Wohnraum*) from private markets to provide it as a socialised good (*Sozialleistung*). In practice this was done by means of leasing flats in cheap low-quality prefabricated *Plattenbau* buildings on very low rents. However, these rents did not cover the costs of maintaining the flats, leading to rapid deterioration of the already scarce, damaged and low-quality housing stock of the GDR: at the time of re-unification in 1990, about 420,000 dwellings were not habitable and complete neighbourhoods were in decay.[89]

After re-unification, it became necessary to dissolve socialist ownership and bring the property rights created according to the ZGB under the scope of the BGB. For collective ownership, this was done through a special entity (the *Treuhand*), tasked with privatising circa 13,000 'people's companies' and making restitution of property to former owners. As to personal ownership, the federal legislator could not ignore the factual reality in the new *Länder*, passing a number of acts[90] that transformed the rights created under the ZGB into forms recognised by the BGB.[91] While not reversing expropriations from the Soviet occupation (1945–49), the unification process asserted the principle of 'return over compensation' for property seized after the creation of the GDR in 1949. This allowed former owners, many of whom had fled to West Germany prior to the building of the Berlin Wall, to recover property, creating regional tensions, as many of these houses were now occupied by easterners.[92]

Seen from a distance, it is surprising that such a radical transformation of the structure of property law faced so little resistance. However, it is worth remembering that the German re-unification did not take place between two parties on equal footing, but by the new *Länder* from the East essentially acceding to a far more prosperous and powerful 'ready-made' state,[93] fueled by the promise of a 'second economic miracle'.[94]

C. Judge-made Property Rights?

According to the principle of *numerus clausus*, the creation of property rights is a matter of legislation. However, the practical acknowledgment by courts of a few rights not contained in the BGB nor its complementary legislation that,

[88] On this, see Baur, Baur and Stürner (n 35) 888–89.

[89] Valesca Maria Molinari, *Die Tradition Staatlicher Interventionen in den Mietwohnungsmarkt* (Mohr Siebeck 2021) 53–54.

[90] See Art 231 § 5 and 233 §§ 1–10 EGBGB.

[91] Baur, Baur and Stürner (n 35) 888–89, 892, 904–05.

[92] David Patton, 'Anus Mirabilis: 1989 and German Unification' in Helmut Walser Smith (ed), *The Oxford Handbook of Modern German History* (OUP 2011) 767.

[93] ibid 765, 768.

[94] Werner Abelshauser, *Deutsche Wirtschaftsgeschichte Seit 1945* (Beck 2004) 402, 405, 448–49.

at the least, strongly resemble property rights, has forced German scholarship to account for the role of the judiciary in the development of the property system.[95] The approach to this issue is not uniform. Sometimes these developments are presented as infringements to the *numerus clausus*,[96] but other times they are seen as an allowed 'extension of the law' (*Rechtsfortbildung*), that does not infringe the principle.[97]

The practical effect of these different views is not too relevant. Despite the way in which these developments are qualified, the substantive outcome is that, in practice, German courts have further developed the property system, and this has not been seen as a massive or problematic invasion of legislative competence. In one view, the judicial creation of property rights should be seen as unproblematic, as the drafters of the BGB seem to have assumed that new property forms would develop by case law.[98] Courts, however, do not seem comfortable openly assuming this power. This is visible in their reluctance to qualify these developments as giving rise to new property rights.[99] This view was confirmed by a 2013 ruling of the Federal Court of Justice (*Bundesgerichtshof*, BGH), holding that the 'creation of private burdens not acknowledged by the *numerus clausus* of property law cannot succeed by means of judicial extension of the law [*Rechtsfortbildung*]'.[100]

In practice, the pressure of changing social and economic circumstances has led courts to enforce rights with third-party effects that are not part of the *numerus clausus*, especially in the field of credit security, including a 'security ownership' over moveable goods (*Sicherheitseigentum*), an 'acquisition right' of buyers (*Antwartschaftsrecht*) and a land charge (*Sicherungsgrundshuld*).[101] To what extent the creation of these rights was an infringement of the *numerus clausus* remains unsettled. For example, a leading *Kommentar* to the BGB describes the acquisition right of buyers as a violation of the *numerus clausus* that has now become part of customary law,[102] while a mainstream property law textbook holds that the same rights developed without breach of this principle.[103] The relevant takeaway is that the coming into existence of these rights shows that the doctrine of *numerus clausus* is either more flexible than assumed or, at least, not always strictly enforced, which, in practice, has very similar results.

[95] Seiler (n 35) 38; Gaier (n 35) [13] and [24].

[96] eg Wiegand, 'Die Entwicklung des Sachenrechts im Verhältnis zum Schuldrecht' (n 49) 128; Gaier (n 35) [13] and [24].

[97] eg Wellenhofer (n 35) 28; Larenz and Wolf (n 81) 95. For discussion, see ch 4, section II.

[98] See Wiegand, 'Funktion und Systematische Stellung des Sachenrechts im BGB' (n 49) 115.

[99] See BGHZ 30, 374, 377–78.

[100] BGH 13.9.2013, NJW 2013, 3515, 3518 (my translation).

[101] Wiegand, 'Numerus Clausus der Dingliche Rechte' (n 37) 624; Seiler (n 35) 38; Gaier (n 35) [11]–13]; Wiegand, 'Die Entwicklung des Sachenrechts im Verhältnis zum Schuldrecht' (n 49) 128. However, note that, since 2008, land charges have been explicitly recognised in §§ 1191 ff BGB.

[102] Gaier (n 35) [11].

[103] Wellenhofer (n 35) 28. In a similar line, Larenz and Wolf (n 81) 95.

This phenomenon is well illustrated by the development of the right of 'ownership for security purposes' as a form of *Treuhand Eigentum*, literally, 'trust-hand ownership'. The *Treuhand* has been described in domestic scholarship as a traditional Germanic form of fragmented ownership,[104] not explicitly acknowledged by the BGB,[105] with strong resemblance to the common law trust.[106] The origin of contemporary security ownership is in the use of the *Treuhand* after purely conventional pledges were disallowed during the second half of the nineteenth century, leading private parties to find new creative ways to allow debtors to retain possession over the pledged asset.[107] In this context a ruling by the Imperial Court (*Reichsgerricht*, RG) predating the entering into force of the BGB set the ground for the 'exceptional treatment of *Treuhand Eigentum*' in cases of security owners,[108] holding that

> an object that has been transferred to the debtor as his ownership, but under the agreement that such object shall not be treated by him as his ownership, might be owned legally by the debtor, but is not in his ownership from a material or economic perspective.[109]

The entering into force of the BGB radically undermined the doctrinal basis of this reasoning. § 1205 enacted the strict Roman principle holding that pledges can only be granted by handing possession of the relevant asset to the creditor (*Faustpfanprinzip)*.[110] This created problems for merchants and industrialists who could not afford to hand over their goods or equipment to access financing nor find professional lenders wishing to keep their assets in storage. However, despite lobbying by trade unions, Parliament did not change this principle.[111] Thus, in order to circumvent this restriction, parties relied on the rules of the *constitutum possessorium* ('constructive delivery')[112] to legally transfer assets from debtors to creditors, but agreeing that such transfer was only 'for security purposes', leaving the asset in possession of the debtor.[113] In this scheme, despite transferring the absolute ownership to the creditor, contractual

[104] Wilhelm (n 35) 12.

[105] Wellenhofer (n 35) 17.

[106] On the difference and similarities of trust and Treuhand, see in general Hein Kötz, *Trust und Treuhand: Eine Rechtsvergleichende Darstellung des Anglo-Amerikanischen Trust und Funktionsverwandter Institute des Deutschen Rechts* (Vandenhoeck & Ruprecht 1963).

[107] Werner Schubert, 'Die Diskussion über eine Reform des Rechts der Mobiliarsicherheiten in der Späten Kaiserzeit und in der Weimarer Zeit' (1990) 107 *ZRG Germ Abt* 132, 133.

[108] Wiegand, 'Die Entwicklung des Sachenrechts im Verhältnis zum Schuldrecht' (n 49) 126; Wilhelm (n 35) 12.

[109] RGZ 45, 80 (my translation).

[110] Carsten Herresthal, 'Das Recht der Kreditsicherung' in Dagmar Kaiser and Markus Stoffels (eds), *J. Staudingers Kommentar zum Bürgerlichen Gesetzbuch mit Einführungsgestetz und Nebengesetzen. Eckpfeiler des Zivilrechts* (6th edn, Sellier & de Gruyter 2018) 666; Karl Larenz and Claus-Wilhelm Canaris, *Methodenslehre der Rechtswissenschaft* (3rd edn, Springer 1996) 233–34.

[111] Schubert (n 107) 138.

[112] See § 930 BGB.

[113] Wilhelm (n 35) 12; Baur, Baur and Stürner (n 35) 785.

limitations restrict the creditor's ownership over the asset to one thing: selling it to pay the debt in case of default.[114] However, when the right of the debtor (who had no formal ownership in the thing) clashed with that of other creditors or successors in title of the lender, the RG continued applying its old doctrine, allowing debtors to assert their rights in relation to the pledged asset against these third parties, and the BGH later followed suit, with some doctrinal modifications and corrections.[115]

German doctrine explains this by distinguishing between the internal and the external relations of the *Treuhand*. From an external perspective (that of third parties), the creditor is the only (and full) owner of the asset and can dispose freely of the thing, while the internal relation between creditor and debtor is governed by their contract.[116] Nonetheless, the internal (obligational) relation of the creditors and debtor might affect third parties in two cases. As explained in chapter six, first, a third party that knows about the relation and still acts in a manner that affects it, can exceptionally become liable in tort.[117] Second, in cases of insolvency of any of both parties or when a third party, who is a creditor of the formal owner of the asset, wants to seize it (*Vollstreckung*), legal ownership of the creditor is not decisive, as the object is not treated as having fully left the patrimony of the debtor.[118]

In scholarship, ownership for security purposes is frequently treated as a property right or together with such rights.[119] Therefore, this right has been seen as strong deviation from the strict separation of the law of property and the law of obligations,[120] developed without proper statutory support (*praeter legem*)[121] and suspected to be a property right outside the *numerus clausus*.[122] In particular, Wiegand argued that this is as an open infraction of the principle, as shown by the comparison with a case in which the Swiss Federal Court solved a similar problem in a analogous form but openly acknowledging that this required disapplying the absolute principle of ownership.[123] Since then, this view has been further developed by authors, arguing that the *Treuhand* is better characterised as contractual fiduciary relation with third-party effects that are

[114] Akkermans, *The Principle of Numerus Clausus in European Property Law* (n 5) 188; Baur, Baur and Stürner (n 35) 787, 805.

[115] Wiegand, 'Die Entwicklung des Sachenrechts im Verhältnis zum Schuldrecht' (n 49) 126.

[116] eg see Wilhelm (n 35) 12; Wellenhofer (n 35) 17, 18; Baur, Baur and Stürner (n 35) 787.

[117] BGH NJW RR 1993, 367.

[118] This was first solved without statutory support, but is now enacted in §771 ZPO and §§ 47 and 51 InsO. Larenz and Canaris (n 110) 235; Wilhelm (n 35) 13, 1091–93; Baur, Baur and Stürner (n 35) 802–03, 805–06.

[119] eg Baur, Baur and Stürner (n 35) 784–824; Wilhelm (n 35) 1091–93.

[120] Akkermans, *The Principle of Numerus Clausus in European Property Law* (n 5) 184.

[121] Larenz and Canaris (n 110) 233–34.

[122] Wilhelm (n 35) 12. In English, Bar, *The Foundations of Property Law* (n 9) 77, especially at fn 267.

[123] Wiegand, 'Die Entwicklung des Sachenrechts im Verhältnis zum Schuldrecht' (n 49) 127–28.

implicitly approved by the legislator.[124] As with leases in land, this creates a legal interest that, despite being described as an obligation, is able to bind successors in title.

Relying on this, some contemporary authors argue that the *numerus clausus* principle does not imply an absolute prohibition to create new property types: courts can treat specific and well-defined fact patterns as having proprietary effects. What judges cannot do is create new property rights through general provisions.[125] The implications of this are ambiguous, but at least two things are clear. First, regardless of claiming a strict adherence to the principle, German courts are exceptionally willing to enforce certain rights outside the *numerus clausus* against some third parties with no clear statutory support. Second, because courts are reluctant to recognise that they are disapplying the *numerus clausus*, such developments are fitted within the pre-existing private law categories, normally by conceptualising these rights as obligations with anomalously expansive effects, rather than property rights.

III. ENGLAND: THE RISE OF A RULE WITH NO NAME

A. The Discovery of the Principle

In the common law tradition, the *numerus clausus* principle has historically received little attention[126] and does not enjoy the same clear status it has in civilian systems.[127] The principle is said to have developed as a 'rule of judicial self-governance' and, for a long time, it did not even have a name.[128] However, thanks to the growing interest in the standardisation of property rights among Anglo-American economic approaches to private law,[129] over the last decades English scholarship has extensively borrowed the civilian label of '*numerus clausus*' to describe the legal limitation on the free creation of novel property rights,[130] especially in land law.[131] However, this is by no means unanimously accepted, not even in land law.[132]

The recognition of the *numerus clausus* principle by case law is also unclear. On the one hand, English judges have been said to follow this principle without

[124] Stefan Grundmann, *Der Treuhandvertrag: Insbesondere die Werbende Treuhand* (Beck 1997) ch 7. In English, see Stefan Grundmann, 'Trust and Treuhand at the End of the 20th Century – Key Problems and Shift of Interests' (1999) 47 *Am J Comp L* 401, 411.

[125] Auer (n 54) 114.

[126] Merrill and Smith (n 2) 4–5; Hansmann and Kraakman (n 3) 373–74.

[127] Milo (n 9) 734.

[128] Merrill and Smith (n 2) 9, 69.

[129] Especially, Rudden (n 2); Merrill and Smith (n 2).

[130] eg Swadling (n 24) 175–77; McFarlane, 'Keppell v Bailey (1834); Hill v Tupper (1863)' (n 4).

[131] eg Swadling (n 24) 175; Ben McFarlane, *The Structure of Property Law* (Hart 2008) 137; Simon Gardner and Emily MacKenzie, *An Introduction to Land Law* (4th edn, Hart 2015) 10–11.

[132] eg Martin Dixon, *Modern Land Law* (12th edn, Routledge 2021) 6–7.

naming it.[133] For example, in *King v David Allen (Billposting) Ltd*,[134] the House of Lords denied the enforcement of a contract to affix bill posters on the side of a cinema building against an assignee to a title of the building because it did not amount to a property right.[135] On the other, however, recently the High Court explicitly held that the *numerus clausus* is a civilian doctrine not accepted by English law. In *Bucknell v Alchemy Estates*[136] HHJ Paul Matthews held that, contrary to civilian systems

> [t]he common law had (and has) no principle of *dominium*, and thus no *numerus clausus* of exceptions to it either. … the existence and protean nature of the trust, giv[es] the owner power to tailor (equitable) property interests to the precise needs of the situation …[137]

However, as argued in this subsection, this conclusion is based on inaccurate understanding of the civilian principle of *numerus clausus* and insufficient attention to the limited nature of the third-party effects of trusts.

Part of this the problem derives from the fact that, in England, the principle of *numerus clausus* is normally not formulated with the same level of abstraction as in Germany, but fleshed out from nineteenth century case law[138] and the LPA 1925.[139] When formulated in general terms, it is normally described as broadly stating that, if private parties want their rights to have third-party effects, such rights have to correspond to one of those legal or equitable property rights recognised by the law.[140] However, the precise content of the English version of the *numerus clausus* is only revealed by close attention to its common law sources and the historical origin of the LPA 1925.

The leading case in this process was *Keppell v Bailey*.[141] This case concerned a 1795 agreement of the owners of three ironworks who formed a stock company to build a railway to link their facilities to a quarry. As part of this, the owners of the ironworks agreed to use the railroad to carry limestone and ironstone to their works, paying a fixed price per ton per mile to do so, binding themselves and their successors in title as covenantors. In 1833 one of the ironworks was

[133] Hanoch Dagan and Irit Samet, 'Express Trust: The Dark Horse of the Liberal Property Regime', *Philosophical Foundations of the Law of Express Trusts* (OUP 2023) 155. However, some classic authorities suggest something different, eg *National Provincial Bank v Ainsworth* [1965] AC 1174, HL, commented by Swadling (n 24) 177.

[134] *King v David Allen (Billposting) Ltd* [1916] 2 AC 54, HL.

[135] Swadling (n 24) 176. Further endorsements mentioned include *Clore v Theatrical Properties Ltd* [1936] 3 All ER 48, CA; *Ashburn Anstalt v Arnold* [1989] Ch 1, CA; and *Rhone v Stephens* [1994] 2 AC 310, HL.

[136] *Bucknell v Alchemy Estates* [2023] EWHC 683 (Ch).

[137] ibid [80].

[138] eg Swadling (n 24) 175, 176; McFarlane, 'Keppell v Bailey (1834); Hill v Tupper (1863)' (n 4) 2; McFarlane, Hopkins and Nield (n 24) 150–71.

[139] McFarlane, Hopkins and Nield (n 24) 150–71.

[140] See McFarlane, 'Keppell v Bailey (1834); Hill v Tupper (1863)' (n 4) 2. Similarly, Gardner and MacKenzie (n 131) 10.

[141] *Keppell v Bailey* (1834) 2 My & K 517.

sold to a third party (Mr Bailey) who started to build a tramway to link its ironworks to another of his facilities. The shareholders relied on the covenant to obtain an *ex parte* injunction to prevent Mr Bailey acting against the terms of the 1795 agreement.[142] In what has been said to be the most eloquent defence of the *numerus clausus* in the common law,[143] Lord Brougham held that agreements that did not create recognised types of proprietary rights were not enforceable against subsequent purchasers as property running with land and granted the motion to dissolve the injunction stating that 'it must not therefore be supposed that incidents of novel kind can be devised and attached to property at the fancy or caprice of any owner'.[144]

The principle laid down in *Keppell* was later expanded in *Hill v Tupper*.[145] In this case,[146] a canal company had granted Mr Hill the sole and exclusive right to hire out pleasure boats on its canal as part of a lease. Mr Tupper, the landlord of a nearby pub also started hiring boats out on the canal for pleasure, leading to a claim for damages by Mr Hill.[147] Relying on *Keppell*, Pollock CB stated that the question of the enforceability of Mr Hill's exclusive rights against Mr Tupper depended on whether new species of property could be created or whether the rights only existed in covenant, that is, as a mere contractual promise. Under the influence of *Keppell*, Pollock CB rejected Mr Hill's claim, holding that

> [a] new species of incorporeal hereditament [a property right] cannot be created at the will and pleasure of the owner of the property, but he must be content to accept the estate and the right to dispose of it subject to the law as settled by decisions or controlled by act of parliament. A grantor may bind himself by covenant to allow any right he pleases over his property, but he cannot annex it to a new incident, so as to enable the grantee to sue in his own name for infringement of such a limited right as that now claimed.[148]

Despite not being always mentioned when accounting for the principle,[149] in England, at least for rights in land, the restriction on the free delineation of property rights was consolidated in a systematic form with the enactment of the LPA 1925. In one view, this act does not contain a *numerus clausus* principle, but only states what pre-existing rights may further qualify as 'legal' and 'equitable'.[150] Nonetheless, by doing this, the act effectively standardised and

[142] McFarlane, 'Keppell v Bailey (1834); Hill v Tupper (1863)' (n 4) 3–5.
[143] McFarlane, 'The Numerus Clausus Principle and Covenants Relating to Land' (n 11) 8.
[144] *Keppell v Bailey* (1834) 2 My & K 517, 535, discussed in ch 5, sections II and III. and ch 7, section II.
[145] McFarlane, 'Keppell v Bailey (1834); Hill v Tupper (1863)' (n 4) 2, 9–12.
[146] *Hill v Tupper* (1863) 2 H & C 121, 159 ER 51.
[147] McFarlane, 'Keppell v Bailey (1834); Hill v Tupper (1863)' (n 4) 5, 6; McFarlane, 'The Numerus Clausus Principle and Covenants Relating to Land' (n 11) 308.
[148] *Hill v Tupper* (1863) 2 H & C 122, 127–28.
[149] eg Swadling (n 24) 175–77.
[150] Martin Dixon, 'Proprietary and Non-Proprietary Rights in Modern Land Law' in Louise Tee (ed), *Land Law: Issues, Debates, Policy* (Willan Publishing 2002) 13.

limited the number of property rights in land, providing that (i) '*the only*' estates and interests that can subsist or be conveyed or created in law are those listed in the LPA 1925, s 1(1) and (2), (ii) any other property right will take the form of an equitable interest (LPA 1925, s 1(3)) and (iii) limiting the permissible equitable interests to those existing before its coming into force (LPA 1925, s 4(1)).[151]

Despite its origin in nineteenth century common law and its enactment in the LPA 1925, the use of the '*numerus clausus*' label to designate the restriction on the free delineation of property rights in England is relatively new. The terminology was first borrowed from civilian systems in England during the late 1980s[152] and its use only took off in the common law world after its 'discovery' in the US, in the early 2000s.[153] Nowadays the *numerus clausus* concept is firmly established in English legal academic literature,[154] and – although they do not use this exact terminology – practitioners texts also acknowledge that 'proprietary interests are fixed by the law, and finite in number'.[155]

The adoption of the civilian '*numerus clausus*' label in the common law tradition has been met with some scepticism.[156] In one view, the proponents of this doctrine have adopted this civilian concept as a 'badge of honour', practically forcing it into the English legal system. The general formula identified by them is a 'rule with no name', which only reflects a general principle of certainty regarding property rights. The civilian *numerus clausus* is only one way of implementing such wider principle, but it has no place in the English common law, especially due to trusts being essentially incompatible with the idea of a closed list of property rights.[157] In *Bucknell* the High Court seems to have endorsed this view. After discarding the existence of the principle in English law, it held that 'the existence and protean nature of the trust, giv[es] the owner power to tailor (equitable) property interests to the precise needs of the situation'.[158] The implication seems to be that the freedom enjoyed by settlors of an express trusts to create 'equitable property rights' is conclusive evidence that common law property systems do not follow a *numerus clausus* principle.

Assessing to what extent this is correct, requires a more nuanced approach to the effects the rights of the beneficiary of a trust have on third parties. As highlighted by some of the proponents of the 'rights against rights theory',[159] the duties that trusts impose on trustees do not affect strangers, because they

[151] McFarlane, 'The Numerus Clausus Principle and Covenants Relating to Land' (n 11) 309; Gardner and MacKenzie (n 131) 11.

[152] See Rudden (n 2) 241, 243.

[153] Especially, with Merrill and Smith (n 2). For discussion, see ch 5, section II.

[154] eg see Swadling (n 24) 175, 180–82; McFarlane, 'Keppell v Bailey (1834); Hill v Tupper (1863)' (n 4); Gardner and MacKenzie (n 131) 11.

[155] Stuart Bridge, Elizabeth Cooke and Martin Dixon, *Megarry & Wade: The Law of Real Property* (8th edn, Sweet & Maxwell 2019) [26-016].

[156] eg Merry (n 29) 455–56 criticising McFarlane. Also see, Dixon (n 150) 13–15.

[157] Sparkes (n 1) 771–72, 774, 790, 799, 804.

[158] *Bucknell v Alchemy Estates* [2023] EWHC 683 (Ch) [80].

[159] For an explanation, ch 2, section III.B.

do not come under any immediate duty to the beneficiary.[160] First, when A sets up a trust in favour of B, the duties X – a stranger – owes to A are not affected, and X does not come under any new duty towards B. Second, even if C acquires the trust property in breach of trust, and is not a *bona fide* purchaser without notice of B's right, if C remains ignorant of any breach of trust until after the point when C disposes of the trust property and any traceable proceeds, B has no claim against C.[161] In this view, this is enough to conclude that there is no incompatibility between trusts and the *numerus clausus*.[162]

The previous argument, however, does not address cases in which C – a third party who acquired in breach of trust and has no *bona fide* purchaser defence – is still in possession. In this scenario 'the court will treat the defendant as holding the property on a constructive trust for the plaintiff and will order the defendant to transfer it in specie to the plaintiff'.[163] In other words, in these cases, B's right *will* bind C, effectively behaving as a property right. This seems to inflict a fatal blow to the *numerus clausus* principle. However, this is not precise, as C will not be subject to the same duties as A (the original express trustee).[164] The only significant duty C will owe to B is transferring the trust property back to A or the person appointed to replace A.[165] C does not come under any other specific duty owed by A to B, including fiduciary duties,[166] nor any idiosyncratic duties created by the settlor, such as investing the funds in a precise manner.[167] This is consistent with the prevalent view in English law holding that the recipient of trust property holds on a distinct type of trust imposed by law, namely, a constructive trust.[168] Thus, although settlors enjoy ample freedom to design the rights of beneficiaries behind the curtain of an express trust, the third-party effects of these rights on successors are imposed by law and are, therefore, always the same: giving up the trust property.[169] This has relevant implications for the *numerus clausus*: the content of B's claim-rights against A (the trustee) is not decisive in establishing the content of the duties C owes to B (the beneficiary), as they are not construed on the basis of A's idiosyncratic duties towards

[160] Simon Douglas and Ben McFarlane, 'Defining Property Rights' in James Penner and Henry Smith (eds), *Philosophical Foundations of Property Law* (OUP 2013) 240–41; Ben McFarlane and Simon Douglas, 'Property, Analogy and Variety' (2022) 42 *OJLS* 161, 179.

[161] Discussed in *Independent Trustee Services Ltd v GP Noble Trustees Ltd and others* [2012] EWCA Civ 195 and *Re Montagu's Settlement Trusts* [1987] Ch 264.

[162] See Ben McFarlane, 'Equity, Obligations and Third Parties' (2008) *Sing J Legal Stud* 308; Ben McFarlane and Robert Stevens, 'The Nature of Equitable Property' (2010) 4 *J Eq* 1, 2.

[163] *Boscawen v Bajwa* [1996] 1 WLR 328, 334–35.

[164] Swadling (n 24) 213.

[165] Graham Virgo, *The Principles of Equity and Trusts* (5th edn, OUP 2023) 287, 639–40; Nicholas J McBride, *Key Ideas in Trust Law* (Hart 2023) 65–67.

[166] Lionel Smith, 'Constructive Fiduciaries?' in Peter Birks (ed), *Privacy and Loyalty* (OUP 1997) 266.

[167] See *Lonrho plc v Fayed (No 2)* [1992] 1 WLR 1, 12 (Millet J).

[168] See Virgo (n 165) 287; McBride (n 165) 53, 81; Charlie Webb and Tim Akkouh, *Trusts Law* (5th edn, Palgrave 2017) 212.

[169] I plan to expand on the implications of this in a future publication.

B under the express trust, but rather by law. This echoes the approach taken by the drafters of the BGB, who understood that a critical function of the *numerus clausus* was ensuring that the acquisition and content of property rights depend entirely on features that are within the domain of property law,[170] excluding any causal regression to contractual autonomy.[171]

B. The Compromised List

In the modern era, common law courts have mostly declined to create new forms of property and there are no relevant examples of judicial abolition of existing property types.[172] For English land law, the core of the modern list of property rights is said to be found in the LPA 1925, ss 1 and 4.[173] As in Germany, this list is more the result of a process of rationalising pre-existing property types than of creating new ones. However, at least superficially, the rights contained in the LPA 1925 look remarkably different to those in the BGB. This is largely the result of the different way the English political system dealt with the inherent complexity involved in transitioning from traditional to modern property types, especially the difficulty in deciding how to treat the pre-existing rights under the new law.[174]

At the beginning of the nineteenth century, England kept much of its medieval land law.[175] Its key concepts were created 'for and by the rich in a time when the bulk of their wealth was invested in land'.[176] For example, at the time, half of England's agricultural land was settled, and these settlements were central to the power of the landed classes.[177] These medieval hangovers created a system that was remarkably complex, as it allowed parties to fragment ownership in manners that created important difficulties for the transfer of land.[178]

During the nineteenth century this system came under heavy pressure by growing middle classes pushing for reform.[179] However, the strong feelings of the aristocracy towards their land acted as a powerful barrier to comprehensive

[170] See ch 2, section II.C and ch 5, section III.A.

[171] For discussion, see ch 5, section III.A.

[172] Merrill and Smith (n 2) 20.

[173] McFarlane, Hopkins and Nield (n 24) 150–71; Gardner and MacKenzie (n 131) 11.

[174] On the structure of these type of problems, Stuart Banner, 'Transitions between Property Regimes' (2002) 31 *J Legal Stud* 359.

[175] AH Manchester, *A Modern Legal History of England and Wales, 1750–1950* (Butterworth 1980) 302.

[176] FH Lawson and Bernard Rudden, *The Law of Property* (3rd edn, OUP 2002) 170.

[177] William Cornish and others, *Law and Society in England 1750–1950* (2nd edn, Hart 2019) 168.

[178] Manchester (n 175) 302; Stuart Anderson, 'The 1925 Property Legislation: Setting Context' in Susan Bright and John Dewar (eds), *Land Law: Themes and Perspectives* (OUP 1998) 110; Elizabeth Cooke, *Land Law* (2nd edn, OUP 2012) 37, 40–41.

[179] Cornish and others (n 177) 135–37, 168–79; Anderson (n 178) 110. For discussion, see ch 5, section III.B.

change.[180] Furthermore, transforming archaic rights into modern property forms was also technically difficult. For example, by the seventeenth century the copyhold was already outmoded.[181] However, when the 1830 Real Property Commission tried to eradicate it, it had to draw back due to the complexity of valuing the interest of the lord, settling for improvements that facilitated its voluntary enfranchisement.[182] This 'remarkably slow'[183] pace of change stands in marked contrast to what was happening in other areas, like the expansion of political representation by the Great Reforms Acts and the liberalisation of trade by the abolition of the Corn, Sugar Duties and Navigation acts.[184] As a result, despite some reforms enacted in the 1880s,[185] by the turn of the twentieth century English land law was remarkably out of step with social needs,[186] even being described as 'absurd and scandalous'.[187] Writing at the time, the liberal jurist AV Dicey, argued – maybe with some exaggeration – that despite having become a democracy, England's land law remained more 'appropriate to an aristocratic state'.[188]

Structural change to rationalise and modernise this system only came about with 1922–25 land law reform. However, this reform was not as much a driver for change, as a result of social, economic and legal transformations that preceded it. On the one hand, the reforms of the 1880s had prepared the groundwork for a more encompassing and ambitious transformation.[189] On the other, after the Great War, prompted by changes in taxation, heavy debts, decreased profitability and desire to diversify their investments, landowners shifted much of their wealth away from land. This created a real estate boom between 1919 and 1921 that transferred a relevant share of land in England to former tenants and 'new men of wealth'.[190] Thus, by the time Parliament discussed the 1922–25 reform, much of the previous hurdles created by vested interests had been lowered. For example, the number of copyholds had dramatically fallen thanks to voluntary enfranchisement, allowing its last vestiges to be disposed of through compulsory purchases.[191] In a process that has been described as 'peculiarly English', the aristocracies had changed their game ahead of the bill.[192]

[180] Manchester (n 175) 326.
[181] Alan Watson, *Society and Legal Change* (Temple UP 2001) 54–55.
[182] Cornish and others (n 177) 135.
[183] Manchester (n 175) 326.
[184] See James Vernon, *Modern Britain: 1750 to the Present* (CUP 2017) 132, 151–54, 205, 210.
[185] eg Settled Land Act 1882.
[186] Watson (n 181) 55–57.
[187] Arthur Underhill, 'Property' (1932) 51 *LQR* 221, 228.
[188] AV Dicey, 'The Paradox of the Land Law' (1905) 21 *LQR* 221, 222.
[189] Based on work in progress by Lorren Eldridge on the history of the LPA 1925.
[190] Cornish and others (n 177) 173; Anderson (n 178) 128; David Cowan, Lorna Fox O'Mahony and Neil Cobb, *Great Debates in Land Law* (3rd edn, Hart 2023) 54, 57–58.
[191] Cornish and others (n 177) 135.
[192] Anderson (n 178) 128.

The chief object of the reform was simplifying land law[193] and making the transfer of a fee simple free of incumbrancers as easy as possible.[194] Despite the changes that predate it, passing such a reform still required a relevant degree of political compromise and technical skill to bring the more conservative elements of Parliament on board.[195] The result was an apolitical and neutral bill, carefully affirmed on all sides, that did not affect the relation between landlords and tenants nor between the state and private owners.[196] The bill was mostly drafted by professional conveyancers with no input from the public[197] and has been described as a 'monument of legal wisdom'.[198]

The structure of the list contained in the LPA 1925 reflects this elaborate compromise. The act is not a code nor a fresh start, as it presupposes knowledge of a great deal of pre-existing law.[199] To rationalise land law without a radical break with the past, the LPA 1925 introduced a number of reforms that built on the preexisting law, including (i) reducing legal estates to the bare minimum (ie fee simple and leasehold), (ii) allowing the abolished estates (eg fee tail, live estate) to subsist in Equity, thereby dramatically increasing the role of trusts in land law, (iii) closing the list of equitable property rights, and (iv) significantly expanding the scope of overreaching.[200] The result was a severe limitation on the effects that property rights can have on successors in title, reducing the number of legal interests of which a purchaser of land needs to be mindful, at the cost 'downgrading' other rights into weaker and less secure equitable interests.[201]

The rights on this list might sound extremely unfamiliar to a civilian lawyer, but once they are clustered by function the picture is not that different, at least if trusts are left aside. The list is made of 'estates' and 'interests' in land. Underlying this distinction is the 'simple idea' that estates are to do with ownership in land and interests with rights over the land of another.[202] Estates come in two forms, with their conceptual difference being their extension in time: fee simples are indefinite, while leaseholds are subject to a certain term.[203] In contrast, like German 'limited property rights', English property 'interests' provide for rights to make a limited use of a thing owned by

[193] Manchester (n 175) 324–25; Anderson (n 178) 109; Cooke (n 178) 41.
[194] Anderson (n 178) 120.
[195] Anderson (n 178) 120–22.
[196] Cornish and others (n 177) 178.
[197] Anderson (n 178) 123, 125. However, there was plenty of consultation with the legal profession in the many years leading to the reform. See Eldridge (n 189).
[198] RE Megarry and HWR Wade, *The Law of Real Property* (4th edn), 1157, quoted by Manchester (n 175) 325.
[199] Cooke (n 178) 42; Anderson (n 178) 127.
[200] See Anderson (n 178) 108–09. In the same line, Lawson and Rudden (n 176) 102; Cowan, Fox O'Mahony and Cobb (n 190) 57.
[201] Cooke (n 178) 41–43.
[202] Susan Bright, 'Of Estates and Interest: A Tale of Ownership and Property Rights' in Susan Bright and John Dewar (eds), *Land Law: Themes and Perspectives* (OUP 1998) 529.
[203] See ch 2, section III.A.

someone else, such as easements and restrictive covenants, and security rights that make a thing liable to pay a certain debt, such as mortgages. The place of 'acquisition rights' is taken by the doctrine of anticipation,[204] that is, by an equitable doctrine that confers buyers an equitable version of the promised legal right as soon there is an enforceable contract, without having to wait for legal title to pass.

Subsequent changes to the list of property rights in English land law have been mostly achieved thorough Parliamentary action.[205] These include reforms to the law on formalities,[206] trusts in land[207] and registration.[208] However, these changes have not implied a radical transformation of the *numerus clausus*: the current list is almost the same it was in 1925, with only small modifications. For example, since 1997 it has not been possible to create new interests in fee tail,[209] although the existing ones survive in Equity.[210] In turn, the few additions to the list, like the commonhold,[211] have not been very successful in practice.[212] By the same token, courts have been reluctant to change the law, as apparent by the refusal of the House of Lords to create an equitable right in a matrimonial home to protect a wife who had been deserted by her husband,[213] and, more recently, by its reluctance to derogate the certainty of terms rule of leases, and its call on the Law Commission to review the convenience of keeping it.[214]

C. Judicial Development of Property Rights

As in Germany, English courts have occasionally stepped in to solve practical problems derived from having a closed listed of property rights. The most discussed example is the development of restrictive covenants during the mid-nineteenth century. Authors following economic[215] and comparative approaches[216] normally

[204] *Walsh v Lonsdale* (1882) 21 Ch D 9.

[205] Although there are notable examples of judicial ingenuity, especially the development of the common intention constructive trust since the 1970s, see Cooke (n 178) 87–96.

[206] LP(MP) 1989, s 2.

[207] TOLALA 1996.

[208] LRA 2002.

[209] TOLATA 1996, Sch 1.

[210] LPA 1925, s 1. On this, Dixon (n 132) 9.

[211] See Commonhold and Leasehold Reform Act 2002.

[212] See Lu Xu, 'Commonhold Developments in Practice' in Warren Barr (ed), *Modern Studies in Property Law*, vol 8 (Hart 2015).

[213] See *Ainswort* (n 133). However, this resulted in the enactment of special legislation to tackle this problem only two years later. See Matrimonial Homes Act 1967, now Family Law Act 1986, ss 30–32.

[214] *Prudential Assurance Co Ltd v London Residuary Body* [1992] 3 WLR 279, 287.

[215] eg, Merrill and Smith (n 2) 17.

[216] eg Milo (n 9) 736; Akkermans, 'The Numerus Clausus of Property Rights' (n 9) 101.

hold that restrictive covenants emerged from *Tulk v Moxhay*.[217] However, this is not completely accurate, as this was only (part of) the starting point of a process that took more than 60 years.[218]

This development was triggered by the rise of the modern city.[219] By the mid nineteenth century, negative easements were sharply limited in number and responded to the needs of town or village life, while the burden of covenants respecting land could only be enforced against successors in title in the context of landlord-tenant relations.[220] However, as London developed into a modern mega-city, the desire of maintaining a certain general standard of amenity became increasingly important for prospective home owners. In an era when there was no statutory planning,[221] this forced developers to find ways to ensure that neighbourhoods would not deteriorate in the future by, for example, subdivision of houses, re-conversion into shops, and the use of yards for washing lines.[222]

In *Tulk*, for example, the plaintiff had sold the freehold of a plot of land at Leicester Square to a purchaser, who covenanted for him and his successors in title to maintain the garden, not to cut the trees on it, and not to build on the square. After several transfers, Mr Moxhay became the owner of the land and refused to comply with the covenant, despite knowing of its existence when he purchased the land. The court granted an injunction to Mr Tulk, preventing Mr Moxhay from cutting trees and building on the square. In a short judgment, Lord Cottenham clearly rejected the view that equitable intervention was limited to cases in which covenants runs at law, but did not definitely establish under what conditions Equity would bind a third party to covenants that do not run at law.[223]

Initially, this equitable intervention was understood to have been based on Mr Moxhay having notice of the covenant.[224] However, by the end of the 1870s there was strong evidence for a different rationale. Based on a short reference to *Keppell* made by Lord Cottenham, the binding effect of restrictive covenants ceased to be grounded in successors in title having notice of the promise, but rather in identifying the initial promise as a pre-existing equitable property right that, as such, could be asserted against successors in title.[225] This re-interpretation of *Tulk* vindicated the argument made by Lord Brougham in *Keppell* holding that notice is not enough to bind third parties[226] and shifted the test for the

[217] *Tulk v Moxhay* (1848) 2 Ph 774, 41 ER 1143.
[218] Ben McFarlane, 'Tulk v Moxhay (1848)' in Charles Mitchell and Paul Mitchell (eds), *Landmark Cases in Equity* (Hart 2012) 203, 224.
[219] See Merrill and Smith (n 2) 16–17; McFarlane, 'Tulk v Moxhay (1848)' (n 218) 204–11.
[220] Merrill and Smith (n 2) 16; Cornish and others (n 177) 152–53.
[221] Cooke (n 178) 34.
[222] Cornish and others (n 177) 153.
[223] McFarlane, 'Tulk v Moxhay (1848)' (n 218) 207–19, 217–18.
[224] ibid 219. For example, see *de Mattos v Gibson* (1849) 45 ER 108 or *Lucker v Dennis* (1877) 7 Ch D 227.
[225] McFarlane, 'Tulk v Moxhay (1848)' (n 218) 220. For an example, *Wilson v Hart* (1866) 1 Ch App 463.
[226] McFarlane, 'Keppell v Bailey (1834); Hill v Tupper (1863)' (n 4) 19.

enforceability of covenants against successors in title to the content of the promise, thereby shaping the modern rules on restrictive covenants:[227] a promise only counts as a restrictive covenant if it imposes a duty consisting in not making a particular use of the land, it benefits other land of the promisee, and is not intended to be merely personal.[228]

More recently, English law witnessed a new development regarding property rights in land that could be described as a *de facto* creation of a new category of 'recreational easement'.[229] In English law, an easement is a proprietary right of the owner of 'dominant land' to enjoy a limited use of a plot of land owned by another, the 'servient land'. Following *Re Ellenborough Park*,[230] a decisive issue for a right to qualify as an easement is whether it 'accommodates land', meaning whether, as a matter of fact, it serves the 'normal enjoyment of the [dominant] property'.[231] In *Ellenborough Park*, the court held that the right of an urban dwelling to use a neighbouring garden did accommodate the dominant tenement, because in the residential context using a garden serves a normal use of the dominant land, not one of mere 'recreation' or 'amusement', implying that the latter do not accommodate land. However, in *Regency Villas Title Ltd v Diamond Resorts (Europe) Ltd*,[232] the Supreme Court upheld a decision of the Court of Appeal holding that the right granted to the owner of a time share (purported dominant land) to use certain facilities in neighbouring (servient) land that might seem 'purely recreational' (eg tennis courts, swimming pool, etc) *did* accommodate land as an easement, partly relying for this on the social transformation in the value of sport activities in the UK.[233] In this manner, arguably, the Supreme Court created a new form of easement. To what extent this implies a real breach of the *numerus clausus* will be discussed in chapter seven, section II.

IV. SCOPE, ENFORCEMENT AND BREACH OF THE *NUMERUS CLAUSUS*

A. Between Overconfidence and Scepticism

Despite deep differences in style, the basic doctrinal content of the *numerus clausus* principle in Germany and England is surprisingly similar. On the one

[227] See McFarlane, 'Tulk v Moxhay (1848)' (n 218) 221–23.
[228] McFarlane, *The Structure of Property Law* (n 131) 885–91.
[229] See Susan Pascoe, 'Re-Evaluating Recreational Easements- New Norms for the Twenty-First Century?' in Ben McFarlane and Sinéad Agnew (eds), *Modern Studies in Property Law*, vol 10 (Hart 2019).
[230] *Re Ellenborough Park* [1956] Ch 131, CA, at 163.
[231] Anna Lawson, 'Easements' in Louise Tee (ed), *Land Law: Issues, Debates, Policy* (Willan 2002) 73.
[232] *Regency Villas Title Ltd v Diamond Resorts (Europe) Ltd* [2018] UKSC 57.
[233] *Regency Villas Title Ltd v Diamond Resorts (Europe) Ltd* [2017] EWCA Civ 238 [53]–[56].

hand, the words used by Lord Brougham to ground the principle in *Keppell* are not that different from those found in the *Motive* of the BGB: both stress that private parties are not allowed to create new property rights and must content themselves with the property rights made available to them by law. On the other, von Heck's argument that the list of property rights found in the BGB is to be interpreted as exclusive ('these are the only') is very similar to the wording of the LPA 1925, stating that these are 'the only' admissible legal property rights and restricting equitable interests to those that could have been validly created before it. Thus, in both jurisdictions, the core of the principle can be described as a doctrine that determines what rights created by private parties will be binding upon third parties by using a list that can only be amended by Parliament. In other words, the *numerus clausus* principle strongly restricts the freedom of individuals and the power of courts to create new property rights, or adapt the existing ones to new circumstances. The rationale for this will be discussed in chapters four and five.

However, the 'attitude' to the principle in both jurisdictions is remarkably different. German doctrine seems very confident about the place of the principle in its private law. By contrast, in England, the very existence of the principle remains debated, especially due to the impact of trusts. To a relevant extent, this can be explained by the different approach both jurisdictions take to the concept of a property right and the effect this has in assessing the *scope* of the *numerus clausus*. As explained in chapter two, German doctrine has a relatively narrow concept of a property right, that excludes rights that only have limited third-party effects from its scope. Thus, the 'proprietary effects' of leases and ownership for security purpose are normally rationalised as resulting from 'contracts with far-reaching third-party effects'. As a consequence, German doctrine tends to ignore or downplay the conceptual problems these intermediate rights pose for the principle of *numerus clausus*, deriving them to the law of obligations.

If German scholars seems overconfident about the principle of *numerus clausus*, their English counterparts are probably oversceptical. Because it tends to rely on an expansive concept of a property right, English doctrine cannot simply ignore the problem created by rights that only have limited third-party effects, especially the rights of beneficiaries of trusts. The topic has been extensively thematised as part of a long-standing discussion on the nature of equitable property rights, but the issue remains highly contested.[234] This is an important problem, but its impact on the *numerus clausus* should not be overstated. Even if the settlors of express trusts enjoy ample freedom to delineate the rights of beneficiaries, their idiosyncratic effects do not regularly affect third parties: on the one hand, the rights of beneficiaries do not bind trespassers; on the other,

[234] See ch 2, section III.B.

their effects on successors in title are limited and standardised by the imposition of a constructive trust by law.

From a comparative perspective the bottom line is that both systems have entitlements that are hard to bring under the orthodox property rights–obligations divide, making the relevance of the *numerus clausus* in this 'grey zone' uncertain. The dubious applicability of the principle to rights that bind successors in title but not trespassers suggests that the effect this doctrine has on party autonomy is less stringent than normally assumed, as it leaves private parties some room to create atypical rights with some (limited) third party effects. A central implication of this is that assessing the impact of the *numerus clausus* on property law requires distinguishing between its effects on the creation of duties that affect successors in title and trespassers. That distinction is at the base of chapters six and seven.

B. Rationalisation and Creation of Property Types

In both England and Germany, the core of the modern list of property rights is the brainchild of the liberal political ideas that dominated the nineteenth century. Pushed by industrialisation, urbanisation and the expansion of franchise, the rising middle classes decisively campaigned to 'free' land from traditional bonds that allowed an array of duties to run with it, ultimately forging the modern list of property rights. This process should be seen more as one of destruction and rationalisation of old property forms, than one of creation of new types. Thus, the foundational *ethos* of modern property law is probably better described as having fewer and simpler property types, rather than creating more and more complex ones. Furthermore, despite the visible difference in the property types available in England and Germany, from a functional perspective the overall list is not that different. As in most post-feudal societies, property rights come in three basic forms: (i) rights that confer possession over things, (ii) non-possessory, non-security rights that confer limited use of things, and (iii) security rights that provide for the power to get paid with preference from the proceeds of the sale of specific things.[235]

However, the circumstances leading to the configuration of the modern *numerus clausus* in both jurisdictions could hardly be more different. In England 'the land question' was very much at the heart of the nineteenth century political debate. Attempts to rationalise property law started early on, but moved at an extremely slow pace, due to the opposition of vested interest and the intrinsic difficulties of deciding how to value old rights under the new law. Substantial reforms only became possible once the land-owning classes had moved significant parts of their wealth to other types of assets. Consequently, the land

[235] Rudden (n 2) 241–42.

question was only settled in the 1920s, through several acts that required a relevant degree of political compromise and technical skill. The relevant bills were manly drafted by professional conveyancers who made extensive use of Equity to phase out old property form without fully derogating them. In Germany, by contrast, the modern list of property rights came about through a systematic national codification of private law, triggered by the 1871 unification of the Second Empire. The reform counted with widespread support among conservative land-owning and liberal middle classes, while the priorities of the working classes were scarcely considered. The drafting process was led by influential liberal law professors educated in the highly conceptual Pandectist tradition, not by practitioners, and its final version was approved almost with no discussion by the *Reichstag* in 1896. The outcome was a highly stylised list of property rights, based on classical Roman law, that makes little to no compromise with pre-existing Germanic property forms. After their foundational moment, neither list of property rights has suffered radical legislative transformation. In both England and Germany, the list has mainly grown by the enactment of a few new property types. The only relevant exception is the enactment of the ZGB in the GDR and its subsequent replacement with the BGB, once the new *Länder* acceded to the German Federal Republic.

This is consistent with some leading theoretical models on the evolution of property law described in chapter one: reforming property law has extremely high fixed cost and it becomes increasingly harder to change as time passes.[236] Thus, it is easier to add new rights to the list than rationalise or destroy preexisting ones. In this view, structural transformation of property law is normally only possible in exceptional political circumstances,[237] in which an organised group has enough political power to impose the negative consequence of radical changes on weaker groups,[238] as seen during the creation of the German Empire, the GDR or after the German re-unification. By contrast, rationalisation of property law in absence of wider structural institutional change tends to be extremely slow and complex. It is normally preceded by vested interest shifting their attention to other areas and still requires elaborate compromises between different stakeholders, as seen in England.

This finding points to a second features relevant to assess the impact of the *numerus clausus* on the ability of property law to adapt itself to new realities: the principle creates a legislative monopoly over property law, formally precluding the judicial development of the property system. In contemporary democratic societies, this has the obvious implication of making the evolution of property

[236] Yun-chien Chang and Henry Smith, 'An Economic Analysis of Civil versus Common Law Property' (2012) 88 *Notre Dame L Rev* 1.

[237] Ugo Mattei, *Basic Principles of Property Law: A Comparative Legal and Economic Introduction* (Greenwood 2000) 30.

[238] Banner (n 174).

law highly dependent on politics. The problems and justification of this institutional design will be discussed in chapters four and eight.

C. Legal Scaffolding: Breaching the *Numerus Clausus*?

The rigidity that the legislative monopoly created by the *numerus clausus* imposes on property law has led courts in both England and Germany to occasionally deviate from it. Despite being generally reluctant to develop the property system, when economic and social needs are pressing and legislators do not act, both English and German courts have (exceptionally) been ready to step in to provide practical solutions through legal constructs that can be described as 'legal scaffolding'.[239] These are back-up mechanisms in which a complex combination of existing legal categories is used to cure or moderate the divergence between law and social needs, when institutional bodies with fully recognised law-making powers fail to introduce simpler rules that could close the gap.[240]

The use of scaffolding by courts shows that the legislative monopoly over the property system created by the *numerus clausus* is not as strict and inflexible as normally assumed: in practice, judges have some leeway to adapt property law to new circumstances. Despite not being desirable, legal scaffolding is typically tolerated for lack of a better alternative.[241] In English and German property law this is well reflected in the fact that the property rights developed by courts in each jurisdiction point to the comparative weakness of its list of acknowledged property rights. For example, the judicial creation of security ownership in Germany evidences the need for property forms long known in English law, such as the trust and the floating charge. In contrast, the development of English restrictive covenants and recreational easements partially reflects the need to adapt property law to contexts that were consciously addressed by the BGB and by special legislation enacted to deal with housing problems after both world wars.[242]

However, courts almost never openly create new property rights, but claim to only enforce pre-existing private law structures, normally by changing the content inside the pre-existing modules of private law (ie through legal scaffolding). For example, in *Regency Villas* the court did not create a new property right, nor abrogate the rule requiring the right to accommodate land or the rule holding that the mere amusement of the owner does not accommodate land. Instead, it fitted the use of sport facilities into the pre-exiting legal structure of easements. Similarly, German doctrine argues that security ownership is consistent with the unitary notion of ownership, by distinguishing between the internal

[239] Borrowing a term from Alan Watson. See n 240.

[240] Watson (n 181) 87, 91, 122.

[241] See Watson (n 181) 89.

[242] See ch 7, section III.B.

(contractual) relations of the parties and the external (proprietary) effects *vis a vis* third parties. As argued in more detail in chapter eight, reliance of scaffolding on pre-existing categories of private law partially explains why change in property law tends to pass unnoticed. To what extent these developments actually amount to the judicial creation of new property rights is subject to discussion, but the overall result is that, occasionally, English and German courts are willing to develop their property systems. This triggers a further conceptual question: how are these deviations justified? This issue will be addressed in the following two chapters.[243]

[243] Especially, ch 4, section IV and ch 5, section IV.

4

The Governance of Property Rights[1]

ACCORDING TO THE institutionalist framework adopted in chapter one, assessing the impact of the *numerus clausus* principle on legal change requires accounting for the role of the state in delineating and enforcing property rights. From this perspective, chapter three concluded that the main institutional effect of the *numerus clausus* is creating a legislative monopoly that formally precludes the judicial development of property rights. Whether this is a desirable institutional design has been subject to extensive discussion, especially in the context of American property theory. However, evaluating the relevance of these arguments for England and Germany requires a more detailed approach to how legal sources are handled in different jurisdictions. On the one hand, the role played by judges and legislators is often said to be the most apparent fault line between civilian and common law systems. On the other, despite belonging to the same tradition, English and American law conceive the law-making powers of judges differently. Thus, it cannot simply be assumed that the institutional impact of the *numerus clausus* has the same significance across jurisdictions. This chapter discusses these differences by analysing what the *numerus clausus* implies for the wider context of German, English and American law. For this, it focuses on the institutional roles of judges and the style of their legal reasoning. In other words, this chapters looks at the *numerus clausus* 'beyond property law'.

The chapter starts by briefly accounting for the core elements of the normative discussion on the institutional dimension of the *numerus clausus*, arguing that assessing their relevance in a comparative light requires a more fine-grained approach to the role and style of judges in each jurisdiction (section I). Then, it discusses the place the *numerus clausus* principle occupies in the context of the wider continental separation of powers principle and how this impacts the style of judicial legal reasoning in German property law (section II). Afterwards, it analyses the effect of the *numerus clausus* on the English and American *stare decisis* doctrines, focusing on the prevailing approach to the role of judges in the

[1] This chapter partially borrows from Ernesto Vargas Weil, 'The Numerus Clausus and the Governance of Property Law: A Comparative Approach to German, English and American Legal Reasoning' (2024) 11 *EJCL & G* 330. However, the approach of this chapter is different and it also introduces a number of new topics, including a normative discussion on the merits and demerits of legislated property law.

process of legal change and its impact on property law (section III). The chapter ends by discussing the descriptive and normative implications that these differences have on the legislative monopoly over property law created by the *numerus clausus* principle (section IV).

A first conclusion of this chapter is that the institutional impact of the *numerus clausus* varies across jurisdictions. In Germany, its effects are relatively limited, because they are mostly absorbed by the continental separation of powers principle. Hence, the main challenge in this context is not justifying the institutional dimension of the principle, but its occasional breach by courts. By contrast in the American common law, the principle has an uncomfortable institutional position. On the one hand, it has a more visible institutional impact than in Germany because it seems to take inherent law-making powers away from courts but, on the other, it also has a weaker standing as it is essentially conceived as a rule of judicial self-restraint. The relevant implication is that the American version of the principle requires much more external normative support, typically in the form of efficiency and political arguments. Finally, in what might seem an unexpected outcome, due to its stricter *stare decisis* doctrine and the broader role that Parliament plays in developing law in general, the institutional impact of the English version of the *numerus clausus* seems closer to Germany than the US. Consistent with this, the main normative challenge for English law is also justifying judicial deviations from the principle, not the legislative monopoly. These justifications will be discussed in the next chapter.

A second, rather obvious conclusion, is that the *numerus clausus* subordinates the development of property law to the dynamics of legislative politics. Consequently, in practice, the status this legislative monopoly enjoys in each system is highly dependent on the perceived performance of legislators. In the US, where legislators are frequently seen as less responsive or trustworthy than courts, the institutional dimension of the *numerus clausus* is constantly put in question. In contrast, in England and Germany, where legislation is – at least in relative terms – seen as a more legitimate and successful source of legal change, reform by Parliament is the most natural avenue to keep property law in step with social change. The implications of this for the reform of the *numerus clausus* are discussed in chapter eight.

A third conclusion is that, at least in England and Germany, the institutional dimension of the *numerus clausus* is clearly justified by both democratic and technical arguments. On the one hand, regardless of criticism of everyday politics, only legislative law can be conceptually derived from a democratic mandate and ensure representative participation in the law-making process. On the other, the extensive ramifications of reforms that affect rights with inherent third-party effects calls for law-making bodies that have a good overview of the general effects of their actions and possess institutional tools to address them. These arguments are conceptually not less true in America, but they are undermined in practice by prevailing scepticism towards legislators and a certain tendency of scholarship to see judicial law-making as a shortcut to achieve substantively valuable ends, without the need for legislative action. This tension between 'form and substance' is also discussed in chapter eight.

I. THE INSTITUTIONAL DIMENSION OF THE *NUMERUS CLAUSUS*

The *numerus clausus* has been described as a 'constitutional'[2] or 'organisational'[3] rule of property law, because it implies an institutional choice in favour of legislators and against courts as the competent authority to develop new property rights. The justification of this distribution of law-making competences is highly debated, with arguments revolving around two issues. The first is technical: who performs better developing the law? The second is political: is it legitimate for judges to develop property law? In an interesting phenomenon, the available answers to these questions do not align with the division between 'information' and 'progressive' property theorists.[4] This has the outcome of making law and economics and 'liberal' scholars unlikely allies, while at the same time dividing the 'progressive camp'.

On the performance side, the most radical argument against the legislative monopoly over property law relies on economic efficiency. Building on the theory of 'efficient common law',[5] the American law and economics movement traditionally held that judicial development of property law is preferable, because common law rules are more efficient than legislative law.[6] Despite its popularity in America, the descriptive correctness of this theory has been seriously doubted by legal historians[7] and legal theorists;[8] and even if correct, there is no reason to assume it carries the same weight outside this context. Indeed, if anything, comparative-empirical research suggests that judge-made common law property systems do not have a clear efficiency edge over civil-statutory regimes.[9] In line with these empirical findings, leading 'information' theorists justify the institutional dimension of the *numerus clausus* in several technical advantages of

[2] Bram Akkermans, 'The Numerus Clausus of Property Rights' in Michele Graziadei and Lionel Smith (eds), *Comparative Property Law: Global Perspectives* (Edward Elgar 2017) 102; Bram Akkermans, *The Principle of Numerus Clausus in European Property Law* (Intersentia 2008) 407.

[3] Teun Struycken, *De Numerus Clausus in Het Goederenrecht* (Kluwer 2007) 350–56, referring to Dutch law.

[4] On these camps, ch 1, section I.

[5] For this theory, Richard A Posner, *Economic Analysis of Law* (7th edn, Aspen 2007) 249–53, 562–65.

[6] Describing this argument, Thomas W Merrill and Henry E Smith, 'Optimal Standardization in the Law of Property: The Numerus Clausus Principle' (2000) 110 *Yale LJ* 1, 60.

[7] Ron Harris, 'The History and Historical Stance of Law and Economics' in Markus D Dubber and Christopher Tomlins (eds), *The Oxford Handbook of Legal History* (OUP 2018) 38.

[8] eg Ronald Dworkin, *Taking Rights Seriously* (Bloomsbury 2013) 122.

[9] Yun-chien Chang, *Property Law: Comparative, Empirical and Economic Analyses* (CUP 2023) 355.

legislated law, including its ability to convey information to the public, clearer scope, prospective nature and capacity to consider overall costs of reforms.[10]

The proponents of the (progressive) 'liberal theory of property' are not convinced by the technical advantages of legislative law; and, despite relying on a different 'animating principle', they reach a conclusion similar to the one advanced by the efficient common law theory. In this view, save for some exceptions,[11] in an 'autonomy-based' property system there are no performance arguments to prefer legislative over judge-made law, as the creation or modifications of property rights should be triggered by challenges bearing on the desirability of the normative underpinning of property types, their responsiveness to their social context or their effectiveness in promoting their contextually examined normative goals. Thus, as long as rules are not revisited too frequently, there is no reason why judges should not fulfill this task alongside legislators.[12] However, this claim is not justified and its proponents openly accept that it is not grounded on any empirical data.[13] As a consequence, the 'liberal' view should be regarded as a normative 'substance over form' argument, that is more concerned with achieving certain social outcomes than with internal consistency.[14] At its core, this view holds that, as long as judges develop property law for (what these theorists see as) the right normative arguments (ie promoting a certain view of autonomy), judges are competent law makers. Such an argument begs the question, as it assumes what it is supposed to explain: why are judges technically well-placed to develop the property system?

In turn, the political legitimacy discussion divides the progressive camp. On the one hand, the 'democratic property' movement,[15] maintains that the justification for the *numerus clausus* is political, not functional. In this view, the legislative monopoly over the property system is based on the legitimacy that the democratic process provides legislative law.[16] On the other, the proponents of a 'liberal property theory' argue that judges enjoy political legitimacy because adjudication provides a forum that is especially suitable for individuals to participate, thereby creating an instance where the normative and empirical horizons of judges are constantly challenged. In this view, this does not create a problem for the rule of law because judges are also accountable for their decisions. However, no real argument is provided for the latter, other than pointing to the skewed nature of the political process.[17] The latter might be true, but

[10] Merrill and Smith (n 6) 61–66. For the arguments, section III.C.

[11] See section III.C.

[12] Hanoch Dagan, *A Liberal Theory of Property Law* (CUP 2021) 151–56.

[13] See ibid 151.

[14] Dagan explicitly describes himself as a legal realist: ibid 160.

[15] See Joseph William Singer, 'Democratic Estates: Property Law in a Free and Democratic Society' (2009) 94 *Cornell L Rev* 1009, 1046–47.

[16] Avihay Dorfman, 'Property and Collective Undertaking: The Principle of Numerus Clausus' (2011) 61 *U Toronto LJ* 467.

[17] See Dagan (n 12) 157–58.

being an argument about the political system, it says nothing about the legitimacy of judges, and, in any case, it cannot be extended to other jurisdictions without further research. Furthermore, the argument itself is not convincing, as it is far from obvious that interests defended by parties in court are 'representative' of society in any meaningful way: who can bring cases before court is highly contingent and these litigants will typically defend *their* narrow interest.[18] Thus, considering that, in practice, being able to bring a claim is highly dependent on having the means to do, there is no reason to assume that cases heard by courts are less skewed than the political process, especially in jurisdictions where litigating is highly expensive.

Assessing these arguments in a comparative light requires approaching the institutional question of the *numerus clausus* from two perspectives that remain underexplored. The first is to what extent are the civilian and common law versions of the *numerus clausus* principle comparable from a macro-comparative perspective?[19] The scarce scholarship on this issue links the more 'stringent' version of the principle found in some civilian systems, including Germany, to the continental doctrine of separation of powers,[20] and reports that, in common law systems, including England, the judiciary holds the 'prime position' to develop most areas of property law.[21] The second is to what extent the different approach to the authority of courts in England and America impact the institutional standing of the *numerus clausus*. This second point remains practically unexplored.[22]

Addressing these issues in more depth is key to assess the legislative monopoly over property law created by the *numerus clausus*. The sources of law and legal methods of each tradition have traditionally been seen as being at the core of the civil-common law divide. In this view, modern civilian systems are based on the enlightenment idea of having abstract and systematic self-contained codes that anticipate future problems as completely as possible. The operation of these systems relies on a strict separation of powers that seeks to prevent judicial law making, that is currently justified in a democratic law-making rationale.[23] By contrast, in the common law, case law is seen as having a central role as courts are not only tasked with solving individual conflicts, but with developing the law 'from below',[24] with statutory law principally serving to flesh out details of case law on specific points or to overturn individual decisions.[25] Even

[18] In the examples of ch 3: real estate developers, villa owners, merchants and industrialists.

[19] The issue has been raised by Bram Akkermans. Akkermans, 'The Numerus Clausus of Property Rights' (n 2) 103; Akkermans, *The Principle of Numerus Clausus in European Property Law* (n 2) 407.

[20] Akkermans, 'The Numerus Clausus of Property Rights' (n 2) 103–06.

[21] Akkermans, *The Principle of Numerus Clausus in European Property Law* (n 2) 407.

[22] But see n 1.

[23] Mathias Siems, *Comparative Law* (2nd edn, CUP 2018) 52–53; Uwe Kischel, *Comparative Law* (Andrew Hammel tr, OUP 2019) 361, 364–67.

[24] Siems (n 23) 55.

[25] Kischel (n 23) 242.

if contemporary comparative scholarship has relativised these differences,[26] and domestic doctrine, at least in England, sees legislation as having a much wider role,[27] the different approach to the sources of law across traditions is still a defining starting point to understand their divergence. The civil law is deemed as essentially made of legislated law, applied in a (more or less) positivistic and mechanical manner by judges aiming to interpret statutory law in an impersonal, rational and predictable manner by 'subsuming' individual facts into general rules using syllogisms. In contrast, the common law is described in comparative research as evolving gradually through judicial inductive reasoning, shaped by the rationale of individual decisions that give relevant attention to policy concerns and arguments from economics and other social sciences.[28] However, legal traditions are not monolithic and it cannot be assumed that different jurisdictions within one of them will treat their sources of law in the same manner. For example, since independence, the US has, in many senses, departed from English law.[29]

Moreover, the idea of 'sources of law' is itself problematic. First, because it is a metaphor, not a formal concept, even in the context of a single jurisdiction, its meaning can be ambiguous. Second, to what extent sources of law have an actual impact on shaping legal outcomes depends on how these sources are applied in the judicial process, that is, on the prevailing 'legal method' or 'legal reasoning' of the relevant jurisdiction.[30] Thus, regardless of the weight of converging trends, the institutional choice of the *numerus clausus* in favour of legislators as competent authorities to develop new property rights cannot simply be assumed to have the same meaning in England, Germany and the US. If the civilian codification was not only an effort to unify and systemise the law of the emerging national states, but a part of a political agenda that included a strict separation of the judicial, executive and legislative branches,[31] in principle, the exclusive authority of legislators in this field seems a necessary consequence of the institutional arrangement in which modern civilian systems came into existence. By contrast, if case law is the main source of private law in common law systems, in such jurisdictions, the *numerus clausus* principle seems to remove inherent lawmaking powers from the courts, radically altering the structure of its sources of law. However, this conclusion cannot be generalised, as there is also relevant

[26] For an updated discussion, ibid 619–30. For a sceptical view, Holger Spamann, 'Civil v. Common Law: The Emperor Has No Clothes' (2024) 24–11, Harvard Public Law Working Paper, https://ssrn.com/abstract=4937647 accessed 17 October 2024.

[27] See David Kelly, *Slapper and Kelly's English Legal System* (19th edn, Routledge 2020) 92.

[28] Siems (n 23) 55–56; Kischel (n 23) 229–32, 361–62, 371–74, 392–97, 412–16.

[29] Kischel (n 23) 333, 336, 344–48; Konrad Zweigert and Hein Kötz, *An Introduction to Comparative Law* (Tony Weir tr, 3rd edn, OUP 1998) 243–49, 259–65; Siems (n 23) 75–78.

[30] Stefan Vogenauer, 'Sources of Law and Legal Method in Comparative Law' in Mathias Reimann and Reinhard Zimmermann (eds), *The Oxford Handbook of Comparative Law* (2nd edn, OUP 2019) 878–79, 884–86, 889, 894.

[31] Jan Smits, *The Making of European Private Law* (Intersentia 2002) 77; Zweigert and Kötz (n 29) 89.

divergence between the English and American approaches to the value of judicial precedents and the style of legal reasoning.

Filling these gaps requires stepping back to see the functioning of the institutional dimension of the *numerus clausus* within the wider context of the legal sources of each tradition. This will lead to some unexpected conclusions, including that English courts do not have the prime position to develop the property system (as sometimes said) and that English legal reasoning is, in many senses, more similar to the German than the American model. From a normative perspective this implies that the arguments advanced in the US against the institutional dimension of the *numerus clausus* are rather weak in other contexts.

II. GERMANY: THE BOUNDED JUDGE

A. The Dogma of Separation of Powers

Assessing the significance of the *numerus clausus* within the broader German legal system requires a closer look at the role of its courts and legislators. In civilian systems, the level of freedom and creativity enjoyed by judges is a permanent matter of controversy.[32] In Germany, even though legislated law (*Gesetz*) is almost always the departure point of private law, the evaluation standards (*Wertungsmaßstäbe*) contained in such statutes can never be complete and need to be laid down by courts in concrete cases.[33] This interaction between law giving and adjudication is said to create challenges for the civilian idea of separation of powers that are not paralleled in the common law mindset.[34] As discussed below, this tension has shaped the way in which German legal culture conceives the role of judges and the nature of their reasoning.

Following the political ideas of the Enlightenment,[35] the nineteenth century codification movement adhered to the basic principle that judges should be strictly bound by legislation.[36] The reason for this was primarily to protect the rational structure of natural law. The drafters of the early codified systems inherited from the monarchs of the eighteenth century the fear that courts might undermine their efforts to enact the 'law of reason'[37] and thus

[32] Kischel (n 23) 371.

[33] Dieter Schwab and Martin Löhnig, *Einführung in das Zivilrecht* (20th edn, CF Müller 2016) 38.

[34] Kischel (n 23) 374. For an example, Rolf Wank, *Die Auslegung von Gesetzen* (6th edn, Vahlen 2015) 86.

[35] Franz Wieacker, *A History of Private Law in Europe with Particular Reference to Germany* (Tony Weir tr, Clarendon 1995) 249–51; RC van Caenegem, *An Historical Introduction to Private Law* (CUP 1992) 115–17, 122–25.

[36] Heinrich Honsell, 'Einleitung zum BGB' in Dagmar Kaiser and Markus Stoffels (eds), *J. Staudingers Kommentar zum Bürgerlichen Gesetzbuch mit Einführungsgestetz und Nebengesetzen: Eckpfeiler des Zivilrechts* (6th edn, Sellier & de Gruyter 2018) 90; van Caenegem (n 35) 122, 130.

[37] On the 'law of reason', Wieacker (n 35) 199–275; van Caenegem (n 35) 117–21.

aimed to deny all space for judicial creativity.[38] For this purpose, the absolutist regimes developed the dogma that all legal disputes must be decided by exclusive reliance on statutory law, forbidding all resort to precedents and scholarly opinions.[39] For example, the 1794 ALR explicitly provided that the 'opinions of legal writers or previous decisions of the courts will be ignored in future decision making'.[40] Following this extreme doctrine of separation of powers (*Gewaltenteilung*), civilian judges sought to restrict their creativity to the minimum, claiming that disputes could be resolved by mere 'subsumption' of fact into rules.[41]

This institutional arrangement was later transferred to continental democratic systems. These see democratically generated law (ie statutory law) as a manifestation of the general will of the nation (*allgemieiner Willen des Volkes*), that shall not be altered in any form by an unelected judiciary.[42] Therefore, the prohibition of judicial development of law is considered a guarantee of citizens' freedom.[43] In contemporary Germany, this view is embodied at a constitutional level as part of the rule of law in Art 20(2) GG, and, according to Art 97(1) GG, it means that judges are (only) bound by legislation.[44]

Art 20(3) GG, however, has a slightly different wording, stating that the exercise of jurisdiction (*Rechtsprechung*) is subject to '*Recht und Gesetz*'. This expression cannot be translated into English without losing its full meaning.[45] The word '*Recht*' has no equivalent in English, as it embodies, at the same time, the idea of law and of justice or correctness, while '*Gesetz*' is literally only legislative law.[46] In German scholarship, this is normally understood as holding that it is not enough for judges to follow the formal content of the law (in the sense of *Gesetz*), as they are also bound by a substantive conception of justice, derived from a natural law ideal. This reading of the constitution is frequently seen as embodying the 'Radbruch formula',[47] as a reaction to the acritical enforcement of Nazi law by the German judiciary.[48] Both contemporary constitutional[49]

[38] Honsell (n 36) 90; Schwab and Löhnig (n 33) 38; Zweigert and Kötz (n 29) 89; Kischel (n 23) 375.

[39] Wieacker (n 35) 258, 265; Schwab and Löhnig (n 33) 38; Kischel (n 23) 375.

[40] § 6 ALR, translation by Stefan Vogenauer, Vogenauer (n 30) 887.

[41] Zweigert and Kötz (n 29) 89–90, 258.

[42] Schwab and Löhnig (n 33) 38.

[43] Honsell (n 36) 90.

[44] Christian Bumke and Andreas Voßkuhle, *Casebook Verfassungsrecht* (8th edn, Mohr Siebeck 2020) 357–58, 597; Wank (n 34) 29, 86.

[45] On this topic, Kischel (n 23) 362–63.

[46] This is lost in the English version of the GG made available by the German Government, which translates the passage as 'legislation and the law'. See www.gesetze-im-internet.de/englisch_gg/englisch_gg.html#p0111.

[47] Gustav Radbruch, 'Gesetzliches Unrecht und Übergesetzliches Recht' (1946) 1 *SJZ* 105.

[48] Honsell (n 36) 92; Jörg Neuner, *Allgemeiner Teil des Bürgerlichen Rechts* (13th edn, Beck 2023) 39, 42.

[49] Bumke and Voßkuhle (n 44) 366.

and private law[50] doctrine widely accepts that this provision enables judges to develop the law to fill gaps in legislation, especially to bring old statutes in step with changing social realities. This view has been endorsed by the BVerfG, holding that Art 20(3) GG authorises judges to fill gaps in the law (*Lückenfüllung*) and extend it (*Rechtsfortbildung*).[51]

However, the power of courts to 'extend' law also has well-defined limits,[52] which are ultimately underpinned by the principles of popular sovereignty (*Volkssouveränität*) and the protection of legitimate expectations (*Vertrauensschutzes*).[53] According to a 2011 decision of the BVerfG,[54] *Rechtsfortbildung* does not allow judges to replace the legislator's conception of justice with their own. While this does not preclude judicial competence to use open-ended provisions to overcome the limited capability of legislators to react to accelerated social change, this power has clear boundaries: judges cannot free themselves from the 'sense and purpose' (*Sinn und Zweck*) of the law. They must respect the basic decision made by Parliament, implementing the legislative will under the new circumstances. Courts cannot appropriate the role of the legislature by imposing their own policy choices.[55]

In this wider context, since early on, continental scholarship developed methodical rules for legal interpretation which aim to avoid the arbitrary application of statutes by courts.[56] Nowadays, Art 20(3) GG is seen as being at the core of this system,[57] as contemporary authors directly link the rules for legal interpretation to the protection of the separation of powers principle and the rule of law.[58] Whether these techniques can fulfil this task has become increasingly doubtful as courts have openly recognised their role in the creation of norms.[59] Thus, in practice, 'no civil lawyer believes he is just applying the law in a mechanical and predetermined way'.[60] As a consequence, the prevailing view in Germany is that courts not only interpret law, but also fill its gaps and sometimes correct it.[61] Nonetheless, German legal culture still evidences a deep aversion to unwritten law.[62] As explained in the next subsection, private law is probably the paradigm of this sceptical approach.

[50] Neuner (n 48) 44–46.
[51] BVerfGE 34, 269, 287.
[52] Honsell (n 36) 93.
[53] Neuner (n 48) 42.
[54] BVerfGE 128, 193, NJW 2011 836.
[55] Bumke and Voßkuhle (n 44) 366.
[56] Jaap Hage, 'Legal Reasoning' in Jan M Smits (ed), *Elgar Encyclopedia of Comparative Law* (2nd edn, Edward Elgar 2012) 531.
[57] Neuner (n 48) 29.
[58] eg Bernd Rüthers, 'Methodenrealismus in Jurisprudenz und Justiz' (2006) 61 JZ 53, 53; Wank (n 34) 86.
[59] Schwab and Löhnig (n 33) 43.
[60] Kischel (n 23) 365.
[61] Schwab and Löhnig (n 33) 44.
[62] Kischel (n 23) 364. For a more sceptical view, Rüthers (n 58).

B. Judicial Thinking in German Private Law

The attitude of German legal culture towards unwritten law can be seen in the evolution of the 'Theory of the Juridical Method' (*Juristische Methode*), a ubiquitous doctrine of the application of the law (*Lehre der Rechtsanwendung*) developed by scholarship and case law.[63] The contemporary aversion to judge-made law in German private law has clear historical roots. The BGB was drafted at a time in which legislative positivism and the dogma of the complete nature of the law were the leading approaches in German scholarship.[64] Despite being opposed to codified law and more open to acknowledging some role for judges,[65] Savigny's Historical School (*Historische Rechtsschule*)[66] was reluctant to give judges power to develop the law outside its romanistic framework.[67] Under this influence, when codification came to be accepted after the 1871 German unification,[68] the scholars in charge of drafting the BGB perpetuated the idea that judges shall have no power to develop the law.[69] From a theoretical perspective, this approach was underpinned by the belief that all legal decisions could be logically deduced from abstract concepts (*Begriffe*) contained in a closed and complete system by simply bringing the facts of the case under a general rule laid down *ex ante* by the law,[70] through a process of 'subsumption' (*Subsumtion*).[71] Because in this method legal consequences result from concepts, this doctrine came to be known as 'Conceptual Jurisprudence' (*Begriffsjurisprudenz*).[72]

Soon after the enactment of the BGB, this strict positivist view came under attack. The inability of Conceptual Jurisprudence to deal with the ambiguity of language and unforeseen problems soon triggered judicial decisions leading to new legal developments,[73] as well as intellectual currents arguing for recognising a broader judicial discretion, including the 'Free Law Movement' (*Freirechtsbewegung*) and 'Interest Jurisprudence' (*Interessenjurisprudenz*).[74]

[63] Honsell (n 36) 52.

[64] ibid 91.

[65] See Friedrich Carl von Savigny, *Vom Beruf Unserer Zeit für Gesetzgebung und Rechtswissenschaft* (Mohr und Zimmer, 1814).

[66] On this school, Nigel Foster and Satish Sule, *German Legal System and Law* (4th edn, OUP 2010) 27–29; Wieacker (n 35) 279–362.

[67] Honsell (n 36) 91.

[68] ibid 2–7; Wieacker (n 35) 375–76. In this book, see ch 3, section II.B.

[69] Kristoffel Grechenig and Martin Gelter, 'The Transatlantic Divergence in Legal Thought: American Law and Economics vs. German Doctrinalism' (2008) 1 *Hastings Int'l & Comp L Rev* 295, 345.

[70] See Karl Larenz and Claus-Wilhelm Canaris, *Methodenslehre der Rechtswissenschaft* (3rd edn, Springer 1996) 91–98; Karl Larenz, *Methodenlehre der Rechtswissenschaft* (6th edn, Springer 1991) 36–86.

[71] Basically, an Aristotelian deductive reasoning based on syllogisms. Honsell (n 36) 52.

[72] Neuner (n 48) 92–93.

[73] Karl Larenz and Manfred Wolf, *Allgemeiner Teil des Bürgerlichen Rechts* (9th edn, Beck 2004) 74. The most famous is probably the doctrine of the disturbance of the basis of the contract developed during the hyperinflation of 1923 (*Störung der Geschäftsgrundlage*).

[74] Neuner (n 48) 93.

The former held that even the most carefully drafted code has countless gaps, arguing in favour of broad judicial freedom to fill them.[75] This movement has been presented as a German version of American legal realism, but its shut down by Nazism prevented it from having the same influence in discrediting legal formalism.[76] In turn, Interest Jurisprudence[77] was more moderate, arguing that the Juridical Method should not be based on deducing logical outcomes from abstract concepts, but on understanding legal rules as purpose-oriented solutions (*zweckbestimmte Lösungen*) of conflicting interests by legislators.[78]

After the Second World War, Interest Jurisprudence was supplemented by the 'Jurisprudence of Value Judgments' (*Wertungsjurisprudenz*). This stream of thought sought to bring the values promoted by the law to the foreground, including a view of private law underpinned by an ideal of ethical personalism and, more generally, the respect of the fundamental rights contained in the GG.[79] Interest and Value Judgement jurisprudence still form the basis of the Juridical Method prevailing in contemporary Germany,[80] and legal theorists often find it difficult to distinguish between them, as both approaches share great confidence in the ability of positive law to bind judges, either by systematic thinking or by resorting to the order of values established in the law and the constitution.[81]

Nonetheless, despite being proven to be an illusion,[82] Conceptual Jurisprudence still plays an essential role in German legal thinking.[83] A decisive aspect of this derives from seeing substantive values as ingrained in legal concepts.[84] As a consequence, the mainstream view on the creative powers of judges is still close to the rather classic positivist paradigm. In this line, the dominating opinion in contemporary German private law is that judges are primarily subject to legislation, either by its text (*Wortlaut*) or its sense (*Sinn*). Only when there is no rule, judges can resort to customary law (*Gewohnheitsrecht*) and, if all else fails, they should decide according to the rule that the legislator would have given to the case at hand.[85] Therefore, consistent with constitutional doctrine,[86] contemporary versions of the Theory of the Juridical Method allow judges to develop the law to fill gaps

[75] Honsell (n 36) 91; Neuner (n 48) 93.

[76] See Grechenig and Gelter (n 69) 308, 348–50.

[77] See Philip Heck, 'Gesetzesauslegung und Interessenjurisprudenz' (1914) 112 AcP 1.

[78] Neuner (n 48) 93.

[79] ibid 93–94.

[80] Larenz (n 70) 120. *Kommentare* also speak of 'restricted' Jurisprudence of Value Judgments, eg Christian Grüneber, 'Einleitung', *Palandt: Bürgerlicher Gesetzbuch mit Nebengesetzten* (80th edn, Beck 2021) 8.

[81] Grechenig and Gelter (n 69) 353–55.

[82] Larenz and Wolf (n 73) 73; Schwab and Löhnig (n 33) 38.

[83] Larenz and Wolf (n 73) 73; Honsell (n 36) 52. For example, standard textbooks present the 'subsumption' paradigm as the primary approach to legal application, eg Hans Brox and Wolf-Dietrich Walker, *Allgemeiner Teil des BGB* (36th edn, Vahlen 2012) 29–33.

[84] Neuner (n 48) 94.

[85] Honsell (n 36) 91. In the same line Brox and Walker (n 83) 33–36.

[86] See Bumke and Voßkuhle (n 44) 366. For discussion, see section II.A.

in legislation, especially to bring old statutes in step with changing social realities.[87] The outcome is that, nowadays, there is a general agreement that judges can 'extend the law' to fill gaps in it.[88]

The previous conclusion suggests that, over the twentieth century, German courts acquired a degree of power to develop private law that could dilute the restrictive impact of the *numerus clausus* in judicial law-making. Nonetheless, German courts are still seen as being under the duty to capture the binding decision made by Parliament and fully apply it to solve the dispute at hand.[89] From the perspective of the Juridical Method, Interest Jurisprudence aims to enforce the purpose objectively laid down by the legislator in the statute itself, while Value Judgment Jurisprudence requires judges to resort to the values embodied in the wider legal system.[90] As a result, the main gateways for judicial creativity in private law are narrowed by the need to conform to the political choices either implied in statutory law[91] or the value system embedded in the fundamental rights laid down by the GG (*Grundrechte als Wertordnung*).[92]

Even when judges are not able to interpret the law in accordance with the constitution,[93] they are not expected to change it themselves, but to refer problems to the BVerfG (Art 100 GG; §§ 80 ff BVerfGG).[94] Accordingly, deviations from legislative intent have been subject to heavy criticisms by authors arguing that a relaxation in the use of the Juridical Method risks converting Germany into an 'oligarchical judicial state'.[95] This might explain why, despite the existence of a certain flexibility, judges are reluctant to openly develop property law, preferring to work, as much as possible, within the forms already provided by the law. In line with this, even when intentionally establishing new legal principles that can then be generalised, German judges almost universally avoid describing themselves as creators of law.[96]

The tension between separation of powers and judicial development of law achieves its maximum with the doctrine of *Rechtsfortbildung* (extension of the law) and the elusive concept of *Richterrecht* (judge-made law). According to recent commentary literature, *Richterrecht* encompasses all decisions that explicitly or implicitly contain rules that do not correspond to the mere repetition of the abstract rules laid down in statutes, with some authors distinguishing between immanent (*gesetzimmanent*) and constructive (*gesetzübersteigend*)

[87] See Rüthers (n 58) 59; Wank (n 34) 35, 83–86.
[88] Grüneber (n 80) 10.
[89] Schwab and Löhnig (n 33) 39.
[90] Neuner (n 48) 93–94.
[91] Schwab and Löhnig (n 33) 39, 43; Wank (n 34) 85–86.
[92] Larenz and Wolf (n 73) 86–90; Schwab and Löhnig (n 33) 44; Honsell (n 36) 69–88.
[93] Honsell (n 36) 69–88.
[94] Brox and Walker (n 83) 30; Neuner (n 48) 42.
[95] eg Rüthers (n 58) 60 (my translation).
[96] Kischel (n 23) 373.

judge-made law.[97] Immanent extension allows judges to fill a gap by extending a rule by analogy to a case not covered by the meaning of the text (*Analogie*) or by excluding from its scope cases that are not covered by its purpose (*teleologische Reduktion*).[98] By contrast, constructive judge-made law corresponds to rules developed by courts, either with no statutory support to fill a gap (*praeter legem*) or against a statute (*contra legem*).[99]

However, the scope of judicial extension is narrow, and courts enjoy limited discretion within it. To start, the concept of 'a gap' (*Lücke*) is restricted. It is not enough that the law is silent on a given issue: there must be an 'unplanned gap in the statute' (*planwidrige Unvollständigkeit des Gesetzes*).[100] For example, the absence of a provision in the BGB allowing for ownership in separate parts of buildings is not such a gap and, thus, could not possibly be overcome by *Rechtsfortbildung*.[101] That is why flat ownership had to be created by a special act.[102] Only if a proper gap is identified using the regular interpretation elements of the Juridical Method, may judges fill it by 'extending the law'. In this process judges must first resort to the original plan of the legislator 'immanent' in the statute. If this fails, judges can fill the gap by 'constructive' extension of the law, which does not rely on the original intention of the legislator, but is still governed by and must result from the general principles of the legal system.[103] Judicial extension that contradicts the text of statute, has no grounding in it, or is at least not indirectly allowed by it, amounts to a violation of Art 20(3) GG.[104]

In practice, this implies that courts sometimes deviate from statutory law, either because the purpose (*Zweck*) of the law does not match its text (*Wortlaut*) or because, since the enactment of a statute, the development of social life and the prevailing views on the law have created new rules. Such developments can be justified by the inevitable needs of legal affairs (*Rechtsverkehr*), 'the nature of things' or the overriding effect of a legal-ethical principle, such as good faith or a constitutional right. Due to this certain relaxation of the subsumption paradigm, German judicial reasoning has opened itself to a (limited) level of consequentialism. However, when doing this, judges remain bounded by legislation, as they can only rely on the consequences intended by the legislator, either by the relevant statute or the legal system in general, especially, by the values laid down in the constitution.[105]

[97] Honsell (n 36) 89–90.
[98] Other textbooks use different terminology. For example, Brox and Walker (n 83) 36–38.
[99] Larenz and Wolf (n 73) 95, 221–22.
[100] Larenz and Canaris (n 70) 191, 194; Grüneber (n 80) 10.
[101] Larenz and Canaris (n 70) 191, 194, 196.
[102] 1951 WEG, discussed in ch 7, section III.B.
[103] For all the process, Larenz and Canaris (n 70) 187–90.
[104] Grüneber (n 80) 10.
[105] For all this paragraph, Larenz and Wolf (n 73) 77–79, 88, 93–96, 221–22; Neuner (n 48) 33–34, 44–46.

C. Impact on Property Law

Despite enjoying only a limited discretion to develop the law, German judges are still credited with having successfully adapted the 'positivist and slightly anachronist nature of the BGB' to new economic and social realities, especially after 1951.[106] Nowadays, German doctrine openly acknowledges that the judiciary has developed a number of private law doctrines with no statutory support via constructive extension.[107] Some of these doctrines were later included in the BGB by the 2002 general reform of the law of obligations,[108] while others remain without positive regulation.[109] However, due to the persistent ideal that, in principle, courts should not develop private law, these doctrines are normally not openly presented as judicial creations, but as conceptually derived from positive law.[110] In the law of obligations, this has frequently worked through the 'escape to the open legal provisions' (*Flucht in die Generalklauseln*),[111] especially the duty to perform contracts in good faith (§ 242 BGB).[112]

Property law lacks the open-ended provisions of the law of obligations, forcing judicial creativity to operate within more rigid legal frameworks. This is especially apparent in German courts occasionally enforcing rights that are not part of the *numerus clausus* in manners that resemble property rights, especially the anticipation right of buyers[113] and ownership for security purposes,[114] but refusing to acknowledge them as judicially developed property rights. The approach underpinning these decisions is well reflected in a recent ruling of the BGH, holding that the 'creation of private burdens not acknowledged by the *numerus clausus* of property law cannot succeed by means of extending the law'.[115] As a consequence it is not always apparent when a new doctrine qualifies as judge-made law and, if so, whether it is the result of immanent or constructive extension of the law. However, at least the anticipation right of buyers, has been described as a case of *praeter legem* constructive legal extension,[116] while the

[106] Wieacker (n 35) 409, 416.

[107] Larenz and Wolf (n 73) 95.

[108] For example, the doctrines of the disturbance of the foundation of the transaction (*Störung der Geschäftsgrundlage*), of *culpa in contrahendo* and of positive breach of contract (*positive Vertragverletzung*).

[109] For example, the doctrines of apparent power of attorney (*Anscheinsvollmacht*) and of abusive exercise of a right (*unzulässige Rechtsausübung*). Larenz and Wolf (n 73) 74.

[110] For example, the doctrine of the disturbance of the foundation of the transaction, as discussed by Simon Whittaker and Reinhard Zimmermann, 'Good Faith in European Contract Law: Surveying the Legal Land Scape' in Reinhard Zimmermann and Simon Whittaker (eds), *Good Faith in European Contract Law* (CUP 2000) 20–21.

[111] Honsell (n 36) 31.

[112] See previous footnotes on the fall of the basis of the contract.

[113] The BGH has held that this is not a property right and it cannot be asserted against everyone, but it still is a very strong right and a step prior to full ownership, BGHZ 30, 374, 377.

[114] See Jan Wilhelm, *Sachenrecht* (5th edn, De Gruyter 2016) 12; Marina Wellenhofer, *Sachenrecht* (34th edn, Beck 2019) 17–18. For discussion, ch 3, section II.C.

[115] BGH 13.9.2013; NJW 2013, 3515, 3518.

[116] Larenz and Wolf (n 73) 95.

development of ownership for security purposes has been said to constitute an open infraction of the *numerus clausus*.[117] In one view, this implies that German judges are not subject to an absolute prohibition on creating new property types. They cannot create new property rights through general provisions, but they can treat specific and well-defined fact patterns as having proprietary effects.[118]

Nonetheless, the overall relevance of judge-made law in German property law should not be overplayed. The formal structure of the BGB imposes strong limits on what even a modern court can achieve.[119] Despite scholarship frequently highlighting the impact that the constitutional concept of ownership[120] and public law reforms[121] had in modernising German property law, changes that implied clear breaks with the original property rights of the BGB have been achieved by legislative reforms. For example, the strong 'accession principle' established in §§ 94(1) and 93 BGB, which provides for the unity of land and building in a single module of ownership, could only be broken by the legislative expansion of the superficies right in 1919[122] and, more radically, by the legislative creation of 'flat ownership' in 1951.[123]

In summary, the increased flexibility of the German Juridical Method over the twentieth century should not lead to the assumption that German judges have a massive power to update private law and, especially, the property system. Despite their importance, private law doctrines developed by judge-made law are relatively few and almost all of them fall within the law of obligations. These innovations were almost never presented by courts as freely created doctrines but were disguised as logical conclusions from positive law and were frequently criticised by their contemporaries as judicial usurpations of legislative powers.[124]

Despite the modern acknowledgment that judicial reasoning cannot be purely mechanical, it is clear that, within the distributions of law-making competences of the German legal systems, Parliament is the one primarily called to develop private law, with courts having only a residual and limited role. Nowhere is this clearer than in property law. In this context, the main impact of the *numerus clausus* seems to be the imposition of stringent doctrinal constraints on the identifications of gaps: if a property right does not exist, in principle, this should not be regarded as a gap, and this precludes the creation of a new property type through *Rechtsfortbildung*. Beyond that, the *numerus clausus* principle does not seem to take any further powers away from German courts.

[117] Wolfgang Wiegand, 'Die Entwicklung des Sachenrechts im Verhältnis zum Schuldrecht' (1990) 1/2 *AcP* 112, 128.

[118] Marietta Auer, *Der Privatrechtliche Diskurs der Moderne* (Mohr Siebeck 2014) 114.

[119] Wieacker (n 35) 419.

[120] eg Friedrich Quack, *Münchener Kommentar zum Bürgerlichen Gesetzbuch. Sachenrecht*, vol 6 (Friedrich Quack ed, 3rd edn, Beck 1997) 3, 18–19.

[121] eg Wieacker (n 35) 431.

[122] ErbbauVO, now ErbbauRG.

[123] WEG, discussed in ch 7, section III.B.

[124] For example, the doctrine of the disturbance of the foundation of the transaction. Whittaker and Zimmermann (n 110) 21–22.

These findings have relevant implication for the comparative and theoretical understanding of the institutional effects of the *numerus clausus*. In German law this principle should be seen as a doctrine that has the limitation of party autonomy as its primary concern, not the curtailing of judicial power. Therefore, the justification of this principle should emerge from the (internal) system of the BGB, the practical goals pursued by it and the values underpinning German private law. Its institutional dimension does not require a strong justification, as its effects are absorbed by the broad principle of separation of powers prevailing in continental systems. By the same token, the question that demands a special explanation in Germany is why courts have (occasionally) infringed this prohibition.

III. ENGLAND AND AMERICA: JURISDICTIONS SEPARATED BY A COMMON DOCTRINE

A. The Meaning of *Stare Decisis*

In common law systems the *numerus clausus* operates in a different institutional context. As in civilian systems, the primary function of common law courts is solving disputes under the existing standards of society.[125] However, in contrast to the civilian separation of powers principle, the *stare decisis* doctrine is said to invest common law judges with an inherent authority to create and develop new legal rules, subject to legislative revision.[126] Thus, in principle, in Anglo-American legal systems, developing the common law is within the province of courts.[127] This is specially the case in private law, which in England and America is still broadly made up of case law, especially in the areas of contracts and torts.[128] As a result, in common law systems, the acknowledgment of a *numerus clausus* of property rights seems to have a deep impact on the basic division of powers between judges and legislators: it takes away from courts the authority to develop a part of private law, placing it under the exclusive power of legislators. This institutional impact might explain why contemporary Anglo-American scholarship shows far more interest than its German counterpart in providing a justification for the principle.

Despite scholarship frequently highlighting convergence across traditions,[129] common law systems are still normally characterised by the importance of case law, the doctrine of *stare decisis*, the weaker role of statutory law and the less prominent place of academic literature. From this perspective, despite their

[125] Melvin Eisenberg, *The Nature of the Common Law* (Harvard UP 1988) 4.
[126] Merrill and Smith (n 6) 10.
[127] Eisenberg (n 125) 1.
[128] Merrill and Smith (n 6) 10.
[129] For an updated discussion, Kischel (n 23) 619–30.

differences,[130] the main characteristic of common law legal systems is still said to be that they are created by judicial decision-making.[131] However, the historical origin of the common law rested in the opposite idea: *stare decisis* was founded in the view that judges did not make law, but only 'declared' it.[132] Indeed, for a long time, judges were said to merely 'discover' the basic principles of the common law,[133] grounded in immemorial custom.[134]

This does not mean that legislation had a prominent role. In contrast to the growing importance that legislation acquired in Europe during the age of the 'law of reason', in England the role of legislation, especially in private law, remained marginal at the time.[135] This only started to change during the nineteenth century, due to procedural reforms[136] and the incorporation of a formal principle of judicial independence.[137] Pushed by Bentham's utilitarian views regarding the rationalisation of the law,[138] during the 1830s the historical English writ system was brought to an end,[139] allowing the emergence of a 'substantive common law'.[140] Because the scope of the old writs was limited and judges were now 'deciding cases on the merits', they started developing the law. Since these judges were also fiercely independent, by the middle of the century they were *actually* making law,[141] even though this might not have been acknowledged until much later. This phenomenon is well captured in comparing the opinion delivered by Lord Parke in 1833, holding that 'the common law system consists in applying … those rules of law which derive from legal principles and judicial precedents … and we are not at liberty to reject them',[142] with a famous speech held by Lord Reid in the early 1970s, acknowledging that view was 'a fairy tale' that cannot longer be believed.[143]

Following in this trend, the English common law has come to accept that judicial activity is inherently creative.[144] To a large extent this seems to result from the conclusive arguments that militate against the declaratory view of the law. First, due to the impossibility of infinite regress, all rules have an origin: at

[130] Kischel (n 23) 333, 336, 344–48; Zweigert and Kötz (n 29) 243–49, 259–65; Siems (n 23) 75–78.
[131] See Kischel (n 23) 228–242; Siems (n 23) 52–57.
[132] Richard Ward, Amanda Wragg and RJ Walker, *Walker & Walker's English Legal System* (10th edn, OUP 2008) 78.
[133] ibid; Martin Partington, *Introduction to the English Legal System: 2018–19* (OUP 2018) 48, 49.
[134] Merrill and Smith (n 6) 10.
[135] van Caenegem (n 35) 135–36.
[136] H Patrick Glenn, *Legal Traditions of the World* (5th edn, OUP 2014) 254–57; Zweigert and Kötz (n 29) 197.
[137] Glenn (n 136) 256–57.
[138] van Caenegem (n 35) 137–38, 162.
[139] John Baker, *Introduction to English Legal History* (5th edn, OUP 2019) 60.
[140] Glenn (n 136) 254–55. For a brief account of the reforms, van Caenegem (n 35) 162–65.
[141] Glenn (n 136) 255, 257–58.
[142] *Mirehouse v Rennell* (1833) 6 ER 1015, 1023.
[143] Lord Reid, 'The Judge as Law Maker' (1972) 12 *JALT (New Series)* 22, 22.
[144] Geoffrey Samuel, 'Common Law' in Jan M Smits (ed), *Elgar Encyclopedia of Comparative Law* (2nd edn, Edward Elgar 2012) 175–76.

some point a court must have made them.[145] Second, the judicial establishment of legal rules would occur even if the sole function of courts was to resolve disputes on the basis of existing ones: if judges are to explicate the application, meaning and implication of the society's existing standards in a new situation, they cannot at the same time by prohibited from formulating rules they have not previously announced. Modern societies are in continuous change, creating a constant need for new legal rules to resolve unprecedented issues. Because of the inevitability of change, the application of an old rule to a new case may constitute a new rule. Finally, even when no social change is involved, old rules sometimes need to be discarded because they were wrongly established. Hence, common law courts have an inevitable secondary function of enriching the supply of legal rules.[146] This law-making power cannot be derived from any theory of representative democracy, at least as long as judges are not elected. Thus, in England, the legitimacy of courts to develop the common law is closely tied to a doctrine of separation of powers that sees their independence as a form of preventing dictatorial powers from being asserted by any one branch of government.[147]

The original idea of *stare decisis* as a process of discovering the law provided the common law with an inductive-deductive judicial reasoning that seems to stand in contradiction with the nominally deductive style of the German Juridical Method:[148] in the common law, judges seeks to induce a rule from a previous decision to later apply it deductively to the case at hand, giving a key importance to the *justification* of the rule. In this scheme, the rules abstracted from individual cases are necessarily broader than those applied, as otherwise such rules could not be applied to different facts. Therefore, this inductive process cannot be strictly logical and irrefutable.[149]

Due to the central place that case law enjoys in this framework, comparative legal research normally describes the role of statutory law in England as remedial or secondary, arguing that courts have historically resisted the power of Parliament[150] and seen statutes as necessary evils that disturb the harmony of the common law.[151] In this line, despite the unique supremacy that Parliament enjoys under the British constitution, courts have always managed to retain the power to interpret the law. For example, until recently, English courts did not admit, in any form, parliamentary debates in aid to legal interpretation.[152] Thus, to confine the power of judges, English statutes

[145] Kelly (n 27) 183–84.
[146] Eisenberg (n 125) 4–5.
[147] Partington (n 133) 49.
[148] Zweigert and Kötz (n 29) 69–71; Samuel (n 144) 174.
[149] For an analysis in a comparative context, Kischel (n 23) 229–32.
[150] ibid 242–43.
[151] Zweigert and Kötz (n 29) 265.
[152] See *Pepper v Hart* [1993] AC 593, allowing resort to Hansard in certain cases.

are drafted in highly technical, detailed and often opaque terms, which are alien to civilian lawyers.[153]

Despite sharing the same basic systems of legal sources, the law-making powers of English and American judges are different. Due, among other things, to their divergent understanding of *stare decisis*,[154] the enduring legacy of legal realism,[155] and the unique power of the US Supreme Court,[156] American courts generally play a more decisive role in the process of legal change than their English counterparts,[157] who are much more willing to defer major legal reforms to Parliament.[158] After the fall of legal realism, this attitude gained new normative support thanks to a leading stream in law and economics, which is sceptical as to the quality of statutory law, favouring the common law as a more efficient source of legal change.[159] This already points to an important difference between the status of the *numerus clausus* in England and the US: in the former this doctrine has been acknowledged by Parliament as part of a major, encompassing and much appreciated reform of land law,[160] while in the latter it normally continues to be seen as a norm of judicial self-restraint.[161] As shown in the two next subsections, these differences have relevant impact on the institutional standing of the *numerus clausus* in both jurisdictions.

B. England: Parliament as Driver of Change

The way in which English judges exercise their power to change the law is regarded as much more circumscribed than that of American courts.[162] This is largely an outcome of English law adhering to a much stricter and formal doctrine of *stare decisis*.[163] Following an old practice established during the nineteenth century and reaffirmed in *London Street Tramways Co Ltd v London County Council*,[164] for most of the twentieth century the House of Lords held that it was bound by its own precedents and that reforms of the law were for Parliament.[165] This situation partially changed with the 1966 Practice Statement

[153] Kischel (n 23) 243; Samuel (n 144) 178; Zweigert and Kötz (n 29) 267.

[154] PS Atiyah and RS Summers, *Form and Substance in Anglo-American Law* (Clarendon Press 1987) 116–17.

[155] ibid 251–57; Zweigert and Kötz (n 29) 245–49; Kischel (n 23) 344–47; Grechenig and Gelter (n 69) 308.

[156] See Kischel (n 23) 338.

[157] Atiyah and Summers (n 154) 134.

[158] ibid 141–42; Ward, Wragg and Walker (n 132) 5.

[159] Especially, Posner (n 5) 249–53, 562–65.

[160] On the appreciation of the reform AH Manchester, *A Modern Legal History of England and Wales, 1750–1950* (Butterworth 1980) 324–25. On the English *numerus clausus*, ch 3, section III.

[161] Merrill and Smith (n 6) 9.

[162] Atiyah and Summers (n 154) 115–56; Kischel (n 23) 333–48.

[163] Atiyah and Summers (n 154) 116–17.

[164] *London Street Tramways Co Ltd v London County Council* [1898] AC 375.

[165] Kelly (n 27) 153.

by which the House of Lords announced that it would, from then on, depart from a previous decision when it appeared right to do so.[166] However, the statement also made clear that the House of Lords would continue treating former decisions as normally binding and that it would bear in mind the danger of retrospectively disturbing the basis on which contracts and property settlements were entered into. Consequent with this, the use of this prerogative by the House of Lords (now Supreme Court) has been very restrictive,[167] while the Court of Appeal is still generally forbidden from departing from its own precedent in civil cases.[168] Thus, even after 1966, the power of English courts to disregard their own precedents is seen as much weaker than that of American courts.[169]

Consistent with this general approach to the law-making process, in the field of property law, the UK Supreme Court,[170] like the House of Lords before it,[171] tends to defer pressing problems to Parliament. A good example is the reluctance of the House of Lords to change the rule requiring leases to be for a defined term of years to qualify as property rights, despite Lord Browne-Wilkinson holding it to be an 'ancient and technical' rule that produces a 'bizarre outcome' and has no 'satisfactory rationale' nor 'useful purpose', expressing the 'hope that the Law Commission might look at the subject to see whether there is in fact any good reason now for maintaining a rule which operates to defeat contractually agreed arrangements'.[172] This judicial deference to Parliament is mirrored by the comparative appraisal of English legal thinking, which has been described as far more positivistic, formal and centred in black letter rules than the American.[173] That is why, like the German Theory of the Juridical Method, the style of English legal reasoning has been held to be more 'internal' to the law than the American.[174] Richard Posner even argued that, in this respect, English law has more in common with continental legal systems than with the American common law.[175]

The English resistance to the judicial development of law is paralleled by the emergence of Parliament as the dominant force in the British Constitution and legislation becoming the major source of change in English law.[176] As a consequence, in comparative research, the idea of case law being the main

[166] Practice Statement [1966] 1 WLR 1234, [1966] 3 All ER 77.

[167] Atiyah and Summers (n 154) 139; Kischel (n 23) 241.

[168] *Davis v Johnson* [1979] AC 264, HL. This court can only depart from its own precedents in the cases laid down in *Young v Bristol Aeroplane Company Ltd* ([1944] 1 KB 718) and in other specific cases, as when previous law conflicts with the HRA 1998.

[169] Atiyah and Summers (n 154) 120–22.

[170] eg *Arnold v Britton* [2015] UKSC 36, [2015] 2 WLR 1593, as discussed by Sarah Blandy, Susan Bright and Sarah Nield, 'The Dynamics of Enduring Property Relationships in Land' (2018) 81 *MLR* 85, 105.

[171] eg overruling Lord Denning's analysis in *National Provincial Bank v Ainsworth* [1964] Ch 665, CA; [1965] AC 1175, HL.

[172] *Prudential Assurance Co Ltd v London Residuary Body* [1992] 2 AC 386, 396.

[173] Kischel (n 23) 333, 347–48.

[174] Grechenig and Gelter (n 69) 303.

[175] Richard A Posner, *Law and Legal Theory in England and America* (OUP 1996) 20.

[176] Ward, Wragg and Walker (n 132) 5; Kelly (n 27) 92.

source of contemporary English law has recently been held to be a myth.[177] Similar to what happens in civilian systems, there is not much doubt that, in England, major legal reforms are for Parliament, not for judges.[178] Furthermore, in England legislative reforms are also much easier and frequent than in the US.[179] This is apparent in the development of English property law since the mid nineteenth century, especially after the 1922–25 Land Law Reform.[180] Even leaving landlord-tenant law aside, over the last half of a century, Parliament has passed a variety of acts aiming to keep property law in step with society, including the Matrimonial Homes Act 1967, the LP(MP)A 1989, the TOLATA 1996, the Commonhold and Leasehold Reform Act 2002 and the LRA 2002 (itself also subject to further reforms),[181] while the Law Commission has more recently proposed or considered reforms, in other fields such as leasehold and commonhold[182] and registration.[183]

In this context, the principle of *numerus clausus* does not seem to imply a major alteration to the way in which modern English law deals with problems of legal change *in general*. Moreover, the embodiment of the principle in the LPA 1925 might be seen as nothing more than a very tangible chapter in the process by which Parliament gradually became the central developer of property law in England. The approach to the law on covenants is a good example. In the early 1830s, the Commissioners of the Law of Real Property stated that the enforcement of freehold covenants against successors in title should be developed by Equity,[184] while during the early twenty-first century the Law Commission held that the admission of positive covenants as new interests in land should occur through statutory recognition.[185] Thus, from an institutional perspective, as in Germany, in England there might be more need to justify the judicial infringement of the *numerus clausus* principle than its existence.

C. America: Challenging the Efficient Common Law

The American approach to the judicial power to develop the legal system diverges from the English, making the place of the *numerus clausus* in America different

[177] Samuel (n 144) 178.
[178] On this, Zweigert and Kötz (n 29) 271.
[179] Atiyah and Summers (n 154) 140–41.
[180] See Manchester (n 160) 304, 310–11; William Cornish and others, *Law and Society in England 1750–1950* (2nd edn, Hart 2019) 135, 168–70.
[181] eg Land Registration Act 2002 (Amendment) Order 2008.
[182] See Wendy Wilson and Casie Barton, 'Leasehold and Commonhold Reform' (House of Commons Library 2021) 8047.
[183] Law Commission, *Updating the Land Registration Act 2002* (Law Com No 380, 2018).
[184] Ben McFarlane, 'Tulk v Moxhay (1848)' in Charles Mitchell and Paul Mitchell (eds), *Landmark Cases in Equity* (Hart 2012) 212.
[185] Law Commission, *Making Land Work: Easements, Covenants and Profits à Prendre* (Law Com No 327, 2011). On this, also see Elizabeth Cooke, 'To Restate or Not to Restate? Old Wine, New Wineskins, Old Covenants, New Ideas' [2009] Conv 448, 460.

again. This is not only explained by a weaker doctrine of *stare decisis*,[186] but by the central place policy arguments acquired in American legal reasoning during the twentieth century, in the wake of the realist movement.[187] There has been much discussion on the precise place that policy arguments have in American judicial reasoning. However, in the end, social propositions (ie policy concerns) seem to always have some role in the American common law, either in the way that rules are first established by courts or in the way in which those rules are then extended, restricted and applied.[188] Consistent with this view, in comparative law, American legal reasoning is generally perceived as much more policy oriented than its English equivalent.[189]

In contrast to what happens in England (or Germany), this view is accompanied by the perception that the capacity of legislatures to provide the legal rules needed by society is limited and that much of that capacity is dedicated to governmental matters, such as taxation, administrative rules, definition of crimes, or regulated industries, and that, in many fields, the flexible form of judicial precedents is preferable to the canonical forms of legislation.[190] In this line, American courts have been described as having an 'inherent policy making authority with respect to private law'.[191] The law and economics movement has endorsed this view with a strong normative support grounded in seeing common law rules as more efficient than legislative law, because courts are not subject to the political pressures of interest groups with narrow distributional goals.[192] In property law, the faith American law places in judges for keeping property law in step with social needs is apparent in the approach taken by the 2000 'Restatement (Third) of Property: Servitudes', which replaces traditional (English) doctrines controlling servitudes *ex ante*, by *ex post* judicial tests based on open-ended terms, such as denying covenants proprietary effect if they are illegal, unconstitutional or against public policy.[193] However, the reformist style of the Restatement has not been embraced by courts. Ironically, at least in one view, this is because judges do not want to cede their control over the development of the common law to academics.[194]

Considering that, in practice, the general division of authority between courts and legislators in the American common law gives the judiciary a much more relevant and legitimate role in developing private law than in England or Germany, in America, the presence of a *numerus clausus* can be seen as placing a

[186] See Atiyah and Summers (n 154) 119–20, 139.
[187] See n 155 and accompanying text.
[188] Eisenberg (n 125) 2–3.
[189] Hage (n 56) 533–34.
[190] Eisenberg (n 125) 5.
[191] Merrill and Smith (n 6) 10.
[192] ibid 60, describing this view.
[193] See Susan French, 'Highlights of the New Restatement (Third) of Property: Servitudes' (2000) 35 *Real Prop Prob & Tr J* 225.
[194] Ronald Rosenberg, 'Fixing a Broken Common Law – Has the Property Law of Easements and Covenants Been Reformed by a Restatement?' (2016) 44 *Florida State U L Rev* 192.

much greater limitation on the inherent powers of courts. However, it must also be considered, first, that the American version of *numerus clausus* essentially results from judicial self-restraint and not from a straightforward legislative decision; and, second, that the American version of *stare decisis* is also weaker than the English. As a consequence, American judges feel less pressure to stick to preexisting property forms, making the *numerus clausus* also weaker. For example, in *Garner v Gerrish*,[195] a New York court faced with an agreement to create a lease for life simply disapplied the common law rule that converts leases with uncertain terms into tenancies at will, arguing that such a rule was outmoded and that applying it would frustrate the intentions of the parties.[196] Probably therefore, the American supporters of the *numerus clausus* have been specially interested in justifying the principle from a policy perspective that is consistent with the idea of courts developing an efficient common law, particularly on its ability to internalise informational externalities and lower transaction costs.[197] These types of arguments, however, are more concerned with explaining why courts should self-restrain when it comes to creating new property forms, than justifying why legislators should have a monopoly over property law.

When it comes to justifying the institutional choice in favour of legislators as the primary force of change in property law, arguments are both technical (ie performance based) and political. The former build on the broader theoretical view that it is impossible for courts to introduce radical reforms based on individual cases,[198] but do not challenge the utilitarian principle underpinning the efficient common law. The point made is simply that, for a number of technical reasons, the nature of property rights makes them more suitable for legislative reform. First, statutory reforms are easier to identify than common law rules, because the former do not need informational intermediaries to disseminate information. Second, legislation is more universal than common law rules in its application, as judge-made law has an ambiguous domain resulting from only being binding in the jurisdiction of the court. Third, legislators can be more comprehensive in addressing a problem, because courts are limited to the specific issues before them and it can take the courts years to flesh out a doctrine. Fourth, legislation is more stable than common law rules, because the greater cost of the legislative production of rules limits the number of reforms. Fifth, statutes have the advantage of always being prospective, avoiding disruptive effects on established reliance interests. Finally, legislation is better in providing implicit compensation because legislators are in a better

[195] *Garner v Gerrish* 473 N.E.2d 223 (NY 1984).

[196] For discussion, Bernie Jones, 'Garner v. Gerrish and the Renter's Life Estate: Teaching A New Concept of "Home"' (2010) 2 *Faulkner L Rev* 1.

[197] Especially, Merrill and Smith (n 6); Henry Hansmann and Reinier Kraakman, 'Property, Contract, and Verification: The Numerus Clausus Problem and the Divisibility of Rights' (2002) 31 *J Legal Stud* 373.

[198] For this view, Joseph Raz, *The Authority of Law: Essays on Law and Morality* (Clarendon Press 1979) 200–01.

position than courts to assess the overall costs of reforms.[199] Indeed, even scholars who are generally sceptical about the advantages of legislative law acknowledge that, at least in some contexts, legislators are in a better position than judges to develop property law, namely, for the creation of complex regulatory schemes, in contexts that require technical knowledge and the annulling of property rights.[200]

Views that highlight the technical advantages of legislation do not deny that the principle of *numerus clausus* comes with the risk of legislative inertia, especially if problems have low visibility and highly dispersed costs. Nonetheless, they see these demerits as the flip side of the stability inherent to legislative action, representing nothing more than the well-known trade off of any legal system between stability and change. For the specific case of property law, they add that the creation of new forms of property might create fewer inducements for rent seeking by interest groups than in other areas of law (eg taxes) because they see new forms of property as creating opportunities for the creation of new wealth, but rarely creating wealth itself or redistributing it. Consistent with this rather optimistic view of the legislative development of property law, when it comes to the law in action, its proponents also argue that the overall American legislative record is not that bad.[201]

On the other hand, political arguments as the advanced in the context of the 'Democratic Property' movement,[202] find the normative base of the *numerus clausus* in the legitimacy that the democratic process provides legislative law, not in its functional or technical advantages[203] The argument is doubted by other progressive scholars who seem sceptical about the quality of contemporary democracy,[204] but this does not point to a conceptual problem of the democratic argument, but to a wider and contingent criticism of the (American) political system. The weakness of the democratic argument lies elsewhere. From the perspective of a common law system, it is hard to see why this argument is specific to property law and not a general criticism of the Anglo-American understanding of the role of courts. By contrast, from the viewpoint of civilian systems, it does not add anything new, as the democratic delineation of private law is one of its foundational dogmas. The bottom line is that, outside some cases of structural transformation, the institutional basis of the *numerus clausus* in the US remains weak and disputed, making efficiency arguments that justify judicial restraint more relevant than in England or Germany.

[199] Merrill and Smith (n 6) 61–66.
[200] eg Dagan (n 12) 154–55.
[201] Merrill and Smith (n 6) 66–67.
[202] See Singer (n 15) 1046–47.
[203] Dorfman (n 16).
[204] eg Dagan (n 12) 157–58.

IV. THE *NUMERUS CLAUSUS* AS CONSTITUTIONAL RULE

A. Varying Meaning of the *Numerus Clausus*

From an institutional perspective, assessing the role of courts and legislators is essential to understand how property law evolves over time. In this view, the relevance of the *numerus clausus* principle can hardly be overstated because it creates a formal legislative monopoly over property law that, at least in principle, precludes the judicial creation of new property types. In a material sense, this principle constitutes something like 'constitutional rule of property law'. However, the impact of this rule varies between different jurisdictions, depending on how they understand their legal sources and handle them in the judicial process.

In Germany, the institutional impact of the *numerus clausus* is relatively limited. Because German law adopts a strong separation of powers principle, denying courts power to create new property rights does not alter its basic distribution of law-making competence. The principle only entails a doctrinal restriction regarding what qualifies as a gap under the German Juridical Method, thereby limiting the scope of 'judicial extension of law' (*Rechtsfortbildung*). This is probably why German scholarship tends not to offer up a justification for the legislative monopoly created by the principle. By the same logic, in this context, the most pressing problem is accounting for the judicial infringements of the principle.

In the American common law, by contrast, the principle has a more visible institutional impact but also a more uncertain position. On the one hand, the *numerus clausus* implies a radical alteration of the basic law-making institutional arrangement, as it drastically limits the inherent power of courts to develop private law. However, on the other hand, this limitation is institutionally weak, as it is mainly based on a principle of judicial self-restraint. As a result, because the principle does not have clear statutory standing and seems to run counter to the theory of efficient common law, in America, the *numerus clausus* requires much more 'external' normative support, either in the form of efficiency, technical or political justifications.

In what might seem an unexpected outcome, the institutional impact of the English version of the *numerus clausus* seems closer to Germany than America. Although England follows a different separation of powers principle, as in Germany, reforms of property law are primarily seen as a matter for Parliament. Therefore, English doctrine also tends to justify the principle in elements that can be described as 'internal' to the law. Consistent with this, the main normative challenge for English law is also justifying judicial deviations from the principle.

B. Institutional Impact: The Role of Politics

An obvious effect of the institutional dimension of the *numerus clausus* is that it subordinates the development of property law to democratic politics. This has relevant implications for the ability of property law to respond to new circumstances. In one view, the price liberal democracies pay for controlling the arbitrary exercise of political power is making modern law less responsive to social demands.[205]

The practical outcome of this depends on the status that legislative law enjoys in each system. In America, where legislation is mistrusted and judges are seen as the main and most competent source of legal change in private law, the rigidity that the *numerus clausus* introduces into the property system implies a structural challenge. In contrast, for jurisdictions like England or Germany, where legislators are seen as the main and more legitimate engine of legal change, the *numerus clausus* does not imply a relevant challenge to its basic distribution of law-making competences.

This difference in the perceived legitimacy and competence of legislators to develop property law seems to have some correlation with their actual performance. In England and Germany property law has been subject to substantive structural reform by legislation, most notably the enactment of the LPA 1925 and the BGB. By contrast, despite optimistic views,[206] the fact remains that main American jurisdictions like New York and California lack milestone reforms like those of other anglophone countries[207] and, needless to say, continental systems.

C. Normative Implications: Legitimacy and Performance

The main implication of these findings is that in Germany and England the natural route for adapting property law to new realities is clearly legislative reform. This is justified by a democratic argument and technical considerations. In the case of Germany, the legal monopoly over the property system is a direct outcome of the continental separation of powers principle. Nowadays, this principle is justified in the democratic legitimacy of statutory law but is worth remembering that it first emerged as a technical device to avoid the judicial undermining of the rational structure of the legal systems created by the Sovereign.

In contemporary England, the central place of statutes in property law can also be explained as an outcome of the role achieved by Parliament as lawmaker since the mid nineteenth century. As in civil law systems, nowadays this is can also be justified in democratic and technical arguments, which were historically put forward by the English radicals of the nineteenth century. In line with this, neither German nor English doctrine really feels pressed to provide any special justification for the legislative monopoly created by the *numerus clausus*.

[205] Philippe Nonet and Philip Selznick, *Law and Society in Transition: Toward Responsive Law* (2nd edn, Transaction Publishers 2001) 53–72.
[206] Like that of Merrill and Smith (n 6) 66–67.
[207] Chang (n 9) 356.

As shown in the next chapter, when some justification for the principle is given, it normally relies on considerations that are embedded in the private law system itself. In this context, the most pressing challenge is not accounting for the existence of the principle, but for its judicial infringement.

The situation is different in America. On the one hand, the principle has a less clear statutory standing, compared to England and Germany. On the other, American legal culture is inherently more suspicious of legislative law. This scepticism cuts across theoretical views, with both mainstream law and economics and some progressive ('liberal') scholars openly placing more faith judges than legislators as the most competent authority to develop property law, although for very different reasons. Consequently, in the American context there is more need of explicit support for the limitation of judicial power resulting from the *numerus clausus* principle. Consistent with the policy-oriented style of American legal reasoning, the core of these justifications lies in the inherent efficiency gains derived from the ability of this principle to control externalities and transaction costs and, to a lesser extent, in the technical advantages of legislative law.

Finally, the different systematic impact of the *numerus clausus* across jurisdictions also generates different attitudes towards its justification. In the US, the controversial standing of the principle is reflected in the vivid attempts to justify it from an (external) policy perspective. By contrast, in England and Germany, the tendency is to account for the principle on the basis of arguments that can be described as much more 'internal' to the law. These arguments will be the topic of the next chapter.

5

Function and Justification of the Numerus Clausus

As discussed in previous chapters, the principle of *numerus clausus* creates two in-built sources of rigidity in modern property law. On the one hand, it restricts the institutional power of courts to develop the property system; on the other, it denies private parties the freedom to create new property forms by contract.[1] Chapter four justified the institutional dimension of this principle in the political legitimacy and technical advantages of legislative law. This chapter addresses the second issue by developing on what justifies restricting party autonomy to invent new property forms. The precise question this chapter seeks to answer is why most modern property systems adopt a *numerus clausus* principle of property rights and why judges sometimes also breach it. In the institutional framework of this book, this corresponds to the 'ideology' of the *numerus clausus*.

After briefly discussing what counts as justification in this context (section I), this chapter addresses the main utilitarian (section II) and rights-based (section III) arguments for the *numerus clausus* made in America, England and Germany. The American debate serves to introduce the discussion in the functional or 'external' style of law and economics. Afterwards, these arguments are pinned down, using the more 'internal' legal methods of English and German doctrine. Contrary to prevailing views, the chapter concludes (section IV) that, in practice, utilitarian and right-based justifications of the principle are largely complementary. Building on this, this chapter offers a new and more encompassing justification for the *numerus clausus* and its exceptional breach.

The key to this argument is the realisation that the different efficiency gains of the *numerus clausus* are better explained as an 'external' reflection of a common single 'internal' rationality, based on the moral value of autonomy. A relevant implication is that the *numerus clausus* does not only aim to bring

[1] Thomas W Merrill and Henry E Smith, 'Optimal Standardization in the Law of Property: The Numerus Clausus Principle' (2000) 110 *Yale LJ* 1, 58; Ben McFarlane, 'The Numerus Clausus Principle and Covenants Relating to Land' in Susan Bright (ed), *Modern Studies in Property Law*, vol 6 (Hart 2011) 309; Bram Akkermans, 'The Numerus Clausus of Property Rights' in Michele Graziadei and Lionel Smith (eds), *Comparative Property Law: Global Perspectives* (Edward Elgar 2017) 102.

standardisation to property law, but a *specific* form of standardisation, namely one that provides property law with a stable but flexible internal structure that maximises the autonomy of private parties to adapt the existing modules of property to new realities. This does not mean that policy arguments are completely irrelevant in adjudication. In practice, utilitarian arguments serve to exceptionally override the *numerus clausus*, typically when legislators fail to adapt property law to new realities. The implications of this are discussed in chapter eight.

I. JUSTIFYING THE *NUMERUS CLAUSUS*

The central topic of this chapter is what *justifies* curtailing the autonomy of private parties to create non-recognised property rights by consent. A relevant difficulty in answering this question is that there is no agreement as to what should count as 'justification' in law nor the role it should play in legal reasoning. Therefore, there is also no single theoretical framework to assess the possible justifications for the *numerus clausus*, especially when more than one jurisdiction is considered. This section remedies this by grouping the available arguments based on three different but overlapping criteria: the civil/common law divide; the distinction between policy and principle-based arguments; and the 'internal-external' debate in private law theory.

In Anglo-American scholarship, where the need for justification is normally seen as a response to the law's claim to authority,[2] explaining legal institutions by resorting to their underlying normative support is a common practice. From a comparative perspective this has been explained as an outcome of the inductive method of *stare decisis*:[3] it is not the decision that sets the precedent, but rule of law in which it is founded.[4] Thus, in English law, a decision carries weight only to the extent it rests on justifying grounds.[5] Nonetheless, in Anglo-American legal theory the relevance and nature of this justification remains unsettled: on the one hand, some strands are deeply sceptical about its role (eg legal realism or critical legal studies), while, on the other, even among those who are classified as 'non-sceptical',[6] there is a substantive disagreement about what should count as justification.[7]

[2] Christopher Gray (ed), 'Justifications', *The Philosophy of Law: An Encyclopedia* (Garland Publishing 1999) 469; Mark Tebbit, *The Philosophy of Law. An Introduction* (2nd edn, Routledge 2005) 91; William Lucy, 'Adjudication' in Jules L Coleman, Kenneth Einar Himma and Scott J Shapiro (eds), *The Oxford Handbook of Jurisprudence and Philosophy of Law* (OUP 2004) 222–23.

[3] eg Uwe Kischel, *Comparative Law* (Andrew Hammel tr, OUP 2019) 230.

[4] David Kelly, *Slapper and Kelly's English Legal System* (19th edn, Routledge 2020) 176.

[5] John Bell, 'Sources of Law' in Andrew Burrows (ed), *English Private Law* (3rd edn, OUP 2013) 23.

[6] See Lucy (n 2) 208–22.

[7] Gray (n 2) 470–71.

One way of ordering this discussion is distinguishing between policy and principle-based arguments. The former justify legal institutions in the advance of some collective good, generally an improvement in some political, economic or social feature, like the greatest aggregate economic benefit.[8] These arguments are normally associated with the utilitarian tradition inaugurated by Jeremy Bentham and John Stuart Mill.[9] In their view, human actions should be assessed by their ability to advance general welfare.[10] Since the rise of legal realism, this approach has had a distinctive influence on American legal thinking,[11] reaching its high point with the law and economics movement.[12] Explicitly relying on Bentham, its dominant current justifies extensive areas of the law as promoting the efficient allocation of resources,[13] typically focusing on the effect that legal institutions have in lowering transaction costs and internalising externalities. In property theory, these arguments come in a variety of forms and typically purport to show that the total happiness of a society will be greater, that the general welfare will be better served, or that markets will be able to promote productive efficiency and social prosperity, if material resources are exclusively owned or controlled by private individuals.[14] This has an obvious but frequently overlooked implication: the imposition of non-consented duties inherent to the creation of property rights has to be justified in a 'common interest in the efficient allocation of resources'.[15]

In contrast, principle-based arguments are founded on respect for the *rights* of individuals as a requirement of justice, fairness or some other dimension of morality, not on the prosecution of collective goals.[16] This view is normally seen as rooted in Kantian moral philosophy. In Anglo-American legal theory, it has been specially put forward by Ronald Dworkin,[17] while in Germany, Kantian-based respect for human dignity is explicitly imbedded in Art 1 GG[18] and held to be the highest principle of the legal system.[19] In contrast to utilitarianism, which is grounded in the human ability to experience pleasure

[8] Ronald Dworkin, *Taking Rights Seriously* (Bloomsbury 2013) 38, 107, 115–16.

[9] See Jeffrie G Murphy and Jules L Coleman, *Philosophy of Law: An Introduction to Jurisprudence* (rev edn, Westview Press 1990) 72–75; Tebbit (n 2) 113, 119–21.

[10] Murphy and Coleman (n 9) 72.

[11] Konrad Zweigert and Hein Kötz, *An Introduction to Comparative Law* (Tony Weir tr, 3rd edn, OUP 1998) 246–49. On realism in this book, see ch 2, section III.C and ch 4, section III.C.

[12] Murphy and Coleman (n 9) 33–36; Ernest J Weinrib, *The Idea of Private Law* (rev edn, OUP 2012) 3.

[13] Especially Richard A Posner, *Economic Analysis of Law* (7th edn, Aspen 2007) 4, 11, 24–26.

[14] Jeremy Waldron, *The Right to Private Property* (OUP 1988) 3–16, 62, 64–68.

[15] Christian von Bar, *The Foundations of Property Law* (OUP 2023) 67.

[16] Dworkin (n 8) 38–39, 115–16.

[17] Murphy and Coleman (n 9) 81; Tebbit (n 2) 119–23.

[18] Christian Bumke and Andreas Voßkuhle, *Casebook Verfassungsrecht* (8th edn, Mohr Siebeck 2020) 73–82.

[19] Jörg Neuner, *Allgemeiner Teil Des Bürgerlichen Rechts* (13th edn, Beck 2023) 96.

and pain,[20] contemporary Kantians hold that people are morally relevant due to their status as free and independent creatures.[21] This gives each human being a capacity to make rational choices that deserve to be respected. Thus, there is something about human beings that makes them uniquely precious ('dignity') and entitles them to a special kind of respect, including the right not to be used without their consent for the benefit of others.[22] This seems at odds with the aforementioned utilitarian idea that the imposition of non-consented duties can be justified in efficiency consideration.

Building on this view, 'right-based' arguments justify private property by showing how it respects or promotes consideration to people.[23] No modern philosopher has produced a discussion on this subject on the scale of the historical theories of Locke and Hegel.[24] In a nutshell, Locke justifies private property in a theory that entitles human beings (subject to certain provisions) to have whatever they are able to take from nature by their labour;[25] while Hegel links the normative grounds of private property to its ability to make personal freedom possible.[26] For modern Kantians, ownership reflects the legitimacy of the usability of things within a regime of equal reciprocal freedom: since things have no rights, freedom alone governs the connection between the owner and the thing owned. In this view, in a regime of equal and reciprocal freedom, ownership is intrinsic to the legal relation of people through things.[27]

In contemporary Anglo-American private law theory, the opposition between policy and principle-based arguments has recently taken the form of a debate around what is 'internal' and 'external' to law. What this means is far from clear, but it is generally accepted that it evokes the distinction between understanding private law on its own concepts (what it *is*) and explaining private law on the basis of its purpose (what it *does*).[28] The former seeks to understand private law by evaluating it in terms of the coherence of its immanent morality, typically a Kantian corrective justice approach, while the latter tries to explain private

[20] Jeremy Bentham, *The Collected Works of Jeremy Bentham: An Introduction to the Principles of Morals and Legislation* (JH Burns and HLA Hart eds, OUP 1998) 11; John Stuart Mill, 'Utilitarianism' in JM Robson (ed), *The Collected Works of John Stuart Mill: Essays on Ethics, Religion and Society*, vol X (University of Toronto Press; Routledge & Kegan 1969) 210.

[21] Ernest J Weinrib, 'Ownership, Use, and Exclusivity: The Kantian Approach' (2018) 31 *Ratio Juris* 123, 128.

[22] Murphy and Coleman (n 9) 76–79.

[23] Waldron (n 14) 3–16, 62, 64–68.

[24] ibid 14–15.

[25] John Locke, 'Second Treatise of Government', *Second Treatise of Government and A Letter Concerning Toleration* (OUP 2016) 16–17, [30].

[26] GWF Hegel, *Grundlinien der Philosophie Des Rechts* (Meiner 2009) 66–69.

[27] Weinrib (n 21) 131, 138. On Kantian property, also see Arthur Ripstein, 'Property and Sovereignty: How to Tell the Difference' (2017) 18 *Theo Inq L* 243, 255.

[28] Andrew S Gold, 'Internal and External Perspectives: On the New Private Law Methodology' in Andrew S Gold and others (eds), *The Oxford Handbook of the New Private Law* (OUP 2021) 4.

law in terms of criteria that are said to be 'outside law', especially, economic efficiency.[29]

From this perspective, the prevailing opinion in comparative law,[30] Anglo-American legal theory[31] and law and economics[32] is that the style of English legal reasoning is more internal than the American, as it tends to prioritise doctrinal consistency over policy concerns. Thus, despite being a common law jurisdiction, English legal thinking is also frequently seen as closer to the German than to the American approach.[33] Nonetheless, the American policy-oriented style has made some relevant inroads in England.[34] Following this tendency, it is not infrequent for English private law scholarship to address legal problems by opposing the involved doctrinal and policy considerations,[35] but these are rarely formalised in microeconomic terms.

In the civilian tradition, the question of what counts as justification is less visible. Civilian judges are normally not seen as being required to find reasons behind rules nor as having inherent powers to develop the law that need to be justified.[36] For example, in Germany, as a consequence of the pervasive influence of Hans Kelsen's thinking,[37] normative decisions have traditionally been seen as part of politics and, therefore, as 'external' to adjudication and unsuitable for legal analysis.[38] Therefore, justification in everyday legal reasoning is highly doctrinal and, in that sense, 'internal' to the law. However, this does not imply that external views are not needed or useful to understand concrete civilian legal institutions. As shown in the previous chapter (at section II), normative arguments are not absent in German law, but only primarily displaced to the legislative process, still playing a key role in adjudication, due to the deference that continental judges owe to legislative intent. Therefore, understanding the

[29] Andrew S Gold and Henry E Smith, 'Sizing up Private Law' (2020) 70 *U Toronto LJ* 489, 489–90; Benjamin C Zipursky, 'Philosophy of Private Law' in Jules L Coleman, Kenneth Einar Himma and Scott J Shapiro (eds), *The Oxford Handbook of Jurisprudence and Philosophy of Law* (OUP 2004) 623.

[30] See Kristoffel Grechenig and Martin Gelter, 'The Transatlantic Divergence in Legal Thought: American Law and Economics vs. German Doctrinalism' (2008) 1 *Hastings Int'l & Comp L Rev* 295, 303, 318; Kischel (n 3) 347, 348; Mathias Siems, *Comparative Law* (2nd edn, CUP 2018) 75–78.

[31] HLA Hart, 'American Jurisprudence through English Eyes: The Nightmare and the Noble Dream', *Essays in Jurisprudence and Philosophy* (OUP 1983); PS Atiyah and RS Summers, *Form and Substance in Anglo-American Law* (Clarendon Press 1987) 409–15.

[32] Richard A Posner, 'The Future of the Law and Economics Movement in Europe' (1997) 17 *Int Rev Law and Econ* 3, 3–4.

[33] Reinhard Zimmermann, 'Savigny's Legacy': Legal History, Comparative Law, and the Emergence of European Legal Science' (1996) 112 *LQR* 576, 584. On this, see also ch 4, section III.

[34] Grechenig and Gelter (n 30) 303.

[35] See JW Harris, 'Legal Doctrine and Interests in Land' in John Eekelaar and John Bell (eds), *Oxford Essays in Jurisprudence: Third Series* (Clarendon 1987) 168–69.

[36] Dieter Schwab and Martin Löhnig, *Einführung in das Zivilrecht* (20th edn, CF Müller 2016) 38. On this, see also ch 4, section II.

[37] See Hans Kelsen, *Reine Rechtslehre. Studienausgabe der 1. Auflage 1934* (Matthias Jestaedt ed, Mohr Siebeck 2008).

[38] Grechenig and Gelter (n 30) 356–58.

ideological forces that influenced the creation and development of the BGB is normally seen as necessary for the correct interpretation and application of German private law.[39]

The diversity of views as to what should count as justification in the law is reflected in the modern discussion on the normative underpinning of the *numerus clausus*. In the Anglo-American context, this discussion is intense, and approaches that start from similar first-principles frequently end up reaching opposite conclusions. For example, from a policy perspective, the main argument against the *numerus clausus* is that restricting the right of parties to make contracts in relation to property undermines the efficiency allocation of wealth.[40] However, by the same token, the leading policy argument in favour of this principle holds that restricting party autonomy is essential to internalise negative economic impacts derived from the free delineation of property rights by private parties.[41] In turn, principle-based arguments that rely on the moral value of autonomy also reach divergent conclusions. For one progressive strand, autonomy as organisational principle requires that individuals have access to a menu of property rights that includes a 'residual' property category that allows parties to 'invent' idiosyncratic private frameworks that are inconsistent with the mainstream understanding of the *numerus clausus*.[42] However, on a more conceptual view, the justification of the *numerus clausus* has been said to be found on a wider legal principle according to which an agreement can generally not impose a duty on someone who is not a party to that agreement,[43] which can easily be related to the respect of third-party autonomy.[44]

In Germany, the discussion about the normative justification of the *numerus clausus* is far more muted.[45] Due to its uncontroversial status, the principle is normally justified in the broad idea that if absolute rights bind everyone, their content and boundaries need to be easily established.[46] However, below this doctrinal surface lie two substantive normative justifications. The first is policy-based and relates to the need of limiting the duties and burdens running with

[39] Karl Larenz and Manfred Wolf, *Allgemeiner Teil Des Bürgerlichen Rechts* (9th edn, Beck 2004) 21; Schwab and Löhnig (n 36) 23.

[40] Richard A Epstein, 'Past and Future: The Temporal Dimension in the Law of Property' (1986) 64 *Wash U LQ* 667–68, 703–04, 710, 713–15; Richard A Epstein, 'Notice and Freedom of Contract in the Law of Servitudes' (1981) 55 *S Cal L Rev* 1353, 1360.

[41] See Benito Arruñada, 'Property as Sequential Exchange: The Forgotten Limits of Private Contract' (2017) 4 *J Inst Econ* 753, 755–56.

[42] Hanoch Dagan and Irit Samet, 'Express Trust: The Dark Horse of the Liberal Property Regime', *Philosophical Foundations of the Law of Express Trusts* (OUP 2023) 140, 144, 148, 151.

[43] McFarlane, 'The Numerus Clausus Principle and Covenants Relating to Land' (n 1) 311.

[44] Ben McFarlane, 'Property: Duties, Diversity and Limits' (2022) 1 *King's LJ* 23, 23.

[45] Holger Fleischer, 'Der Numerus Clausus der Sachenrechte im Spiegel der RechtsÖkonomie' in Thomas Eger and others (eds), *Internationalisierung des Rechts und seine ökonomische Analyse: Festschrift für Hans-Bernd Schäfer zum 65. Geburtstag* (Gabler Verlag 2008) 127.

[46] eg Larenz and Wolf (n 39) 252; Fabian Klinck, 'Sachenrecht' in Dagmar Kaiser and Markus Stoffels (eds), *J. Staudingers Kommentar zum Bürgerlichen Gesetzbuch mit Einführungsgestetz und Nebengesetzen: Eckpfeiler des Zivilrechts* (6th edn, Sellier & de Gruyter 2018) 1274.

land to create modern market economies.[47] The second justification is principle-based and consists in ensuring that property remains essentially 'free' (ie not subject to burdens) to allow individuals to unfold their personality in the material word.[48]

The following sections will unpack these arguments, showing, first, that the policy and principle-based arguments made *against* the *numerus clausus* are flawed and, second, that the policy and principle-based arguments *in favour* of it are conceptually and functionally related. Building on this, the two next sections will argue that the different 'external' efficiency effects of the *numerus clausus* are better explained a reflection of a common single 'internal' rationality relating to the moral value of autonomy. Finally, using a rule-utilitarianism reading of John Stuart Mill's work, the last section will explain this internal-external connection, offering a new and more encompassing justification for the *numerus clausus* principle and its exceptional breach.

II. EXTERNAL EFFECTS: THE CONTROL OF EXTERNALITIES

A. The *Numerus Clausus* in Law and Economics

In the Anglo-American context, utilitarian justifications of the *numerus clausus* are underpinned by an apparent contradiction between property law and economic theory.[49] Since, according to Ronald Coase, freedom of contract is instrumental in efficiently allocating externalities,[50] rules that restrict the right of parties to make contracts in relation to property rights are normally assumed to undermine the maximisation of wealth. As a result, utilitarian justifications of the *numerus clausus* are normally based on the identification of some overlooked negative economic impact derived from the free delineation of property rights. The key to most of these theories is the realisation that the externalities dealt with by Coase derive from *using* things and that there is a separate group of externalities resulting from *making transactions* over things, which are worsened by the freedom to create property rights.[51]

The key to understanding the normative discussion on the *numerus clausus* is that it was preceded by an attack by leading law and economics scholars on what they saw as ancient doctrines undermining freedom of contract for no good reason, in a context in which the *numerus clausus* did not enjoy the standing of a clearly identified doctrine that could be defended. The broad idea that

[47] Fleischer (n 45) 129.
[48] Philipp von Heck, *Grundriss des Sachenrechts* (Mohr 1930) 87.
[49] See Bernard Rudden, 'Economic Theory v. Property Law: The Numerus Clausus Problem' in John Eekelaar and John Bell (eds), *Oxford Essays in Jurisprudence: Third Series* (Clarendon 1987) 239.
[50] Ronald Coase, 'The Problem of Social Cost' (1960) 3 *J Law and Econ* 1.
[51] Arruñada (n 41) 755–56.

property rights come in fixed forms had been familiar to American property law for a long time, but until the end of the twentieth century, American scholars had barely discussed the *numerus clausus* as such. This disconnection between theory and practice led to the lack of an explicit justification for the limitations that property law imposes on the free delineation of property rights,[52] facilitating the unchallenged development of economic arguments against the *numerus clausus* principle.

For classic economic analysis of law, the only social justification to limit the rights of private parties to create whatever interest they need is the protection of strangers to the title, that is, avoiding negative externalities. Following this view, Richard Epstein argued that this can be achieved entirely by means of registration and trusts, proposing the abolition of all other restraints on alienation. In this view, legal limitations on the free delineation of property rights wrongly focus on protecting the free disposition by successors in title, neglecting that that the proper time to assess the value of contractually binding limitations of property rights is when the original owner wants to sell the land. At that moment, conventional restrictions on property might be valuable, for example to develop land, and no restriction of this freedom is justified when there is no externality.[53] Epstein argued that, on the one hand, once a robust registration system is in place there is no justification for limiting the free creation of property rights, as all the arising externalities could be internalised by a recordation system that serves to give notice: if the seller wants to attach personal covenants to the land, the seller will also have to accept a reduction in price, making standardisation superfluous.[54] On the other hand, modern trust law has made the need of restrictions on alienation obsolete by turning beneficial interests in land into rights in a fund, thereby lifting restrictions blocking the free allocation of individual assets.[55]

This view only started to be challenged after Bernard Rudden first used the civilian label of '*numerus clausus*' as part of an effort to explain why most modern legal systems did not allow private parties to freely create new property rights.[56] Besides accounting for legal and philosophical arguments, Rudden mentioned seven different economic reasons,[57] that in different ways, highlight the effect of the *numerus clausus* in improving a market economy. Most of these arguments were later developed in sophisticated economics terms by American scholars who focused on the negative externalities of contracting over property rights.[58] Their views can be grouped in (i) antifragmentation, (ii) optimal standardisation and (iii) verification for conveyance arguments.

[52] Merrill and Smith (n 1) 1, 4–7, 9.
[53] Epstein, 'Past and Future' (n 40) 668, 703–04, 710, 713–14.
[54] Epstein, 'Notice and Freedom of Contract in the Law of Servitudes' (n 40) 1360.
[55] Epstein, 'Past and Future' (n 40) 714–15.
[56] Rudden (n 49).
[57] ibid 252–60.
[58] Akkermans (n 1) 108.

B. External Arguments

i. Antifragmentation

As early as the seventeenth century, the uncontrolled attachment of obligations to land was perceived as uneconomic, as it jeopardises its efficient use and circulation in the market.[59] That is why the abolition of feudal duties running with the land was seen as a precondition for the development of modern land markets.[60] As explained later in this chapter,[61] this is closely related to the historic origin of the *numerus clausus* in the civilian tradition,[62] and similar reasons can be found at the roots of contemporary common law property systems.[63] The idea still carried weight in the twentieth century, as evidenced by the warning against the danger that proprietary burdens have on the marketability of land made in the American Restatement of the Law of Property (1944) and the English Law Commission's Report (1984) on Land Obligations.[64]

By the end of the twentieth century the best economic arguments available in the context of Anglo-American property law to justify the sort of restrictions created by the *numerus clausus* were still based on concerns over the excessive splitting of property rights over durable assets.[65] In England, for example, Peter Birks argued that the strict control of the content of property rights is grounded in avoiding sterilising the economic value of land.[66] However, this did not have a deep impact in the way Anglo-American legal scholarship understood the relation between freedom of contract and property law until Michael Heller framed it as part of his 'tragedy of the anticommons'. His basic idea is that an excessive fragmentation of property rights over the same resource gives rise to an excessive number of veto-rights holders, which may lead to collective waste by under-consumption. Thus, in this view, the ability of an owner to break up the bundle of rights is subject to the restriction that the owner does not decompose it in ways that impair the object's marketability.[67] The point is illustrated with the Humpty Dumpty nursery rhyme: it is very easy to break an egg, but once it is shattered into pieces, there is no force that can reassemble its parts.[68]

[59] Rudden (n 49) 250, 257; Akkermans (n 1) 104.

[60] Francesco Parisi, 'Entropy in Property' (2002) 50 *Am J Comp L* 595, 601.

[61] See section III.A.

[62] Akkermans (n 1) 104.

[63] See AH Manchester, *A Modern Legal History of England and Wales, 1750–1950* (Butterworth 1980) 304, 310–11; William Cornish and others, *Law and Society in England 1750–1950* (2nd edn, Hart 2019) 135, 168–70.

[64] Rudden (n 49) 252–53.

[65] Merrill and Smith (n 1) 6.

[66] Peter Birks, 'Five Keys to Land Law' in Susan Bright and John Dewar (eds), *Land Law: Themes and Perspectives* (OUP 1998) 475.

[67] Michael Heller, 'The Tragedy of the Anticommons: Property in the Transition from Marx to Markets' (1998) 111 *Harv L Rev* 621, 677, 664.

[68] Michael Heller, 'The Boundaries of Private Property' (1999) 108 *Yale LJ* 1163, 1169.

According to Francesco Parisi, this implies that the mandatory standardisations of property rights can be justified in avoiding fragmentations that might lead to Heller's tragedy of the anticommons. In this view, economic forces subject property rights to a fundamental 'law of entropy'. Such law induces a one-directional bias towards their inefficient fragmentation, because splitting the bundle of property rights is relatively easy, while re-uniting it is subject to high transaction and strategic costs. As a result, initially, contractual limitations of ownership look reasonable, but then, when an opportunity arises that requires exploiting the complementarities now fragmented, the initially attractive fragmentation proves suboptimal, due to the great costs of reunification. In this context, the *numerus clausus* functions a legal device that avoids the dysfunctional fragmentation of property.[69]

Arguments as this have been questioned for a long time by scholars holding that this is not a problem for courts, but for markets and registration:[70] if the seller wants to attach idiosyncratic covenants to the land, as long as an effective registration system is in place, the fragmentation problems will simply be reflected in a reduction in the price.[71] However, for Parisi, this assumption does not work. Rational owners that anticipate the costs and benefits of fragmentating property rights might charge a higher price for the sale of the fragmented parcels. However, this does not facilitate optimal allocation of proprietary entitlements because the higher price charged by the original seller of the fragments will not affect the costs of reunification: no matter how much surplus was captured by the original seller, higher prices will have to be paid to restore the original unity. In simpler terms, the party creating the novel right will not bear the fall in the value of the thing, as the re-unification costs will need to be incurred by successor in title, at a later moment. In this view, that is why all modern legal systems have doctrines that work as a 'gravitational force' that limits the disintegration of property rights and promote the re-unification of its bundle.[72]

ii. Optimal Standardisation

Anti-fragmentation arguments were subject to a different criticism by Merrill and Smith, in one of the first papers that explicitly borrowed the civilian nomenclature of '*numerus clausus*' in America.[73] They stated that antifragmentation arguments do not hold, because the system of estates is flexible enough to always find a way to make a complicated conveyance possible, arguing that these problems are addressed by other doctrines. They looked into the English common

[69] Parisi, 'Entropy in Property' (n 60) 595–96, 613–14, 622, 627–28; Francesco Parisi, 'Freedom of Contract and the Laws of Entropy' (2003) 10 *Sup Ct Econ Rev* 65, 67–75.

[70] Rudden (n 49) 253.

[71] Epstein, 'Notice and Freedom of Contract in the Law of Servitudes' (n 40) 1359–60, 1368.

[72] Parisi, 'Entropy in Property' (n 60) 613–14, 627–28.

[73] Merrill and Smith (n 1).

law for a better rationale, which they found in a passage from *Keppell v Bailey* holding that:

> [t]here can be no harm in allowing the fullest latitude to men in binding themselves and their representatives, that is, their assets real and personal, to answer in damages for breach of their obligations …; but great detriment would arise and much confusion of rights if parties were allowed to invent new modes of holding and enjoying real property, and to impress upon their lands and tenements a peculiar character, which should follow them into all hands, however remote. Every close, every messuage, might thus be held in several fashion; and it would hardly be possible to know what rights the acquisition of any parcel conferred, or what obligations it imposed.[74]

In Merrill and Smith's view, restated in modern terminology, what the Lord Chancellor held was that, permitting unprecedented covenants 'would create unacceptable information costs to third parties'.[75] When individuals encounter property rights, they face measurement problems, either for acquiring them or to avoid violating them. In consequence, when idiosyncratic property rights are created, three different groups of people are affected: originating parties; potential successors in interest; and other market participants. For the two first groups, the measurement costs will be mediated by the price system, but the measurement costs imposed on other market participants will not be fully internalised in the price. In this view, standardisation of property rights stems from the need of controlling such externality.[76]

This model goes one further step forward, as it also acknowledges that standardisation comes with its own costs, as mandatory rules might sometimes prevent parties from achieving legitimate goals in cost-effective manners. Nonetheless, although the *numerus clausus* might frustrate some of these objectives, often those goals can still be accomplished by more complex combinations of the available property forms. This does not make the principle trivial, because parties willing to have tailored property interests can only achieve this by incurring higher planning and implementation costs. This trade-off between measurement and frustration costs should lead legal systems to reach an optimal standardisation of property rights. In this process, more simple forms will be adopted first, and more complex forms will gradually appear until marginal costs equal the benefits.[77]

iii. Verification for Conveyance

The optimal standardisation argument installed the *numerus clausus* as a central object of interest in contemporary private law scholarship. Hansmann

[74] *Keppell v Baily* (1834) 2 My & K 517, 39 Er 1042, at 1049. On this case, see ch 7, section II.A.
[75] Merrill and Smith (n 1) 26.
[76] ibid 26–34.
[77] ibid 35–40.

and Kraakman agreed with Merrill and Smith that third party information costs are at the core of the justification of the *numerus clausus*. However, they argued that this principle does not aim to avoid externalities on other market participants, but rather to allow successors in title to verify the existence of third-party property rights in the asset they acquire. They take the key to property rights to be that such rights are enforceable against subsequent owners. Thus, when two persons have rights in a single asset, there needs to be a common understanding of those rights (coordination problem). Even without this problem, they might need to be assured that the other party will not make opportunistic use of its right in the same asset (enforcement problem). Solving the coordination problem requires each party to understand the other parties' respective rights, while solving the problem of enforcement implies that judges must be able to understand (verify) the parties' understanding of the involved rights. In contractual rights, the agreement itself is the way to solve both problems, so there is no need for restrictions;[78] although it might be more precise to say that, in pure contractual obligations, verification turns into a problem of evidencing and construing the content of contracts.

Hansmann and Kraakman argue that the problem of verification is more difficult for property rights, because the holders of rights in the same asset might not be in privity of contract. In their view, property law solves these problems by setting out certain 'verification rules' that address under which conditions a given right will run with the asset. These rules involve costs for users (the parties), non-users (third parties) and the system (the courts), which can be allocated in different manners. Rules that allow parties to tailor property rights to their needs ('accommodating rules') imply relatively low costs for users, but impose high costs on non-users and the system; while rules that limit the discretion of private parties to accommodate property rights allocate relatively more costs on users, and less on non-users and the system. They argue that a property regime should maximise the aggregate value of assets to rights holders, less the cost for users, non-users and the system. Thus, an efficient legal system will offer special accommodation to divided property rights only where the benefits to users exceed the overall costs.[79]

C. In Search for a Common Principle

The three arguments grounding the *numerus clausus* in efficiency considerations discussed in the previous subsection present themselves as largely incompatible. However, if it is realised that they focus on different effects of property rights, the opposite becomes apparent. The three theories work on the implicit assumption

[78] Henry Hansmann and Reinier Kraakman, 'Property, Contract, and Verification: The Numerus Clausus Problem and the Divisibility of Rights' (2002) 31 *J Legal Stud* 373, 374, 378–78, 382–83.
[79] ibid 383–84, 396–97, 419.

that a legal doctrine can serve only one function, and that one practical purpose can only be served by one doctrine. However, as shown by other legal disciplines that specialise in functional approaches to the law,[80] this is not true. Utilitarian arguments are justifications that relate legal institutions to their effects in the real world (to what they *do*) and one institution can do more than one thing at the time. If proper attention is given to the different nature of the transaction costs discussed by each of these theories, it will soon be noted that they perform different but complementary functions within the context of a market economy.

The main conceptual argument to reject the anti-fragmentation policy as part of the underpinning of the *numerus clausus* is that the involved parties could also solve these problems by direct dealings,[81] turning the anti-fragmentation justification into a mere incidental effect.[82] As suggested by Parisi, this argument overlooks that this sort of private dealing can be subject to incredibly high transaction costs. Even if only two clearly identified parties are involved, both hold a monopoly position that allows them to exercise speculative behaviours in their negotiations, which creates high transaction costs that might prevent them from a reaching a deal.[83] These problems are only increased when parties are not clearly identifiable, difficult to reach, made up of many individuals, etc. Indeed, chapter seven will show that *Keppell*, the case Merrill and Smith rely on to build the optimal standardisation theory, is better explained by an antifragmentation rationale.[84]

The *numerus clausus* also plays a key role in reducing transaction costs related to the transfer of assets. Epstein argued that a robust recordation system that serves to give notice would make standardisation superfluous[85] and Merrill and Smith accept that the impact of idiosyncratic property rights on successors in title is internalised in the price.[86] Even if they have a point, both views overlook that, in practice, the transfer of rights is subject to relevant transaction costs, arising from the need of verifying that sellers have good title to the asset and identifying the possible duties or liabilities associated with its acquisition, which is, more or less, the point made by the verification argument. These costs might well be reflected in a lower price, but they still must be incurred by

[80] See Roger Cotterrell, *The Sociology of Law: An Introduction* (2nd edn, OUP 1992) 72–73; Kischel (n 3) 90–91.

[81] Rudden (n 49) 257. The other argument made by Merrill and Smith, that the fragmentation problem is tackled by other doctrines, is unconvincing. It not only assumes that the antifragmentation cannot be served by more than one doctrine, but grounds its points by reference to doctrines that also operate in cases in which there is no fragmentation, as adverse possession.

[82] Merrill and Smith (n 1) 6.

[83] On this sort of strategic behaviour, Guido Calabresi and A Douglas Melamed, 'Property Rules, Liability Rules, and Inalienability: One View of the Cathedral' (1972) 85 *Harv L Rev* 1089, 1106–10; Richard Epstein, 'A Clear View of The Cathedral: The Dominance of Property Rules' (1997) 106 *Yale LJ* 2091, 2093–94.

[84] See ch 7, section II.A.

[85] Epstein, 'Notice and Freedom of Contract in the Law of Servitudes' (n 40).

[86] Merrill and Smith (n 1) 32–33.

someone and, because they are transaction costs, they will not be fully transferred as part of the price to the other party, resulting in a net efficiency loss. Of course, having a robust registration system that serves to give notice to third parties regarding the existence of such rights would contribute to lowering these costs, but this still might not be enough.

One reason that justifies the *numerus clausus* principle from the perspective of the transaction costs associated with conveyancing is that registration of non-standardised rights only allows others to find out that a right exists, but does not tell buyers, *per se*, anything about its nature and content. In other words, registration solves the problem of finding out about the existence of the contract, but it does not solve the problems of its construction (eg interpretation, gap filling). This marketability problem is efficiently tackled by the *numerus clausus* by limiting and standardising the problems associated with the transfer of wealth. This is apparent in an example of everyday legal practice: when one company is acquiring another, the complexity, risks and workload associated with carrying out due diligence on the contracts of the acquired company is normally much higher than that for its property rights.[87] This difference does not arise from a problem of notice (all relevant information being handed over by the seller to the buyer), but from the fact that the possible contingencies associated with contracts are infinite and their forms unforeseeable, while with property rights, the buyer has a very clear idea of what will be the possible problems and their boundaries. That is also probably why German courts see the mandatory standardisation of property rights as a doctrine that helps to provide clarity regarding their content, arguing that this function is different but complementary to the notice effect achieved by registration.[88]

Finally, the criticism made of the optimal standardisation theory is not fatal. The three basic arguments against it mainly relate to aspects of the standardisation of property rights that such a theory fails to explain.[89] However, the failure to explain some features does not imply that a thesis is wrong in regard to those elements it actually accounts for, in this case, that the mandatory standardisation of property rights serves to reduce the overall costs of people dealing in the same market. What this criticism is truly pointing to is that *numerus clausus* might be serving a wider array of purposes regarding the circulation of wealth in the market, and that each of these three narrow economic justifications might simply be one external outcome of a common internal rationality. However, the highly formalised and abstract approach of economic analysis of law makes it difficult to look for this common conceptual justification. The next section attempts to finds this more concrete underpinning by switching to a comparative method to look for the meaning and

[87] Drawing from my previous experience as corporate lawyer working on mergers and acquisitions.
[88] BayObLG, NJW 1967, 1373. See section III.A and ch 7, section III.A.
[89] See Hansmann and Kraakman (n 78) 380–82.

functioning of the principle of *numerus clausus* in two of the main jurisdictions where it originally developed: England and Germany.

III. INTERNAL RATIONALITY: EFFICIENT AUTONOMY

Right-based justifications for the *numerus clausus* available in Germany and England are largely underpinned by domestic doctrinal elements and concrete historical problems. This has relevant consequences. First, in contrast to modern efficiency-based arguments, which are framed in the abstract and universalist terms of microeconomics, right-based justifications for the *numerus clausus* seem, at least on the surface, extremely dependent on arbitrary considerations of national doctrine. Second, as these right-based arguments did not develop in the 'aseptic' environment of law and economics, they are also frequently linked in very tangible manners to their historical context, making them appear as somehow contingent to no-longer relevant problems from early industrial societies. Therefore, these arguments cannot be presented in isolated terms, without losing much of their grasp. Considering the well-known divergence in the style of German and English property law, the two following subsections will discuss these arguments in the context of their contemporary national doctrine and then make some comparative remarks.

A. The German Approach

The universal inclusion of the *numerus clausus* among the foundational principles of German property law accounted for in chapter three,[90] stands in strong contrast with its normally only apodictic justification in textbook and commentary literature.[91] When justification is provided, it normally relies on the broad idea that, if absolute rights must be respected by everyone, the content and boundaries of their zone of protection need to be easily established.[92] In a common view, this reflects that the *numerus clausus* is so entrenched in German law that it does not need any material legitimation.[93] The fact that, until recently, the attempts of law and economics to provide a clear efficiency justification for the principle have barely been noticed in Germany is a good example of this.[94]

[90] See ch 3, section II.A.

[91] Fleischer (n 45) 127.

[92] eg Larenz and Wolf (n 39) 252; Klinck (n 46) 1274; Bar (n 15) 69; Neuner (n 19) 105, 245.

[93] eg Wolfgang Wiegand, 'Numerus Clausus der Dingliche Rechte. Zur Entstehung und Bedeutung eines Zentralen Zivilrechtlichen Dogmas' in Gerhard Köbler (ed), *Karl Kroeschell zum 60: Geburtstag dargelegt von Freunden, Schülern und Kollegen*, vol 60 (Verlag Peter Lang 1987) 623; Fleischer (n 45) 127.

[94] Although it might also be a consequence of the continental hostility towards law and economics.

This does not imply that the German version of the *numerus clausus* has no justification or that it is unimportant or uncontroversial. Indeed, most of its justifications are linked to some core ideas of German private law. Holger Fleischer has grouped them into traditional and modern justifications, the former including a dogmatic, an historical and a philosophical argument; and the latter corresponding to a policy argument identified with the protection of the 'circulation of wealth'.[95] He presents these theories as different justifications of the principle, but a careful analysis shows that the four can be linked by a common rationality: the dynamic preservation of personal freedom regarding the use of things. In this subsection this link will be built backwards, starting from the superficial dogmatic layers, then moving through its historic dimension, until reaching its ultimate policy and philosophical foundations.

i. The Dogmatic Argument

According to Philipp von Heck,[96] neither the BGB nor the *Motive* provide an explicit justification for the principle of *numerus clausus*. However, this is only the case when the analysis is restricted to the *Motive*, as the drafters' motivations for adopting a *numerus clausus* principle become clear once it is seen in its historical context. Following Wolfgang Wiegand, this rationale can be found in the general viewpoints of the *Motive*, which present the *numerus clausus* as a logical consequence of what the drafters saw as substantive dogmatic improvements over the pre-existing ALR: the creation of a self-sufficient property system that works fully independently from the law of obligations.[97]

According to this argument, the adoption of a *numerus clausus* principle by the BGB was predated by the development of two key doctrinal ideas during the nineteenth century: the autonomy of property law (developed here) and the abstract concept of ownership (developed below as 'historical argument'). In the *Motive*, the *numerus clausus* is presented as an apodictic deduction of the main idea behind the first: the inherently correct strict division of rights over things and persons.[98] The starting point for this development is found in Savigny's 'System of Roman law', where he argued for a universal and clear-cut division between property law and the law of obligations.[99] Building on this view, the drafters of the preliminary version of the property section of the BGB understood that a necessary consequence of this strict separation was that the acquisition of property rights must depend on features that are entirely within the domain of property law, excluding any causal regression to contractual

[95] Fleischer (n 45) 127–31.
[96] von Heck (n 48) 88.
[97] Wiegand, 'Numerus Clausus der Dingliche Rechte' (n 93) 625.
[98] ibid 627, 630.
[99] Friedrich Carl von Savigny, *System des Heutigen Römischen Rechts*, vol 1 (Veit & Comp 1840) 331–45, 367–79. For details, see ch 2, section II.C.

autonomy in establishing the content of property rights.[100] In this line, Wiegand argues that the *Motive* saw as obvious that parties could not be allowed to freely create property rights over things, a point from which the principle of *numerus clausus* followed like a theorem.[101]

ii. The Historical Argument

The other doctrinal concept that had a key influence in the birth of the German version of the *numerus clausus* is the absolute or abstract concept of ownership.[102] The European *Ius Commune* inherited a fragmented understanding of property law from feudal law. In this system both the tenant and the landlord could have ownership rights over the same land which the Glossators and Post-glossators, called *dominium utile* and *dominium directum*. If one of these positions was to be seen as more important, it was that of the landlord who did not physically hold the land (*dominium directum*). Led by Grotius and using the concepts of Roman law, the Natural Law School tried to overcome this fragmentation, arguing for a 'unitary notion of ownership', in which only one person could have 'ownership' of land, with any other property right becoming a *ius in re aliena* (a right in a thing owned by someone else). This idea was then adopted by the French Revolution and the *Code Civil* as part of the political process to bring feudalism to an end, making the *dominium utile* (that of the vassal) the only form of ownership.[103]

In a similar spirit, the BGB was the product of the liberal political ideas that became dominant in Germany during the nineteenth century, including the desire to overcome feudalism.[104] In this process the unitary notion of ownership gained immense popularity, coming to be seen as the cornerstone of a desirable property system.[105] Therefore, the drafters of the BGB were explicitly required

[100] Including the clear separation between the sale of a thing (a contract) and the transfer of its property. See §§ 433 and 929 BGB.

[101] Wiegand, 'Numerus Clausus der Dingliche Rechte' (n 93) 630, 635; Wolfgang Wiegand, 'Die Entwicklung des Sachenrechts im Verhältnis zum Schuldrecht' (1990) 1/2 *AcP* 112, 113; Wolfgang Wiegand, 'Funktion und Systematische Stellung des Sachenrechts im BGB' in Michael Martinek and Patrick L Sellier (eds), *J. von Staudingers Kommentar zum Bürgerlichen Gesetzbuch mit Eiführungsgesetz und Nebengesetzen. 100 Jahre BGB – 100 Jahre Staudinger* (Sellier & de Gruyter 1999) 111.

[102] Wiegand, 'Numerus Clausus der Dingliche Rechte' (n 93) 627, 628; Wiegand, 'Die Entwicklung des Sachenrechts im Verhältnis zum Schuldrecht' (n 101) 117; Wiegand, 'Funktion und Systematische Stellung des Sachenrechts im BGB' (n 101) 112. For discussion, see ch 2, section II.

[103] Bram Akkermans, *The Principle of Numerus Clausus in European Property Law* (Intersentia 2008) 19, 20, 56–81. For details on how this idea was received in the *Code* and later evolved in French doctrine, Anna Di Robilant, *The Making of Modern Property Law: Reinventing Roman Law in Europe and its Peripheries* (CUP 2023) 131–66.

[104] Schwab and Löhnig (n 36) 25–26; Zweigert and Kötz (n 11) 144–49; Di Robilant (n 103) 169–70.

[105] Wiegand, 'Numerus Clausus der Dingliche Rechte: Zur Entstehung und Bedeutung eines Zentralen Zivilrechtlichen Dogmas' (n 93) 628. For an intellectual history on how this idea was received in Germany, Di Robilant (n 103) 167–203.

to shape its property law as a system that ensures a 'free ownership'.[106] In strong contrast with the Anglo-American 'bundle picture',[107] in this conception, 'ownership is no longer understood as an aggregate of powers or rights, but as an encompassing and total dominion, that is indivisible and always the same'.[108] Thus, ownership can only be restricted by personal rights or by creating one of the limited real rights accepted by the *numerus clausus*. Any unauthorised fragmentation of ownership infringes the *numerus clausus*,[109] making the principle a guardian of a unitary notion of ownership.[110] This justification still carries force in German law, as evidenced by a leading *Kommentar* holding that 'the sense and purpose of the prohibition on the free configuration of property rights is to preserve their essential content …'.[111]

iii. The Policy Argument

In recent times these traditional 'doctrinal' justifications of the *numerus clausus* have been seen as insufficient by German scholars, leading them to develop a more 'external' policy-oriented grounding for the principle.[112] However, in contrast to the American law and economics movement, this approach gives more attention to explaining how this policy goal is embedded in the doctrinal structure of the BGB, rather than isolating and explaining its precise economic benefits in formal terms.

History plays a key role in this approach. During the second half of the nineteenth century, Germany experienced a radical economic and social transformation that left modern industrialised areas existing side by side with regions dominated by traditional economic relations.[113] Against this background, Wiegand showed that, during the nineteenth century, the burdens and fragmentations allowed by the ALR came to be seen as having a deeply negative impact in the circulation of wealth, arguing that the rapid success of the doctrinal concepts associated with the *numerus clausus* are better explained by the fact that they were in step with the leading policy ideas of the time, especially with

[106] See Heinrich Honsell, 'Einleitung zum BGB' in Dagmar Kaiser and Markus Stoffels (eds), *J. Staudingers Kommentar zum Bürgerlichen Gesetzbuch mit Einführungsgestetz und Nebengesetzen. Eckpfeiler des Zivilrechts* (6th edn, Sellier & de Gruyter 2018) 7–8, 13.

[107] See ch 2, section III.C.

[108] Wiegand, 'Die Entwicklung des Sachenrechts im Verhältnis zum Schuldrecht' (n 101) 117 (my translation).

[109] Sjef van Erp, 'Comparative Property Law' in Mathias Reimann and Reinhard Zimmermann (eds), *The Oxford Handbook of Comparative Law* (2nd edn, OUP 2019) 1044.

[110] Wiegand, 'Numerus Clausus der Dingliche Rechte' (n 93) 635.

[111] Hans Hermann Seiler, 'Einleitung zum Sachenrecht' in Elmar Bund and others (eds), *J. von Staudingers Kommentar zum Bürgerlichen Gesetzbuch mit Einführungsgesetz und Nebengesetzen* (Sellier & de Gruyter 2007) 26 (my translation).

[112] Fleischer (n 45) 129.

[113] Cornelius Torp, 'The Great Transformation: German Economy and Society, 1850–1914' in Helmut Walser Smith (ed), *The Oxford Handbook of Modern German History* (OUP 2011) 336–37.

the protection of free trade advanced by the Manchester School.[114] For Wiegand, that this 'interest in legal traffic' (*Verkehrsinteresse*) is the real justification of the *numerus clausus* becomes apparent in a number of doctrinal elements of the BGB, including the provision declaring that obligations not to dispose of things have no effect on third parties, the choice for an abstract transfer system, and a wide protection for good faith acquirers.[115]

At the beginning of the twenty-first century, this seems to be the leading justification for the *numerus clausus* in German doctrine,[116] evidencing some degree of convergence with the arguments of the law and economics movement. The core of the argument is as follows: third parties must be able to rely on that the things they acquire will only be subjected to the limitations and burdens explicitly allowed by the law. Protecting the circulation of wealth becomes especially important when it comes to property rights, because they affect third parties, normally, with no time limitation. Thus, by restricting the free delineation of property forms, the law protects legal security, clarity and simplicity.[117] In this view, standardisation of limited property rights plays a different role from registration, as it seeks to protect legal traffic by creating abstract types that are known beforehand by parties, forcing idiosyncratic agreements to rely on the law of obligations.[118] Thus, in the words of Marietta Auer, 'the basic function of the *numerus clausus* is defining the types and content of property rights, with the view of promoting efficiency and easing legal traffic'.[119]

iv. The Philosophical Argument

The current emphasis on 'legal traffic' and its economic rationale should not obscure that, for the contemporaries to the drafting of the BGB, the doctrinal package made of absolute ownership, *numerus clausus* and autonomous property law also had a strong philosophical underpinning of a less utilitarian nature, linked to the importance of ownership for the effective exercise of personal freedom.[120]

[114] On this, also see ch 2, section II.B.

[115] Wiegand, 'Die Entwicklung des Sachenrechts im Verhältnis zum Schuldrecht' (n 101) 118–19, 131; Wiegand, 'Funktion und Systematische Stellung des Sachenrechts im BGB' (n 101) 112–13; Wiegand, 'Numerus Clausus der Dingliche Rechte' (n 93) 628, 638–39.

[116] eg Jan Wilhelm, *Sachenrecht* (5th edn, De Gruyter 2016) 10; Marina Wellenhofer, *Sachenrecht* (34th edn, Beck 2019) 27; Klinck (n 46) 1274.

[117] Fleischer (n 45) 130.

[118] Jörg Mayer, 'Dienstbarkeiten' in Wolfgang Wiegand (ed), *J. von Staudingers Kommentar zum Bürgerlichen Gesetzbuch mit Einführungsgesetz und Nebengesetzen. Buch 3. Sachen Recht. EbbVo; §§ 1018–1112* (Sellier & de Gruyter 2002) 222–23, referring to servitudes.

[119] Marietta Auer, *Der Privatrechtliche Diskurs Der Moderne* (Mohr Siebeck 2014) 114 (my translation).

[120] eg, von Heck (n 48) 87.

As discussed in previous chapters,[121] the ideas of political liberalism that became dominant in Germany during the nineteenth century were indissolubly tied to the notion of 'free ownership' (*Freiheit des Eigentum*). The philosophical justification for this link between ownership and freedom can be traced to the loose influence of Kant and Hegel in Savigny's Theory of Will.[122] Hegel, in particular, argued that private property is justified because it contributes to personal freedom.[123] For him, human freedom is brought into existence by means of abstract freedom of ownership.[124] Therefore, in this view, limiting and standardising the proprietary interests that can burden ownership are part of a struggle to free ownership from its feudal content.[125] The philosophical underpinning behind this view can be found in §§ 41–45 of Hegel's 'Elements of the Philosophy of Right'.[126] According to it, the distinctiveness of the person is far from mere subjectivity (§§41 and 42) and needs an external sphere of freedom in which to be expressed (§ 41). Thus, 'free will' only becomes actual by its exercise as possession over things of the outside world (§45). Therefore, for Hegel, a free ownership is a necessary requirement of personal freedom.[127] Building on these ideas, the Romanist scholars that dominated nineteenth century German legal academia sought to give property law conceptual and normative coherence by organising it around the principle that the owner's will is absolute. In this view ownership gives individuals a sphere in which the will is the absolute master.[128] Despite this principle being softened during the twentieth century,[129] its core idea is still visible in classic sentences of the BVerfG, holding that 'ownership is … a guarantee of personal freedom … that provides its holder with a space of patrimonial freedom to live an autonomous life'.[130]

v. Dynamic Preservation of Personal Freedom as Unifying Idea

Despite being presented separately, these four different justifications for the *numerus clausus* can be understood as reflecting different aspects of a single general idea. The dogmatic and historical justifications are two technical sides of the same phenomenon: organising property law around a type that concentrates as many powers as possible in a single hand. However, this is not the ultimate normative justification of the *numerus clausus*, but rather a legal means to achieve two substantive ends that are at the core of modern thinking. On one

[121] See ch 2, section II.A and ch 3, section II.B.
[122] Larenz and Wolf (n 39) 21–22, 240–42.
[123] Dudley Knowles, *Hegel and the Philosophy of Right* (Routledge 2002) 116.
[124] Joachim Ritter, 'Person und Eigentum' in Ludwig Siep (ed), *G. W. F. Hegel – Grundlinien der Philosophie des Rechts* (3rd edn, De Gruyter 2014) 61.
[125] Rudden (n 49) 250.
[126] Hegel (n 26) 66–69.
[127] Knowles (n 123) 112–13, 117; Ritter (n 124) 55, 61.
[128] Di Robilant (n 103) 175, 188–90, 204.
[129] See ch 2, section II.B.
[130] BVerfGE 24, 367, 389 (my translation). Also see BVerfGE 50, 290, 339.

hand, the unitary notion of ownership and the *numerus clausus* principle are justified by their positive effects in creating modern market economies. In other words, one possible justification for the principle is the broad utilitarian idea that aggregate social efficiency is increased by reducing the transaction costs of the market allocation of wealth. On the other hand, the German *numerus clausus* also has a principle-based justification underpinned by the idea that respecting personal freedom requires that individuals are, in principle, not subject to non-consented duties.

The market and the freedom-based justification are not necessarily exclusive but are also not the same and might conflict.[131] However, in most cases both are not only compatible, but also highly complementary: to remain valuable for economic and legal traffic, things and people need to remain essentially unburdened. In most cases, people acquire things to use them, either for economic purposes (eg to rent out a house) or direct satisfaction of personal needs (eg to live in the house). Following the Hegelian justification of ownership, in both cases, things are valuable and circulate in the market because they enable people to exercise their freedom by using them. Therefore, property rights that burden ownership must be limited and exceptional.

This justification has, at least, two gaps. First, it does not develop on the different third-party effects of property rights. The Hegelian and the policy arguments implicitly focus on restricting successor liability and facilitating conveyance. In line with this, German scholarship does not discuss the impact of the *numerus clausus* on trespassory liability.[132] However, as recently shown by English scholarship (see next subsection), this does not imply that it has no relevance. Indeed, chapter six, section III will show that, although German doctrine does normally not directly link the principle of *numerus clausus* to tort law, this principle still plays a key role in this context as a means of protecting strangers from liability arising from non-consented duties.

Second, although German scholarship recognises that it is possible to enforce rights outside the *numerus clausus* against third parties subject to very high argumentative burden,[133] it does not offer a developed conceptual argument as to what justifies this occasional judicial infringement. Wiegand explains these deviations as a consequence of the inherently flawed project of the drafters of the BGB of having a fully self-sufficient property system. According to him, property was the central figure in feudal times but, after the end of the *ancien régime*, its relative importance decreased, as more and more patrimonial relations were taken over by the law of obligations. By the end of the nineteenth century this process was complete: thanks to industrialisation, the enormous growth of the law of obligations had displaced property law as core field of private law.

[131] See Rolf Stürner, 'Dienstbarkeit Heute' (1994) 194 AcP 265, 275–76.
[132] See ch 6, section III.
[133] Auer (n 119) 119.

For example, the contemporaries to the drafters of the BGB already held that its property law might be too formal and abstract to satisfy new economic needs,[134] as exemplified with the development of the security ownership during the early twentieth century.[135] This suggests that the deviations from the principle of *numerus clausus* are most likely underpinned by policy considerations, which is consistent with the growing (but also limited) regard that German judges are expected to have for the consequences of their decisions.[136]

B. The English Approach

Due to the historical absence of a consciously developed *numerus clausus* doctrine, English law lacks the explicit long-standing justifications for this principle available in Germany. Indeed, some even argue that the function of the *numerus clausus* in England remains unknown.[137] Nonetheless, clear attempts to justify its substance can be found in two different contexts. The first does not normally deal explicitly with the principle but emerges from the actual historical rationality underpinning *Keppell v Bailey*,[138] *Hill v Tupper*,[139] and the list of rights contained in LPA 1925.[140] To a large extent, this rationality ties the *numerus clausus* to the broad idea of protecting the marketability of land. The second justification is more recent and corresponds to a conscious reaction to the growing influence of the utilitarian justifications discussed in section II. Its core idea is shifting from the economic effects of the principle to its conceptual underpinning.[141] Since the conceptual argument builds on the historical development of the principle, this subsection will first provide a brief view of the historic origin of the principle in England and then systemise these historical elements based on the conceptual approach.

i. Historical Policy Concerns

The origin of the common law doctrine of *numerus clausus* is closely linked to some deep problems in the marketability of land found in nineteenth century England. At the beginning of the century, England still kept much of its medieval land law. This system was remarkably complex,[142] tending to fragment

[134] Wiegand, 'Die Entwicklung des Sachenrechts im Verhältnis zum Schuldrecht' (n 101) 131–34.
[135] See ch 3, section II.C.
[136] See ch 4, section II.
[137] eg Simon Gardner, '"Persistent Rights" Appraised' in Nicholas Hopkins (ed), *Modern Studies in Property Law*, vol 7 (Hart 2013) 351.
[138] *Keppell v Bailey* (n 74).
[139] *Hill v Tupper* (1863) 2 H & C 121, 159 ER 51.
[140] For details, see ch 3, section III.
[141] McFarlane, 'The Numerus Clausus Principle and Covenants Relating to Land' (n 1) 311, 314.
[142] See Manchester (n 63) 302.

ownership in manners that created important difficulties for the transfer of land.[143] As a result, the 'land question' became a topic of major public concern, with Benthamite radicals, including Lord Brougham,[144] permanently pressing for reforms. In this context, the Real Property Commissioners of the 1829–33 period – the time of *Keppell* – saw the conveyancing system as the central problem. The 'land question' remained a contested problem for the rest of the century and by the 1860s – the time of *Hill* – radicals were campaigning for 'free land'. For example, the Land Law League had the free transfer of land and the restriction of the power of tying it up among as its main goals. Parliament tried to tackle these problems by a variety of legislation, but no substantial nor successful reform was achieved,[145] until the 1922–25 property legislation.[146]

The doctrinal foundations of today's common law version of the *numerus clausus* are still found in this context.[147] Even if *Keppell* did not identify the principle by name, Lord Brougham offered a tangible justification as to why courts should reject attempts to enforce idiosyncratic rights against third parties, already quoted above when discussing the optimal standardisation argument.[148] As argued in chapter seven,[149] whether this passage also has the implications these authors attribute to it is a different story. For now, it is worth noting that, very much in tune with his time and radical views, Lord Brougham was concerned with both doctrinal and policy issues, seeing idiosyncratic property rights as 'clearly inconvenient both to the science of the law and to the public weal'.[150] The harm to the public good not only involved 'confusion' (the point highlighted by the optimal standardisation argument), but also problems relating, first, to conveyancing as, 'it would hardly be possible to know what rights the acquisition of any parcel conferred, or what obligations it imposed'; and, second, to impairing the free use of land by successors in title, as 'great detriment would arise ... if parties were allowed to invent new modes of holding and enjoying real property ... which should follow them into all hands, however remote'.[151]

In *Hill*, Pollock CB was less explicit in providing an underlying justification to deny the enforcement of idiosyncratic rights against 'pure strange' third parties (ie trespassory liability).[152] However, the key substantive consideration

[143] See Stuart Anderson, 'The 1925 Property Legislation: Setting Context' in Susan Bright and John Dewar (eds), *Land Law. Themes and Perspectives* (OUP 1998) 110; Elizabeth Cooke, *Land Law* (2nd edn, OUP 2012) 41.

[144] Cornish and others (n 63) 69, 168, 175.

[145] For all the historical background, Manchester (n 63) 302–26.

[146] Cooke (n 143) 39. In this book, ch 3, section III.B.

[147] See William Swadling, 'Property: General Principles' in Andrew Burrows (ed), *English Private Law* (3th edn, OUP 2013) 174–77; McFarlane, 'Keppell v Bailey (1834); Hill v Tupper (1863)' (n 139).

[148] See section II.B.

[149] See ch 7, section II.A.

[150] *Keppell v Bailey* (n 74) 137.

[151] ibid.

[152] *Hill v Tupper* (n 139) 127–28. For details, see ch 3, section III.A and ch 6, section II.A.

seems to have been that the company that had granted the rights was not entitled to create novel entitlements that would bind the defendant. The link between both cases is not clear, but the rejection of the claim in *Hill* has been said to be better explained as an expansion of the principle stated in *Keppell*: if a right is not able to bind successors in title (if it fails the *Keppell* test), *a fortiori*, it cannot bind a stranger.[153]

This brief analysis of *Keppel* and *Hill* suggests that the origin of the English version of the *numerus clausus* relates to three different elements: first, pure conceptual legal correctness (allowing idiosyncratic property rights would be 'inconvenient ... to the science of the law'); second, providing clarity as to the content of property rights in order to facilitate their marketability; and third, a conceptual reluctance to subject both successors in title and pure strangers to duties to which they have not consented. The last of these elements is the cornerstone of the conceptual argument recently advanced in England.

With the LPA 1925 the *numerus clausus* finally found its way into statutory law.[154] However, the main purpose of the act was not limiting the free creation of new property forms, as this restriction was already a part of the common law.[155] Its chief goal was to simplify the property system.[156] This is apparent in the fact that the only legal estates that the Act allowed to subsist are the fee simple and the leasehold, that is, property rights with *certain* temporal extensions: either indefinite (the fee simple) or subject to a strict temporal limitation (the leasehold).[157] On Peter Birks' view, this choice aimed to ensure the free alienability of land by subjecting the temporal slicing of ownership to extremely certain limits and forcing anyone wanting to deal in other (complex) time slices to act 'behind the curtain of a trust'.[158] Thus, the statutory enactment of the *numerus clausus* in England does not seem to add a new justification for such principle as it already existed in the nineteenth century common law but it suggests that its substantive delineation of the estates aims to provide certainty as to the boundaries of property rights to facilitate their marketability *over time*. The practical implications of this are developed in chapter seven.

ii. The Conceptual Argument

In England, the policy rationale based on preserving the economic usability of land has often been accompanied by arguments that see property rights as

[153] McFarlane, 'Keppell v Bailey (1834); Hill v Tupper (1863)' (n 139) 12. Although in *Stockport* Bramwell B (dissenting) argued for the opposite rationale. See nn 172–174 and accompanying text.

[154] See ch 3, section III.A.

[155] Note that Swadling does not mention the LPA 1925 when accounting for the principle. Swadling (n 147) 175–77.

[156] See Manchester (n 63) 324; Anderson (n 143) 109; Cooke (n 143) 41.

[157] See LPA 1925, s 1(1).

[158] Birks (n 66) 463.

'invisible threats' to strangers that need to be strictly controlled.[159] In this vein, in recent times, Ben McFarlane has attempted to explain the piecemeal case law that limits the free creation of property rights by means of a principle-based argument. In this view, law and economics approaches tend to neglect trespassory liability, focusing only on successor liability. However, in *Hill* this liability was completely absent as the issue at stake was whether B, who had acquired rights relating to the land from A, could enforce such rights against a stranger (X). Since the claim was rejected under the argument that not-recognised forms of covenant could not impose duties on strangers, any justification of the *numerus clausus* must also be able to account for its effects on trespassory liability. Relying on this, McFarlane holds that the justification for the *numerus clausus* is conceptual rather than consequentialist and corresponds to a more general legal principle holding that, generally, an agreement cannot impose duties or liabilities on someone outside that agreement.[160]

This general principle is not absolute but requires that compelling reasons are provided for its exceptions. In McFarlane's view, which has been advanced in similar terms in Germany,[161] these good reasons are policy arguments: new property rights are recognised when the overall utility is increased by having third parties bound to such claims. Acquisition by first possession provides a clear example: once B takes control over a previously ownerless asset, all others (X) lose their pre-existing privileges in it, at least in regard to B, without consenting or even knowing it, and become subject to a new duty to B of keeping off the asset.[162]

This need for a special justification for the non-consented loss of privileges is felt in many contexts, providing a solid intuitive grounding to the reluctance of private law to bind parties to new non-consented duties. For example, Locke's theory of appropriation by first possession puts a lot of effort into justifying the existence of a general tacit mutual consent to the appropriation of assets previously held in common.[163] Contemporary Kantians, in turn, justify these non-consented burdens in the existence of a system that allows everyone to actually or potentially acquire new things.[164] However, in modern times,[165] justifications for acquisition by first possession have moved from these fictional forms of consent or reciprocity to utilitarian arguments. These include (i) internalising the beneficial and harmful effects of the use of open access goods;[166]

[159] eg ibid 475.

[160] McFarlane, 'The Numerus Clausus Principle and Covenants Relating to Land' (n 1) 311.

[161] See Bar (n 15) 67.

[162] McFarlane, 'The Numerus Clausus Principle and Covenants Relating to Land' (n 1) 311–12, 314. Similarly, JE Penner, 'Property' in *The Oxford Handbook of New Private Law* (OUP 2021) 281–82, 288–89.

[163] Locke (n 25) 16, [28]–[29].

[164] eg Weinrib (n 21) 134. For discussion, see section IV.B.

[165] Although the roots of the argument are old. See James Gordley, *Foundations of Private Law* (OUP 2006) 9.

[166] Harold Demsetz, 'Toward a Theory of Property Rights' (1967) 57 *Am Econ Rev* 347.

(ii) incentivising the discovery, identification and characterisation of valuable resources that would otherwise remain hidden;[167] and (iii) allocating resources to the person who, with its effort in finding the resource, has evidenced having the knowledge and capacity to take advantage of it in a context that no one else has.[168]

In contrast, when new non-consented duties are imposed on third parties by the simple transfer of the pre-existing correlative right, this effect is not seen as requiring any special justification. The reasons for this is that this new duty does not take any further privileges away from them, as it only changes the identity of the correlative right holder. Thus, in practice, the problem of the contractual creation of non-consented duties on third parties only arises when the owner of an asset (A) is allowed to retain the property and, at the same time, grant a property right in the same asset to another party (B), as then the rest of the world (X) become subject to a *new* duty they have not consented to. This has a direct detrimental effect on third parties (not a mere informational externality), as they are now exposed to liability *vis a vis* two persons for the breach of two different rights[169] – a phenomenon Rudden named 'claim cloning'.[170]

Avoiding this cloning effect played a key role in *Hill*,[171] as later made apparent in *Stockport Waterworks Co v Potter.*[172] In this case, a riparian owner (A) granted the claimant (B) all its rights in a water flow, including the right to take water from an adjacent river, without transferring the riparian land to him. The defendant (X) polluted the river and was sued by B. The claim was rejected by Pollock CB arguing that it is not possible for a riparian owner to keep his land and deal separately with the water. For this, he relied on *Hill* as an authority holding that a person cannot create by grant new property rights that give the grantee the right of suing the third party in his own name for the interruption of the right.[173]

It is not completely clear whether the court in *Stockport Waterworks* understood that A's separate dealing with the water rights attempted either to clone its right or to make an atypical transfer of (part of) it.[174] If it was a cloning case, the holding would be underpinned by the idea that private dealings cannot invent types of property rights that will impose novel forms of non-consented liability on strangers. If this principle is restricted to the paradigmatic case, it implies that parties can only clone claims that will affect strangers when the law has

[167] Richard A Epstein, 'Possession as the Root of Title' (1979) 13 *Ga L Rev* 1221, 1237–38; Randy E Barnett, *The Structure of Liberty: Justice and the Rule of Law* (OUP 2000) 68–69.

[168] Epstein, 'Possession as the Root of Title' (n 167) 1238–39; Barnett (n 167) 68–69.

[169] McFarlane, 'The Numerus Clausus Principle and Covenants Relating to Land' (n 1) 312–13.

[170] Rudden (n 49) 251.

[171] McFarlane, 'The Numerus Clausus Principle and Covenants Relating to Land' (n 1) 312.

[172] *Stockport Waterworks Co v Potter* (1864) 3 H & C 300, 159 ER 545.

[173] ibid (H&C 300 at 326–327, 159 ER 545 at 566). For discussion, Joshua Getzler, *A History of Water Rights at Common Law* (OUP 2006) 316–20.

[174] At least Baron Bramwell (dissenting) seemed to understand that A had passed its property to B, see *Stockport* (n 172) H&C 300 at 327, 159 ER 545 at 566.

previously authorised the creation of such property rights. As in the case of first possession, the reasons why the law authorises this is to be found in pure policy concerns: whether the overall utility will be increased if B is allowed to assert her right against X.[175] If this was a case of attempted ('fragmentary') transfer, then the protection of third parties seems to be more closely associated with information problems: if the right to use the water could be traded in gross, it would be very hard for X to find out who is the owner of such right. This would create uncertainty as to the content of the right, imposing information costs on X that could prevent the achievement of a Coasean bargain.

C. Comparative Remarks

At first sight, the German and English justifications given for adopting a *numerus clausus* of property rights seem very different. In Germany, the principle is historically bound to the emergence of the unitary notion of ownership as part of the political project of bringing feudal rights to an end and the strong academic push of the Pandectist School to provide property law with a self-sufficient doctrinal structure within the system of the BGB. None of these elements are present in England. English property law developed from feudal law with little romanistic influence and, by the time of *Keppell*, feudal duties had been abolished for a long time.[176] As a result, English land law did not develop a unitary notion of ownership and still relies on the traditional theory of estates.[177]

However, once the historical motivations of the drafters of the BGB, the LPA 1925 and the judges in *Keppell* and *Hill* are detached from the specific doctrinal constraints in which they developed and understood in their broader context, it becomes apparent that both versions of the *numerus clausus* share a relevant functional and ideological similarity. With the arrival of modernity, the traditional personal bonds of static agricultural economies lost their purpose and started to be seen as unnecessary and prejudicial burdens to the free use and trade of land. As industrialisation spread from England to Germany,[178] the kind of personal ties with enduring third-party effects allowed by traditional land law came to be seen as jeopardising its circulation and transformation. Faced with similar problems, both jurisdictions came up with an analogous solution: to limit the real burdens that owners could impose on their land. Thus, the general interest of 'protecting legal traffic' that justifies the German version of the *numerus clausus* can also be seen as underpinning *Keppell*, *Hill*

[175] McFarlane, 'The Numerus Clausus Principle and Covenants Relating to Land' (n 1) 313–14; McFarlane, 'Keppell v Bailey (1834); Hill v Tupper (1863)' (n 139) 16.

[176] 1660 Statute of Tenuere.

[177] See ch 2, section III.

[178] Torp (n 113) 337.

and the LPA 1925. The difference in the way the doctrine developed in both countries is better explained as an effect of their dissimilar political history and legal tradition.[179] In England, it developed slowly and progressively, led by the practical and piecemeal approach that characterises the judge as the motor of the common law, reaching statutory law at the end of the journey. By contrast, in Germany, the concept developed from academic scholarship, finding its way into private law in a single discrete legislative act: the entering into force of the BGB.[180]

This generic interest in protecting legal traffic (efficient allocation) broadly encompasses all the narrow and highly formalised justifications for the *numerus clausus* put forward by the law and economics movement. However, in the German and the English case, this justification is embedded in legal doctrine, reflecting the actual historical ideology that shaped the principle, namely, a broad hostility to imposing duties on people who have not consented to them. Such argument holds that, in principle, people have an essential *right* not to be subject to duties to which they have not consented. In Germany, this idea is explicit in Savigny's Theory of Will, especially when it comes to strangers, and in the Hegelian justification of ownership, especially in regard to successors of title. In England a similar conceptual argument can be found in McFarlane's reading of *Keppell* and *Hill*.

Unlike theories grounded on democratic values or utilitarian considerations, this argument is deeply internal to property law, as it forms the bedrock of modern private law systems. Due to the systematic nature of codified law, this idea is especially apparent in civilian private law systems. For example, the BGB is built upon a basic principle of self-determination or private autonomy emerging from a Kantian-based personalist ethic (*ethischer Personalismus*) according to which parties are free to decide on their relations with other people.[181] In the common law, the fragmentary nature of private law makes this less conspicuous, but it is self-evident that consent is central to contract law, while tort and unjust enrichment law are essentially concerned with providing a justification to impose non-consented obligations. As a result, similar to what happens in German private law, in the common law, theoretical right-based approaches explicitly hold that private law is underpinned by the protection of autonomy.[182]

These findings also undermine the autonomy-based argument against the *numerus clausus* recently put forward by some progressive scholars under the rubric of a 'liberal theory of property law'.[183] Their focus on the autonomy of

[179] On these differences, Zweigert and Kötz (n 11) 181, 191, 193, 138–44, 257–59; Siems (n 30) 53–61.

[180] On this, see ch 3, section IV.B.

[181] Neuner (n 19) 96.

[182] eg Peter Cane, 'Rights in Private Law' in Donal Nolan and Andrew Robertson (eds), *Rights and Private Law* (Hart 2011).

[183] Dagan and Samet (n 42) 140, 144, 148, 151; Hanoch Dagan, *A Liberal Theory of Property Law* (CUP 2021) 15–16, 24.

owners obscures the heavy impact that property rights have on the autonomy of third parties, including *other owners*. Every time a new property right is created, an indefinite number of people is subject to a new non-consented duty to stay-off and exposed to non-consented liability for their breach. Thus, by definition, the creation of new property rights imposes new duties on third parties that curtail their freedom. For example, in the case of trespassory liability, if A grants a new property right to B, then an indefinite number of strangers (X), who might or might not be holders of property rights in other things, will lose the correlative liberty and be made liable to B in manners they have not consented to and have no knowledge of. This is hard to reconcile with one of the central pillars of the 'liberal theory', namely, the 'compliance of owner's powers with relational justice to verify that property does not offend the principle of reciprocal respect for self-determination'.[184] Thus, far from limiting party autonomy, the *numerus clausus* seems to strike a balance between the autonomy of the owner of an asset and that of strangers affected by the rights the owner can create on that asset.[185] This compromise is explored in chapter six.

This deeper principle-based justification is not *per se* opposed to policy justifications based on the protection of legal traffic. As discussed above, the value that human beings attach to having freedom regarding how they use things is central to classic utilitarian arguments that justify the *numerus clausus* in the protection of the marketability of land and the Hegelian thesis that links ownership to the effective exercise of personal liberty.[186] Thus, in both traditions, the moral status that the free will achieved in the private law of post-feudal societies was historically implemented by two closely linked principles: 'free' ownership and limits to non-consented obligations. The *numerus clausus* plays a key role in making both principles operative. In Germany this seems so obvious that it is frequently overlooked, while in England, the essentially pragmatic approach to legal problems has historically prevented the full articulation of this idea.

However, this principle-based justification does not provide any guide to explain the occasional infringement of the principle by courts. In German scholarship, the development of new property forms is clearly explained by the pressures to deal with practical economic needs that surpass the rigid nature of the property system of the BGB, but this does not amount to a justification, only to an explanation. The same happens in England, but this is less relevant, as the development of private law by pragmatic solutions to specific problems is essential to the common law. However, the broad policy justifications found across jurisdictions to allow imposing duties on third parties without their consent in general[187] can also be extended to the emergence of property rights outside the

[184] Dagan (n 183) 4.

[185] Similarly, McFarlane, 'Property: Duties, Diversity and Limits' (n 44) 33.

[186] A similar reading has been suggested by Gordley (n 165) 16.

[187] See McFarlane, 'The Numerus Clausus Principle and Covenants Relating to Land' (n 1) 311–12, 314; Bar (n 15) 67; Penner (n 162) 281–82, 288–89.

numerus clausus. In a line similar to the optimal standardisation theory, in both England and Germany the infringement of the principle seems to be justified by pure utilitarian considerations: when the structure of the existing property law is not capable of satisfying new social and economic demands, courts behave *as if* the creation of non-legislative property rights is justified. The next section accounts for the place of this policy-based argument in English and German property law.

IV. TOWARDS A SUBSTANTIVE JUSTIFICATION

A. The Internal: Justifying the *Numerus Clausus*

The *numerus clausus* seems to be one of those doctrines that can be justified by either utilitarian or principle-based arguments.[188] However, there is a wide agreement in modern philosophical thinking that there is no deep compatibility between both type of arguments, as they value rights for different reasons. For utilitarianism, rights are ultimately protected and justified due to their capacity to increase general utility,[189] while principle-based arguments are ultimately based on the respect of individuals, for their own sake.[190] Despite this, the superficial compatibility of both strands of thought is enough to provide a consistent justification of the practical operation of the *numerus clausus* principle in England and Germany. The path for this resembles, but also deviates from other views that seek to connect the internal structure of private law with elements external to it, like managing information cost[191] or ideologies.[192]

The first key to reach the operative reconciliation of both justifications is found in the role that JS Mill attributes to 'secondary moral principles' in his effort to make his utilitarian doctrine compatible with the existence of liberal rights. At Mill's time, the distinction between act and rule utilitarianism had not yet been developed and he offers apparently contradictory views on this subject.[193] In some passages he holds that 'actions are right in proportion as they tend to promote happiness',[194] while in others he holds that actions are right if they conform to 'rules and precepts of conduct by the observance of which … the greatest extent [of happiness might be] secured to all mankind'.[195] However, both views can be reconciled by noting that they answer different questions: the

[188] On this compatibility, Gold and Smith (n 29).
[189] Murphy and Coleman (n 9) 74–75, 79–80; Tebbit (n 2) 121.
[190] Dworkin (n 8) 107.
[191] eg Gold and Smith (n 29).
[192] eg Cane (n 182).
[193] Michael Schefczyk, 'John Stuart Mill: Ethics' in James Fieser and Bradley Dowden (eds), *The Internet Encyclopedia of Philosophy*, https://www.iep.utm.edu, accessed 15 March 2020.
[194] Mill (n 20) 210.
[195] ibid 214.

first deals with the problem of moral rightness, while the second is part of a theory of moral obligation.[196]

As to the latter, Mill holds that the utilitarian calculations that would be needed to adjust action to the principle of utility, even if possible, would be time consuming and subject to bias and distortion.[197] Thus, much moral reasoning should be governed by 'secondary principles' about such things as fidelity, fair play and honesty, which do not have a direct reference to utility but still promote it.[198] However, Mill's utilitarianism seems to collide with his wider view of liberty. For him, humans should live under conditions that assure sufficient self-governance. Thus, the only valid reason to limit the personal liberty of any individual is the avoidance of harm to third parties ('Harm Principle'). However, even if necessary, the Harm Principle is not enough to limit liberty: to do so, the harm avoided must also outweigh the negative effect of the restriction, making utilitarian calculations the ultimate criteria for protecting or restricting liberal rights. Nonetheless, in Mill's view this does not deprive liberty from moral value. As a secondary moral principle, the protection of others' liberty is morally justified, unless it is shown that the harm created by such regulation outweighs its benefits.[199]

In this classical-liberal framework, the English and German versions of the principle of *numerus clausus* can be seen as doctrinal devices underpinned by an 'internal' secondary moral principle holding that people should not be subject to a duty to which they have not consented, unless the creation of such rights is allowed by the law. The ultimate justifications for this can be found in the ideology of nineteenth century economic and political liberalism. By the same logic, judges are not required – in fact, are forbidden – to assess whether, in a particular case, the benefits of creating a particular property right would outweigh the cost it imposes on third parties: they can only enforce the property rights that exist in the law.

Thus, under the principle of *numerus clausus*, English and German judges are not called to overrule this secondary moral principle based on utilitarian arguments. That decision is for legislators, who – as argued in chapter four – are in a structurally better position to evaluate the cost and benefits of introducing new property rights. In this view, even if the *numerus clausus* might ultimately be justified by 'external' utilitarian policy goals, its justification in the context of English and German adjudication works *as if* it is underpinned by a non-utilitarian morality internal to private law. In contrast to what happens in

[196] JO Urmson, 'The Interpretation of the Moral Philosophy of J. S. Mill' (1953) 3 *Phil Q* 33.

[197] Schefczyk (n 193); for direct reference, see Mill (n 20) 219–21, 225, 226.

[198] For a full development, see David Brink, 'Mill's Moral and Political Philosophy' in Edward N Zalta (ed), *Stanford Encyclopedia of Philosophy* (Winter 2018) https://plato.stanford.edu/archives/win2018/entries/mill-moral-political/.

[199] John Stuart Mill, 'On Liberty' in JM Robson (ed), *The Collected Works of John Stuart Mill: Essays on Ethics, Religion and Society*, vol XVIII (University of Toronto Press; Routledge & Kegan 1977) 223–26, 260–75, 292–93.

America, where the principle does not have the same legislative standing and policy arguments play a much more important role in adjudication, in England and Germany, the ultimate policy justification of the principle is found *outside* the law.

B. Justifying Deviations: Internal or External?

Grounding the direct justification of the *numerus clausus* in right-based arguments or secondary moral principles does not imply that utilitarian considerations will lose all importance in adjudication. Even for advocates of rights-based views, in some cases, rights might also have to yield in favour of other rights or urgent policy concerns.[200] However, when it comes to property law, contemporary supporters of right-based approaches tend to ignore this, making huge efforts to justify the imposition of non-consented duties by non-utilitarian arguments. For example, faced with the puzzle created by original acquisition, Ernst Weinrib justifies the imposition of non-consented duties on third parties arising as a consequence of the emergence of new specific property rights in a systematic reciprocity consideration. In his view, every act of acquisition – and thus, the correlative imposition of non-consented duties – is justified by the others' actual or potential act of acquisition.[201]

These arguments are unconvincing.[202] Weinrib's thesis does not amount to a justification for the imposition of non-consented obligations, but to a moral minimal requirement of any liberal democratic society: if the law allows someone to impose non-consented duties on third parties, such power must be made available to everyone in equal terms. However, this argument does not provide any reasons as to *why*, in the first place, people should be able to act in such a way as to acquire rights that impose new non-consensual duties on third parties. Indeed, Weinrib's argument can be reduced to the following: A can create a right in favour of B that will bind C and X without their consent, because C and X can do the same in regard to A. This seems rather tautological and denies the strong intuition that the imposition of non-consented duties is exceptional.

The non-consented duties arising with the creation of new property rights are better justified by utilitarian considerations, which is widely consistent with experience, as evidenced by the development of restrictive covenants in England and ownership for security purposes in Germany.[203] In particular, Mill's acceptance of the exceptional overriding of secondary moral principles by utilitarian considerations provides a simpler and more intuitive explanation of the

[200] Dworkin (n 8) 117.

[201] Weinrib (n 21) 134.

[202] For a general criticism, NW Sage, 'Original Acquisition and Unilateralism: Kant, Hegel, and Corrective Justice' (2012) 25 *CJLJ* 119, 126–29.

[203] See ch 3.

occasional breach of the *numerus clausus* principle by English and German courts. This view is also consistent with Nonet and Selznick's socio-legal model described at the end of chapter four. According to this model the formal (internal) structure of the law tends to yield to substantive policy arguments when it is pressed by litigators aiming to make it more 'responsive' to social change.[204] In this sense, policy arguments that override the *numerus clausus* do have a place in adjudication, although exceptional and unsystematic.

Whether the justification for these deviations is better described as 'internal' or 'external' depends on a further consideration, namely, on whether the law is approached from a 'doctrinalist' or 'conceptualist' perspective. The former starts with cases and other legal materials and, from there, induces principles and taxonomies that bring order to legal reality. Hence, it is not dogmatic about 'substantive' reasons and is willing to consider them if they are 'part of the law', for example, because courts *actually* rely on them.[205] From this perspective, the policy arguments that justify the deviations to the *numerus clausus* would seem to be internal to the law. That seems to be the case of England. In contrast, conceptualism starts with *a priori* inherent principles and taxonomies and seeks to fit the law in them.[206] Thus, in this view, utilitarian arguments that justify the deviations to the *numerus clausus* would seem to be external. German law seems to lean towards this view.

What Weinrib's Kantian argument adds to this picture is a conceptual limitation: if someone is allowed to create a property right due to its social convenience, then this ability must be available for all. Thus, when enforcing a right not contained in the *numerus clausus* against third parties, judges must think beyond the effects of the case at hand. This also explains why judges are and should be reluctant to develop the property system: admitting a new type of rights might shake the whole edifice of property law, and the casuistic nature of adjudication prevents judges from having complete view of the edifice. As argued in chapter four, judges are simply not in a good position to make these policy decisions.

C. Towards a Substantive *Numerus Clausus*

A final takeaway of this chapter is that the English and German versions of the principle of *numerus clausus* are not underpinned by a mere aim to standardise property rights for its own sake, but rather by the goal of standardising them *in a precise manner*, namely, in a form that ensures that they impose as few

[204] See Philippe Nonet and Philip Selznick, *Law and Society in Transition: Toward Responsive Law* (2nd edn, Transaction Publishers 2001) 73–114.

[205] Dan Priel, 'Two Forms of Formalism' in Andrew Robertson and James Goudkamp (eds), *Form and Substance in the Law of Obligations* (Hart 2019) 168, 171.

[206] ibid.

as possible non-consented duties on third parties. In other words, the *numerus clausus* might be a formalistic doctrine, but it exists to protect the substantive design of modern property law. This is a key finding for the rest of the book: in a sense, the *numerus clausus* collapses the form and substance of property rights in one. This is especially visible in German law, where the *numerus clausus* is explicitly said to exist to preserve the substantive structure of property rights.[207] The same can probably be said for English law.

In this framework, consistent with the optimal standardisation thesis, new property rights are only admitted to this list when there are strong policy reasons for doing so, which is normally a choice to be made by legislators. On the assumptions that legislative activity in this field is infrequent, this makes property law look static and rigid. However, once it is acknowledged that the *numerus clausus* has an historical commitment to standardise property law in a manner that keeps broad spaces of freedom available, a different explanation emerges. Property law might be static, but it is not rigid, as its (internal) doctrinal structure is designed to allow private parties to accommodate new social and economic realities. In this view, property law does not often change, because *it does not need to change*. This triggers a first question is: how does this happen in practice?

Acknowledging the role of policy arguments as normative justifications for the expansion and breach of this principle also provides property law with a 'principle of growth'. The basic idea that parties shall not be subject to non-consented duties is not absolute and must, on occasions, yield to utilitarian considerations. In principle, this decision is for legislators, but in practice both English and German courts have occasionally assumed this task when Parliament has failed to do so. Thus, a second question is why these developments have not altered the prevailing perception of property law as a static field?

The two next chapters will answer both questions, distinguishing between the impact that the *numerus clausus* has in trespassory (chapter six) and successor liability (chapter seven). On the one hand, they will demonstrate that the English and German *numerus clausus* provide property law with a substantive 'modular' structure that allows and facilitates private parties to accommodate new realities into pre-existing legal forms through a process of 'functional transformation'. On the other hand, they will also show that the flexible structure of these modular design has limits as to the changes it can accommodate, by discussing some cases in which the list of property rights has been expanded by legislation.

[207] See nn 111 and 119 and accompanying text.

6

Numerus Clausus *and Trespassory Liability*

THE PREVIOUS CHAPTERS have shown that in England and Germany property rights are characterised by their ability to bind third parties[1] and that, in both jurisdictions, the principle of *numerus clausus* aims to contain such effects by standardising them.[2] As submitted in chapter five, the ultimate justification of this principle remains contested but, at least in English and German law, its direct or 'internal' justification is the protection of the personal autonomy of third parties.

As explained in chapter two, property rights have two clearly differentiable third-party effects: successor liability and trespassory liability. Despite its analytically clear nature, this distinction has not been widely explored. In Germany, it was neatly identified by some scholars during the mid twentieth century,[3] but it is rarely mentioned in contemporary literature, although the idea is sometimes used when discussing the third-party effects of leases.[4] In Anglo-American scholarship, Tony Honoré also mentioned the distinction in the late 1950s, with a direct reference to German scholarship.[5] Nonetheless, in the common law, the limits between both effects remained unexplored until James Penner re-introduced the distinction in the mid 2000s.[6] Since then, the distinction gained traction in England, especially as an analytical device to distinguish equitable and legal property rights.[7]

[1] See ch 2.

[2] See ch 3.

[3] eg Heinz Hübner and Joachim Riegner, *Sachenrecht* (Translatia 1948) 7; Hermann Eichler, *Institutionen des Sachenrechts*, vol 1 (Duncker & Humblot 1954) 6–7.

[4] eg Fritz Baur, Jürgen Baur and Rolf Stürner, *Sachenrecht* (18th edn, Beck 2009) 393–99.

[5] AM Honoré, 'Rights of Exclusion and Immunities Against Divesting' (1959) 34 *Tul L Rev* 453, 467.

[6] James Penner, 'Duty and Liability in Respect of Funds' in John Lowry and Mistelis Loukas (eds), *Commercial Law: Perspectives and Practice* (LexisNexis Butterworths 2006) 215.

[7] eg Ben McFarlane and Robert Stevens, 'The Nature of Equitable Property' (2010) 4 *J Eq* 1; William Swadling, 'Property: General Principles' in Andrew Burrows (ed), *English Private Law* (3rd edn, OUP 2013) 180; Simon Douglas and Ben McFarlane, 'Defining Property Rights' in James Penner and Henry Smith (eds), *Philosophical Foundations of Property Law* (OUP 2013) 240, 241.

As shown in chapter five, in England, identifying the effects of the *numerus clausus* on trespassory liability has been of key importance in developing a conceptual justification of this principle based on the protection of party autonomy,[8] which makes its parallels with the German justification of the principle apparent. Nonetheless, the wider implications of this distinction for the *numerus clausus* remain underdeveloped. In England this seems to result from a lingering scepticism towards describing common law phenomena using terms taken from the civil law,[9] while in Germany the well-established conceptual status of the principle seems to have discouraged further developments.[10] In this line, broader theoretical accounts aiming to explain the flexible nature of standardised property rights, particularly Karl Renner's 'functional transformation' of property rights and Henry Smith's 'Modular Theory',[11] tend to overlook the importance of the distinction.

The next two chapters fill this gap by explaining how the mandatory standardisation of property rights provides flexibility to private law in the context of trespassory (chapter six) and successor liability (chapter seven). This chapter addresses the former by developing on its conceptual and functional elements (section I), applying them to concrete case studies coming from England (section II) and using German doctrine to account for their conceptual underpinning (section III). The chapter concludes showing how, by limiting the free creation of trespassory liability, the *numerus clausus* not only protects the general liberty of strangers, but also the specific Hohfeldian liberty of owners (including the owners of other property) to functionally transform their property in light of changing social and economic circumstances (section IV).

I. THE STRUCTURE OF TRESPASSORY LIABILITY

A. Doctrinal Elements

As shown in chapter three, German doctrine and modern Anglo-American legal theory broadly conceptualise property rights by the power of a holder of such a right to exclude everyone else from a thing and the correlative duty of third parties to keep off it. In Germany this is seen as a straightforward outcome from the doctrinal structure property rights. In this system, these rights are described as one specific kind of 'absolute right', namely an absolute right in a tangible

[8] Ben McFarlane, 'The Numerus Clausus Principle and Covenants Relating to Land' in Susan Bright (ed), *Modern Studies in Property Law*, vol 6 (Hart 2011) 311.

[9] eg Malcolm Merry, 'Landmark Cases in Land Law (Review)' (2013) 5 *Conv* 455, 455–56.

[10] See ch 3, section II and ch 5, section III.A.

[11] For these theories, see ch 1, section IV.

thing, with 'absoluteness' meaning that such rights are good against everyone.[12] In Anglo-American theory the path to reach the same conclusion is more convoluted and only (re)emerged clearly with the conceptual revolution against the bundle of rights described in chapter two.[13] In this context, Penner argued that a property right is a right to exclude others from a thing based on the interest of its holder in using such thing.[14] This link between 'right to exclude' and 'liberty to use' (using Hohfeld's terms), might be less salient in German doctrine but it is not ignored: it is apparent in accounts of property rights as 'generic private law relations'[15] and in the Hegelian underpinning of ownership.[16] For example, in the 1950s, Hermann Eichler argued that property rights have an 'internal side' that enables the owner to act over the thing (*Einwirkungsmacht*) and an 'external' side, that empowers the owner to exclude third parties from it (*Ausschließungsbefugnis*).[17]

Despite this basic similarity, claim-rights protecting property holders against strangers have a remarkably different systematic position in German and English law. In Germany, the trespassory protection of ownership is made effective by duties imposed on all others[18] which result from three different clusters of 'remedies' (*Ansprüche*):[19] (pure) proprietary claims, property claims with an obligational effect, and pure tort law claims.[20] 'Proprietary' or 'real' claims (*dingliche Ansprüche*)[21] confer primary protection for property rights by providing for strict liability legal actions that are seen as specific to property law, including an action to recover the thing unlawfully possessed by a third party, ie a *vindicatio* (§ 985 BGB), and an action to prevent third parties disturbing the owner's use of the thing by means different than dispossessing her (§ 1004 BGB).[22] For disputes only concerning the physical recovery of

[12] Hans Hermann Seiler, 'Einleitung zum Sachenrecht' in Elmar Bund and others (eds), *J. von Staudingers Kommentar zum Bürgerlichen Gesetzbuch mit Einführungsgesetz und Nebengesetzen* (Sellier & de Gruyter 2007) 23; Reinhard Gaier, 'Einleitung zum Sachenrecht' in Franz Jürgen Säcker and others (eds), *Münchner Kommentar zum BGB* (7th edn, Beck 2017) [4], [11]; Marina Wellenhofer, *Sachenrecht* (34th edn, Beck 2019) 2.

[13] See ch 2, section III.C.

[14] Especially JE Penner, *The Idea of Property in Law* (OUP 1997) chs III and VI; JE Penner, *Property Rights: A Re-Examination* (OUP 2020) ch 7.

[15] eg Karl Larenz and Manfred Wolf, *Allgemeiner Teil des Bürgerlichen Rechts* (9th edn, Beck 2004) 228. On this, see ch 2, section II.

[16] On this, see ch 5, section III.A.

[17] Eichler (n 3) 6.

[18] eg Wellenhofer (n 12) 2.

[19] Using English terminology from Christian von Bar, *The Foundations of Property Law* (OUP 2023) 5.

[20] Seiler (n 12) 43.

[21] Translation by Bar (n 19) 5 at fn 23. Its worth noting that the concept of a 'proprietary claim' was not mentioned in the original text of BGB (although, since 2010 it has been used in the new versions of §§ 197 and 198 BGB) and remains ill-defined in contemporary literature, see Seiler (n 12) 16–17.

[22] Seiler (n 12) 16–17; Gaier (n 12) [7].

things from unlawful possessors and injunctions against third parties otherwise disturbing the owner's use of the thing, these 'pure' proprietary claims'[23] would suffice but, in practice, this is often not enough. That is why the BGB also provides for 'statutory' or 'complementary' obligational claims (*gesetzliche Schuldverhältnisse* or *Begleitschuldverhältnisse*), regulating what needs to be handed over by the possessor, in addition to the thing itself, once she is defeated by the owner in a *vindicatio* trial (§ 987 BGB).[24] Finally, German tort law provides a general protection for property rights against fault-based damage inflicted by third parties. According to § 823(1) BGB '[a] person who, intentionally or negligently, unlawfully injures the life, body, health, freedom, *ownership* or another right of another person is liable to make compensation to the other party for the damage arising from this' (added emphasis). As discussed below, this provision only protects absolute rights (excluding personal rights), and German doctrine sees in this a key difference between property and personal rights. Following a textbook example, if a third party (X) damages the thing before title has passed from seller A to buyer B, the latter has no claim under tort law against X. Because B's (personal) right is only enforceable against A, such right cannot impose duties on X.[25] Nonetheless, this neat system is distorted in the case of land by the possessory protection of personal rights.[26]

The common law lacks 'pure proprietary remedies' like a Roman *vindicatio*, yielding the bulk of the protection of property rights to the law of obligations, especially the law of wrongs.[27] As a consequence, in Anglo-American theory there is not much doubt that tort law is the conceptual starting point to explain the third-party effects of property rights. For example, Penner holds that 'it is obvious that the law of property in a sense depends on the law of wrongs. … It defines the contours of the right to property, and it determines, in part, who has a property right'.[28] Thus, from a conceptual and a practical perspective, the third-party effects of common law property rights are defined by civil wrongs resulting from the duty not to physically interfere with a thing. 'Those duties are expressed in the tort law rules governing trespass, conversion, negligent damage, nuisance and so on' and make up the 'Basic Property

[23] Using Peter Birks' words referring to the Roman *vindicatio*. Peter Birks, 'Personal Property: Proprietary Rights and Remedies' (2000) 11 *King's LJ* 1, 4–5.

[24] Seiler (n 12) 20.

[25] Wellenhofer (n 12) 2. Similarly, Jan Wilhelm, *Sachenrecht* (5th edn, De Gruyter 2016) 49.

[26] See section III.B.

[27] Birks (n 23) 4, 6; Simon Douglas, *Liability for Wrongful Interferences with Chattels* (Hart 2011) 9, both discussing personal property. For discussion, Nicholas J McBride, 'Vindicatio: The Missing Remedy?' (2016) 28 *Sing Ac LJ* 1052. In land law this panorama is altered by the summary procedure for possession of land now incorporated into CPR rule 55. Note that the defendant in these cases is still referred to as a trespasser, suggesting that a tort is required. See CPR rule 55.1(b) and *Secretary of State for Environment, Food, and Rural Affairs v Meier and another (FC) and others* [2009] UKSC 11 [8].

[28] Penner, *The Idea of Property in Law* (n 14) 139. Similarly, Henry E Smith, 'Property as the Law of Things' (2012) 125 *Harv L Rev* 1691, 1693.

Norm' for tangible property.[29] All these torts impose 'strict liability' on third parties, meaning that the defendant is liable for interfering with the claimant's property, regardless of her fault.[30] In this manner, these torts impose a broad duty on strangers consisting in not physically interfering with the property of others.[31]

As in Germany, the access to tort law remedies in England is one of the salient differences between property and personal rights: in principle, the holder of a mere personal right cannot sue a third party in tort.[32] English tort law is not structured in the systematic manner of the BGB, but the idea that a claim needs to be based on interference with an interest defined as *in rem* by the law is not alien to it. In *Allen v Flood*,[33] a case involving the claim of two shipwrights against a union that pressed their employer to dismiss them, the claim was rejected because the claimants did not suffer any damage relative to their 'mind, body, [or] estate'.[34] Cave J acknowledged that the latter category, which can be 'substituted for "property" … is very general',[35] but the conceptual and practical resemblance with § 823(1) BGB is apparent. For example, in the landmark case *Hunter and others v Canary Wharf*,[36] a dispute involving nuisance caused to London residents by the construction of the Canary Wharf Tower, the House of Lords granted damages for claimants holding property rights in land, but rejected the claims of those who only held licences. Similarly, in *Leigh and Sillavan Ltd v Aliakmon Shipping Co Ltd ('The Aliakmon')*,[37] the modern leading authority for chattels,[38] a tort claim by a buyer (B) who had purchased goods from a seller (A) that were carelessly damaged by the defendant (X) prior to the passing of title, was rejected because the claimant only had a contractual right to the goods, not a property right. The resemblance with the German textbook example mentioned above is obvious. However, as discussed below,[39] in England this clear boundary between property and personal rights is distorted once Equity comes into the picture.[40]

[29] Penner, *Property Rights* (n 14) 16.

[30] Penner, *The Idea of Property in Law* (n 14) 139, 141. In cases of unintentional interference with chattels, 'fault' by the defendant is still needed. In English law, its precise meaning is contested, but it involves the defendant's failure to meet an objective conduct standard in relation to the foreseeable consequences relating to the claimant's chattel. Douglas (n 27) 141, 149, 168–70.

[31] Strict liability does not exclude the requirement of a mental state by the breacher, but it does not refer to the lawfulness of her conduct, only to her action. Douglas and McFarlane (n 7) 224–25.

[32] Penner, *The Idea of Property in Law* (n 14) 141.

[33] *Allen v Flood* [1898] AC 1.

[34] ibid 29.

[35] ibid.

[36] *Hunter and others v Canary Wharf* [1997] AC 665, HL.

[37] *Leigh and Sillavan Ltd v Aliakmon Shipping Co Ltd ('The Aliakmon')* [1986] AC 785.

[38] Douglas (n 27) 13.

[39] See section II.B.

[40] For example, the opinion expressed by Pill LJ in the Court of Appeal decision in *Hunter*, that beneficial rights of spouses should be protected against nuisance. *Hunter v London Docklands Development Corporation* [1996] 2 WLR 348, 365, CA.

B. Excluded Fact Patterns: Tortious Protection of Contractual Rights

In the framework developed above, the role of the *numerus clausus* seems simple: a stranger (X) can only become liable for interfering with the right B acquired from A, when this right is contained in the list of property rights. Other rights, especially personal rights created by freedom of contract and, in England, (most) equitable property rights, are not protected against strangers by tort law.[41] However, this outcome is not absolute. In both Germany and England personal rights *might* deserve *some protection* against third parties under tort law. However, these cases are few, they are subject to a high threshold and only impose a mild form of liability, revealing that B's initial right is not protected in the same way as a property right.

In England, the most readily apparent case is the tort of procuring a breach of contract, this is, the duty of X to refrain from inducing A to breach a contractual promise she has made to B. Due to the limitation on its ambit imposed by a conduct and a mental element,[42] the duty this tort imposes on X is different in nature from the one arising for A.[43] First, X's duty does not have the same content as that of A, as it only consists in restraining from inducing A to breach its contractual duty to B, but it does not impose on X the duty to fulfil A's obligation towards B. Following the example of the leading case in this regard,[44] when A promises B to deliver an exclusive performance at a concert hall, X is only subject to a negative and ancillary duty to B consisting in not inducing A to breach such contract, for example by entering into a second contract with A. X is not subject to the same exclusive performance duty as A. Second, to become liable to B, X must have a precise mental state, namely, believing that her conduct will lead to the breach of A's obligation to B. Finally, X's liability is dependent on an actual breach by A of its contractual duty to B.[45] Therefore, this tort is said to only create an 'accessorial liability', that is 'parasitic to a primary breach of contract'.[46] The relevant implication is that, despite providing contractual rights with a 'secondary protection' that Lord Hoffmann described as implying treating 'contractual rights as a species of property which deserve special protection …',[47] this 'special protection' does not undermine the distinction between personal and property rights.[48]

[41] Swadling, 'Property' (n 7) 180. The situation of equitable property rights is discussed in detail in section II.B.

[42] See Paul S Davies, *Accessory Liability* (Hart 2015) 132.

[43] Ben McFarlane, 'Equity, Obligations and Third Parties' (2008) *Sing J Legal Stud* 308, 315, 317; McFarlane, 'The Numerus Clausus Principle and Covenants Relating to Land' (n 8) 311.

[44] *Lumley v Gye* (1853) 2 E & B 216.

[45] *OBG Ltd v Allan* [2007] UKHL 21, [2008] 1 AC 1 [39], recently discussed by Lewison LJ in *Allen v Dodd* [2020] EWCA Civ 258 [11]–[37].

[46] Davies (n 42) 141.

[47] *OBG v Allan* (n 45) [32].

[48] McFarlane, 'Equity, Obligations and Third Parties' (n 43) 317; Ben McFarlane and Simon Douglas, 'Property, Analogy and Variety' (2022) 42 *OJLS* 161.

The situation is not that different in Germany. Since personal rights and abstract patrimonial integrity are not protected interests under § 823(1) BGB,[49] liability for inducing the breach of a contract can only be brought under § 826 BGB, which provides for intentional harm caused by a wrongful conduct *contra bonos mores*.[50] This provision has a wide objective scope that includes personal rights, but has very strict subjective requirements. Courts resort to it only when the behaviour of the offender is especially improper: 'not simply unreasonable but actually unethical, really deplorable and disgusting'.[51] Thus, to create tortious liability under § 826 BGB, the breach of the contract must be caused by a conduct consisting in a lack of consideration incompatible with decency or the basic requirements of a proper view of the law,[52] which is normally equated to intention to cause an unlawful harm.[53] Thus, as in England, under § 826 BGB, the content of X's duty in relation to the contractual rights owned by A to B is negative and ancillary, and can only be breached by fault-based conduct. However, different from Lord Hoffmann's argument seeing contractual rights as a 'species of property', in Germany the protected interest is (arguably) good morals, not B's contractual right.[54]

From a comparative perspective, this general similarity has been attributed to the circumstances that neither German nor English law hold defendants liable for pure economic harm caused by mere negligence to a person with whom the defendant has no contract.[55] However, at least from an historical perspective, the causality seems to have been the other way around. In both jurisdictions this rule is better explained as an outcome of a simple conceptualist (internal) argument developed during the nineteenth century: if X interferes with A's duty to B, the latter cannot recover from X because X owes no duty to B.[56] Accordingly, the similarity between both systems is best explained by this shared doctrinal structure, although the policy argument might be necessary to explain why X has no duty to B.

The relevant implication for this chapter is that the strict requirements of the English tort of inducing the breach of a contract and of § 826 BGB when applied to similar cases, have a function akin to that of the *numerus clausus*: both limit the effects private dealings have on third parties. This also explains why it is normally so important to establish whether the interest held by the claimant

[49] See section III.A.

[50] RG, JW 1913, 866; RG, RGZ 78, 14, 17; BGH, NJW 1981, 2184; BGH, NJW 1994, 128; BGH, JZ 1996, 416.

[51] Tony Weir, *Economic Torts* (OUP 1997) 46.

[52] Basil S Markensis, John Bell, André Janssen (eds), *Markesinis's German Law of Torts: A Comparative Treatise* (5th edn, Hart 2019) 78–81, 85.

[53] Weir (n 51) 46.

[54] James Gordley, *Foundations of Private Law* (OUP 2006) 273.

[55] Weir (n 51) 45.

[56] Gordley (n 54) 270–80.

qualifies as a right *in rem*. If it does not, the defendant will normally not be liable for the economic damage she caused to the claimant.

C. Functional Structure: ABX Patterns

Building on the doctrinal elements of the previous subsection, 'trespassory liability' can be functionally characterised as a negative duty that *prima facie* everyone owes to the holder of a property right, unconditionally of time and regardless of their position in respect to the owner. In Penner's words, all others (X) have a duty 'not to interfere', 'keep-off' or 'leave alone' the things that are not their own.[57] That is why Merrill and Smith described the rights correlative to this duty as 'pure *in rem* rights', meaning cases where the duty holders are numerous and indefinite.[58]

It is important to note that the emergence of a conflict between B and X does not depend on X having or claiming a property right over the same thing as B: X's interference with B's right in the thing might or might not be backed by a claim of X's own property rights in the thing. In fact, frequently X has no pre-existing property claims to the thing or relies on her property right in a different thing.[59] As shown in chapter seven, this is a structural difference from successor liability, as these cases only arise when a third party (C) claims to have or have had, at the relevant moment, a competing property right over the same thing as B, typically also acquired from A.[60]

If property rights are explained through trespassory liability, a simple functional structure emerges: when A grants B a right in connection to a thing, if this right qualifies as a property right, then all others (X), regardless of their relation to A, B or the thing, will immediately come under a *prima facie* duty to B not to interfere with such thing. Thus, despite being a *stranger* to the AB dealing, X is bound by the right A conferred on B (see Figure 2). The content of this duty is always negative and is typically made of three specific duties: not depriving B of her possession of the thing (eg § 985 BGB and the tort of conversion); not physically interfering with or disturbing B's use of the thing (eg § 1004 BGB and the tort of trespass); and not otherwise unreasonably physically interfering with B's enjoyment of the thing (eg §§ 1004 and 823(1) BGB and the torts of

[57] Penner, *The Idea of Property in Law* (n 14) 28, 73; Penner, 'Duty and Liability in Respect of Funds' (n 6) 215; JE Penner, 'Property' in *The Oxford Handbook of New Private Law* (OUP 2021) 238.

[58] Thomas W Merrill and Henry E Smith, 'The Property/Contract Interface' (2001) 101 *Colum L Rev* 773, 784–85.

[59] For example, discussing the law of nuisance, the tortfeasor might be a non-owner. Penner, *Property Rights* (n 14) 145.

[60] See ch 7, section I.

nuisance and negligence). In this book, fact patterns following this structure are labelled 'ABX cases'.

Figure 2 ABX patterns ('trespassory liability')

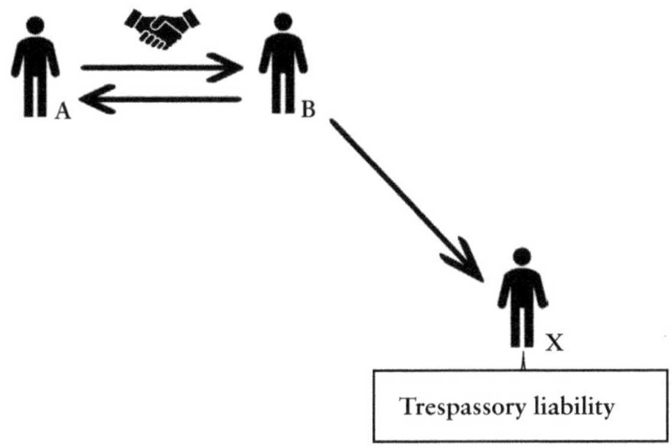

The most salient effect of trespassory liability is that it permits A and B to bind people they may have never seen, heard or known about. In other words, the ABX effect of property rights binds *complete strangers*. This is made possible because ABX relations are mediated through things, permitting people to interact through dealings that are not personal in any significant way. Thereby property law provides the basic framework for the general and impersonal practices upon which modern societies largely depend.[61] The paramount importance of the impersonal nature of property rights is reflected in the vocabulary of German limited property rights: 'things' are burdened (*Dinge werden belasstet*), not people.[62] In the Anglo-American context Honoré explains the same by describing property interests as rights that cannot be divested by alienation of the property.[63] This feature of property rights plays a central role in Henry Smith's Modular Theory.[64] According to the latter, property law organises the world by packaging legal relations around useful attributes that tend to be strong complements. The property system defines these things by using an 'exclusion strategy' and then enriches the system using 'governance strategies', for more sophisticated relations.[65] In this model the 'exclusion strategy' is essentially trespassory liability explained by its function of lowering informational costs.

At first impression, the *numerus clausus* only plays the trivial function of identifying which of B's rights will have ABX effects. However, the implications of this go well beyond. As discussed in chapter five, different arguments have

[61] Penner, *The Idea of Property in Law* (n 14) 27, 30, 128.
[62] Eichler (n 3) 2–4.
[63] Honoré (n 5) 464.
[64] For details, see ch 1, section III and IV.
[65] Smith (n 28) 1693–94, 1709.

been put forward to explain the deeper rationale that underpins the *numerus clausus*. For example, economic analysis emphasises the efficiency gains achieved by limiting and standardising property rights, but neglects that the *numerus clausus* also limits trespassory liability. In contrast, conceptual accounts tend to bring the protection of trespassers (X) against non-consented duties to the forefront. Building on this, some elements of Smith's Modular Theory and the conclusions submitted in chapter five, the rest of this chapter will show how, by containing the ABX effects of AB dealings, the *numerus clausus* not only lowers transaction costs and protects X's liberty as a matter of principle, but also facilitates the functional transformation of property rights. For this, English law will provide most of the examples, while German law will serve to flesh out their conceptual underpinning.

II. ENGLAND: *IN PERSONAM* AND EQUITABLE PROPERTY RIGHTS *VIS A VIS* STRANGERS

A. The Protection of Innovative Activities

A thorough assessment of the practical impact of a legal doctrine over time requires an historical approach that goes beyond the scope of this book. This chapter (and the next) can only suggest how the *numerus clausus* might shape the operation of private law over time by discussing a few examples and developing arguments based on them. In the case of English law, this is facilitated by the rich casuistic reasoning of its law and the historical depth of its doctrine. In this specific case, this is further eased by a happy coincidence: the leading case discussing the impact of the *numerus clausus* on trespassory liability can be linked, without field research, to a well-known historical process, while another more recent landmark case dealing with the protection of interests in land is connected to an extensively documented urban development in London.

i. From Georgian Transport to Victorian Leisure

In *Hill v Tupper*,[66] Mr Hill (B) had acquired the exclusive right to hire out pleasure boats on a canal from a canal company (A). After Mr Tupper (X), the owner of an adjacent pub, also started hiring boats out for pleasure, B sued X for damages. B's claim was rejected by Pollock CB holding that X was not bound by the right B acquired from A, because such a right is not a property right acknowledged by the law. In other words, even if the principle was not

[66] *Hill v Tupper* (1863) 2 H & C 121, 159 ER 51.

mentioned as such, the court refused to enforce B's right against X because it was not in the *numerus clausus* of property rights.[67]

Within the boundaries of the case, Pollock CB's argument seems the narrow outcome of a formalistic doctrine. However, its impact in preserving the flexibility of property rights becomes apparent as soon as the case is seen in its wider context. The canal involved in the dispute was built in 1794,[68] that is, during the second outburst of the British 'canal-mania' of the late eighteenth century.[69] Due to their ability to provide high-capacity transport that was both reliable and low-cost, the transformation of Britain's inland waterways during this age has been described as one of the most spectacular innovations of the First Industrial Revolution,[70] and has been credited with a decisive role in Britain's shift from an organically powered economy to a coal-fueled economy.[71] However, by the time of *Hill*, the canal age was largely over, as the massive development of rail transport after 1830 had made Britain's inland waterways largely obsolete for trade.[72] At the same, the increased per head economic output brought about by the second industrialisation implied that, after 1850, living standards in Britain were growing rapidly.[73] Both trends can be seen at play in this case. The deal between the Canal Company and Mr Hill seems to have been motivated by the company's attempt to replace its decaying transport business with the increasingly popular activity of pleasure boating.[74] In other words, while the changes triggered by the Second Industrial Revolution made canals increasingly less useful for trade, they also made them more appealing as places to provide leisure activities for the new urban population of Victorian times, eager to spend their new free time and higher wages visiting the countryside.[75]

It is tempting to see Pollock CB's decision to deny the enforceability of Mr Hill's right as a hurdle to the re-conversion of the canal into a leisure attraction. However, this would be a mistake. Mr Tupper was the owner of a pub opened beside the same canal only three years before the deal between the Canal Company and Mr Hill. Thus, by allowing the visitors of his pub to use his boats for fishing and bathing, Mr Tupper was already playing a relevant role

[67] Also see, ch 3, section III.A.

[68] McFarlane, 'The Numerus Clausus Principle and Covenants Relating to Land' (n 8) 5.

[69] Phyllis Deane, *The First Industrial Revolution* (2nd edn, CUP 1980) 78.

[70] ibid 78–80.

[71] James Vernon, *Modern Britain: 1750 to the Present* (CUP 2017) 94–95; Brian A'Hearn, 'The British Industrial Revolution in a European Mirror' in Roderick Floud, Jane Humphries and Paul Johnson (eds), *The Cambridge Economic History of Modern Britain*, vol I 1700–1870 (CUP 2014) 44.

[72] Mark Casson, *The World's First Railway System: Enterprise, Competition, and Regulation on the Railway Network in Victorian Britain* (OUP 2009) 2, 4, 31.

[73] A'Hearn (n 71) 4.

[74] McFarlane, 'The Numerus Clausus Principle and Covenants Relating to Land' (n 8) 6.

[75] See Judith Flanders, *Consuming Passions: Leisure and Pleasure in Victorian Britain* (Harper 2006) 205–10, 216–19.

in adapting a canal from the Georgian period to the new reality of Victorian Britain. If Mr Tupper had been found liable to Mr Hill, the liberty of private parties to adapt their land to new circumstances would have been diminished, not increased: thanks to the freedom preserved by the principle of *numerus clausus*, there were more people (an indefinite number of Xs) with the liberty (as against B) to change the use of their land to satisfy the new leisure needs of a modern and more affluent urban society.

It is worth stressing that the problem of enforcing the claimant's right in *Hill* does not seem to have been the creation of a monopoly over the use of the canal for pleasure boating, but the allocation of such a monopoly to a person different than its owner. Discussing this case in the context of the operation of the *numerus clausus* in the law of easements, Lord Briggs recently argued that, even if the right to put pleasure boats in the canal had accommodated the land (one of the requirements of an easement),[76] suing for 'an infringement of it by another pleasure boat operator would had required the plaintiff to sue in his landlord's name as the owner of the canal'.[77] This suggests that the problem of enforcing Mr Hill's right against Mr Tupper is that it would have separated the decision as to who can put pleasure boats on the canal from the ownership of the canal itself, including all other decisions over it. This would have affected not only Mr Tupper and other strangers owning land adjoining the canal, but also the modular structure of the ownership of the canal itself. The wider implications of this type of arrangement, including the potential anti-commons scenarios, will be discussed in chapter seven.

ii. From Nineteenth Century Trade to Twenty-first Century Global Finance

Hunter v Canary Wharf[78] offers a contemporary example of the same mechanism. The area known as the Isle of Dogs was originally developed at the turn of the nineteenth century by the West India Docks Company to satisfy the pressing need for new port infrastructure in a period in which London was at the heart of global trade. The area boomed with business for the following one and a half centuries: 'Canary Wharf' was the name of a dock built in this area in 1936 to serve the fruit trade.[79]

Despite massive investment in reconstructing the area after the Second World War, by the 1960s the future of London's up-river docks had turned bleak, due to the emergence of containers for cargo handling, changes in the patterns

[76] See *Re Ellenborough Park* [1956] Ch 131, CA.

[77] *Regency Villas Title Ltd v Diamond Resorts (Europe) Ltd*, [2017] EWCA Civ 238 [56].

[78] See section I.A.

[79] 'The West India Docks: Historical Development', *Survey of London: Volume 43 and 44, Poplar, Blackwall and the Isle of Dogs* (Hermione Hobhouse 1994) www.british-history.ac.uk/survey-london/vols43-4/pp248-268, accessed 9 December 2020.

of world trade, its relative distance from the sea, and increasing competition from other British ports.[80] During the 1970s, as the individual docks started to close, the Isle of Dogs became one of the largest failing areas in the UK. Finally, in 1980, the whole area was shut down, turning it into a 'disconnected continent' that looked 'dark and isolated'.[81] At the same time, after decades of being mostly relegated to the domestic market, London was entering into a new era of 'financial globalisation'.[82] In this context, the construction of the Canary Wharf Tower (officially, One Canada Square) during the late 1980s and early 1990s was the spearhead of a redevelopment project that made the London docklands flourish again, this time not with trade, but with global finance. In 2012 the Financial Times even reported that Canary Wharf was overtaking the City of London as the largest employer of bankers in Europe.[83]

The spectacular shift of the Isle of Dogs from abandoned nineteenth century trade port to twenty-first century financial services hub can obviously not be explained by *Hunter* alone, as other factors, including liberal zoning, subventions, tax benefits and the extension of public transport services, surely played a more decisive role.[84] Nonetheless, this case still played its part. By holding that only claimants having property rights were entitled to damages and denying actions to claimants who only held licences,[85] the House of Lords preserved important liberties of the developers as against licensees: if the residents-claimants (B) had been allowed to cluster actions based on property and personal rights, such claims would have effectivity 'cloned' the duties the developers (X) owed to those with property rights in the affected land. The court did not explicitly rely on the *numerus clausus* principle to avoid this end, but on the idea that 'nuisance is a tort to land'.[86] Nonetheless, the decision is underpinned by the same principle: only parties holding a direct right in land (*in rem*), that is, a property right, are protected against strangers.

The relevance of this principle in preserving the liberty of third parties might seem to fade away when the remedy sued for by B is an injunction, which is likely in nuisance cases.[87] In such scenarios, if a single claimant holding

[80] ibid.

[81] Moore Rowan, *Slow Burn City* (Picador 2017) 46, 49.

[82] David Chambers, 'The City and the Corporate Economy since 1870' in *The Cambridge Economic History of Modern Britain*, vol II 1870 to the Present (CUP 2014) 257.

[83] Rowan (n 81) 49, 52.

[84] On the relevance of regulation, see Maria Lee, 'Hunter v Canary Wharf Ltd (1997)' in Charles Mitchell and Paul Mitchell (eds), *Landmark Cases in the Law of Tort* (Hart 2010).

[85] The actual reasoning in *Hunter* (n 36) is more complex. Lord Goff held that a 'licensees with exclusive possession' would also be entitled to a tort claim (at 692), which in turn seems to run against the basic authority holding that exclusive possession leads to a lease (*Street v Mountford* [1985] AC 809). Nonetheless, the holding seems to be pointing to the direct proprietary effect of direct exclusive possession (see Lord Hoffmann in *Hunter* (n 36) at 705–06), not to the personal rights of a licensee.

[86] *Hunter* (n 36) 687.

[87] eg *Coventry v Lawrence* [2014] UKSC 13.

a property right succeeds in stopping X's activity, all other affected parties, including those not holding property rights, will benefit from the injunction. However, this does not really undermine the effect of the *numerus clausus*, as only those holding property rights will be able to obtain an injunction. This imposes a structural limit on the number of Bs X will have to deal with, for example, when obtaining their consent to develop the adjacent land via a 'Coasean bargain'. Thus, the 'freeride' that those not holding property rights might obtain from B's injunction is largely irrelevant for X's liberty to functionally transform her land.

This rationale also addresses a common argument made against the *numerus clasusus*. In *Stockport Waterworks Co v Potter*,[88] the majority rejected the claim of B, who had acquired a right to use a waterway from a riparian owner (A), against a stranger (X) who had polluted the stream. The court held that, as A had retained the riparian land and could not deal separately with the water right, only A had been wronged by X. Dissenting, Bramwell B criticised this view, arguing that, if X committed a wrong against A by polluting the stream, there is no reason X should not also be liable to compensate B.[89] This suggests the following argument: if X is already barred from using its property in a certain way (eg polluting the water) as a result of a duty towards A, enforcing B's right against X, does not take any new liberty away from X. However, this is not accurate: allowing B to directly claim in her own name against X multiplies the number of right holders X must indemnify or deal with to achieve a 'Coasean bargain'.

B. Accounting for Deviations

The basic idea put forward in the previous subsection is challenged by a few cases in which rights that are not within the closed list of property rights have been allowed to create trespassory liability, including personal rights and equitable property rights. On its face, this implies an open breach of the principle of *numerus clausus* as, according to it, personal and equitable property rights do not have the ability to bind trespassers. This subsection accounts for these deviations, arguing that some are justified exceptions, while others are simply wrongly decided cases. After briefly discussing the case of licensees in possession, this subsection will expand on cases involving equitable property rights, because these represent the most important challenge to the *numerus clasusus* principle in England.[90]

[88] *Stockport Waterworks Co v Potter* (1864) 3 H & C 300.
[89] ibid 319.
[90] See ch 3, section III.

i. Licence to Occupy v Licensee in Occupation

As discussed in chapter two,[91] a basic principle of English private law is that only property rights can bind third parties. This principle seems to have been openly breached in *Manchester Airport plc v Dutton and others*.[92] In this case, the National Trust (A), the owner of a piece of land, gave Manchester Airport plc (B), and its subcontractors contractual permission to enter such land to carry out some works (ie A gave B a contractual licence). Before B entered onto the land, a group of environmental protestors (X) occupied it, and B applied for an order of possession against X. Despite acknowledging that B had a purely personal right against A, the majority of the Court of Appeal decided to enforce B's right against X. The three judges sitting on this case agreed that if B had been in possession under the licence *before* X's interference, B could have brought the claim for possession against X. Building on this, the majority opinion delivered by Laws LJ argued that not extending this protection to the licensee not yet in possession was based on a 'false assumption' and that the 'true principle is that a licensee not in occupation may claim possession against a trespasser if that is a necessary remedy to … give effect to such … licence'.[93]

Dutton has been met with heavy criticism for breaching the *numerus clausus* of property rights. According to William Swadling,[94] by excessively focusing on making a remedy available to B, Laws LJ failed to notice that contractual licensees in possession (B) have two different rights coming from different sources. The first has its origin in contract and entitles B to demand possession from the licensor (A), while the second comes from the fact of possession and grants B a property right which is therefore binding on strangers (X). Thus, commentators have argued that Chadwick LJ's dissent, which made this distinction, should be preferred. In this view, the same outcome could have been met by arguments consistent with the *numerus clausus*: B could have forced A to seek possession against X to comply with A's contractual obligation to B.[95] If the critics are correct, cases such as *Dutton*[96] do not amount to a conceptual challenge to the *numerus clausus*, but only to poorly reasoned cases.

ii. Trespassory Protection of Equitable Property Rights?

In principle, equitable property rights only bind successors in title,[97] not imposing duties on strangers that might restrict their freedom to use their

[91] See ch 2, section III.
[92] *Manchester Airport plc v Dutton and others* [2000] QB 133, CA.
[93] ibid 149–50.
[94] William Swadling, 'Opening the Numerus Clausus' (2000) 116 *LQR* 354.
[95] Ben McFarlane, *The Structure of Property Law* (Hart 2008) 345, fn 22. Also see Oscar Han, 'Licensee versus Trespasser: Hill v Tupper Resuscitated' (2016) 6 *Prop L Rev* 87.
[96] eg Lord Neuberger *in obiter* in *Mayor of London v Hall and others* [2010] EWCA Civ 817 [27].
[97] Swadling, 'Property' (n 7) 180. Also see FW Maitland, *Equity: A Course of Lectures* (AH Chaytor and WJ Whittaker eds, 2nd rev, CUP 1936) 169–70.

property. For example, if A grants B an equitable lease in Blackacre, this right might bind A's successor in title (C), but it does not impose any new duty on the owner of Whiteacre (X). However, case law evidences the existence of a handful of holdings that have allowed different forms of equitable property rights to bind strangers. This subsection discusses these deviations, by distinguishing between (i) cases that create true exceptions to the effect of the *numerus clausus* on ABX liability (ie the restrictive covenant) and (ii) holdings that seem better explained as wrongly decided cases (cases involving rights held on trust).

a. Restrictive covenants as a 'Legal Scaffolding'

As explained in chapter three,[98] probably the main breach to the principle of *numerus clausus* in English law was the emergence of the restrictive covenant during the second half of the nineteenth century. By means of a line of cases that can be traced to *Tulk v Moxhay*,[99] the Court of Chancery developed a new equitable property right that facilitated the sale of, and release of capital from, urban land by enforcing negative duties regarding the use of land against successors in title,[100] and thereby permitting the seller to exercise some control on future developments.

However, the development of the restrictive covenant did not stop there. After the turn of the twentieth century, in *Re Nisbet and Potts Contract*[101] the courts expanded the binding effect of restrictive covenants beyond the natural ABC scope of equitable rights. *Nisbet* concerned a piece of land transferred by someone holding only possessory title to the land, that is, a squatter (X1) to X2 who had no knowledge that prior to her possession, the paper-title owner (A), had granted a restrictive covenant to another person (B). The court held that, even though A's title to the land was barred by adverse possession, B could still enforce her covenant against X2, despite the latter not being a successor in title to the grantor of the covenant nor being aware of its existence. As a result, English doctrine acknowledges restrictive covenants as an exception to the principle holding that equitable property rights do not have ABX effects.[102]

Nisbet has been said to be indefensible from a purely conceptual perspective.[103] The decision was subject to early criticism,[104] and contemporary English scholars who argue for the recognition of equitable property rights

[98] See ch 3, section III.C.
[99] *Tulk v Moxhay* (1848) 2 Ph 774, 41 ER 1143.
[100] Ben McFarlane, 'Tulk v Moxhay (1848)' in Charles Mitchell and Paul Mitchell (eds), *Landmark Cases in Equity* (Hart 2012) 204–11.
[101] *Re Nisbet and Potts Contract* [1906] 1 Ch 386, CA.
[102] Swadling, 'Property' (n 7) 180.
[103] McFarlane, 'The Numerus Clausus Principle and Covenants Relating to Land' (n 8) 319.
[104] Maitland (n 97) 166–67, 169–70.

as a discrete category ('persistent rights') conceptually different from (legal) property rights and obligations,[105] acknowledge that the trespassory effect of restrictive covenants makes them difficult to accommodate with other 'persistent rights',[106] forcing them to treat restrictive covenants as 'a special case'.[107] For them, this does not imply that the decision in *Nisbet* is necessarily a bad one, but that it is dangerous to rely on it to reach broader conclusions regarding the nature of equitable property rights.[108] In this view, the trespassory effects of restrictive covenants can only be justified by their practical outcomes: the restriction is offset by the increase in the amenity of the neighbouring land;[109] an argument already present in Cozen-Hardy LJ's opinion in *Nisbet*, who openly argued that the value of an estate in a city depends upon 'the continuance of the mutual restrictive covenants affecting the user and enjoyment of property'.[110]

In Smith's Modular Theory, this utilitarian justification of the ABX effect of restrictive covenants seems to be captured by the basic 'exclusionary strategy'. In order to reduce informational costs, this strategy divides the world into chunks and delegates the decisions over them to the owner, with exclusion from third parties.[111] In this case, the exclusionary rule protecting B's land is expanded to the land subject to the restrictive covenant in favour of B, thereby reshaping its property module. From B's perspective, this expansion makes sense: the covenant is highly complementary to her use of the land. However, in practice, B can only rely on this benefit if the covenant binds *all* third parties, including squatters (X). In the modern urban context, when B buys a part of A's land, B not only needs to be sure that A and A's successors (C) will not use the rest of the land for a particular purpose, but also that pure strangers (X) will be precluded from doing so. This certainty is evaporated if B cannot assert her rights against X. Thus, by allowing restrictive covenants to bind squatters, the law facilitates that parties deal separately with a piece of land pertaining to larger plot: on the one hand, the purchaser (B) can functionally transform the separated piece, while, on the other, A can raise funds to functionally transform the section of the plot she retains.[112] Of course, this means that X is not only liable towards A for trespassing on the land, but also towards B for breaching the restrictive covenant. This is justified by the benefits that this form of liability has for private urban development, that is, by pure policy reasons.

[105] See ch 2, section III.

[106] See McFarlane, 'Equity, Obligations and Third Parties' (n 43) 322, fn 67.

[107] See McFarlane and Stevens (n 7) 14.

[108] McFarlane, 'Tulk v Moxhay (1848)' (n 100) 231.

[109] McFarlane, 'The Numerus Clausus Principle and Covenants Relating to Land' (n 8) 319; McFarlane and Stevens (n 7) 14.

[110] *Nisbet* (n 101) 409.

[111] Smith (n 28) 1693, 1694, 1702, 1703; Henry E Smith, 'Economics of Property Law' in Francesco Parisi (ed), *The Oxford Handbook of Law and Economics: Volume 2: Private Law and Commercial Law* (OUP 2017) 149, 150, 159, 160.

[112] McFarlane, 'Tulk v Moxhay (1848)' (n 100) 228.

However, the trespassory effects of restrictive covenants could also be accounted for in a different manner. Instead of justifying its exceptional effects in utilitarian considerations, one could argue that the oddity of this right lies in a conceptual problem: these rights are described as 'equitable', despite having the essential hallmarks of 'legal' interests in land. This becomes apparent in the attempts to categorise restrictive covenants and easements from a comparative perspective, as their civilian counterparts make one single category of servitudes.[113] Furthermore, that restrictive covenants might have more in common with legal interest is apparent in the strange position they occupy among equitable property rights. According to English scholarship, equitable property rights fall in three groups: equitable versions of legal rights (equitable lease, equitable easement, etc); beneficial rights held in trust; and 'other equitable rights',[114] which do not really seem to have any conceptual unity. The need for a catch-all term to accommodate restrictive covenants within equitable property rights suggest that it does not have much in common with the rest of them. Indeed, the Law Commission has suggested that legislation should acknowledge that covenants in freehold land operate as legal rights,[115] which would complete the transition of the restrictive covenant from purely personal to legal property right.[116]

If the foregoing is correct, what needs to be explained is not why restrictive covenants bind strangers, but why they remain equitable rights. Such reasons are not obvious and, certainly, cannot be based on the conceptual structure of restrictive covenants. Nonetheless, from the perspective of the *numerus clausus*, the restrictive covenant is better explained as a full member of the list: in English land law, the rights that have ABX effects are legal property rights and restrictive covenants. This could be seen as the (almost) final stage of a process by which successive 'legal scaffolding'[117] used to solve urban policy challenges converted restrictive covenants, first, from pure personal right, only binding A, into equitable rights, also binding successors in title (C), and then, into entitlement entirely functionally equivalent to legal property right, by making them binding on X; a path that resembles that of the right of lessees from personal to property rights.[118]

[113] eg see Bernard Rudden, 'Economic Theory v. Property Law: The Numerus Clausus Problem' in John Eekelaar and John Bell (eds), *Oxford Essays in Jurisprudence: Third Series* (Clarendon 1987) 242.

[114] Swadling, 'Property' (n 7) 180, 181.

[115] Law Commission, Making Land Work: Easements, Covenants and Profits à Prendre' (Law Com No 327, 2011).

[116] See McFarlane, 'The Numerus Clausus Principle and Covenants Relating to Land' (n 8) 320–21.

[117] This is a back-up mechanism in which a complex combination of existing legal categories is used to cure or moderate the divergence between law and social need. Alan Watson, *Society and Legal Change* (Temple UP 2001) 87, 91, 122. For details, see ch 8, section III.C.

[118] On leases, Simon Gardner, '"Persistent Rights" Appraised' in Nicholas Hopkins (ed), *Modern Studies in Property Law*, vol 7 (Hart 2013) 328.

b. Beneficial Rights in Trusts

The other challenge to the *numerus clausus* created by rights with ABX effects derives from cases in which beneficial rights under trusts have been enforced against strangers (X). When Merrill and Smith put rights held in trust in a *continuum* between personal and property rights, they attributed the oddity of these rights to their quasi-multital effects, that is, to the ability of beneficial rights to bind a small number of indefinite people, who essentially correspond to the successors in title of the trustee. From the perspective of tort law, they did not see any grey-area problem, as they relied on the general view that the right to sue in tort is exclusive to legal owners.[119] In the same line, when Penner distinguished between trespassory and successor liability, he held that the trustee has all the trespassory rights to the trust property, while the beneficiaries' rights are good only against successors.[120] Thus, a Hohfeldian analysis shows that when a trust is declared, the trustee (A) comes under a duty towards the beneficiary (B), while strangers (X) remain only bound to A. Consistent with this, A can declare a trust in favour of B without altering X's position. That is why, according to Douglas and McFarlane, there is no need for a *numerus clausus* of beneficial rights in trusts.[121] This does not imply that the beneficiary (B) is not protected against damage to the trust property, but only that the party entitled to sue in tort is the trustee and that the damages recovered from X will be held by A on trust for B.[122] The picture that emerges is that beneficial interests in trusts behave as obligations *vis a vis* strangers: X can simply ignore B's beneficial rights, because these only bind A. Thus, since rights held in trust do not impose duties on strangers, there is no need to protect their liberty by having a closed list of beneficial rights. By the same token, the problems rights held in trust create for the *numerus clausus* are, primarily, a matter of successor liability.[123]

This understating of the operation of trusts has been recently challenged in England by the Court of Appeal, forcing a re-evaluation of the meaning of the *numerus clausus* in ABX contexts. In *Shell UK Ltd and others v Total UK Ltd and others*,[124] the defendant (X)[125] damaged infrastructure held by two services companies (A) in trust for beneficiaries, including Shell (B). Shell sued X for the loss resulting from not being able to supply its clients. Relying on precedents that prevent beneficial owners from directly suing in tort for damage to the trust property,[126] the first instance court held that X did not have any duty of

[119] Merrill and Smith (n 58) 846.
[120] Penner, 'Duty and Liability in Respect of Funds' (n 6) 216.
[121] Douglas and McFarlane (n 7) 240–41.
[122] See *Lord Compton's Case* (1568) 3 Leo 196; *Earl of Worcester v Finch* (1600) 4 Co Inst 85; *The Aliakmon* (n 37); *MCC Proceeds Inc v Lehman Bros* [1998] 4 All ER 675.
[123] See ch 7, section II.
[124] *Shell UK Ltd and others v Total UK Ltd and others* [2010] EWCA Civ 180, [2011] QB 86.
[125] Also a beneficiary but that did not make any difference here.
[126] *The Aliakmon* (n 37).

care towards Shell. The tribunal argued that the latter did not hold legal rights in the infrastructure nor in the land where it was placed, therefore describing the damage suffered by Shell as pure economic loss,[127] which is not usually indemnifiable in negligence in English law.[128] Nonetheless, the Court of Appeal reversed this decision arguing that the precedent did not cover the case of a joint lawsuit by beneficial and legal owners. Building on this, the court granted damages to Shell, arguing that it would be 'legalistic' to deny compensation under the exclusionary rule. After acknowledging that such claims can only succeed if there is a 'special relation' that creates enough proximity between the defendant (X) and person suffering the economic loss (B), the court found that beneficial ('real') ownership of the damaged property did give rise to such relation.[129] Permission to appeal to the Supreme Court was given, but the case was settled.

The reasoning of *Shell* has been met with criticism for both doctrinal and policy reasons. As to the first, the holding not only goes against precedents and overlooks the conceptual structure of trusts,[130] but is also internally inconsistent, as its treatment of Shell's damages as pure economic loss precisely assumes that Shell did *not* have any kind of property right in the pipes or the land.[131] Moreover, the reliance of the Court of Appeal on the existence of 'a special relation' allowing a derivative action against the defendant is also flawed, as the existence of a trust does not by itself create the 'special circumstances' that enable a beneficiary to sue directly in tort.[132] Thus, it is probably safe to disregard the challenge that *Shell* imposes on the *numerus clausus* arguing that it is wrongly reasoned, especially since it did not reach the Supreme Court.

Contrario sensu, *Shell* also shows how a strict enforcement of the *numerus clausus* helps to keep property law flexible by preserving the liberty of strangers to deal with their own property. If private parties are allowed to freely create rights with trespassory effects, the indefinite liability such rights might impose on strangers will make it increasingly hard for everyone else to develop any new activity with their own property. This is apparent when the outcome of *Shell* is contrasted with both *Hill* and *Hunter*. In the latter cases, the limitation of the trespassory effects of B's rights was instrumental in enabling the

[127] *Colour Quest Ltd and others v Total Downstream UK plc and others* [2009] EWHC 540 (Comm) [518]–[520].

[128] James Edelman, 'Two Fundamental Questions for the Law of Trusts' (2013) 129 *LQR* 66, 69.

[129] *Shell* (n 124) [136], [144].

[130] Edelman (n 128) 71.

[131] Ben McFarlane, Nicholas Hopkins and Sarah Nield, *Land Law: Text, Cases and Materials* (5th edn, OUP 2021) 192.

[132] William Swadling, 'In Defence of Formalism' in Andrew Robertson and James Goudkamp (eds), *Form and Substance in the Law of Obligations* (Hart 2019) 109–10; Ben McFarlane, 'Form and Substance in Equity' in Andrew Robertson and James Goudkamp (eds), *Form and Substance in the Law of Obligations* (Hart 2019) 205–06. Note that the trust creates a relation between A and B, not B and X.

defendants to continue with projects that served to functionally adapt their property rights to new realities, while the effect of *Shell* would be multiplying the potential liability for those acting on their own property.

This raises an obvious question: how can a rule that preserves the liberty of X to damage B be justified?[133] From the perspective of economic analysis of law, the answer would be simple: the rule is justified if the benefit to X exceeds the costs it imposes on B.[134] However, this is not relevant here. The point of the *numerus clausus* is not that it allows X to efficiently damage B, but that it denies A and B the right to create a *new* and *additional* liability for X: the latter is *already* liable for damaging A's property. The *numerus clausus* is not aimed as a rule that allows X to be careless, but to prevent A from cloning its rights in favour of an indefinite number of Bs, as this will impose new non-consented duties on all Xs. In *Shell*, B could have also chosen to be the legal owner of the damaged site, but for good reasons it did not. B cannot have the benefits of the trust and at the same time have the rights of the legal owner.

III. GERMANY: PERSONAL RIGHTS *VIS A VIS* STRANGERS

A. The Protection of Personal Freedom

This section shows how the basic mechanics of English law discussed in the previous section is replicated by German law. Due to the more systematic nature of German private law, this will provide a much clearer conceptual framework to explain why the *numerus clausus* is insolubly tied to the protection of strangers and the functional transformation of property rights. However, analysing the impact of the *numerus clausus* on trespassory liability in German law presents challenges of its own. Whilst comparative lawyers see English tort law as a collection of separate wrongs developed by case law since the Middle Ages,[135] the German law of 'illicit actions' (*Recht der Unerlaubte Handlungen*) or 'law of delicts' (*Deliktsrecht*) is a consciously designed statutory system that entered into force at a precise moment in time (1900) and has not significantly changed since then.[136] The manner in which German scholarship explains this system emphasises the exegesis of black-letter rules and accounts for its practical operation by the creation of stylised 'case groups' (*Fallgruppen*) which are discussed detached from its broader socio-historical context, making it harder to locate history-laden examples such as those found in English tort law.

[133] For example, in *Stockport*, discussed above (see section II.A.ii).

[134] Moreover, in a world with no transaction costs, the initial allocation of the right to damage would be irrelevant. See Ronald Coase, 'The Problem of Social Cost' (1960) 3 *J Law and Econ* 1.

[135] Konrad Zweigert and Hein Kötz, *An Introduction to Comparative Law* (Tony Weir tr, 3rd edn, OUP 1998) 605.

[136] This does not mean that there have not been legal reforms (eg 1909 Unfair Competition Act, 1909 Road Traffic Act or 1959 Atomic Energy Act), only that they have not altered its core.

However, by the same token, German doctrine offers an explicit systematic account of the principles that underpin its tort law that is not readily available in England.[137] Despite normally not relying on the *numerus clausus* of property rights,[138] this explanation provides a clear conceptual account as to why having a closed number of fixed property types ensures the wider flexibility of private law, serving to rationalise the more casuistic English approach. This cross-fertilisation is facilitated by the great resemblance between some German and English cases.

i. Freedom of Action

As in other civilian systems,[139] the main aim of German tort law is indemnifying people who suffer damage caused by third parties.[140] However, this system also has the 'freedom of action' (*Handlungsfreiheit*) of strangers as one of its central concerns.[141] As mentioned above,[142] the cornerstone of this system is § 823(1) BGB, which provides for a limited list of interests deserving protection against damage caused by fault-based conduct. This basic rule is supplemented by two general provisions both with a very narrow scope. One deals with damage arising from the breach of a legislative norm intended to protect another person (§ 823(2) BGB) and the other with intentional harm that breaches a legal-ethical minimum (§ 826 BGB).[143]

From a comparative viewpoint, the manner in which German law defines the scope of protection of tort law has been seen as closer to the Anglo-American limitation of the duty of care than to the general clause of the other civilian systems, especially France.[144] From an historical perspective, this solution was a compromise between those who wanted a general liability clause similar to the original Art 1382 of the French *Code Civil* (today Art 1240), holding that '[a]ny human action whatsoever which causes harm to another creates an obligation

[137] On the different style of English and civilian tort law, Pierre Catala and John Antony Weir, 'Delict and Torts: A Study in Parallel – Part IV' (1964–5) 39 *Tul L Rev* 701, 781.

[138] But the link has been explored by Marietta Auer, *Der Privatrechtliche Diskurs der Moderne* (Mohr Siebeck 2014) 118–19, 126.

[139] Gerhard Wagner, 'Comparative Tort Law' in Mathias Reimann and Reinhard Zimmermann (eds), *The Oxford Handbook of Comparative Law* (2nd edn, OUP 2019) 996.

[140] Johannes Hager, 'Das Recht der Unerlaubten Handlungen' in Dagmar Kaiser and Markus Stoffels (eds), *J. Staudingers Kommentar zum Bürgerlichen Gesetzbuch mit Einführungsgestetz und Nebengesetzen. Eckpfeiler des Zivilrechts* (6th edn, Sellier & de Gruyter 2018) 100; Hartwig Sprau, 'Unerlaubte Handlungen', *Palandt: Bürgerlicher Gesetzbuch mit Nebengesetzten* (80th edn, Beck 2021) 1410.

[141] See Stephan Lorenz, 'Grundwissen – Zivilrecht: Deliktsrecht – Haftung aus § 823 I BGB' [2019] *JuS* 852, 852.

[142] See section I.

[143] Hager (n 140) 1191, 1192. For a general explanation in English, see Bell, Jansen and Markensis (n 52) 72–86.

[144] eg Wagner (n 139) 1005.

in the person by whose fault it occurred to make reparation for it',[145] and those who favoured a casuistic approach similar to the English. The outcome reflects a conscious aim to avoid the judicial development of tort law and a deep scepticism towards the open-ended case law developed by the French judiciary under the general liability clause of the *Code*.[146] According to James Gordley, this is underpinned by a conceptual not a consequentialist argument. In this view, third parties can only become liable in tort for affecting an absolute right because only those rights are good against everyone: contractual rights cannot be violated by anyone other than the debtor. Thus, the protection § 826 BGB offers in cases of inducement of a breach of a contract is not explained by the unlawful violation of the claimant's personal rights, but by the violation of good morals.[147] After the entering into force of the GG, the narrow scope of German tortious liability gained a further constitutional underpinning in the general right to the free development of personality contained in Art 2 GG.[148]

Due to this conscious design, even if this system is not explained from the perspective of property rights, contemporary German doctrine is very much aware of the tension that trespassory liability creates between the holder of a property right (B) and the freedom of strangers (X). For example, a leading *Kommentar* holds that the more intense the protection tort law provides victims, the more the liberty of the perpetrator is curtailed.[149] The BGB strikes this balance by allowing tortious liability only for the injury of well-defined legal interests: life, body, health, freedom and ownership (§ 823(1) BGB). The list also contains one open-ended term providing for the injury of 'other rights' (*Sonstige Rechte*), but this does not mean that any right held by a person will be subject to protection. Leading *Kommentare* agree that only interests that share the absolute nature of the other rights in the list, that is, rights that have an exclusionary character (*Ausschließlichkeitscharakter*)[150] or function (*Ausschlussfunktion*),[151] deserve protection under this section. Accordingly, the most salient examples of 'other rights' are limited property rights, property rights in intangible assets and personality rights. By the same token, scholarship and case law consistently hold that relative rights and abstract patrimonial integrity are not protected by § 823(1) BGB.[152] Some textbooks even hold that this provision itself follows

[145] Translation by John Cartwright and Simon Whittaker, available at http://translex.uni-koeln.de/601101/highlight_john_cartwright_simon_whittaker/french-civil-code-2016/, accessed 31 January 2022.
[146] Wagner (n 139) 1000; Bell, Jansen and Markensis (n 52) 16.
[147] Gordley (n 54) 272–73.
[148] Lorenz (n 141) 852.
[149] Hager (n 140) 1191.
[150] Sprau (n 140) 1419.
[151] Hager (n 140) 1204.
[152] ibid 1419; Sprau (n 140) 1204, 1205.

a *numerus clausus* rule,[153] although doctrine does normally not invoke the *numerus clausus* of property rights in this context.[154]

For German doctrine, the most salient outcome of this system is that, beside those exceptional cases that might arise under §§ 823(2) and 826 BGB, strangers are not subject to liability for causing 'primary patrimonial damage' to others,[155] which has been held to be broadly equivalent to the English treatment of pure economic loss.[156] As explained, this was not a consciously established policy of the drafters of the BGB, but emerged from case law after the entering into force of the code, as a logical consequence of the conceptual structure of German tort law.[157] Cases confirming this are abundant. For example, an ice skater, whose partner suffers an accident that impedes him from skating with her, cannot obtain damages for the economic loss she experienced because they were not able to perform together.[158]

The line between what constitutes an injury to a property right and what only qualify as pure patrimonial damages is very fine. This is apparent in the so called 'cable cases' (*Kabelbruchfälle* or *Kabelfälle*).[159] In the *Hatching Eggs* case (*Bruteierfall*)[160] a stranger (X) damaged some electricity cables when cutting trees, interrupting the energy supply to an incubator and spoiling most of the eggs owned by the claimant (B). The BGH upheld the damage claim under § 823(1) BGB because the spoiled eggs were within the ownership of the claimant. However, in another cable case,[161] a building company (X) conducting excavations on private land damaged some cables, interrupting the energy supply of a neighbouring printer (B). B sued for the damages caused by the interruption in its production, but the BGH dismissed the claim, arguing that B's ownership had not been injured. The similarity of these cases with English landmark holdings in the same field is striking. In *Spartan Steel & Alloys Ltd v Martin & Co (Contractors) Ltd*,[162] a case involving the interruption of the energy supply to a steel company, the Court of Appeal reached the same basic outcome based on a very similar reasoning that distinguished the ingots that could not be processed (pure economic loss) from the ingots owned by the claimant that suffered damage because they were already in the melt when power was lost.

Due to this foundational decision of reserving tort law for the protection of absolute rights, in Germany, the duty not to damage the patrimony of another

[153] eg Karl-Nikolaus Peifer, *Schuldrecht: Gesetzliche Schuldverältnissse* (5th edn, Nomos 2016) 42–43.

[154] But see n 138.

[155] See Sprau (n 140) 1410, 1419; Hager (n 140) 1191, 1192; Lorenz (n 141) 852, 854.

[156] Weir (n 51) 45; Wagner (n 139) 1008.

[157] See RG, 11 Apr 1901, ERGZ 48, 114; RG 27 Feb 1904, ERGZ 58, 24, as discussed by Gordley (n 54) 272.

[158] BGH NJW 2003, 1040, 1041 as discussed by Hager (n 140) 1192.

[159] Hager (n 140) 1201.

[160] BGHZ 41, 123. NJW 1964, 720.

[161] BGHZ, 66 388. NJW 1976, 1740.

[162] *Spartan Steel & Alloys Ltd v Martin & Co (Contractors) Ltd* [1973] 1 QB 27.

person can normally only arise within the context of contractual relations.[163] In practice, this means that A cannot give B a right that imposes a new duty on X, unless such right is either contained in the closed list of property rights or the correlative duty is accepted by X, converting it into an AB case. In this manner, German private law ensures that X retains a broad freedom to do as she wishes, including the exercise of a Hohfeldian liberty over her own property. Probably due to the neat structure of § 823(1), German law does not directly link this effect to the *numerus clausus* of property rights, but case law reveals a reasoning that is underpinned by the same conceptual logic. For example, in a case in which the managing director (B) of a hospital was unlawfully fired by his employer (A) due to pressure applied by a group of its physicians (X) and could not later find a job, the Federal Court for Labour Law (*Bundesarbeitsgericht*, BAG) denied B's claim against X, arguing that the right to a workplace that A owed to B was a relative right and therefore excluded from the protection of § 823(1).[164] This case has some resemblance to *Allen v Flood*,[165] as in that case the claim of the shipwrights (B) against the union (X) for pressing their employer (A) to dismiss them was rejected because B were hired on a day-by-day basis and, therefore, had no right that could be damaged by X.

This rationality is not limited to labour law cases. In the more recent *Gewinn.de* case,[166] the claimant (B) acquired from the German Internet Domain Administrator (A) the right to use a certain internet domain. Later, the domain ceased to be listed under B's name and was registered by the defendant (X). B sued X, requesting to be reinstalled in the domain, but the BGH denied the claim, arguing that the holder of an internet domain only has a relative right against A and, therefore, cannot enforce its rights against X. Thus, as in *Hill*,[167] despite not making an explicit link to the *numerus clausus* principle, by limiting tortious liability to violation of absolute rights, these cases show how the very structure of German tort law ensures that, within the general framework of the law, X retains a broad liberty to do as she wishes, including the general liberty to act upon her property, and does not have more duties than those arising from her own will or from the closed list of property rights. In this manner § 823(1) BGB seems to operate in a fashion similar to *Allen v Flood*.

ii. Implications for 'Borderline Cases'

Once the effect of the *numerus clausus* in trespassory liability is clearly identified, the significance of the deviations from it come under a different light. For example, as discussed in chapter three,[168] German doctrine tends to see the

[163] Hager (n 140) 1192–93.
[164] BAG, NJW 1999, 164.
[165] See n 33 and accompanying text.
[166] BGH, I ZR 187/10.
[167] One can assume that the domain registration was intended to be exclusive.
[168] See ch 3, section II.C.

judicial creation of security ownership as one of the most relevant breaches of the principle of *numerus clausus*. In a transfer for security purposes (*Sicherungsübeignung*) B transfers its full ownership over a specific (normally) moveable asset to A by means of constructive delivery (*constituto posessiorio*), with B retaining 'possession for another' (*Fremdbesitz*) and A acquiring 'indirect possession' over it (*mittelbarer Besitz*). Thus, on one side, under the rules of property law, A becomes the full owner of the thing thanks to the constructive delivery and, on the other, A also comes under a purely contractual obligation towards B to only exercise such ownership to sell the thing if B defaults and only for the purpose of covering the outstanding debt, giving rise to a case of *Treuhand*.[169] However, despite only holding a personal right against A, B might enforce its 'indirect right' to the thing against third parties in two scenarios.

The first are cases in which other creditors of A (C) want to enforce their rights over the asset B transferred to A for security purposes (*Einzelzwangsvollstreckung*). In these cases courts have held that A is still bound by its agreement with B, implying that B can prevent the creditors from selling the thing to satisfy their debts under § 771 ZPO, thereby authorising B to enforce 'its indirect right on the thing' against third parties. Similarly, if A becomes insolvent (*Insolvenzverfahren*), B can directly claim the thing under §§ 47 and 51 InsO, as long she has not defaulted on the secured transaction.[170] A second group of cases are those in which A breaches its duty towards B and sells the thing to a third party (C). In these cases, B *might* be able to claim damages from C under § 826 BGB, if the latter had knowledge of the AB agreement.[171]

In none of these scenarios does the AB dealing create a new duty upon a stranger (X) who might become liable for breach without fault. In the first group of cases the AB dealing does not impose any new duty on the creditors, who only lose the chance to sell one of the assets in A's possession to repay their credit.[172] The significance of this should not be overstated. When A is not insolvent, the creditor might proceed to sell any of the other assets owned by A and, when A is insolvent, B can only recover the thing if she has paid her debt to A. As to the second case, in principle, strangers (X) are not encumbered by B's right in the goods transferred to A for security purposes. As with the English trusts, in principle only A's property right exists for X. The only exception to

[169] Carsten Herresthal, 'Das Recht der Kreditsicherung' in Dagmar Kaiser and Markus Stoffels (eds), *J. Staudingers Kommentar zum Bürgerlichen Gesetzbuch mit Einführungsgestetz und Nebengesetzen Eckpfeiler des Zivilrechts* (6th edn, Sellier & de Gruyter 2018) 695–702; Sebastian Herrler and Hartmut Wiecke, 'Sachenrecht', *Palandt Bürgerlicher Gesetzbuch mit Nebengesetzten* (80th edn, Beck 2021) 1619–22.

[170] Wilhelm (n 25) 1091–93, describing both cases. See also Herrler and Wiecke (n 169) 1622.

[171] BGH NJW RR, 1993, 367.

[172] For example, the RG ruled security transfers over whole deposits and inventories of changing goods invalid. Werner Schubert, 'Die Diskussion über eine Reform des Rechts der Mobiliarsicherheiten in der Späten Kaiserzeit und in der Weimarer Zeit' (1990) 107 *ZRG Germ Abt* 132, 142–45. Currently, the viability of these general guarantees is seen, at least, as 'problematic' as a result of the difficulties in identifying the goods, eg Herresthal (n 169) 697.

this is the possible liability of X under § 826 BGB, but as discussed above, this is an extremely exceptional, very low intensity duty that responds to a different rationale. Thus, from the perspective of trespassory liability, security ownership does not really seem to breach the *numerus clausus* of property rights. When adapting their property to new circumstances, strangers do not need to mind non-consented duties arising for them as a result of security transfers. Hence, the real significance of security ownership as a property right 'outside the *numerus clausus*' is found in its ability to bind successors in title, which will be discussed in chapter seven.

B. The Impact of Possession

The general exclusion of trespassory liability for personal rights is distorted by the role that possession plays in German property law. The nature of possession has been said to be one of the most radical differences between civil and common law systems.[173] In contrast to common lawyers who tend to equalise possession with title,[174] civilian lawyers see possession as a mere fact that does not *per se* give any right to the possessor of a thing;[175] although they also acknowledge that it is a factual circumstance which might have relevant legal implications.

In the case of Germany, the factual nature of possession (*Besitz*) is seen as positively recognised in § 854(1) BGB, which holds that possession over a thing is acquired through the exercise of actual power over it. Such possession is different from ownership and does not amount to a property right.[176] However, the possessor of a thing still enjoys a certain level of protection against third-party interference that is independent of her having title to the thing (see §§ 858 to 864 BGB). In particular, § 858 BGB protects the possessor from non-consented deprivations or disturbances of her possession.[177]

The protection property law provides to possessors *regardless of title* has led to possession being considered one of the 'other rights' protected under § 823(1) BGB.[178] This raises a problematic question: if possession is only a fact (and not a right), why should it be protected? The nature and extent of this protection is

[173] eg Gordley (n 54) 47–51.

[174] ibid 50–51.

[175] Except for first possession cases, see § 958 BGB.

[176] In the context of property law: Herrler and Wiecke (n 169) 1537; Fabian Klinck, 'Sachenrecht' in Dagmar Kaiser and Markus Stoffels (eds), *J. Staudingers Kommentar zum Bürgerlichen Gesetzbuch mit Einführungsgestetz und Nebengesetzen: Eckpfeiler des Zivilrechts* (6th edn, Sellier & de Gruyter 2018) 1278–79, 1306–07; in the context of tort law: Wolfgang Fikentscher and Andreas Heinemann, *Schuldrecht: Allegemeiner und Besonderer Teil* (11th edn, De Gruyter 2017) 930.

[177] In this context, Dieter Schwab and Martin Löhnig, *Einführung in das Zivilrecht* (20th edn, CF Müller 2016) 140–41. In general, Herrler and Wiecke (n 169) 1541–45; Klinck (n 176) 1289–1303.

[178] Klinck (n 176) 1306, 1307; Wellenhofer (n 12) 64; Schwab and Löhnig (n 177) 140. For an explanation in English, see Bell, Jansen and Markensis (n 52) 37.

highly contested[179] and there is no agreement on whether protection is provided to possession or to the right to possess,[180] nor on whether the unlawful possessor is also entitled to such protection.[181] Nonetheless, it is generally accepted that a possessor with no title who can use the thing in a manner similar to the owner is entitled to protection under tort law.[182] For example, based on his possession of a rented flat, the BGH allowed a tenant (B), who only held a personal right against the landlord (A), to recover damages under § 823(1) BGB from another tenant (X) whose construction activity negatively affected B's medical practice.[183]

This has far-reaching consequences for the structure of German private law. Although doctrinal accounts do not state it in this manner, from a functional perspective, even when B's possession is based on a mere contract with A, B's possession will be protected against strangers (X). For example, shortly after German re-unification a *Gemeinde* of Saxony hired an architecture firm to redevelop a site into an industrial park, which in turn sub-contracted execution of the works to a building company (*Building Company* case).[184] The day the works were scheduled to begin, protestors blocked the access of the builders to the site. The BGH granted damages to the building company under § 823(1) BGB arguing that it was in rightful possession of the site.[185]

The *Building Company* case has an obvious resemblance with *Dutton*, but some relevant distinctions must be made. In English law, possession gives a property right to the possessor. According to Chadwick LJ's dissent, in *Dutton*, the problem was that the claimant had not yet entered in possession and, therefore, could not *yet* have a property right. By contrast, in German law, possession is not a subjective right nor gives the possessor any property right until the prescription term has elapsed and, in the case of land, the possessor is registered as owner.[186] Thus, in the *Building Company* case the BGH did not argue that the claimant had or was entitled to a property right because of its possession, but relied on the direct protection of possession of the land *as a fact*.

From the perspective of the division between relative and absolute rights, probably the most salient effect of the possessory protection of the non-owner arises in the context of leases. As discussed in chapter two,[187] in German law,

[179] Schwab and Löhnig (n 177) 141.

[180] Lorenz (n 141) 854.

[181] Fikentscher and Heinemann (n 176) 930.

[182] Sprau (n 140) 1419; Lorenz (n 141) 854; Hager (n 140) 1206; Fikentscher and Heinemann (n 176) 930; Schwab and Löhnig (n 177) 141. For an explanation in English, Bell, Jansen and Markensis (n 52) 37.

[183] BGH, JZ 1954, 613, discussed by Eberhard Wieser, 'Der Schadensersatzanspruch des Besitzers aus § 823 BGB' [1970] Juristische Schulung 557.

[184] BGHZ 137, 89.

[185] From the holding it is not clear whether the building company was already in possession of the site, but the reasoning of the court assumed that it was.

[186] Ownership is not acquired by possession, but by *usucapion*. See § 927 BGB for land and § 937 BGB for movables.

[187] See ch 2, section II.C.

leases only provide lessees (B) with a personal right against lessors (A) to obtain possession, which is enforceable against A's successors in title (C). However, once B enters in possession, B's relation to the land becomes protected under § 823(1) BGB, making her position 'absolute' and, therefore, binding on strangers (X).[188] From a functional perspective, this brings the position of German tenants far closer to that of English leaseholders than normally assumed: after entering in possession, the tenant is also protected against strangers. Nonetheless, as explained below, the (doctrinal) justification for this protection is not based on the proprietary nature of possession – or at least not directly.

The impact that possessory protection has on the number of people who are bound by B's rights seems a massive erosion to the German version of the *numerus clausus*: once the holder of a relative right (B) enters in possession, all strangers (X) become bound by something that is not a property right. However, German doctrine does not see in this a breach of the *numerus clausus*. To a certain extent this can be explained by the overlap of the values safeguarded by the *numerus clausus* and by the protection of possession as a fact.

This cannot be explicated without accounting for the (unclear) position that possessory protection has in German law. The conceptualist approach that underpins civilian systems defines an owner as a person with the right to use a thing as she wishes. In this view, the owner has the right to possess. The implicit outcome is that possessors without ownership are persons without a proprietary right to possess. At least since the nineteenth century, this has led to an unsettled debate as to why bare possessors deserve protection. One position, normally associated with Rudolf von Jhering, bases this protection in ensuring the continuous access of the possessor to the thing as its most probable owner. This so called 'Personality' or 'Continuity Theory' (*Persönlichkeits* or *Kontinuitätstheorie*) was the leading position during the nineteenth century and was supported by the Pandectist scholars who drafted the BGB. However, following Friedrich Carl von Savigny's 'Peace Theory' (*Friedenstheorie*), nowadays the majoritarian view grounds the protection of possession in keeping social peace and avoiding private violence.[189]

Despite their merits, neither of these two views provides a reason to protect possessors 'as such'.[190] At least from a conceptual perspective, this is a relevant difference with English law. Because the protection granted to lessees by §823(1) BGB is presented as derivative from the general protection of possession, this might shed some light on the situation of the *numerus clausus*. According to the Peace Theory, the trespassory protection of the lessee is not grounded on making her personal right against A proprietary, but in the general social interest of protecting *any* possessor from the private violence of strangers, including

[188] See Schwab and Löhnig (n 177) 141.
[189] See Klinck (n 176) 1288–90; Gordley (n 54) 53–58.
[190] Gordley (n 54) 57.

purely contractual tenants. Following the Personality or Continuity Theory, this protection could be seen as mere manifestation of the general duty not to interfere that strangers owe to the (most probable) owner of the thing. From the perspective of the *numerus clausus*, this suggests that the trespassory protection of lessees in possession does not aim to create a new and additional duty on strangers, but to protect the thing, regardless of whether it is possessed by the owner or by someone having a purely contractual right to possess derivative from that of the owner.

This idea is reinforced by the doctrinal structure of possession in Germany. When an owner (A) gives a tenant (B) a personal right to possesses her thing, strictly speaking, possessory rights are not cloned but functionally divided: A retains 'indirect possession' (*mittelbarer Besitz*) in the object, relevant for *usucapio*, while B is in 'possession for another' (*Fremdbesitz*), which entitles her to file injunctions to protect or recover her possession from strangers under §§ 858 to 863 BGB.[191] Hence, the possessory protection of lessees does not seem to multiply duties on X. What this 'functionally divided possession' implies for claims under § 823(1) BGB – in particular, to what extent X interference with the thing makes her liable to A or B – requires in-depth research on German tort law that is beyond the scope of this book. However, considering the broad functional and ideological similarity underpinning the limitation of trespassory liability in English and German law, it would not be surprising if the German outcome would be similar to the English.

IV. FUNCTIONAL TRANSFORMATION: THE IMPORTANCE OF HOHFELDIAN LIBERTIES

As discussed in chapter three,[192] comparative research argues that the principle of *numerus clausus* has different degrees of stringency across jurisdictions,[193] especially once Anglo-American equitable property rights come into the picture.[194] This chapter suggests that such a conclusion might be too broad to be fully accurate, as it does not pay sufficient attention to the different effects that property rights have on strangers and successors in title. Although German doctrine does not link it to the *numerus clausus* of property rights, and English scholarship has only recently started to explore this relation, this chapter has

[191] Klinck (n 176) 1316.

[192] See ch 3, section I.

[193] eg Bram Akkermans, 'The Numerus Clausus of Property Rights' in Michele Graziadei and Lionel Smith (eds), *Comparative Property Law: Global Perspectives* (Edward Elgar 2017) 105, 106; Christian von Bar, 'The Numerus Clausus of Property Rights: A European Principle?' in Louise Gullifer and Stefan Vogenauer (eds), *English and European Perspectives on Contract and Commercial Law: Essays in Honour of Hugh Beale* (Hart 2014) 454.

[194] See Peter Sparkes, 'Certainty of Property: Numerus Clausus or the Rule with No Name?' (2012) 20 *Euro Rev Priv L* 769.

shown, that in both jurisdictions, if analysis is restricted to trespassory liability, from a functional perspective, this principle has very stringent effects on the creation of new duties upon strangers. Despite some minor deviations that can be accounted for, trespassory liability can only be created in the cases foreseen by the law: private parties cannot create new ABX cases by pure contractual freedom.

The restriction that the *numerus clausus* imposes on the contractual creation of trespassory liability ensures that property law remains stable and flexible at the same time. From this perspective, the key is in limiting the cases in which X will become liable to B to (i) cases where B has a recognised property right; and (ii) standardised low-intensity duties. The protection that the *numerus clausus* gives to X is partially underpinned by the same rationality of the protection that trespassory liability provides to B. For example, nuisance, is a tort that aims to keep B's land 'usable'.[195] In a similar fashion, by limiting the liability of the tortfeasor (X) *vis a vis* B, the *numerus clausus* ensures that X will be able to use her own property (and the property of any other party) without incurring liability to an indefinite number of parties (B1, B2, etc). Thus, thanks to this principle, A and B cannot take a liberty from X, unless in the limited cases and in low intensity forms authorised by the law.

On the surface, this seems to be nothing else than a piece in the internal legal machinery of the exclusionary strategy of the Modular Theory (ie the concentration in one person of a bulk of complementary uses of a thing). However, the effects of the *numerus clausus* go beyond this. The main concern of the Modular Theory is lowering of informational costs. Nonetheless, the limits that the *numerus clausus* imposes on private dealing also prohibit A and B from changing the structure of A's module, at least *vis a vis* all Xs. Despite rare cases that respond to a different rationale as inducing the breach of a contract, this implies that X's freedom is effectively protected by the *numerus clausus*, including her liberty to act upon her property according to the circumstances. By this means, the *numerus clausus* ensures that 'functional transformation' of property rights identified by Karl Renner as instrumental to the shift from an agricultural to an industrial economy in the nineteenth century[196] remains in operation in the twenty-first century.

The internal rationale of these systems is well explained by the systematic style of German doctrine, while its practical effects are better accounted by the historically loaded English case law. According to German doctrine, limiting tort law claims to the protection of a closed list of well-defined interests is central to protecting the 'freedom of action' of the general public, while English case law of the mid nineteenth and the late twentieth century reveals how the protection

[195] Donal Nolan, 'The Essence of Private Nuisance' in Ben McFarlane and Sinéad Agnew (eds), *Modern Studies in Property Law*, vol 10 (Hart 2019).

[196] Karl Renner, *The Institutions of Private Law and their Social Functions* (Agnes Schwarzschild tr, Routledge and Kegan Paul 1976).

of strangers facilitates the 'functional transformation' of old property rights in practice: from Georgian transport to Victorian leisure, from imperial trade to contemporary global finance.

A key element of this system is that it works 'through the thing'. Due to the very concept of a property right in German law and the rise of thing-based conceptions of property in Anglo-American theory, this might sound obvious, but its implications have not been fully developed, especially in a comparative context. In England, the doctrine of relativity of title seems to make possession the ultimate reason for the direct protection of B's right over the thing against X. In German law, the same effect is achieved by the protection of possession *as a fact*, even if its justification remains unsettled. The implications of this are twofold: on the one hand, X does not need to know whether things are owned by A, B1 or B2. If things are not hers, she simply must stay off them.[197] On the other hand, this also protects X. As things cannot be subject to multiple competing possessions at once,[198] at any point in time, only one party can be in possession.[199] Thus, the mediation of ABX liability through possession of things imposes a structural limitation on the number of parties that can have a claim against X and thereby permits the latter to easily buy them out through Coasean dealings.[200]

The resulting mental image is that of the *numerus clausus* acting as a firewall that protects X from the effects of AB dealings. This firewall ensures that, some low-intensity duties aside (eg liability for procuring a breach of contract), X will not be subject to new additional duties (or liabilities) that restrict her freedom, other than those arising from a limited set of clearly identified rights, justified by well-thought-out policy considerations, normally decided by legislators giving due consideration to the general operation of the system. In England, this *numerus clausus* is made of legal property rights and restrictive covenants; while in Germany, where the list is built differently, it compromises property rights and possession, as one of the 'other rights' mentioned in § 823(1) BGB.

[197] Penner, *The Idea of Property in Law* (n 14) 75–76.

[198] This is straightforward in Germany, see Klinck (n 176) 1284. In England this is more complex, but a similar picture emerges from co-ownership of land: a legal estate can only be held by co-owners in joint tenancy, which is defined by the unity of possession. Tenancy in common in land can only exist behind the trust curtain (LPA 1925, ss 1(6), 36(2)).

[199] This party can be made of more than one person, as when A and B have a joint right to exclusive possession, see *Antoniades v Villiers* [1990] 1 AC 417, HL.

[200] Other limited property rights, not dependent on possession (eg servitudes), follow a different rationale. The cloning effect of these rights is limited by controlling their content.

7

Numerus Clausus *and* *Successor Liability*

As explained in previous chapters, one of the key features of property rights is their ability to create successor liability: when A grants a property right in a thing to B and then A grants or transfers a new property right in the same thing to C, B's right is (or can be) binding on C. In simple term, the basic effect of successor liability is that older property rights bind subsequent acquirers of rights in the same thing. However, as shown in chapter two, the conceptual place of this liability in Germany and England is different. In the former, the impact of B's property right on A's successor in title (C) does not play a relevant role in accounting for the conceptual nature of property rights, as this is seen as a self-evident outcome from their absolute nature. In contrast, in England, successor liability is at the heart of the doctrinal concept of a property right, evidencing an odd disconnection with the emphasis Anglo-American property theory places on trespassory liability for conceptual purposes.

This chapter discusses the impact that the *numerus clausus* has on the contractual creation of successor liability, regardless of how it is labelled in domestic doctrine. It starts by unearthing the functional structure of successor liability (section I). Then, it addresses how the *numerus clausus* controls this liability in England (section II) and Germany (section III). Finally it concludes (section IV) putting forward three main ideas: first, that the substantive form in which the *numerus clausus* standardises English and German property rights provides property law with a doctrinal structure that is inherently capable of accommodating new realities; second, that in neither jurisdiction does the *numerus clausus* control all forms of successor liability, providing further (although limited) space for party autonomy; and third, that there also are limits as to what private parties can achieve through the functional transformation of property rights, making the legislative creation of new modules of property necessary in certain contexts.

I. THE STRUCTURE OF SUCCESSOR LIABILITY

A. Doctrinal Elements

In German law, successor liability seems extremely straightforward: older property rights simply take priority over newer rights (eg § 879 BGB).[1] Due to the basic 'publicity principle' (*Publizitätsgrundsatz*) that underpins German property law,[2] in land law, this temporal priority is normally easy to establish because transfers of land are subject to registration in the Land Book (*Grundbuch*), while limited property rights in land can only be granted by registration in it (§ 873(1) BGB).[3] So, when A grants a limited property right in land to B and then transfers ownership of the land to C, the latter acquires subject to B's right, or in technical terms, to the 'real rights that burden the land'. In the case of moveable property, when registration is not available, the publicity principle is normally satisfied by possession (see § 929 BGB),[4] which is why under the original design of the BGB, goods could only by pledged by handing them over (§ 1205 BGB).[5] Accordingly, in Germany, successor liability tends to be absolute in the sense that it binds all successors, without having an elaborate system of priorities or defenses that creates fine-grained exceptions to the basic temporal criteria.

In this context, the real puzzle that successor liability poses to the German version of the *numerus clausus* arises from a few borderline cases. First, as shown in chapter two,[6] despite not being property rights, under § 566 BGB, the rights that lessors of immovable property (A) grant lessees (B) are enforceable against successors in title (C). Second, as discussed in chapter three,[7] when B transfers ownership over a moveable asset to A with the sole purpose of securing a loan, B's interest in the thing might be enforced against A's creditors and successors, despite not being a legally acknowledged property right. However, German doctrine normally rationalises these intermediate forms as personal rights with anomalously extensive third-party effects,[8] placing the need for their justification in the law of obligations, not in property law.

English law is less straightforward. From a technical perspective, this derives from equitable property rights and statutory priorities. However, this complexity

[1] Marina Wellenhofer, *Sachenrecht* (34th edn, Beck 2019) 258–59, 283, 244.

[2] Fritz Baur, Jürgen Baur and Rolf Stürner, *Sachenrecht* (18th edn, Beck 2009) 168, 170.

[3] Wellenhofer (n 1) 246, 261; Fabian Klinck, 'Sachenrecht' in Dagmar Kaiser and Markus Stoffels (eds), *J. Staudingers Kommentar zum Bürgerlichen Gesetzbuch mit Einführungsgestetz und Nebengesetzen: Eckpfeiler Des Zivilrechts* (6th edn, Sellier & de Gruyter 2018) 1355.

[4] Wellenhofer (n 1) 27; Klinck (n 3) 1274.

[5] Carsten Herresthal, 'Das Recht der Kreditsicherung' in Dagmar Kaiser and Markus Stoffels (eds), *J. Staudingers Kommentar zum Bürgerlichen Gesetzbuch mit Einführungsgestetz und Nebengesetzen: Eckpfeiler Des Zivilrechts* (6th edn, Sellier & de Gruyter 2018) 665–66. On this, see ch 3, section II.C.

[6] See ch 2, section II.C.

[7] See ch 3, section II.C.

[8] See n 24.

is underpinned by a subtle but essential conceptual difference from German law. In England, the ability of property interests to bind successors does not imply that such rights will *always* bind third parties, but only that they *prima facie* will. The most notable example is the right of the beneficiary of a trust: in general, if the trustee (A) who holds a property right for the benefit of B, conveys such right to C in breach of trust, B will not be able to recover from C if the latter acquired the right in good faith, for value and without actual, implied or constructive notice of the breach.[9]

In land law, statuary overreaching and priorities add further complexity.[10] Not that different from German law, the starting point of English law is that the first right in time prevails (eg LRA 2002, s 28).[11] However, in registered land, successors in title have two relevant defences against pre-exiting property rights that, in practice, make this principle far less decisive. The first is inbuilt in the registration system. Under LRA 2002, s 29 a registrable disposition of a registered estate made for a valuable consideration is not affected by previous unregistered interests, bringing the practical operation of the English Land Registry closer to the German Land Book, especially as the entrance of a notice for rights under a trust is not possible (LRA 2002, s 33(a)(i)).[12] However, C cannot rely on this defence when B has an 'overriding interest', including, for example, a legal lease for seven years or less, this is, a non-registrable lease (LRA 2002, Sch 3, para 1)[13] or a property right in actual occupation (LRA 2002, Sch 3, para 2). The second exception comes from general land law: statutory overreaching enables C to acquire registered and unregistered land free from most pre-existing equitable interests, including especially beneficial interests under trusts, provided that certain requirements as to the payment of any capital money are met (LPA 1925, ss 2 and 27).

B. Functional Structure: ABC Patterns

At a doctrinal level, these defences make successor liability in English and German land law very different. When the analysis is restricted to those rights that each system labels as 'property rights' the following picture emerges: in Germany, property rights in land can only be acquired by registration and are always binding upon successors. By contrast, in England, registration is not always required for the acquisition of property rights in land and, under certain circumstances, non-registered interests, both legal and equitable, can also bind

[9] William Swadling, 'Property: General Principles' in Andrew Burrows (ed), *English Private Law* (3rd edn, OUP 2013) 213. Also see *Pilcher v Rawlins* (1872) 7 Ch App 259.

[10] The same is true for movable property. See Richard Calnan, *Taking Security* (4th edn, LexisNexis 2018) ch 8.

[11] For movable property, see ibid, para 8.17.

[12] Although entry of a restriction is possible (LRA 2002, s 40).

[13] That is, leases not subject to registration (LRA 2002, s 4(c)(i)).

successors. However, if German law is seen from a purely functional perspective that considers all rights that might have ABC effects, regardless of the way they are classified by doctrine, it becomes apparent that successors can also be bound by interests that are not part of the *numerus clausus* nor subject to registration, including leases in land and non-possessory pledges. Considering that in both England and Germany the effect that the *numerus clausus* on trespassory liability is more stringent,[14] this implies that both systems recognise some interests that do not have ABX effects (at least nor *per se*),[15] but that are still capable of binding specific successors in title ('pure ABC rights').

Due to the different conceptual starting points that English and German doctrines take to the concept of a property right, this similarity has not been highlighted enough in comparative law. In England, 'pure ABC rights' are seen as a part of property law and form a self-standing analytical category that needs to be explained, namely equitable property rights.[16] By contrast, in Germany, where the doctrinal starting point of property rights is their absolute nature and successor liability is seen as a logical consequence, rights that *only* have ABC effects cannot be easily accommodated as part of property law. Hence, such rights are normally accounted for as anomalous personal rights, with far reaching third-party effects.[17] The implication is that in both systems successor liability is not only triggered by rights that have ABX effects, but also by a group of rights that *only* give rise to successor liability or 'pure ABC rights'.

However, there is subtle difference on how German and English law conceptualise successor liability. In German law this protection is apparent in the persistence and enforceability of the right itself: the acquirer of a thing burdened with a real right (C) must simply accept that such a right impacts her: property rights are enforceable against successors in title, despite the fact that they are not bound through a personal dealing with the new proprietor.[18] In contrast, in the Anglo-American context, successor liability is not characterised by all others *presently* owing a duty to B, but by the fact that all *may* become successors in title of A at some point.[19]

Thus, once successor liability is stripped of doctrinal elements, the following (preliminary) functional structure emerges: when A grants or transfers a right in a thing to B, anyone else that later acquires a right in the same thing from A or its successors in title (C) will (or may) become subject to B's rights. Thus, if C acquires A's title, the former *may* come under the same duty to B, despite being

[14] See ch 6.

[15] See ch 6, section III on the possessory protection of German leases.

[16] See ch 2, section III.

[17] See n 24.

[18] Hermann Eichler, *Institutionen Des Sachenrechts*, vol 1 (Duncker & Humblot 1954) 6–7.

[19] James Penner, 'Duty and Liability in Respect of Funds' in John Lowry and Mistelis Loukas (eds), *Commercial Law: Perspectives and Practice* (LexisNexis Butterworths 2006) 215.

a third party to the AB dealing (hereinafter, 'ABC cases'). Whether C is *actually* bound by B's right will depend on doctrinal aspects that are unique to each legal system but normally include the content of the rights (ie whether it is on the list of property rights), formalities (including registration), occupation and C having knowledge or notice.

Figure 3 ABC patterns ('successor liability')

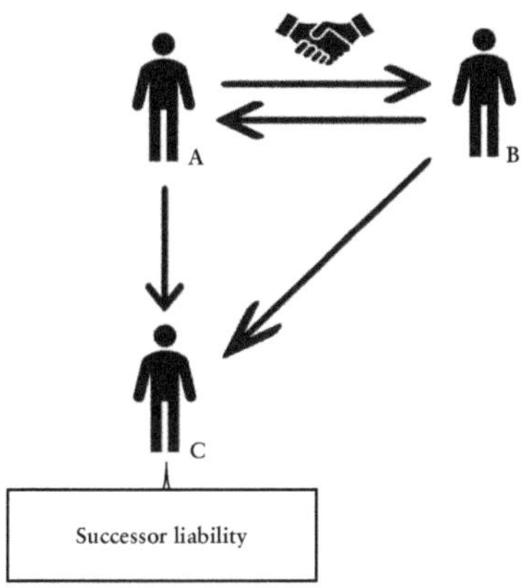

C. The Place of the *Numerus Clausus*

The role of the *numerus clausus* in regulating successor liability is not as clear as in ABX cases. In England and Germany, rights that give rise to trespassory liability always also have ABC effects. This outcome seems fairly intuitive: if B's right binds strangers, why would it not (*prima facie* at least) bind successors? Finally, before becoming a successor, C was also a stranger and, thus, already under the duty to respect B's rights. However, in both jurisdictions there are some rights that produce ABC effects, but do not trigger trespassory liability. As explained in this chapter, these 'pure ABC rights' are the ones posing the most relevant problem to the *numerus clausus* principle. Most of them – if not all – arise from borderline forms that cannot be fully explained by the canonical division between property rights and obligations.

In England, these borderline forms are normally framed in the language of (equitable) property law, making their challenge to the *numerus clausus* easy to see. However, an overlooked feature in this field is that most equitable property rights have a standardised content. Rights arising under the 'doctrine of anticipation'[20] essentially mirror legal property rights and, thus, are also defined by the content of those legal property rights, while 'other equitable rights', as restrictive covenants, must meet specific requirements as to their content.[21] This restricts the challenge that equitable property rights pose to the *numerus clausus* to beneficial rights in a trust. Not without good reason, English scholarship sometimes describes trusts as being on the border of property law and the law of obligations.[22]

In Germany, the absence of an equitable system makes this problem seem alien. However, German law also knows of cases with similar structures, but simply labels them differently. In this context,[23] the most salient examples are the aforementioned rights of lessees of immoveable property and rights of debtors who have transferred moveable property to their lender for security purposes. Nonetheless, because German law tends to describe such rights not as a property right, but as personal rights with far reaching effects against successors,[24] the problems they create for the principle of *numerus clausus* seem less obvious,[25] even though, at least for security ownership, they are not ignored.[26] For example, German doctrine is fully aware that the ABC effect of leases and security ownership is incompatible with the strict separation between property law and the law of obligations.[27]

Contemporary Anglo-American property theory has made relevant efforts to develop models that account for the conceptual structure of these borderline cases. For example, Thomas Merrill and Henry Smith place many of them along a continuum they name the 'property/contract interface'. In their view, one pole of this continuum is made of pure *in rem* rights, meaning rights that impose duties on numerous and indefinite third parties. The other pole is composed by pure *in personam* rights, this is, rights that give rise to few and specific duty

[20] See *Walsh v Lonsdale* (1882) LR 21 Ch D 9, CA).

[21] See ch 3, section III. Similarly, an equity by proprietary estoppel typically involves assurance as to the grant or transfer of a property right and, when it crystalises, it takes the form of a property right.

[22] eg Swadling (n 9) 210.

[23] There are other specific cases where obligations can become binding upon successors, as with the *actio pauliana*, see § 129 InsO.

[24] For the lease, see Volker Emmerich, 'Miete' in Dagmar Kaiser and Markus Stoffels (eds), *J. Staudingers Kommentar zum Bürgerlichen Gesetzbuch mit Einführungsgestetz und Nebengesetzen. Eckpfeiler Des Zivilrechts* (6th edn, Sellier & de Gruyter 2018) 982; Sjef van Erp, 'Comparative Property Law' in Mathias Reimann and Reinhard Zimmermann (eds), *The Oxford Handbook of Comparative Law* (2nd edn, OUP 2019) 1041. For the *Treuhand*, see Stefan Grundmann, *Der Treuhandvertrag: Insbesondere die Werbende Treuhand* (Beck 1997) ch 7; Stefan Grundmann, 'Trust and Treuhand at the End of the 20th Century – Key Problems and Shift of Interests' (1999) 47 *Am J Comp L* 401, 411; Bram Akkermans, *The Principle of Numerus Clausus in European Property Law* (Intersentia 2008) 184.

[25] See ch 2, section II and ch 3, section II.

[26] See Wolfgang Wiegand, 'Die Entwicklung des Sachenrechts im Verhältnis zum Schuldrecht' (1990) 1/2 *AcP* 112, 131–35. Discussed in ch 3, section II.

[27] See ch 2, section II.C and ch 3, section II.B.

holders. Because numerosity and definiteness are contingent variables, the interface is made of two intermediate cases that Merrill and Smith explain using a Hohfeldian terminology: indefinite and singular ('quasi-multital') and definite and numerous ('compound-paucital') rights.[28]

Despite its attractiveness, this account has two problems. First, it inadvertently collapses two continuums into one. By definition, a continuum is based on one single variable that can be arranged linearly. In HLA Hart's famous example, being bald or not is in a continuum depending on one variable: how many hairs a person has on his head.[29] However, Merrill and Smith's 'property/contract interface' is made of two variables: definiteness and numerosity. Second, this model defines rights by their effects, assuming too readily that the difference between pure *in rem* and pure *in personam* rights is simply a matter of degree. If these criticisms are correct, Merrill and Smith's interface is better explained as a double entry table with discrete variables (see Table 1), not a continuum.

Table 1 Property/contract double entry table

	Many people	**Few people**
Indefinite	*In rem* (ABX/ABC)	Quasi-multital (pure ABC, not ABX)
Definite	Compound-paucital (?)	*In personam* (AB)

Once the property/contract interface is transformed into a double entry table, it becomes clear that quasi-multital rights correspond to pure ABC rights: successor liability involves a duty for a specific holder that remains indefinite at the moment of its creation. For Merrill and Smith, the essential problem of quasi-multital rights is one of information: short of standardisation, the law opts for strategies based on notice or the protection of uninformed parties.[30] Advancing the thesis put forward at the end of chapter five, the following sections will show that information problems are only a part of a wider network of issues that are ultimately explained by the need to protect the freedom of successors in title.

The property/contract interface offers two important inputs for the view advanced in this chapter: it provides a clear account of the effects that make pure ABC rights appear as borderline cases and delineates some of the strategies the law uses to deal with the information problems they create. However, due to its exclusive focus on the (external) *effects* rights have on people, it fails to provide a conceptual account of their (internal) structure. As mentioned before,[31] in

[28] Thomas W Merrill and Henry E Smith, 'The Property/Contract Interface' (2001) 101 *Colum L Rev* 773, 774, 777, 785.

[29] HLA Hart, *The Concept of Law* (3rd edn, OUP 2012) 4.

[30] Merrill and Smith (n 28) 805–08.

[31] See ch 2, section III, ch 4, section IV and ch 6, section II.

recent years authors such as Ben McFarlane and Robert Stevens have advanced a new understanding of equitable property rights that might help to fill this gap. They argue that these rights are fundamentally different from both legal property rights and personal rights, and therefore transcend the property-obligations divide. The core of their view is that equitable rights are neither 'rights against things' nor 'rights against persons', but *rights against rights*. In this, they see the key to understanding why equitable rights can be enforced against (some) successors, but not strangers. For example, when A holds a property right on trust for a beneficiary (B), B does not hold a right in the thing, but rather a right against A's right in the thing. Because B has no rights in the thing, B cannot exclude strangers (X) from it, and needs to rely on A for this purpose. However, B's right against the trustee (A) does, *prima facie*, bind a party who later acquires the right from A (C). Thus, B has a right against C's right in the thing, giving rise to a phenomenon McFarlane and Stevens label as 'persistence'.[32]

For Simon Douglas and Ben McFarlane this also explains why there is no *numerus clausus* of rights held in trust. First, when A sets up a trust in favour of B, the duties that X owes to A are not affected. Second, even if C acquires the trust property and is not a bona fide purchaser without notice of B's right, if C remains ignorant of any breach of trust until after the point when C disposes of the trust property and any traceable proceeds, B has no claim against C.[33] In their view, this is consistent with Henry Smith's modular strategy, although the organising module in these cases is not the thing, but the right held by the trustee.[34]

However, this does not account for the place of the *numerus clausus* in cases when the rights of the beneficiary of a trust (B) *actually* bind successors (C), who acquire trust property in breach of trust and have no access to the good faith purchaser defence: sometimes third parties will be bound by B's rights, that is, by rights not subject to the *numerus clausus* principle. Nonetheless, the impact of these cases should not be overstated. As discussed below,[35] although the creation of these rights is not strictly policed by a content test like the *numerus clausus*, their effects against successors in title are still subject to doctrines that protect the position of C, typically limiting or standardising the duties running with the asset. In this sense, even if the *numerus clausus* does not impose a full restriction on the creation of rights with (some) ABC effects, the creation of successor liability outside the *numerus clausus* is not free.

The functional structure that results of all of this is the following: in both English and German law, in principle, A can only grant B a right binding upon

[32] Ben McFarlane and Robert Stevens, 'The Nature of Equitable Property' (2010) 4 *J Eq* 1.

[33] Discussed in *Independent Trustee Services Ltd v GP Noble Trustees Ltd and others* [2012] EWCA Civ 195 and *Re Montagu's Settlement Trusts* [1987] Ch 264.

[34] Simon Douglas and Ben McFarlane, 'Defining Property Rights' in James Penner and Henry Smith (eds), *Philosophical Foundations of Property Law* (OUP 2013) 241.

[35] See section II.B.

A's successor in title (C) if such right is contained in the list of ABX rights. Exceptionally, in both systems, A can grant B a right binding upon C that is not contained in this 'menu'. The creation of such rights is not limited by a stringent content test, but their effects upon C are still controlled by other doctrines that standardise and limit their impact on third parties.

As discussed in chapter five,[36] the role that the *numerus clausus* principle *should have* this context is disputed. On the one hand, the circumstance that successor liability can be controlled by knowledge or registration has led law and economics scholars to argue that the *numerus clausus* is an obsolete doctrine that undermines (efficient) freedom of contract without justification and that its purpose would be better served by relying on strong registration systems made possible by contemporary technology.[37] Some progressive scholars have reached a similar conclusion about the role of registration, although based on 'liberal theory' that brings the value of individual autonomy to the forefront.[38] However, as shown in chapter five, registration and notice cannot fully replace the role of *numerus clausus*, because the functions of this principle go beyond addressing information problems. On the other hand, some authors have argued that freedom of contract and the protection of successors in title would be better balanced by stronger reliance on a judicial *ex post* control based on open ended terms such as 'reasonableness'.[39] However, as argued in chapter five, *ex post* controls of open-ended terms are subject to high administrative costs and create great uncertainty.

To properly assess the impact of the *numerus clasus* on private law it is essential to realise that this doctrine fulfils a broad structural function consisting in preserving property rights as essentially unburdened spaces of personal freedom.[40] In cases of trespassory liability, the relevance of this for property law is contingent on X exercising her liberty on her own property.[41] However, in cases of successor liability, this effect is inherent to property law, as it always serves to preserve the modular structure of the property right owned by C. The rest of this chapter will test the relevance of this conclusion by discussing how the English and German *numerus clausus* ensure that private law retains a doctrinal structure that allows a list of seemingly old and rigid property forms to satisfy new real-life problems in a number of ABC scenarios.

[36] See ch 5, section II.

[37] Especially, Richard A Epstein, 'Notice and Freedom of Contract in the Law of Servitudes' (1981) *55 S Cal L Rev* 1353; Richard A Epstein, 'Past and Future: The Temporal Dimension in the Law of Property' (1986) 64 *Wash U LQ* 667.

[38] See Hanoch Dagan and Irit Samet, 'Express Trust: The Dark Horse of the Liberal Property Regime', *Philosophical Foundations of the Law of Express Trusts* (OUP 2023) 148–49, 154.

[39] eg Akkermans (n 24); Susan Pascoe, 'Re-Evaluating Recreational Easements- New Norms for the Twenty-First Century?' in Ben McFarlane and Sinéad Agnew (eds), *Modern Studies in Property Law*, vol 10 (Hart 2019).

[40] See ch 5, section IV.

[41] See ch 6, section IV.

II. ENGLAND: COVENANTS, EASEMENTS, LEASES AND TRUSTS

A. The Dynamic Protection of Freedom

As explained in chapter six, this book can only suggest how the *numerus clausus* might shape the intertemporal operation of private law in practice by discussing some real-world examples and developing arguments based on them. As with trespassory liability, in English law this is facilitated by the ease with which its doctrine can be related to well-studied historical and social processes, spanning from the Industrial Revolution to the development of contemporary holiday villas.

i. Divestment by Alienation: From Horses to Steam Engines

As mentioned in chapter three,[42] the leading case discussing the impact of the *numerus clausus* principle on successor liability is *Keppell v Bailey*.[43] The case concerned an agreement entered into in 1795 by the owners of three ironworks located in South Wales, who formed a stock company to build a railroad (the Trevil Railroad), authorised by the Monmouthshire Canal Act. The purpose of the railroad was to link their facilities to a nearby limestone quarry. As part of a four-party agreement with the corporation, the owners of the ironworks agreed to satisfy all the requirements of their works by the use of the railroad under a certain price scheme, binding themselves and their successors in title as covenantors. In 1833 the heir of one of the original owners (A) sold the Beaufort Ironworks to Mr Bailey (C), who then started to build a tramway to link it to his mill in Nantyglo. Relying on the covenant contained in the 1795 agreement, the owners of the other ironworks and shareholders of the Trevil Railroad (B), tried to obtain an injunction to prevent Mr Bailey from building the tramway.[44] The injunction was rejected by Lord Brougham, holding that such an agreement did not create a recognised type of proprietary right and, therefore, was not enforceable against a subsequent purchaser of the ironworks.[45]

When this outcome is assessed in its wider context, it becomes apparent that preserving Mr Bailey's right to supply his ironworks or remove goods from it as he saw fit (this is, a 'Hohfeldian liberty') had a decisive impact in allowing property law to accommodate a massive economic transformation without altering its basic structure. Before the Industrial Revolution, Britain's iron production was fairly modest. However, during the second half of the eighteenth century, war and the rise of a fuel economy gave the British iron industry a market

[42] See ch 3, section III.A.
[43] *Keppell v Bailey* (1834) 2 My & K 517.
[44] Ben McFarlane, 'Keppell v Bailey (1834); Hill v Tupper (1863): The Numerus Clausus and the Common Law' in Nigel Gravells (ed), *Landmark Cases in Land Law* (Hart 2013) 3–5.
[45] See ch 3, section III.A for details.

strong enough to incentivise constant technical improvements.[46] By the late eighteenth century, the juxtaposition of superficial coal, ironstone and limestone had given South Wales a unique position to take advantage of these new technologies.[47] As with most economic activities predating the First Industrial Revolution,[48] the main challenge of the South Welsh iron industry seems to have been the high costs of transport.[49] Thus, the Industrial Revolution only really kicked off in this area with the opening of the Monmouthshire Canal in 1796.[50]

Benefiting from the canal required entrepreneurs to build additional infrastructure to access the waterway.[51] At that time, this was normally horse-drawn tramways.[52] Due to the economic structure of investments in transport infrastructure (large initial capital outlays, long periods before seeing returns and dispersed social benefits), financing these works required collective capital that historically could only be raised by governments. However, in a phenomenon characteristic of the First Industrial Revolution in Britain, this capital was primarily raised by private entrepreneurs who expected to benefit from the new infrastructure.[53] The financing of the early industrial railroad followed the same structure.[54] Against this background, it is not hard to see that the covenant contained in the 1795 agreement was aimed to secure a revenue stream to repay the financing of the Trevil Railroad.[55]

By the late 1820s smelting with coke, the invention of 'hot blast' smelting and 'puddling and rolling' had raised the overall capacity of the British iron industry,[56] taking away much of the comparative advantages of the Welsh ironstone.[57] In parallel, the construction of lines for the new steam railway gave the iron industry a constantly growing demand for its product[58] and, at the same time, also created new transport routes to supply it: before 1825 the typical railway involved a (local) short line of wooden rails from a mine or quarry to a neighbouring waterway, while after 1830 citizens all over Britain were anxious to connect their towns, ports and industries to a new integrated national rail network.[59] Thus, by the time of *Keppell*, the horse-drawn wagons of the

[46] Eric Hobsbawm, *Industry and Empire* (3rd rev edn, Penguin 1999) 48.
[47] Michael Atkinson and Colin Baber, *The Growth and Decline of the South Wales Iron Industry 1760–1880* (University of Wales Press 1987) 4–5, 36–38.
[48] See Phyllis Deane, *The First Industrial Revolution* (2nd edn, CUP 1980) 76–77.
[49] See Atkinson and Baber (n 47) 74–75.
[50] McFarlane (n 44) 3; Atkinson and Baber (n 47) 75.
[51] Atkinson and Baber (n 47) 75.
[52] Mark Casson, *The World's First Railway System: Enterprise, Competition, and Regulation on the Railway Network in Victorian Britain* (OUP 2009) 51–52.
[53] Deane (n 48) 72–73, 80.
[54] Casson (n 52) 49–50.
[55] See McFarlane (n 44) 26.
[56] Hobsbawm (n 46) 48.
[57] See Atkinson and Baber (n 47) 32–33, 38–45.
[58] Hobsbawm (n 46) 48–49.
[59] Casson (n 52) 53–54.

South Welsh ironworks must have been becoming relatively slow, expensive and disconnected. Indeed, in 1829 locomotives had already been tried in some lines adjoining the Monmouthshire Canal.[60]

When Mr Bailey decided to acquire the Beaufort Ironworks in 1833, he must have been aware of the growing competition faced by the Welsh ironworks, the new demand for iron, and the emergence of new supply routes. One can safely assume that he planned to take advantage of scale and network economies of using such ironworks together with his neighbouring mill at Nantyglo to reach new markets and access them through a better transport route.[61] Thus, by relying on the *numerus clausus* principle to reject the injunction against Mr Bailey, Lord Brougham allowed the new owner of an industry born in an era of waterways, horse-drawn wagons and wood rails, to adapt his business to a new age of iron railways and steam engines by 'resetting' his property rights or, to use Honoré's terminology,[62] by recognising that the rights of Mr Keppell and the other shareholders of the Trevil Railroad had been 'divested by alienation'. The broader significance of this example of functional transformation can hardly be overestimated as it coincides with the final stage of a shift from an organically powered to a fossil-fueled economy[63] and an historically unprecedently sharp acceleration in Britain's economic growth.[64]

Keppell also exemplifies the tension between contractual freedom and the protection of successors in title that triggered the economic approaches to the *numerus clausus*:[65] at first, the covenant agreed by the partners of the Trevil Railroad may have been the most efficient solution to secure capital for the tramway, but in the long run, this deal prevented the parties from taking advantage of new (more efficient) opportunities. Thus, at first sight, the *numerus clausus* seems to sacrifice present and certain efficiency for future and eventual gains, which is hard to justify. However, this is not an accurate description of the tension. As frequently argued in the law and economics debate,[66] by making a more careful use of the modules of private law, the initial partners could have structured their business in a manner that allowed them to secure the revenue to refund the capital costs, without indefinitely restricting the use of the ironworks, for example, by binding themselves to repay the investment in 30 years, securing the debt with a collateral over the ironworks and making the debt assignable to its future owners.

[60] See John Hodge, *Railways and Industry in the Western Valley* (Pen & Sword 2016) ch 1.

[61] See ibid ch 1.

[62] AM Honoré, 'Rights of Exclusion and Immunities Against Divesting' (1959) 34 *Tul L Rev* 453.

[63] James Vernon, *Modern Britain: 1750 to the Present* (CUP 2017) 94.

[64] Brian A'Hearn, 'The British Industrial Revolution in a European Mirror' in Roderick Floud, Jane Humphries and Paul Johnson (eds), *The Cambridge Economic History of Modern Britain*, vol I 1700–1870 (CUP 2014) 2.

[65] See ch 5, section II.

[66] eg Thomas W Merrill and Henry E Smith, 'Optimal Standardization in the Law of Property: The Numerus Clausus Principle' (2000) 110 *Yale LJ* 1, 35.

ii. Channelling Successor Liability: Changing Social Value of Sport and Recreations

In *Keppell*, the *numerus clausus* allowed the functional transformation of the Beaufort Ironworks by liberating C's land from an AB dealing. However, the *numerus clausus* does not always work by excluding successor liability. With the exception of rights under a trust,[67] this principle also operates by limiting this liability to a well-established list of property rights defined by their content. According to the thesis advanced in chapter five, the substantive design of these rights ensures that, even if C remains liable to B, C will retain enough freedom to decide how to use 'the thing' and any limitations on such freedom will be justified by sound policy considerations. This subsection discusses the doctrinal elements that make this substantive control possible, by offering a new interpretation of some key elements of the English law of easements and then applying them to *Regency Villas Title Ltd v Diamond Resorts (Europe) Ltd*,[68] a Supreme Court case on 'recreational easements'.

Easements, together with restrictive covenants, make up the core of the English law of servitudes. The defining feature of servitudes is that they are property rights that bind one piece of land and benefit another, regardless of who owns them. Thus, this is one of the few areas of English property law that allows the creation of duties binding successive owners of land.[69] However, the creation of these rights is not free. The content of entitlements of dominant owners is strictly controlled by the law, ensuring that the correlative duties of servient owners are always negative.[70] For example, the paradigm of a grant excluded from being an easement under this rule are duties that imply spending money,[71] while restrictive covenant are *per se* negative.[72] The bottom line is that private parties are not free to create servitudes as they wish: they have to use the types established by the law.

Along with a 'certainty' requirement,[73] the negative nature of the duties that servitudes impose on servient owners plays an obvious role in ensuring that successors in title will not be subject to burdens that will substantively jeopardise their liberty to use or transfer the land. However, from a doctrinal perspective, the constraints that the law imposes on the free delineation of servitudes are far more complex and sophisticated, playing a central part in allowing the owners of both servient and dominant land to accommodate new social and economic needs through process of functional transformation

[67] Discussed in section II.B.

[68] *Regency Villas Title Ltd v Diamond Resorts (Europe) Ltd* [2018] UKSC 57.

[69] FH Lawson and Bernard Rudden, *The Law of Property* (3rd edn, OUP 2002) 152–58; Elizabeth Cooke, *Land Law* (2nd edn, OUP 2012) 211–35.

[70] Save for the obligation to maintain a fence. Lawson and Rudden (n 69) 153–56.

[71] See ibid 153; Cooke (n 69) 215.

[72] *Tulk v Moxhay* (1848) 2 Ph 774, 41 ER 1143, discussed in ch 3, section III.C.

[73] See *Burrows v Lang* [1901] 2 Ch 502.

of their property rights. To a certain extent, this seems grounded in a paradox. For example, William Swadling explains that the list of easements is not closed, but also states that this must be read in the context of the *numerus clausus*: new types of easements can be brought into being, but they must conform to a standard model.[74] To see how this operates, it is necessary to approach the doctrinal elements of servitudes more closely.[75]

To qualify as such, an easement must, among other things, be 'capable of forming the subject matter of a grant' and 'accommodate' the dominant tenement.[76] The content control that the *numerus clausus* imposes on the creation of easements arises mainly from these two requirements, but both serve different functions. As argued below, the former ensures that successors in title of the servient land will retain sufficient freedom to use and deal with it, while the latter safeguards that that the burdens imposed on the land are justified from a policy perspective.

a. Subject Matter of a Grant

The requirement that the right must be 'capable of being the subject matter of a grant' has been said to only mean that the right must be 'the sort of thing that can be an easement'[77] and has been described as an 'inept shorthand'[78] for number of criteria that is 'both obscure and unhelpful',[79] and 'not entirely logical'.[80] Contrary to this view, the following lines argue that the criteria required by the law for a right to qualify as an easement do have a clear rationality: safeguarding the freedom of successors in title to servient owners.

The first criterion of the 'capable of forming the subject matter of a grant' requirement is that such grant cannot impose a positive duty on the servient owner.[81] Its relevance has already been discussed.[82] Here there is only need to highlight that the prohibition of imposing on servient owners duties that involve spending money resembles the goal of the civilian codification to avoid feudal burdens,[83] and that English scholarship has seen in this a precondition of modern property rights oriented to protect personal liberty from interference.[84] For example, the refusal of the House of Lords to enforce positive freehold

[74] Swadling (n 9) 195.
[75] Focusing on easements also makes comparisons with German land servitudes easier as both share a common Roman influence.
[76] *Re Ellenborough Park* [1956] Ch 131, 163.
[77] Cooke (n 69) 215.
[78] Simon Gardner and Emily MacKenzie, *An Introduction to Land Law* (4th edn, Hart 2015) 309.
[79] Albert McClean, 'The Nature of an Easement' (1966) 5 *W L Rev* 32, 61.
[80] Cooke (n 69) 215.
[81] *Schwann v Cotton* [1916] 2 CH 459; *William Old International Ltd v Arya* [2009] EWHC 599.
[82] See above.
[83] See section III, ch 3, section II and ch 5, section III.A.
[84] Swadling (n 9) 199.

covenants on successors in title,[85] has been said to be justified in avoiding the feudal-like domination potential inherent to positive duties.[86]

The second element of the 'capable of forming the subject matter of a grant' requirement, this is, the limitation on the creation of new negative easements (ie those that simply prevent A doing something in her land),[87] follows the same logic. Negative easements seem to be strictly numbered[88] and, even if the list is not closed, courts are cautious to recognise new forms. As held by Lord Denning MR in a case in which he rejected a new form of easement imposing a duty not to demolish a house that was protecting a neighbouring dwelling from the weather, 'the reason ... is that if such an easement were to be permitted, it would unduly restrict your neighbour in his enjoyment of his own land. It would hamper legitimate development'.[89]

The same idea seems to also underpin the third element of this test, namely, the 'ouster' principle. According to it, a right to exclusive or joint possession or occupation over the servient land cannot qualify as an easement.[90] From a doctrinal perspective, the most common explanation for this is that, otherwise, the right in question would be an estate.[91] The precise content, rationale and utility of this requirement is highly contested,[92] and the Law Commission has recently even recommended its derogation.[93] Discussing its detailed content is beyond the scope of this book, but if the focus is placed on the duty bearer instead of the right holder,[94] it is apparent that the ouster principle ensures that servient owners retain a well-defined space of freedom that is broad enough to provide them with agency in the management of the land (or the part of the land) not subject to exclusive occupation. For example, in a recent opinion delivered in a Scots law case, the House of Lords explicitly approached the ouster principle focusing on whether the 'servient owner is left with any reasonable use of his land'.[95]

The three previous criteria might be obscure and lack systematicity, but they are far from unhelpful or irrational. When due attention is given to their effect on the ownership of duty-bearers, it becomes apparent that the elements clustered in the requirement that easements are 'capable of forming the subject matter of a grant' serve to establish a substantive control on the creation of

[85] *Rhone v Stephens* [1994] 2 AC 310.
[86] eg JW Harris, *Property and Justice* (OUP 1996) 328.
[87] See *Phipps v Pears* [1965] 1 QB 76, CA.
[88] Lawson and Rudden (n 69) 154.
[89] *Phipps* (n 87) 82.
[90] *Copeland v Greenhalf* [1952] 1 Ch 488.
[91] Susan Bright, 'Of Estates and Interest: A Tale of Ownership and Property Rights' in Susan Bright and John Dewar (eds), *Land Law: Themes and Perspectives* (OUP 1998) 534–36.
[92] eg see Peter Luther, 'Easements and Exclusive Possession' (1996) 16 *Legal Studies* 51.
[93] Law Commission, '*Making Land Work: Easements, Covenants and Profits à Prendre*' (Law Com No 327, 2011) 65.
[94] On this, see Luther (n 92) 62.
[95] *Moncrieff v Jamieson* [2007] 1 WLR 2620, HL [59].

successor liability that ensures that subsequent owners of land will retain a significant degree of discretion regarding to it. Thus, contrary to intuition, these restrictions on the creation of new property types do not make property law more rigid, but instead ensure that the flexible modular structure of ownership is preserved over time. As in *Keppell*, by curtailing freedom in the creation of easements, the *numerus clausus* protects the flexibility associated with the basic exclusionary structure of property law.

However, it is worth noting that the 'subject matter of a grant' requirement does not completely freeze the available types of easements. Because its criteria are not strictly defined by the content of the liberty of the dominant owner over the servient land, but rather by their impact on the duty bearer, novel types of easements that only impose negative duties on the servient owner and are not incompatible with her meaningful possession, might qualify as easements. This is not a new realisation. In the nineteenth century there was a wide acceptance that old types of easement could and should accommodate new examples within the existing forms, allowing them to 'alter and expand with the changes that take place in the circumstance of mankind'.[96] However, this idea lost visibility during the twentieth century, as a result of changes in the way the law of easements was presented in the leading English textbook on this matter, *Gale on Easements*.[97] As argued at the end of this subsection, making this older view visible again is a better way to bring flexibility to property law than getting rid of the *numerus clausus* or converting it into an *ex post* test.

b. Accommodation Test

What remains unanswered is towards which direction the law of easements should develop, that is, what principle should govern the admission of new types of easements. The answer for this is in the requirement that the grant must 'accommodate land'. According to this test, to qualify as an easement, a grant must serve whoever is the owner of the land *as owner*, as opposed to providing a personal advantage to a particular owner.[98] As shown below, this substantive requirement works as an interface between the internal (doctrinal) structure of easements and their external (policy) effects, creating a safety valve that releases the pressure social change imposes on the doctrinal structure of easements. In this view, at the risk of oversimplification, the elements of easements can be visualised as 'buckets':[99] on the one hand, the 'subject-matter of a grant' requirement provides the bucket with a rigid, stable but also opened-ended structure aimed to protect the freedom of whoever will have to carry the

[96] As per Lord St Leonards in *Dyce v Hay* (1852) 1 *Macq* 305, 312.

[97] McClean (n 79) 33–34; cf Graham Glover, *Gale on Easements* (12th edn, Sweet & Maxwell 1932) 21–22.

[98] See *Moody v Steggles* (1879) 12 Ch D 261.

[99] This analogy was suggested to me by Professor Kenneth Reid in the 2019 Edinburgh-UCL PhD Workshop.

bucket. On the other, since the bucket is still a burden on the person who has to carry it, 'the accommodation test' provides a flexible criterion to ensure that the bucket will only be filled with elements that, according to a long-term utility test, are worth being carried for a, potentially, indefinite time.

In English law, the basic elements that define the structure and use of these 'buckets' were borrowed from the Roman law of servitudes,[100] and experienced a significant development during the nineteenth century.[101] As the enclosure movement was coming to an end,[102] landowners realised that land could be exploited in an even more efficient manner by a collaborative use of plots owned by different owners. In the urban context, intensive building of mills and factories also called for similar solutions,[103] that is, for supplementing the basic 'exclusionary strategy' of the enclosures with fine-grained 'governance strategies' to regulate sophisticated relations between neighbours.[104] However, cross-exploitation of land comes at a cost and, therefore, must be restricted to cases where it does more good than harm: the broader the scope of the duty imposed on the servient land, the more the servient land ceases to be 'owned' in a meaningful way by the servient owner, diminishing her chances to make an efficient use of the land as a separate module.[105] Thus, easements undermine the basic modular structure of property law in the simple sense that they allow one module to permanently interfere with another.

From a static perspective, when easements originate in an agreement, the effect on the servient land is not problematic, as the bargain guarantees that the servient owner will be compensated for the negative impact on her land. However, from a dynamic perspective, ensuring that the gain for the dominant owner will continue to outweigh the alternative use of the servient land is not that easy.[106] This is of paramount practical importance because easements are not restricted in time and also explains why legal systems have developed doctrines to police the creation of easements, either *ex ante*, as in England,[107] or *ex post*, as in the US.[108]

[100] Lawson and Rudden (n 69) 153.

[101] Gardner and MacKenzie (n 78) 315.

[102] See Mark Overton, *Agricultural Revolution in England: The Transformation of the Agrarian Economy* (CUP 1996) 147–92; Karl Polanyi, *The Great Transformation* (2nd edn, Beacon 2001) 36–42.

[103] Gardner and MacKenzie (n 78) 315.

[104] Using terminology from Henry E Smith, 'Property as the Law of Things' (2012) 125 *Harv L Rev* 1691, 1693–94, 1709. For an explanation, ch 6, section I.C.

[105] Gardner and MacKenzie (n 78) 315–316.

[106] In similar terms, James Gordley, *Foundations of Private Law* (OUP 2006) 81–82; Ben Depoorter and Francesco Parisi, 'Fragmentation of Property Rights: A Functional Interpretation of the Law of Servitudes' (2003) 3 *Global Jurist* i, 1–2.

[107] Pascoe (n 39) 184–86. English law has methods to extinguish restrictive covenants that have become obsolete (LPA 1925, s 84(1)(a)), but despite the proposal of the Law Commission, there is no mechanism for a court or another body to put an end to an easement, no matter how useless or troublesome it may be, Cooke (n 69) 224.

[108] Susan French, 'Highlights of the New Restatement (Third) of Property: Servitudes' (2000) 35 *Real Prop Prob & Tr J* 225, 226, 228, 214–42.

For example, in *Re Ellenborough Park*,[109] the easement subject to litigation was granted more than 90 years before the case was tried. In a world of zero transaction costs this would not be a problem, as parties could always contract around it.[110] However, as shown in chapter five,[111] in the real world, this might not happen because property rights are subject to a 'law of entropy' that makes the reunion of all the fragments back into one bundle hard to achieve.[112] Hence, even if an AB dealing for cross-exploitation of land can be efficient at the time of the agreement, it locks the servient land into a situation that undermines its functional transformability, as what would have happen in *Keppell*, if the court had enforced the covenant.

Faced with this dynamic balancing problem, the accommodation test aims to ensure that the policy reasons that justify the imposition of duties on C will subsist over time, especially if B wishes to change the use of the dominant land or transfer it. As a result, the accommodation test operates as a utility control on the free creation of easements that imposes a significant restriction of the content of ABC rights. The function of this requirement is to ensure that the AB dealing will remain justified over time, especially when the dominant land is in new ownership. However, due to its open-ended nature, the accommodation test also provides the law of easements with a principle of growth: what rights accommodate the dominant land can change over time.

This is apparent in some recent developments triggered by changes in the social significance of sports and outdoors activities. *Ellenborough Park* involved a number of houses that had been sold in the 1860s together with a right to fully enjoy a surrounding park. During the Second World War, the park was requisitioned and, to decide whether the owners of the houses were entitled to compensation, it became necessary to establish whether their rights to enjoy the park qualified as easements. According to what were held to be the relevant authorities at the time,[113] to accommodate land, the right had to be 'of utility and benefit and not of mere recreation and amusement'.[114] In *Ellenborough Park*, in a reasoning that already implied a relaxation of previous criteria, the court held that, in a residential context, the right to use a garden fulfilled this test, but explicitly excluded 'rights to indulge in such recreations as … horse racing or … playing games'[115] from being easements.

[109] *Re Ellenborough Park* [1956] Ch 131, 163.
[110] See Ronald Coase, 'The Problem of Social Cost' (1960) 3 *J Law and Econ* 1.
[111] See ch 5, section II.
[112] Francesco Parisi, 'Entropy in Property' (2002) 50 *Am J Comp L* 595; Michael Heller, 'The Tragedy of the Anticommons: Property in the Transition from Marx to Markets' (1998) 111 *Harv L Rev* 621.
[113] *Mounsey v Ismay* (1865) 3 H& C 486, *Lady James Hay* (1852) 1 Macq 305, *Dempster v Cleghorn* (1813) 2 Dow 40.
[114] *Re Ellenborough Park* (n 109) at 177, citing Theobald's *The Law of Land* (2nd edn, 1929) 263.
[115] *Ellenborough Park* (n 109) 178.

Since *Ellenborough Park*, the perceived social value of sports and outdoor activities has changed dramatically.[116] At least since the 1960s, physical activities have come to be seen as instrumental for health and social wellbeing. In 1966 the Council of Europe implemented the 'Sport for All' policy to achieve physical and mental health and social benefits, later consolidated in 1975 by the European Sport for All Charter, and the 1991 and 2001 European Sports Charter. This development has been reflected in policy initiatives in the UK,[117] revealing the growing value that people in contemporary Britain attribute to having access to sporting facilities. However, the valuation of sports as a 'mere recreation' under *Ellenborough Park* seemed to make it impossible for a right to use such facilities to qualify as an easement, making the *numerus clausus* a hurdle for adjusting property law to new social preferences.

Nonetheless, recent case law shows how the open-ended structure of the 'accommodation test' allows property law to account for social changes,[118] without altering its basic structure. In *Regency Villas*,[119] a time share development granted the owners of a number of villas a right to use different sporting facilities, triggering the question as to whether these rights were granted as personal rights against the developer or as easements over the land. Faced with *Ellenborough Park*'s exclusion of sports and recreation from the scope of easements, in *Regency Villas* the Court of Appeal held that the right to use outdoor facilities qualified as property rights, arguing that

> [e]asements in the modern world must … retain their essential legal qualities. But the views of society as to what is mere recreation or amusement may change … Physical exercise is now regarded by most people in the United Kingdom as either essential or at least desirable part of their daily routines. It is not a mere recreation or amusement.[120]

The Supreme Court upheld the decision (although it departed from the distinction between indoor and outdoor activities), adding that time shares are a recent concept – another acknowledgment to social change – and that even if sporting facilities were primarily recreational, the fact that timeshares are typically occupied for holidays, shows that they provided utility and service to the apartments.[121]

Regency Villas has been celebrated for introducing flexibility into the law of easements, inspiring scholars to propose new frameworks that depart from the anti-feudal and anti-fragmentation rationality that has traditionally been

[116] See Pascoe (n 39).

[117] See Paul Downward, Kirstin Hallmann and Simona Rasciute, 'Exploring the Interrelationship between Sport, Health and Social Outcomes in the UK: Implications for Health Policy' (2017) 28 *Eur J Public Health* 99, 99.

[118] See Pascoe (n 39).

[119] See n 68.

[120] *Regency Villas Title Ltd v Diamond Resorts* [2017] EWCA Civ 238 [54].

[121] *Regency Villas* (n 68) [53].

used in England to explain the law of easements.[122] However, the open-ended texture of the accommodation test does not imply that the doctrinal structure of easements needs to be altered to keep the law in step with society. Following Lord Carnwath's dissent, *Regency Villas* would have been better decided if the court had distinguished between the use of facilities that required positive actions by the servient owner and those that only required her tolerance.[123] The relevant implication is that a robust 'capable of a grant' test should provide judges with more leeway when assessing the 'accommodation test', and *vice versa*.

The analysis put forward in this subsection suggests that new theories are not needed to account for the ability of the law of easements to accommodate new social realities. To start, it is not obvious that the law of easements required any change to accommodate the new social perception of sporting activities. In *Regency Villas*, as suggested by the Supreme Court,[124] probably the same practical effect could have been reached by using traditional leasehold covenants to structure the time-share development. However, even if this was not true, the old 'bucket structure' of easements could be used to accommodate the change. On the one hand, by denying admission into the list to rights that impose positive duties on C, the *numerus clausus* safeguards the ability of successors to functionally transform land, as in *Keppell*. On the other hand, by having an open-ended accommodation test, the *numerus clausus* also provides judges with some discretion to assess policy arguments that justify the imposition of new proprietary duties on third parties, in light of the changing values of society, like in *Regency Villas*.

B. Successor Liability Outside the *Numerus Clausus*?

The scheme presented in the previous subsection is challenged by, at least, two elements of English property law that allow creating non standardised rights with ABC effects: first, leases admit the almost free creation of positive covenants running with the land and, second, trusts allow the almost unlimited creation of property rights behind the trust curtain. This subsection accounts for both cases. In the case of leases, it argues that the substantive control operates at a different level due to the different economic function served by this relationship. In the case of the trust, it argues that successor liability is standardised by functionally equivalent doctrines that are better tailored to the need of wealth and resource management.

[122] See Pascoe (n 39).
[123] *Regency Villas Title Ltd* (n 68) [94]–[115].
[124] See *Regency Villas* (n 68) [9], [23] and [80].

i. ABC Effects of Leases

Leases almost always begin in contract by an agreement between two parties. However, these contracts also confer an alienable property interest on lessees (a leasehold), which is valid against successors in title of the freeholder. To qualify as a leasehold, the grant must comply with some stringent requirements of content and form.[125] As to the content, only agreements that confer a right to exclusive possession ('exclusive possession rule') subject to a term certain from the onset ('term of years rule') qualify as leases.[126] Whenever these two elements are found, they give rise to a lease, irrespective of the intention of the parties or the name they give to their deal.[127] The latter has been recently criticised as an excessive commitment to a 'substance over form' rationality, arguing that there is no good reason to deny parties the liberty to grant a personal right to exclusive occupation.[128] This argument is not without merit, but is not relevant for this book, as it does not engage with the limitation on the creation of property rights, but with the unreasonable restriction on the creation of personal rights.

The content requirements of leases lack a well-established justification. On the one hand, the 'exclusive possession' rule is aimed to provide 'ownership' to the tenant in the form of 'an indefinitely large set of use privileges and control-powers over the land',[129] distinguishing it from other property interests in land[130] (like easements) and personal rights (like licences).[131] However, doctrinal accounts have been more concerned with establishing what amounts to a right to exclusive possession in practice,[132] than with its justification or function. On the other hand, the 'term of years' rule has been heavily criticised for having no rationale at all.[133] In *Prudential Assurance Ltd v London Residuary Board*[134] Lord Templeman described its effect as the

> bizarre outcome … from the application of an ancient and technical rule of law which requires the maximum duration of a term of years to be ascertainable from the outset. No one has produced any satisfactory rationale for the genesis of this rule. No one has been able to point to any useful purpose that it serves at the present day.[135]

[125] Lawson and Rudden (n 69) 117.

[126] *Street v Mountford* [1985] AC 809, HL.

[127] ibid.

[128] Birke Häcker, '"Substance Over Form": Has the Pendulum Swung Too Far?' in Andrew Robertson and James Goudkamp (eds), *Form and Substance in the Law of Obligations* (Hart 2019) 38–45.

[129] Harris (n 86) 69.

[130] Bright, 'Of Estates and Interest: A Tale of Ownership and Property Rights' (n 91) 538.

[131] See *Westminster City Council v Clarke* [1992] UKHL 11, [1992] 2 AC 288, HL.

[132] eg see Swadling (n 9) 186–89.

[133] Although efforts have been made to explain it based on the *nemo dat* principle, eg Ian Williams, 'The Certainty of Term Requirement in Leases: Nothing Lasts Forever' (2015) 74 *CLJ* 592.

[134] *Prudential Assurance Ltd v London Residuary Board* [1992] 3 WLR 279, HL.

[135] *Prudential Assurance Ltd* (n 134) 287.

Contrary to this view, this subsection will show that the control of content that these two rules impose on leases is critical to keeping the modular structure of property law and enabling the functional transformation of property rights.

In England, leases are widely credited with providing property law with a flexible structure that allows the 'temporal slicing' of ownership, while subjecting these temporal segments to an extremely certain limit, forcing anyone wanting to deal in other (complex) time slices to act 'behind the curtain of [the] trust'.[136] By these means, leases allow the temporal deployment of the basic exclusionary module of ownership in an almost unlimited number of real-life contexts, including housing, commerce and agriculture. Depending on their practical purpose, the temporal extension of leases is subject to great variation. Shorter leases normally involve the payment of market rent by leaseholders, leaving the capital value of the property with the freeholder. Longer leases typically involve the payment of a substantial initial premium and very low or nominal rents, thereby allocating the capital value of the property to the leaseholder.[137]

From a doctrinal perspective, these leases are a collection of reciprocal contractual obligations between landlord and tenant known as 'covenants'.[138] In contrast to freehold covenants, leasehold covenants do not need to be negative to bind successors in estate and, after the passing of the Landlord and Tenant (Covenants) Act 1995, parties can agree on almost any possible obligation.[139] These covenants can be very complex, especially in shared buildings of flats. In some cases, especially in commercial contexts, they even impose duties as to the use of land.[140] As long as they remain within 'privity of contract', leasehold covenants do not challenge the *numerus clausus*. However, once the original parties alienate their interest, their successors in estate will become automatically subject to such covenants as duties running with the estate, provided that the obligations relate to the property and not to the specific individuals.[141] By this means, leasehold covenants give rise to a type of successor liability that English law captures in the idea of 'privity of estate': successors to landlords and tenants remain bound by the covenants.[142]

In England, the broad liberty that private parties enjoy to create leasehold covenants plays a central role in allowing ownership of flats and offices in buildings: because the common law has historically not admitted the notion of *condominium* available in other jurisdictions, ownership in individual units

[136] Peter Birks, 'Five Keys to Land Law' in Susan Bright and John Dewar (eds), *Land Law: Themes and Perspectives* (OUP 1998) 463.

[137] See Susan Bright, *Landlord and Tenant Law in Context* (Hart 2007) 5–6.

[138] See Cooke (n 69) 187–92.

[139] See Landlord and Tenant (Covenants) Act 1995, s 3.

[140] Cooke (n 69) 187–89.

[141] See the LPA 1925, ss 141 and 142 and the Landlord and Tenant (Covenants) Act 1995, s 3.

[142] Lawson and Rudden (n 69) 120–21; Cooke (n 69) 192–93.

that form part of a larger building is almost invariably structured by leases with attached positive covenants that ensure that the long leaseholder will keep the property in good shape[143] and that landlords will make such repairs in the case of short-term leases. Thus, there seems to be little doubt that the ABC effect of leasehold covenants is justified because they are 'necessary for the effective operation of the law of landlord and tenant',[144] this is, by policy reasons.

Although the ABC effects of leasehold covenants are contained within the privity of estates, the broad discretion private parties enjoy to shape their content seems fatal for the thesis advanced in chapter five, as it suggests that the *numerus clausus* is not aimed to ensure that successors in title will only be subject to low-intensity negative duties that preserve the basic exclusionary structure of property rights. However, this is not the relevant approach. In contrast to servitudes, leases do not give rise to 'cross-exploitation' of two different property modules, but to the 'temporal slicing' of a single module. The challenges that the latter creates for the preservation of the functional transformability of property rights are different from those of 'cross-exploitation' and, therefore, call for a different substantive control.

In English law, the control of 'temporal slicing' relies on the exclusive possession and the term of years rules. The former ensures the functional transformability of the land by guaranteeing that leases will have the basic exclusionary structure of ownership. This effect is achieved by denying the nature of a lease, and therefore successor liability, to rights to occupy land that do not grant a right to exclusive possession to the tenant.[145] In turn, the term of years rule has a double effect: first, it ensures that there is total certainty as to who will have ownership (and the ability to functionally transform the module of property) at any given point in time; and, second, it provides certainty to the freeholder as to the value of her reversion, therefore enabling her to trade it without having to negotiate with the leaseholder. In this manner, as in the case of easements, the substantive content-control that the *numerus clausus* imposes on leases ensures that there always exists a clearly identifiable person with broad powers to functionally transform the thing. Using Larissa Katz's terminology,[146] it ensures that property remains 'an office' whose holder has the exclusionary powers to 'set the agenda' for the thing.

This mechanism is well illustrated by *Prudential Assurance*. By denying that a right to exclusive possession over a narrow strip of land for an uncertain term qualified as a lease, the court freed a piece of property that had been subject for more than half a century to a deal designed to solve a situation expected to last

[143] Lawson and Rudden (n 69) 121.

[144] *City of London Corp v Fell* [1994] 1 AC 458, HL 464.

[145] eg *Clarke* (n 131).

[146] Larissa Katz, 'Exclusion and Exclusivity in Property Law' (2008) 58 *U Toronto LJ* 275; Larissa Katz, 'The Regulative Function of Property Rights' (2011) 8 *Econ Journal Watch*; Larissa Katz, 'Property's Sovereignty' (2017) 18 *Theo Inq L* 299.

for a very short period: until the strip of land was required by the local authority for – what at the time was thought to be – an imminent expansion of a road. Its 'bizarre outcome', consisting of having a shop with no access to the street and a strip of land too narrow to be useful, was not created by the *numerus clausus*, but by poor expropriation and urban planning, and could be easily solved by the parties by entering into a new lease. Arguably, the real force acting behind this case was the need to give the landlord a way out of a bargain that had become extremely one-sided over time, due to the impact of more than half a century of inflation over a fixed rent designed to last for a short time.[147]

ii. ABC Effects of Trusts

As explained,[148] beneficial rights under a trust are not subject to the principle of *numerus clausus*.[149] Thus, discussing the role of this principle in preserving the modular structure of beneficial rights might seem out of place; however, this is not the case. Because the rights of the beneficiary of a trust have the ability to impose successor liability despite being idiosyncratic, accounting for the mechanisms used by trust law to control and limit the duties that trusts impose on recipients of trust property is still relevant. The central doctrines that trust law relies upon to this end are constructive trusts and overreaching.

First, when A transfers the property it holds for the benefit of B in breach of trust to C and the latter has no access to the good faith purchaser defence, then C becomes liable to B as 'constructive trustee'. Under this constructive trust, the court will order the defendant (C) to transfer the property back in specie to the claimant (B),[150] but will not subject C to any of the idiosyncratic duty A might owe to B.[151] Hence, even if settlors enjoy ample freedom to design the duties that trustees (A) owe to beneficiaries (B) behind the trust curtain, the third-party effect of B's rights against C is standardised by law,[152] making the precise content of B's rights irrelevant to C.

Second, as least since the nineteenth century, English law has developed an array of doctrines that facilitate ownership passing from A to C free from B's beneficial rights.[153] As discussed in chapter two,[154] recent comparative research has seen in this a development that paralleled the rise of the unitary notion of ownership in civilian systems,[155] which is indissolubly tied to the continental

[147] See Susan Bright, 'Uncertainty in Leases – Is It a Vice?' (1993) 13 *Legal Stud* 38.
[148] See section I, ch 2, section III.A and ch 6, section II.B.
[149] Douglas and McFarlane (n 34) 240–41.
[150] *Boscawen v Bajwa* [1996] 1 WLR 328, 334–35.
[151] *Lonrho plc v Fayed (No 2)* [1992] 1 WLR 1, 12 (Millet J).
[152] I plan to expand on this in a future publication.
[153] William Cornish and others, *Law and Society in England 1750–1950* (2nd edn, Hart 2019) 171, 176–77.
[154] See ch 2, section I.
[155] Michele Graziadei, 'The Structure of Property Ownership and the Common Law/Civil Law Divide' in Michele Graziadei and Lionel Smith (eds), *Comparative Property Law: Global Perspectives* (Edward Elgar 2017) 81–82, 87.

version of the *numerus clausus*. This suggests that, when successor liability is not limited by its substantive content, modern legal systems developed other mechanisms to preserve the functional transformability of the basic modules of property.

Besides the protection historically afforded to the *bona fide* purchaser acquiring for value from a trustee,[156] in contemporary English law the most salient case in relation to land is probably statutory overreaching. In a nutshell, statutory overreaching allows the purchaser of land to take free from beneficial interests held under a trust even if she has notice of the trust, as long as certain requirements as to the payment of capital money are met, shifting B's beneficial right from the sold thing to the proceeds of the sale.[157] Thereby, overreaching insulates C from any third party effect of the AB dealing by divesting the property upon conveyance, while at the same time, it preserves the value of the AB dealing by shifting its object to a new right. In the late twentieth century this scheme was altered by the TOLATA 1996, arguably the 'most significant measure of property law reform since the legislation of 1925',[158] to account for the fact that, in contemporary England, most dwellings are now owner-occupied by co-owners holding the land for residential purposes (not as investments),[159] but this reform did not alter the core of this doctrine.

The practical importance of trusts cannot be overstated. If servitudes allow a 'cross-utilisation' of different properties and leases allow the 'temporal slicing' of ownership, trusts provide for its 'functional split': one or more parties manage the property while other parties get its benefits. In the two first cases, the ABC effects are contained by controlling the content of B's right. Trust law does not resort to this technique, because it would undermine its very core as a flexible instrument for the third-party management of wealth and resources. This does not deny the thesis advanced in this chapter, but confirms its main argument: preserving the functional transformability of property rights requires the law to contain and channel successor liability. In contexts where the *numerus clausus* is not applicable, other legal devices fulfil this function. In the case of trust law, this is done by limiting the effects of the rights of the beneficiary to remedies that are not dependent on the content of her rights against the original express trustee (ie through constructive trust) and by doctrines that allow third parties to easily take free from her beneficial right (eg statutory overreaching).

[156] On this, see Andreas Televantos, *Capitalism before Corporations: The Morality of Business Associations and the Roots of Commercial Equity and Law* (OUP 2021) 102–06.

[157] Payment of capital must be made to two persons, except when it is made to a trust corporation (LPA 1925, s 27).

[158] Charles Harpum, 'The Law Commission and the Reform of Land Law' in Susan Bright and John Dewar (eds), *Land Law: Themes and Perspectives* (OUP 1998) 169.

[159] Law Commission, *Transfer of Land: Trusts of Land* (Law Com No 181, 1989) [3.1]–[3.5].

III. GERMANY: LAND SERVITUDES, LEASES AND FLAT OWNERSHIP

A. The Doctrinal Machinery of the Dynamic Protection of Freedom

Analysing the impact of the *numerus clausus* on successor liability in German law presents challenges that are different from the English case. On the one hand, German doctrine offers a much clearer conceptual approach. In this jurisdiction the *numerus clausus* has enjoyed a well-established place for more than a century;[160] its historical origin can be easily traced to the protection of freedom of successors in title;[161] there is case law that explicitly applies it in ABC scenarios;[162] and scholarship has directly addressed the impact of changing circumstances on the law of servitudes.[163] On the other hand, however, due to the emphasis German doctrine puts on conceptual aspects of law and the rather uncontroversial status of the *numerus clausus* principle, the latter is normally approached in an abstract manner that obscures its interactions with the wider context. As a consequence, scholarship frequently provides no meaningful discussion of cases applying the principle[164] and, when it does, it normally focuses more on its doctrinal account by courts than its relevance for broader social and economic phenomena.[165] In addition, because decisions directly applying the principle normally deal with refusals of the Landbook Office (*Grundbuchamt*) to register idiosyncratic property rights,[166] concrete examples of the impact of the principle in a context different to that of the original AB dealing are difficult to find.

As a result, despite the clear link between the principle of *numerus clausus* and the control of successor liability, finding historically loaded examples to illustrate how this doctrine enables the functional transformation of property rights in Germany is not as easy as in England. This subsection overcomes this difficulty by discussing some cases where the *numerus clausus* was applied to scenarios that entailed *potential* BC conflicts and extrapolating what this might imply for the transformability of ownership.

[160] See ch 3, section II.

[161] See ch 5, section III.A.

[162] See below.

[163] eg Rolf Stürner, 'Dienstbarkeit Heute' (1994) 194 *AcP* 265; Hermann Amann, 'Grunddienstbarkeiten im Wandel der Zeit und von Verjährung Bedroht – Zugleich Anmerkungen zu den Urteilen des BGH v. 18. 7. 2014 – V ZR 151/13 und v. 22. 10. 2010 –V ZR 43/10' [2015] DNotz 164.

[164] eg Wellenhofer (n 1) 27, 28; Hans Hermann Seiler, 'Einleitung zum Sachenrecht' in Elmar Bund and others (eds), *J. von Staudingers Kommentar zum Bürgerlichen Gesetzbuch mit Einführungsgesetz und Nebengesetzen* (Sellier & de Gruyter 2007) 23, 24; Klinck (n 3) 1274; Reinhard Gaier, 'Einleitung zum Sachenrecht' in Franz Jürgen Säcker and others (eds), *Münchner Kommentar zum BGB* (7th edn, Beck 2017) [7].

[165] eg Jan Wilhelm, *Sachenrecht* (5th edn, De Gruyter 2016) 10; Holger Fleischer, 'Der Numerus Clausus der Sachenrechte im Spiegel der RechtsÖkonomie' in Thomas Eger and others (eds), *Internationalisierung des Rechts und seine ökonomische Analyse: Festschrift für Hans-Bernd Schäfer zum 65. Geburtstag* (Gabler Verlag 2008) 126–27, 135 both discussing BayObLG NJW 1967.

[166] See below.

i. Protecting the Exclusionary Structure of Ownership

Due to the central role of the Landbook in granting property rights,[167] German case law explicitly applying the principle of *numerus clausus* frequently relates to registration problems. For example, the case normally cited by German scholarship to account for the judicial application of the *numerus clausus* concerned the registration of a mortgage that aimed to secure a number of obligations different than paying a sum of money, including constructing and maintaining a building, obtaining insurances and allowing inspection visits.[168] In this case, the BayObLG primarily relied on a purely doctrinal argument to uphold the refusal of the Landbook Office to register the mortgage, holding that § 1313 BGB only allows mortgages to secure obligations consisting in the payment of money and that the *numerus clausus* principle did not allow the creation of real rights for cases not foreseen in the law. However, the court also provided a policy argument to back its conclusion, arguing that, otherwise, the Landbook could not fulfil its function consisting in accounting in reliable terms for all legal relations relating to land, emphasising that legal traffic in the Landbook must be clear and certain to avoid third parties having any doubt as to the substantive content of the relevant property right.

Cases involving other limited property rights follow a similar pattern. In a relatively recent case before the Chamber Court of Berlin (*Kammergericht*, KG Berlin),[169] an owner (B) transferred the 'bare ownership' of a plot of land to A, while retaining the 'usufruct' for himself.[170] In the grant, the parties agreed that B would not be liable to A under the rules set forth in the BGB regarding the conservation of the thing (see §§ 1036, 1037 and 1041 BGB), that is, rules fulfilling a function similar to the common law of waste. The KG Berlin upheld a first instance ruling denying registration to B's right, arguing that, according to the *numerus clausus* principle, parties could not contractually create usufructs that abrogated the usufructuary's duty of care.[171]

In these two cases, the court relied on the *numerus clausus* to prevent the grant of idiosyncratic property rights by denying registration in the Landbook to the AB dealings aiming to create them. Since in German law property rights in land can only be acquired by registration, in all these cases an actual ABC conflict, such as in *Keppell*, never arose. However, these cases can still show how the *numerus clausus* preserves a doctrinal structure that enables the functional transformation of property rights by discussing how it protected *potential* successors to A (C) from liabilities towards B.

[167] See section I.A.

[168] BayObLG, NJW 1967, 1373, 1374.

[169] KG DNoZ 2006, 470.

[170] A usufruct (*Nießbrauch*) is a real right to use and obtain the profits of a thing. This right leaves its owner with 'bare' or 'nude' ownership of land, see §§ 1030, 1059, 1061 BGB.

[171] For a more recent case containing similar arguments, NJW-RR 2011, 1587.

In the case before the BayObLG, if registration had been permitted, an eventual successor of the grantor of the mortgage (C) would not have come under the duty to comply with the obligations that her predecessor in title (A) secured by the mortgage. However, C would still have been exposed to losing her ownership in the thing if A failed to comply with A's obligations towards B. Thus, in practice, this would have made C liable to B for a breach by A. The policy argument put forward to deny proprietary nature to such a grant holds that it would jeopardise the free circulation of land. This already points to how, in this case, the *numerus clausus* protects the functional transformation of property rights: by providing certainty, it facilitates the acquisition of land by people who can better use it under new circumstances.

However, the real question is why A is allowed to grant a mortgage that binds C to secure her obligations to pay a sum of money, but not for other types of obligations. From the perspective of the functional transformation of land, an answer can be found in the ease with which C can comply with the liability the mortgage imposes on her: in practice, C can achieve an effect equivalent to divesting the mortgaged land by paying the money A owes to B (see §§ 1143, 1153, and 1177(2) BGB), freeing the land for new uses and facilitating its circulation in the market. This effect could not be as easily achieved if parties were allowed to create mortgages to secure other type of obligations. For example, in the BayObLG case, an eventual C would have needed to fulfil several detailed tailored obligations crafted for a specific developer or building company, including constructing and preserving a building, which is the exact opposite of freeing the land.

Similarly, in the case before the KG Berlin, the refusal of the Landbook Office to register an idiosyncratic usufruct avoided the creation of a property right that might have jeopardised the functional transformability of land. German doctrine is well aware of the problem usufructs create for the circulation of wealth, seeing the rules that forbid its transfer and limit its maximal duration to the life of its holder as the main substantive control to ensure that the land will become fully disposable by one single person at some point not too far removed in time.[172] However, these rules might not be enough to ensure that the ownership split by usufructs retains a high level of functional transformability. For example, in the KG Berlin case, B attempted to create a non-standard usufruct by gifting the bare ownership to A. Before the court, A and B defended their agreement arguing that it did not make sense that B, being originally the full owner, became forced to assume more liability regarding the use of the thing than he had before because of gifting the bare ownership over it to A. From a static perspective, the argument of the claimants seems sound. Due to the gratuitous nature of their deal, it is possible to assume that A and B were

[172] eg Klinck (n 3) 1385; Jörg Mayer, 'Dienstbarkeiten' in Wolfgang Wiegand (ed), *J. von Staudingers Kommentar zum Bürgerlichen Gesetzbuch mit Einführungsgesetz und Nebengesetzen. Buch 3. Sachen Recht. EbbVo; §§ 1018–1112* (Sellier & de Gruyter 2002) 221.

personally related (probably, parent and child) and, for sure, the deal made sense *for them*, probably for tax reasons.[173] However, from a dynamic perspective, the creation of usufructs that impose only minimal liability on possessors creates significant problems. Usufructs last for the life of its holder (§ 1061 BGB), giving her absolutely no incentive to preserve the thing in a manner that will allow new uses of it after the expiration of her right. As long as A and B have a personal relation, as in the KG Berlin case, this might not be a problem, because B will have an idiosyncratic reason to care for the thing. However, if A transfers the bare property to C, B might have no reason to care for it. For the same reason, if A wants to transfer the bare ownership to a third party, she will struggle to find a buyer.

The effects avoided by the KG Berlin show the negative impact of allowing non-standardised usufructs: such usufructs would freeze the use of property into idiosyncratic AB deals until the expiration of the right, jeopardising its marketability and functional transformability. The *numerus clausus* avoids this effect by standardising the core of the relation between the holder of the usufruct and the bare owner by means of 'statutory obligational relations'[174] and denying ABC effects to agreements that deviate from this core.[175] This does not impede the creation of a right that suits the personal nature of the relation between A and B. As suggested by the court, they could have relied on the law of obligations for that purpose.[176] By this means, the *numerus clausus* allows complex interactions between parties that are tailored for a specific scenario, while it also keeps such deals contained within their original module, allowing successors in title to take free from its idiosyncratic aspects.

ii. Content of Successor Liability

In the BayObLG and the KG Berlin cases, the *numerus clausus* preserved the functional transformability of land by preventing the creation of idiosyncratic forms of successor liability. However, as shown above with the example of English servitudes, the German *numerus clausus* works not only by excluding successor liability, but also by channelling it into standardised forms that ensure that, even if C becomes liable to B, she will retain enough freedom to decide how to use 'the thing' and that any limitations on her freedom will be justified by sound policy considerations. For many limited property rights, including usufructs and personal limited servitudes, this works in an extremely simple manner: such rights cannot be transferred by B and expire upon her death, ensuring that

[173] On the tax motivation for usufructs, Baur, Baur and Stürner (n 2) 411.

[174] On these relations, see ch 6, section I.A.

[175] Sebastian Herrler and Hartmut Wiecke, 'Sachenrecht', *Palandt: Bürgerlicher Gesetzbuch mit Nebengesetzten* (80th edn, Beck 2021) 1677. Although some modifications of this relations are admitted, as long they are registered, Baur, Baur and Stürner (n 2) 414.

[176] KG DNoZ 2006, 470 [3].

the full ownership will be reunited sooner or later, either in A or C. However, German law also provides for limited property rights that permanently split the use of land, most notably, land servitudes (*Grunddienstbarkeiten*). This subsection will account for the mechanism by which German law channels successor liability in these cases, focusing on the problem of the 'eternal servitude' (*ewige Dienstbarkeit*').[177]

In German law, land servitudes belong to the larger group of 'servitudes' (*Dienstbarkeiten*), which also comprises 'limited personal servitudes' and 'usufructs'.[178] Personal and land servitudes, unlike usufructs, can only exist in land and only admit a limited use of it. Land servitudes, unlike personal servitudes and usufructs, need to be attached to a dominant land and can have an everlasting nature. By contrast, personal servitudes and usufructs can be granted in gross, but cannot be transferred and expire upon the death of their holder.[179]

As in England, the doctrinal elements of German servitudes (see § 1018 BGB), were borrowed from Roman law,[180] reflecting the same basic structure of easements and restrictive covenants. Servitudes can only impose duties to withhold from doing something (*zu unterlassen*) or to tolerate the dominant owner doing something on the servient land (*zu dulden*), but not a positive doing.[181] The BGB also restricts the content of these duties in manners that resemble the English ouster principle. First, 'duties to withhold' must be specific and cannot give an encompassing right to use the servient land, not even a section of it, as this would amount to a usufruct. Second, 'duties to tolerate' must leave a meaningful use of the land to the servient owner, including freedom to dispose of the land, grant contracts over it, transform it, etc.[182] Finally, as with the English accommodation tests, according to § 1019 BGB, land servitudes also require that the burden on the servient land provides an 'advantage' for the use of the dominant land. However, in contrast to English law which does not admit easements in gross,[183] if this fails the burden can normally still be created in the form of a limited personal servitude. According to German scholarship, a further difference is that what amounts to an advantage to land in German law is broader than in England.[184] Indeed, German doctrine holds that land servitudes have a 'surprisingly open content'.[185]

[177] See Mayer (n 172) 222.
[178] Wellenhofer (n 1) 523; Mayer (n 172) 200–04. For a slightly different categorisation including 'real charges' (*Reallasten*), Baur, Baur and Stürner (n 2) ch 4.
[179] Baur, Baur and Stürner (n 2) 415, 416; Herrler and Wiecke (n 175) 1666.
[180] Mayer (n 172) 205–06.
[181] Baur, Baur and Stürner (n 2) 417, 418, 422; Wellenhofer (n 1) 525–28; Herrler and Wiecke (n 175) 1667–69.
[182] Herrler and Wiecke (n 175) 1668–99.
[183] *London County Council v Allen* [1914] 3 KB 642, CA.
[184] eg Stürner (n 163) 278. Whether *Regency Villas* closed this gap remains to be seen.
[185] eg Mayer (n 172) 199–220 (my translation).

Unlike English easements and restrictive covenants, which are essentially based in the common law and Equity, the structure of German servitudes is the outcome of a conscious legislative choice. The drafters of the BGB considered two opposed models of servitudes: that of the pre-existing ALR, which had an open system that allowed the 'proprietarisation' (*Verdinglichung*) of practically any personal right; and the Roman tradition followed by the Pandectist School, which favoured a closed system of standardised rights. They opted for the latter.[186]

This choice was not only a result of the 'academic triumph' of the Pandectist School over the Germanic school,[187] but also an ideological choice in favour of modernity.[188] Traditional Germanic law admitted entitlements called *Gerechtigkeiten*, which focused on the right of the holder, not on the correlative duty. They came in a variety of forms and created heavy duties on landholders. The restrictions on the content of servitudes imposed by BGB were explicitly aimed to avoid the creation of these rights and should be seen as part of the wider effort to 'free land' from pre-modern agrarian proprietary structures.[189] Indeed, somehow paralleling the English discussion on cross-exploitation of land,[190] contemporary German doctrine often frames the same problem in terms of 'freedom'. For example, a leading author explains that 'ownership is a piece of personal freedom and servitudes, by their own nature, restrict such freedom for the benefit of the freedom of someone else'.[191]

German scholarship often discusses to what extent the restrictions that the *numerus clausus* imposes on servitudes prevent and *should* prevent private parties from creating new types of rights that adjust to new needs.[192] Pushed by relatively recent case law, currently, the most debated topic in this field is the risk entailed by the everlasting nature of land servitudes for the flexibility of property law.[193] Textbooks[194] and *Kommentare*[195] invariably discuss to what extent already existing land servitudes granted in a certain factual context can be adapted to new circumstances, which is a phenomenon sometimes labelled as 'dynamic modification' (*dynamische Veränderung*) of servitudes.[196]

As in *Regency Villas*, the requirement that land servitudes provide an advantage to the dominant land holds the key to this doctrine: as long as a servitude

[186] Stürner (n 163) 276.

[187] RC van Caenegem, *An Historical Introduction to Private Law* (CUP 1992) 155–56. Also see ch 3, section II.B.

[188] Franz Wieacker, *Privatrechtsgeschichte der Neuzeit unter besonderer Berücksichtigung der deutschen Entwicklung* (3rd edn, Vandenhoeck & Ruprecht 2016) 620; Mayer (n 172) 220.

[189] Baur, Baur and Stürner (n 2) 429.

[190] See section II.A and ch 6, section II.B.

[191] Stürner (n 163) 265 (my translation).

[192] eg Stürner (n 163).

[193] See Mayer (n 172) 222.

[194] eg Wellenhofer (n 1) 529, 530; Baur, Baur and Stürner (n 2) 420–22.

[195] eg Herrler and Wiecke (n 175) 1671; Mayer (n 172) 222.

[196] eg Mayer (n 172) 222.

can be exercised according to its original purpose, it will subsist, and it might even impose a heavier burden on the servient land, if this burden has the same 'scope'.[197] Thus, changes caused by technical developments that remain in the same framework are allowed.[198] The flexibility that this rule impresses on the law of servitudes is apparent in a recent holding of the BGH.[199] The case concerned a servitude to pass through a driveway with 'wagons of any kind' (*Fuhrwerke jeder Art*),[200] that is, vehicles pulled by animals. The holding does not provide the date of the grant, but it is apparent that this was before motorised vehicles were of importance,[201] probably at least hundred years before the case reached the court. The defendant claimed that the servitude had expired, arguing among other things, that it did not allow the passing of motorised vehicles. The BGH rejected the argument, holding that 'the content and scope of a temporally unlimited easement … is not fixed in every aspect from the outset for all times, but is subject to changes resulting from economic and technical developments', concluding that a 'right of way granted to drive "wagons", today, includes driving both cars and lorries' and that the 'resulting increase in the burden [on the servient owner] remains within the scope [… as] driving with a wagon corresponds to driving with a motor vehicle today'.[202] The key implications of this is that courts can use the open-ended terms of a grant to adapt existing servitudes to new setting. In other words, the doctrine of dynamic modification of servitudes is a piece of the machinery that allows the functional transformation of concrete property rights.

B. The Modern Home: Social Lease and Flat Ownership

The previous subsection argued that the restrictions that the German *numerus clausus* imposes on successor liability keep property rights ready for change by preserving the exclusionary nature of the basic modules of property law. As in English law, this is mainly achieved by ensuring that property rights running with land will be negative in nature and will not deprive C from meaningful ownership. However, German law has cases that do not follow this rationale. As in England, these cases primarily arise in the context of modern housing. For examples, the BGB rules on land leases allow the creation of successor liability outside the *numerus clausus* of property rights; while the WEG provides for the creation of duties running with flats that are not controlled by the content of those duties. This subsection discusses what this implies for the thesis advanced in chapter five.

[197] Wellenhofer (n 1) 529; Baur, Baur and Stürner (n 2) 421.
[198] Mayer (n 172) 222.
[199] BGH 18.7.2014 – V ZR 151/13.
[200] ibid [1].
[201] Amann (n 163) 164.
[202] BGH 18.7.2014 – V ZR 151/13 [7] (my translation).

i. Social Lease Law

The social and economic importance of leases in Germany can hardly be overestimated. As of 2018, about 60 per cent of Germans 'lived on leases' (*zur Miete wohnen*),[203] with this proportion being much higher in large cities as Berlin or Hamburg.[204] This might not impress a common lawyer used to thinking of leases, especially long-term leases, as temporal ownership. However, in Germany, leases are not legally conceived nor socially perceived as property rights,[205] giving rise to one of the most distinctive features of German homeownership within the European context: an uncommonly low rate of homeownership.[206]

The fact that German law does not conceptualise leases as property rights seems to place them outside the scope of this book. Nonetheless, German doctrine acknowledges that leases have 'some proprietary elements',[207] especially in the residential context.[208] In public law, the most visible feature of this is the 1993 BVerfG decision holding that the right to possession of tenants counts as a property right protected by Art 14 GG.[209] From the perspective of private law, the most salient proprietary element of leases is contained in § 566(1) BGB, which provides that the successor in title to the lessor 'takes over the rights and duties that arise under the lease agreement during the period of his ownership'. However, because German leases are not formally categorised as property rights by private law doctrine, this ABC effect is not subject to the principle of *numerus clausus*.

This does not undermine (nor advance) the general thesis advanced in chapter five. However, it points to a different implication: as in England, the German *numerus clausus* simply does not control all aspects of successor liability. In these scenarios, ABC effects are controlled by other means, which might respond to different rationalities. In the case of German leases, this is best explained by a longstanding 'tradition of state intervention in residential lease markets',[210] reflected on dense and rapidly evolving mandatory legislation on leases.

The depth of this phenomenon can only be properly understood from an historical perspective. Following the heavily Romanised approach of the Pandectist School,[211] the EI adopted the basic principle that acquirers of land were not bound by pre-existing leases and were free to evict tenants at any time.

203 Emmerich (n 24) 954.

204 Valesca Maria Molinari, *Die Tradition Staatlicher Interventionen in den Mietwohnungsmarkt* (Mohr Siebeck 2021) 5.

205 To understand why, see below.

206 Molinari (n 204) 5. For a non-academic comment, James Hawes, *The Shortest History of Germany* (Old Street 2018) 214–15.

207 Baur, Baur and Stürner (n 2) 393; Emmerich (n 24) 566–67.

208 Emmerich (n 24) 956.

209 BVerfGe 89, 1. On this, see ch 2, sections II.B. and II.C.

210 Using the words of Molinari (n 204) (my translation).

211 See Reinhard Zimmermann, *The Law of Obligations: Roman Foundations of the Civilian Tradition* (OUP 1996) 378–79.

This created an outrage in public opinion, leading the BGB to adopt the rule that 'a sale does not break a lease'.[212] However, the rules on leases of the original BGB were mostly dispositive and provided that both parties were normally allowed to terminate the contract at any moment.[213] In the early twentieth century this implied that the far greater bargaining power of lessors enabled them to impose standard forms on tenants that allowed the former to terminate leases unilaterally on very short notice.[214] In the mental framework of Wilhelmine Germany, § 566(1) BGB did probably not pose any serious threat to the preservation of the freedom of owners. In the spirit of the political ideas that inspired the code,[215] its drafters assumed that the market would provide a steady supply of homes for rent that would allow tenants to rapidly find new accommodation.[216]

However, in practice, the market did not provide enough homes for rent. There are many explanations for this: destruction of capital by the 1923 hyperinflation; competition with armament production during the 1930s; destruction during the war; massive influx of refugees from the east in the aftermath of Second World War; arrival of 'guest workers' (*Gastarbeiter*) during the postwar period; cultural changes leading to an increase of one-person homes; and, more recently, incoming of asylum seekers. This structural housing shortage led to the development of a 'law for the protection of tenants' (*Mieterschutzrecht*), which is essentially concerned with limiting the rights of lessors to give notice to terminate a contract and raise rents.[217] This state intervention started in 1917, pushed by the growing housing needs created by the First World War, and resumed in 1936. This created a massive 'emergency lease law' (*Mietnotrecht*) that provided for a 'forced housing economy' (*Wohnungsbewirtschaftung*) that was only dismantled progressively after 1966 and replaced with a 'social lease law', based on strong protection of lessees *vis a vis* lessors. During the 1970s a renewed rise in rents led to the passing of new acts strengthening the protection of lessees that were embodied in the BGB, becoming 'permanent law' (*Dauerrecht*).[218]

The constitutionality of these rules was upheld by the aforementioned 1993 decision of the BVerfG holding that the position of lessees counts as ownership

[212] Emmerich (n 24) 982.

[213] See Baur, Baur and Stürner (n 2) 934; Emmerich (n 24) 954.

[214] See Christoph Bernhardt, *Bauplatz Groß-Berlin. Wohnungsmärkte, Terraingewerbe und Kommunalpolitik im Städtewachstum der Hochindustrialisierung (1871-1918)* (De Gruyter 1998) 20.

[215] See Heinrich Honsell, 'Einleitung zum BGB' in Dagmar Kaiser and Markus Stoffels (eds), *J. Staudingers Kommentar zum Bürgerlichen Gesetzbuch mit Einführungsgestetz und Nebengesetzen. Eckpfeiler Des Zivilrechts* (6th edn, Sellier & de Gruyter 2018) 13–14.

[216] Baur, Baur and Stürner (n 2) 394.

[217] ibid 395. For single-occupancy, Molinari (n 204) 5.

[218] On the evolution of lease law, see Baur, Baur and Stürner (n 2) 395; Emmerich (n 24) 955; Stefan Kofner, *Wohnungsmarkt und Wohnungswirtschaft* (Oldenburg Verlag 2004) 158–74. In this book, also see ch 8, section III.

under Art 14 GG. The court argued that the right to possession of tenants is as significant and worthy of protection as that of owners, especially considering the high proportion of the Germans who rely on leases to cover their dwellings needs.[219] In 2001 leases were newly regulated in the BGB (§§ 549ff BGB),[220] further strengthening the position of lessees.[221] Since then, the law of leases has experienced further reforms, including the passing of an act to facilitate some modernisations in the context of the German 'energy transition' and, after 2015, a variety of special acts limiting the raising of rents, the so-called 'rent brakes' (*Mietpreisbremsen*).[222]

From an internal perspective, the rule that 'a sale does not break a lease' has been regarded as a 'dogmatic anomaly'.[223] It is widely accepted in German sholarship that the ABC effect of leases is justified by its 'social function', particularly by the protection of the 'status of lessees' (*Bestandsschutz des Mieter*),[224] which was confirmed by the line of cases leading to the 1993 ruling of the BVerfG.[225] In other words, the successor liability of leases is justified by pure (external) policy considerations. From a technical perspective, this effect is achieved through a 'contractual transfer ordered by law', that is not dependent on registration nor notice.[226] Bringing to mind the protection of interests of those in actual occupation under the LRA 2002,[227] the operation of § 566 BGB only requires the lessee to be 'in possession at the time of the transfer'. There are different views on the doctrinal operation of this mechanism,[228] but whatever option is followed, its basic effect has been described as creating an outcome similar to a limited property right for the use of land.[229]

As civilian leases do not create property rights, the *numerus clausus* does not play any role in controlling their ABC effect. Notably, in the case before the KG Berlin mentioned above, the court held that the agreement derogating the duty of care of the holder of the usufruct would have been admissible if the parties had agreed on a lease, as these only give rise to obligations.[230] However, this does not imply that parties can use leases to freely create duties running with land. Rights and duties running with leases are only those 'pertaining by nature to the lease' (*mietvertragliche Rechte und Pflichten).* The decisive factor for this is whether the agreement in question 'forms a part of the lease'

[219] BVerfGE 89, 1. See Molinari (n 204) 83. In this book, see ch 2, section II.B.
[220] 2001 Mietrechtsreformgesetz, BGB1 I 1149.
[221] Baur, Baur and Stürner (n 2) 395.
[222] Emmerich (n 24) 955; Walter Weidenkaff, 'Einzelene Schuldverhältnisse. Titel 5. Mietvertrag, Pachtvertrag', *Palandt. Bürgerlicher Gesetzbuch mit Nebengesetzten* (80th edn, Beck 2021) 765.
[223] Zimmermann (n 211) 382.
[224] Baur, Baur and Stürner (n 2) 392.
[225] On this, see ch 8, section III.C.
[226] Baur, Baur and Stürner (n 2) 398.
[227] See LRA 2002, Sch 3, para 2.
[228] See Emmerich (n 24) 982.
[229] eg Baur, Baur and Stürner (n 2) 399.
[230] KG DNoZ 2006, 470 [3].

(*ob die Abreden Teil des Mietvertrag bilden*).[231] Scholarship has systematised the relevant criteria to decide whether an agreement 'forms a part of the lease' through case groups.[232] However, the general picture seems too vague to draw a general conclusion as to what duties will run with the lease.

On the surface, the weak control of the ABC effect of leases seems at odds with the substantive modular view of property rights advanced in chapter five. However, this is not the relevant reading. The key factor controlling the ABC effects of leases is closely linked to the longstanding German tradition of state intervention in residential lease markets. Due to the intense and detailed legislative intervention that has characterised German lease law since the early twentieth century,[233] the content of residential leases is essentially established by statutory law that provides limited space for idiosyncratic agreements, turning the discussion about the 'nature' of the obligations running with land and the protection of C secondary. By the same token, keeping the law of leases in step with social needs also requires constant legislative intervention, rather making this a (controversial) topic of housing policy. For example, in March 2021, a 'rent brake' enacted by the City of Berlin[234] was struck down by the BVerfG, arguing that this was a matter already covered by the 2015 Rent Brake Federal Act (*Gesetz zu Mietpreisbegrenzungen und neuen Regeln für Maklergebühren*).[235] In such context, the control of the free delineation of duties running with leases simply does not seem to be an important issue.

ii. Re-modularisation of Ownership

The relatively little attention that German doctrine devotes to the positive obligations that run with leases can be explained by the scarce importance leases have in articulating 'horizontal ownership' in civilian systems. In contrast to the position of common law leaseholders, in most civil law jurisdictions tenants do not own a right they can transfer: B's lease is binding on A's successor in title C, but B cannot transfer its right to B2. Thus, as other civilian jurisdictions, German law has developed a specific type of property right to allocate individual ownership in separate parts of buildings, namely, 'flat ownership' (*Wohnungseigentum*). This right was enacted by the 1951 WEG as part of a wider effort to overcome the housing crisis of postwar Germany and shows that, sometimes, the modular structure of property law preserved by the *numerus clausus* is not capable of accommodating the demands of social and economic change, making the legislative creation of brand-new property modules indispensable to cope with new realities.

[231] Emmerich (n 24) 983–984.
[232] eg see Weidenkaff (n 222) 865.
[233] In general, see Molinari (n 204).
[234] MietenWoG Bln.
[235] BVerfGE 157, 177.

The background to see this is in the rigid structure of the original BGB. Following the Roman 'accession' principle, the code established that buildings are part and parcel of the land and cannot be subject to separate property rights (§§ 94(1) and 93 BGB),[236] save for a very weak form of *superficies* right.[237] This decision was motivated by both doctrinal and practical considerations. On the one hand, the drafters of the BGB saw undivided ownership of land and building as essential for fluid legal traffic and safeguarding the personal autonomy of individual owners.[238] On the other, they wanted to avoid the frequent disputes created by the pre-existing French-inspired 'floor ownership' that existed in some parts of Germany.[239] Thus, it is not hard to see that the design of the BGB was underpinned by the desire to create stable and robust modules of land ownership that could be easily conveyed in the market[240] and re-deployed to new uses, without having to face anti-commons problems,[241] including letting individual parts through (purely contractual) leases, subject to a permissive regulation.

To what extent this model worked as planned is hard to assess. The growth of German population peaked during the Second Empire (1871–1918), leading to massive migration into cities, especially the new capital, Berlin.[242] In practice, the model of the BGB implied that only people with financial means to buy a plot of land *and* build or buy a *complete* building could become 'homeowners', forcing the vast majority of the population to live as tenants,[243] frequently in overcrowded and insalubrious *Mietkasernen* (literally, 'rental barracks').[244] However, it is uncertain whether an alternative property design would have led to better outcomes. At the time, the main constraint for housing was not the price of land, but the costs of construction[245] and, at least in some places, including Berlin, the early twentieth century saw a massive construction boom that even caused an oversupply of homes in 1912.[246]

[236] Manfred Rapp, 'Einleitung zum Wohnungseigentumgesetz' in Wolf-Rüdiger Bub and others (eds), *J. von Staudingers Kommentar zum Bürgerlichen Gesetzbuch mit Einführungsgesetz und Nebengesetzen* (13th edn, 2005) 64–65.

[237] Manfred Rapp, 'Ebrbaurecht' in Wolfgang Wiegand (ed), *J. von Staudingers Kommentar zum Bürgerlichen Gesetzbuch mit Einführungsgesetz und Nebengesetzen. Buch 3. Sachen Recht. EbbVo; §§ 1018–1112* (2002) 3–4.

[238] Rolf Stürner, 'Sachenrechtsbereinigung Zwischen Restitution, Bestandsschutz und Rechtssicherheit' (1993) 48 *JZ* 1074, 1075.

[239] Baur, Baur and Stürner (n 2) 375.

[240] On 'verification for conveyance', Henry Hansmann and Reinier Kraakman, 'Property, Contract, and Verification: The Numerus Clausus Problem and the Divisibility of Rights' (2002) 31 *J Legal Stud* 373, discussed in ch 5, section II.

[241] For anti-commons, Heller (n 112), discussed in ch 5, section II.

[242] Bernhardt (n 214) 13–14.

[243] Baur, Baur and Stürner (n 2) 374.

[244] For a powerful description, Joachim Käppner, 'Wohnungsnot in der Kaiserzeit – Berliner Häuserkampf' *Süddeutsche Zeitung* (Munich, 10 May 2019).

[245] See Bernhardt (n 214) 102–04.

[246] ibid 6, 145–60.

Whatever this oversupply meant, the neat property model based on the Roman accession principle was not able to cope with later social and economic changes. This system was first cracked with the housing crisis of the last years of the First World War, when the *Reichstag* passed an act that fully regulated the *superficies* rights (ie the granting of property rights over buildings separate from land).[247] However, the real blow came after the Second World War. By the end of the war, Germany was experiencing a catastrophic housing crisis. On the side of supply, from the 10.84 million homes that existed in 1939 in what later became the allied occupation zones, 2.2 million (20.3%) had been completely destroyed and, between 2 to 2.5 million (about another 20%), most of them in cities, had varying degrees of damage. On the side of demand, western Germany was also suffering great pressure, due to the massive influx of people escaping from the eastern zones occupied by the Red Army. The crisis was first dealt with by the same compulsory means that were used during the war: 'forcing complete strangers to share kitchen and bath'.[248]

The only way out of the crisis was to create new housing space, which became one of the central concerns of the first elected Federal Parliament (*Bundestag*).[249] The main goals of the *Bundestag* were to re-activate construction in a depressed economy, promote influx of private capital and expand homeownership. However, it also wanted to ensure that public funding for reconstruction reached extensive segments of the population, instead of flowing directly to building companies and, not least, to achieve an efficient allocation of the, now, scarce living space in cities.[250] Within this broader policy design, the widespread distribution of homeownership was seen as central. However, with most people having lost almost all their savings due to the 1948 currency reform,[251] the 'accession' ownership model of the BGB seemed hopeless. Thus, it soon became clear that homeownership could only be achieved by allowing the acquisition of property rights in individual flats, this is, by creating a new and smaller module of property.[252] Such a right was enacted by the 1951 WEG, providing for a 'flat ownership' that is equivalent to ownership in land,[253] but insolubly united with co-ownership over communal property (eg the land) and membership in a community of flat-owners that manages the communal property.[254] Scholarly commentaries on the relation of flat and regular ownership vary. On the one hand, this development is sometimes described as a total break with the

[247] 1919 *Erbbaurechtsverordnung* (ErbbauVO), now2007 *Erbbaurechtsgesetz* (ErbbauG). See ch 3, section II.B.

[248] Kofner (n 218) 151–54.

[249] Rapp (n 236) 65, 67.

[250] Baur, Baur and Stürner (n 2) 375–76.

[251] See Christoph Buchheim, 'Die Währungsreform 1948 in Westdeutschland' (1988) 36 *Vierteljh Zeitgesch* 189.

[252] See Rapp (n 236) 8.

[253] ibid 15.

[254] ibid 8; Hartmut Wiecke, 'Gesetz über das Wohnungseigentum und das Dauerwohnrecht', *Palandt: Bürgerlicher Gesetzbuch mit Nebengesetzten* (80th edn, Beck 2021) 3001.

ownership concept of the BGB[255] that could never have been achieved through judicial gap filling.[256] On the other hand, however, it is worth noting that, even if flat ownership is a 'new legal institution' created by statute, it is also considered a form of 'true ownership',[257] equivalent to ownership in the BGB.

A detailed review of the WEG is beyond the scope of this book, but it worth outlining its basic framework. According to standard accounts, flat ownership is based on the insoluble union of (i) individual ownership over the flat (ii) co-ownership over communal property (eg land, stairs, lifts, etc) and (iii) membership in a community of flat owners (*Wohnungseigentümergemeinschaft*) that manages the communal property.[258] Each flat must be a separate and self-contained unit (*Abgeschlossene Wohnung*), established by plans registered in the Land Book (§ 3 (1) (2) WEG). Ownership in the flat is equivalent to ownership in land[259] and its holder is entitled to the same set of actions to defend her property against third parties as regular landowners.[260] The flat cannot be transferred separately from the shares in the communal property nor the membership in the flat-owners community (§ 6 WEG). In this design, the core function of the statute is regulating the rights and duties between flat owners by means of 'statutory obligations' and creating the governance structure of the community, especially, establishing which decision can be taken by simple majority and which require unanimity (see §§ 10-29 WEG). In Smith's modular framework, this seems to be a combination of a basic exclusionary strategy over the flat (the module) and a dense and sophisticated governance strategy to rule the relations between co-owners (ie between modules).

The 'modular design' of the WEG had decisive impact in solving the postwar housing crisis. During the 1950s the previously depressed construction sector boomed. As early as 1954, 500,000 new homes were built annually, a construction rate that would not decrease until 1969, most of it financed by generous public spending. As a result, by the mid 1960s, it was no longer possible to speak of a housing crisis.[261] Of course, this was the effect of a wider policy framework, but the WEG played a relevant role in it. Beside facilitating reconstruction, coupled with a restrictive lease legislation, it incentivised the owners of buildings that rented flats to convert them into separate units for sale.[262] Later the WEG found additional functions, including structuring rights in terraced houses and condominiums.[263]

[255] Rapp (n 236) 67.

[256] Karl Larenz and Claus-Wilhelm Canaris, *Methodenslehre der Rechtswissenschaft* (3rd edn, Springer 1996) 191, 194, 196. On gap filling in this book, see ch 4, section II.

[257] Johannes Bärmann, 'Zur Theorie des Wohnungseigentumsrechts' (1989) *NJW* 1057, 1057.

[258] Rapp (n 236) 8; Wiecke (n 254) 3001.

[259] Rapp (n 236) 15.

[260] Baur, Baur and Stürner (n 2) 377.

[261] Kofner (n 218) 154, 157–58.

[262] Baur, Baur and Stürner (n 2) 376.

[263] Herbert Grziwotz, 'Gesetz über das Wohnungseigentum und das Dauerwohnrecht (Wohungseigentumgestz)' in Harm Peter Westernmann, Barbara Grunewald and Georg Maier-Reimer (eds), *Erman Bürgerliches Gesetzbuch* (15th edn, Otto Schmidt 2017) 6331.

The main lesson of this development is that even modules of property that guarantee that successors in title will be able to exercise broad liberty to functionally transform their property, sometimes fail to accommodate legal change. The robust land ownership concept of the BGB was simply not capable to cope with Germany's post war housing needs: its Roman accession model, designed for an agricultural economy, was too large and rigid for dense urban development. However, this does not fully undermine the thesis advanced in chapter five. A second and less obvious aspect of the WEG is that flat ownership itself has a modular structure. The WEG avoided the problems of the old French-inspired 'floor ownership' by replicating the strong exclusionary ownership concept of the BGB: each flat must be an enclosed and self-sufficient home and is subject to the same constraints when it comes to burdening it with real rights, that is, the *numerus clausus*. Thus, beside the issue of managing the communal property, the essential difference between the BGB and the WEG concept of ownership is found in the technical approach to the creation of successor liability in the context of relations among the co-owners, who are essentially neighbours. Instead of fully following the *numerus clausus* principle, the WEG opted for a different strategy, more akin to company law: it provides for 'corporate governance' for the communal property that can impose persistent duties on flat owners, delegating discretion on the community to deal with new circumstances at a local level.

IV. FUNCTIONAL TRANSFORMATION AND ITS LIMITS

In both England and Germany property rights create successor liability. However, the doctrinal relevance of this form of liability varies between both jurisdictions: in England successor liability is enough to classify a right as proprietary, while, in Germany it is not.[264] Nonetheless, from a purely functional perspective, both jurisdictions provide, in one way or another, for a category of rights that can bind successors in title (C), but not strangers (X). In England these are typically equitable property rights, while in Germany they are a handful of anomalous obligations.

It is beyond doubt that in both England and Germany the *numerus clausus* imposes substantive constraints on the successor liability that AB dealings can create. Overall, the content of these constraints is very similar in both jurisdictions. For property rights that provide for the cross-exploitation of land (eg servitudes), the impact of the *numerus clausus* is straightforward: the principle is aimed to ensure that duties running with land will be essentially negative and will not deprive the holder of the servient land from meaningful ownership. Rights that fail this test will not come into existence or will only be enforced

[264] See ch 2, section IV.

as obligations (ie will not trigger ABC effects). Similarly, property rights that provide for the temporal slicing of ownership (eg English leases and German usufructs) must also fulfill substantive requirements that ensure that there will, at any point in time, be a party with a broad degree of freedom to 'set the agenda' of the thing,[265] as apparent in the requirement that both English leases and German usufructs provide 'exclusive possession' to its holder and have a limited duration. Temporal slicing that does not comply with this requisite will fail to become a property right.

This substantive design provides property law with three inherent sources of flexibility. At the most basic level, the *numerus clausus* forbids the creation of idiosyncratic property rights that might jeopardise the transferability and functional transformability of land. In the short run, this might seem to bring rigidity into property law, as it limits the ability of private parties to deal with new circumstances. However, in the long run, it preserves the flexibility of property law by 'resetting' ownership upon transfer. This effect is very tangible in cases such as *Keppell*, and a similar outcome is achieved in the German cases dealing with Landbook Offices refusing to register agreements aiming to create non-standardised property rights. The impact of this on party autonomy should not be overestimated, as often a similar practical outcome can be achieved by a thoughtful use of the existing modules of property. For example, in *Regency Villas*, the court suggested that a practical outcome equivalent to an easement which had previously not been allowed could have been achieved by using leasehold covenants, while in the KG Berlin case the court argued that a similar outcome could have been achieved through a lease.

Second, by the same token, the *numerus clausus* works by channeling successor liability into standardised forms that are inherently designed to preserve the freedom of the party burdened with the duty. In England and Germany this mechanism is best seen at work in doctrines imposing *ex ante* controls on the creation of servitudes. In both jurisdictions, servitudes can regularly only impose abstention duties on the servient owner and cannot deprive her from meaningful freedom in the use of her land. A similar rationality is seen in the control of the content of property rights that provide for the temporal slicing of ownership, although the main concern in these cases is providing clear limits on the duration of the temporal right. In England, this is accomplished by the term of years rule, while in Germany a similar effect is achieved by making usufructs expire upon death of the holder and forbidding their transfer.

Third, English and German property law deal with changes in economic and social circumstances by relying on some open-ended doctrinal elements as gateways for the incremental judicial re-configuration of property rights through

[265] Using the terminology of Katz, 'Exclusion and Exclusivity in Property Law' (n 146); Katz, 'The Regulative Function of Property Rights' (n 146); Katz, 'Property's Sovereignty' (n 146).

'legal scaffolding'.[266] This can also be seen at work in the laws of servitudes. On the one hand, the open-ended nature of the accommodation test has allowed English courts to admit new forms of easements that had previously been seen as mere obligations, as in *Regency Villas*. On the other, the German doctrine of dynamic modification of land servitudes has allowed courts to adapt property rights granted a century ago to contemporary circumstances, as in the case of the horse-drawn wagons.

However, another part of the capability of English and German property law to adapt to new circumstances is not explained by the *numerus clausus*, but by its absence. Both jurisdictions have broad areas in which the creation of pure ABC rights by private parties is not subject to strong content-controls. In English law, the most obvious case is the trust, which offers private parties a residual category to freely delineate rights with some ABC effects,[267] but subject to strict restrictions that ensure the idiosyncratic effects of these rights do not run with the asset. Another relevant case is the flexibility that parties enjoy in creating leasehold covenants within the privity of estates. In Germany, the latter is partially mirrored by the effect of the rule that 'a sale does not break a lease', although its practical importance is less acute, as leases are not required to articulate horizontal ownership. This shows that the *numerus clausus* is less pervasive than frequently assumed, as it does not cover all aspects of successor liability.

Finally, the brief discussion on German flat ownership shows that, despite their flexibility, modular property systems have a limited ability to deal with social and economic change: sometimes legislative 're-modularisation' is required, which is entirely consistent with having a *numerus clausus*. This does not make modularity irrelevant. To the contrary. Part of the success of the WEG can be explained by the sound modular design of 'flat ownership', which in turn relies on the general module of ownership contained in the BGB.

These remarks trigger an unavoidable question: if property law is as flexible and dynamic as suggested, why is its static and rigid image so persistent? This question will be answered in chapter eight, as part of a broader discussion about the place of form and substance in property law.

[266] Using a term from Alan Watson, *Society and Legal Change* (Temple UP 2001) 87, 91, 122. For details, see ch 8, section III.C.

[267] Dagan and Samet (n 38) 148–49.

8

Form and Substance of the Numerus Clausus

THE STARTING POINT of this book is an apparent paradox inherent to many contemporary property systems: how can an area of private law made of a fixed list of rights, frequently described as static, rigid and formalistic, accommodate the demands created by a vast array of social and economic changes, without undergoing noticeable transformations?[1] Instead of denying the paradox, this book has opted to embrace it, arguing that the very legal principle that creates the paradox – the principle of *numerus clausus* – provides modern English and German property law with an 'internal' or 'doctrinal' structure that allows them to deal with changing social needs, while retaining their stability.

The previous chapters have argued that the *numerus clausus* is a doctrine that exists to ensure that property law retains a modular design made of 'substantive forms' that preserve personal autonomy over time[2] and shown how, in practice, these forms can accommodate a vast array of new realities.[3] In doing so, the previous chapters have outlined the operation and connections of the key building blocks of an institutional theory that seeks to explain economic performance over time:[4] 'property rights', understood as human-created devices that reduce transaction costs and organise exchange, 'the state', as the body in charge of designing and enforcing property rights, and 'ideology', that is, the underlying world view that determines the costs of maintaining and enforcing the property system.[5]

This chapter presents all these elements in a unified and coherent manner, in the context of the contemporary 'form and substance' debate. It starts by discussing what is 'formal' and what is 'substantive' in the *numerus clausus* doctrine (section I). Then, it outlines how the form and substance of the English and German *numerus clausus* enables individuals and the state to use a limited set of property types to accommodate new realities through a process of 'functional'

[1] See ch 1, section I.
[2] See ch 5, section IV.
[3] See chs 6 and 7.
[4] See Douglass C North, *Structure and Change in Economic History* (WW Norton 1981).
[5] For details, see ch 1, section IV.B.

transformation of its modules (section II). Afterwards, it explains the role of form and substance in the 'structural' transformation of the *numerus clausus* by legislators, regulators and courts (section III). The chapter ends highlighting the importance of formalism for the sound operation of property systems with modular designs (section IV).

I. HOW IS THE *NUMERUS CLAUSUS* FORMAL?

A. Form and Substance in Private Law

The 'form and substance' debate has a central role in contemporary Anglo-American private law theory.[6] However, what is meant by 'substance' and 'form' in this context remains uncertain.[7] Nonetheless, its core is a framework that sees 'formal reasoning' as the application of rules without reference to the justifications that underlie them and 'substantive reasoning' as making direct reference to consideration of justice, purpose, welfare or convenience.[8] The distinction seems to have been less explored in German private law, but 'formalism' has been associated with the excesses of Conceptual Jurisprudence, while 'substantivism' has been linked to the reaction to it by Interest Jurisprudence[9] and the development of the doctrine of horizontal application of human rights, during the post-war era.[10]

In common law academia, the 'form and substance' debate normally builds on the work of PS Atiyah and RS Summers, who used this distinction to flesh out the difference between the more 'substantive' American and more 'formal' style of English law.[11] In this view, substantive reasons can be 'goal', 'rightness' or 'institutional' arguments. The first are future oriented and derive their force from serving a social good. As such, they tend to overlap with the 'policy' justifications for the *numerus clausus* discussed in chapter five. The second, in

[6] For example, this was the topic of the IX Biennial Obligations Conference held in Melbourne in 2018.

[7] Andrew Burrows, 'Form and Substance: Fictions and Judicial Power' in Andrew Robertson and James Goudkamp (eds), *Form and Substance in the Law of Obligations* (Hart 2019) 17. Also see Kit Barker, 'Form and Substance: Three Observations of the State of the Debate' in Andrew Robertson and James Goudkamp (eds), *Form and Substance in the Law of Obligations* (Hart 2019) 433.

[8] Andrew Robertson and James Goudkamp, 'Between Form and Substance' in Andrew Robertson and James Goudkamp (eds), *Form and Substance in the Law of Obligations* (Hart 2019) 1.

[9] Birke Häcker, '"Substance Over Form": Has the Pendulum Swung Too Far?' in Andrew Robertson and James Goudkamp (eds), *Form and Substance in the Law of Obligations* (Hart 2019) 60. On Conceptual and Interest Jurisprudence, see ch 4, section II.

[10] See Stefan Grundmann, Hans-W Micklitz and Moritz Renner, *New Private Law* (CUP 2021) 193, 196.

[11] PS Atiyah and RS Summers, *Form and Substance in Anglo-American Law* (Clarendon Press 1987). Although a good part of the framework comes from previous work, especially Robert Summers, 'Two Types of Substantive Reasons: The Core of a Theory of Common-Law Justification' (1978) 63 *Cornell L Rev* 707. For details, see ch 4, section III.

contrast, accord to sociomoral norms that assess how a situation came about, typically focusing on categories as 'culpability' or 'fairness'. Thus, these reasons tend to have a close association with 'principle' or 'right-based' justifications of the *numerus clausus*, also discussed in chapter five. Finally, 'institutional' reasons are not conceptually independent from those already mentioned. These are either goal or rightness reasons, tied to specific institutional roles. These normally state that, for a given goal or rightness reason, some decision must be made by a specific body.[12] An example of this is the discussion on the institutional dimension of the *numerus clausus* contained in chapter four.

In contrast, formal reasoning is based on 'authoritative' arguments which judges are required to use to base their decision, normally with 'exclusion' of any others. These arguments are not identified by their substantive content (ie goals or morals), but rather by their 'source': they are binding because they are embodied in statute or precedent. However, this does not imply that formal rules do not have 'second-level' substantive reasons that justify them, including 'closing the debate', containing costs, minimising errors and ensuring that the right people or bodies are making relevant decisions.[13]

In contemporary Anglo-American private law theory, the form and substance debate can be linked to the distinction of what is 'internal' and 'external' to law. As mentioned in chapter five, in this framework, 'the internal' is associated to understanding private law on its own concepts (what it *is*), while 'the external' to explaining private law on the basis of its purpose (what it *does*).[14] Because, 'the internal' relies on legal concepts and categories, its reasoning tends to be more formal. In contrast, the concern of the 'the external' with the efficiency or fairness of outcomes, tends to make its arguments more substantive.[15] Recently, elements from both approaches have been successfully combined as part of the (mostly) American New Private Law movement, which claims to take conceptual or 'internal' aspects of private law seriously, but without relinquishing the use of elements coming from other 'external' disciplines, including philosophy and economics.[16] For example, Merrill and Smith's 'optimal standardisation' justification of the *numerus clausus* discussed in chapter five, section II has been said to follow this approach: by showing how the inflexibility of a formal rule supplies utility, it reflects deference to doctrine (form), while explaining the functions its serves (substance).[17]

[12] On substantive reasons, Summers (n 11) 716–25.

[13] Atiyah and Summers (n 11) 12–26.

[14] On the internal and the external, Andrew S Gold, 'Internal and External Perspectives: On the New Private Law Methodology' in Andrew S Gold and others (eds), *The Oxford Handbook of the New Private Law* (OUP 2021) 4.

[15] Andrew S Gold and Henry E Smith, 'Sizing up Private Law' (2020) 70 *U Toronto LJ* 489, 489–90.

[16] John CP Goldberg, 'Introduction: Pragmatism and Private Law' (2012) 125 *Harv L Rev* 1640, 1663; Gold (n 14).

[17] Barak Richman, 'New Institutional Economics' in Andrew S Gold and others (eds), *The Oxford Handbook of New Private Law* (OUP 2021), referring to Merrill and Smith's work.

The German discussion on 'form and substance' requires a longer explanation. In this jurisdiction, the debate normally takes an evolutionary or historical approach. The jurisprudential paradigm dominating at the time of the drafting of the BGB assumed that the content of legal rules could be logically inferred from well-defined concepts.[18] This was underpinned by a broader approach holding that 'values' – this is, considerations of substance – have no place in law.[19] The paradigm of this view is Hans Kelsen's Pure Theory of Law,[20] which is 'pure' in the sense that it seeks to account for law without reference to criteria of substance, like morals or politics. In private law, this was reflected on the dominance of Conceptual Jurisprudence at the time of the enactment of the BGB.[21]

The first reactions against this rather 'formalistic' view of private law came soon after the enactment of the BGB. In theorical discussions, this is reflected in the emergence of the Free Law Movement and Interest Jurisprudence.[22] From a practical perspective, it was visible in courts seeking to protect weaker parties in the economic turmoil of the interwar years by re-introducing natural law concepts rejected by the BGB.[23] This trend gained momentum after the foundation of the GFR in 1949, thanks to the open irruption of fundamental rights in private law adjudication[24] and their growing instrumentalisation to protect weaker parties in a modern consumer society.[25]

Behind this trend lies a relevant shift in the perceived status of private law *vis a vis* constitutional law.[26] At the time of the enactment of the BGB, private law was seen as a politically neutral,[27] self-standing and complete system, entirely independent from constitutional law.[28] However, after the Second World War, scholars reacting to the acritical application of Nazi law by German courts, especially Gustav Radbruch,[29] pushed for the introduction of substantive natural law ideas of justice into the very concept of law. This view was enshrined in the GG through Art 20(3), which subjects judges not only to '*Gestez*' (*lex*), but also to '*Recht*' (*ius*).[30] The implication is that corrupt (statutory) law

[18] Jörg Neuner, *Allgemeiner Teil des Bürgerlichen Rechts* (13th edn, Beck 2023) 92.

[19] Grundmann, Micklitz and Renner (n 10) 156, 158.

[20] Hans Kelsen, *Reine Rechtslehre. Studienausgabe der 1. Auflage 1934* (Matthias Jestaedt ed, Mohr Siebeck 2008).

[21] Neuner (n 18) 93. For Conceptual Jurisprudence, see ch 4, section II.B.

[22] ibid. On these movements, see ch 4, section II.B.

[23] Grundmann, Micklitz and Renner (n 10) 199. For example, the doctrine of the fall of the basis of the contract, see ch 4, section II.B, fn 110.

[24] Neuner (n 18) 48.

[25] Grundmann, Micklitz and Renner (n 10) 27.

[26] See Mattias Kumm, 'Who is Afraid of the Total Constitution? Constitutional Rights as Principles and the Constitutionalization of Private Law' (2006) 4 *German LR* 341, 360.

[27] Dieter Schwab and Martin Löhnig, *Einführung in das Zivilrecht* (20th edn, CF Müller 2016) 23.

[28] Grundmann, Micklitz and Renner (n 10) 24.

[29] Gustav Radbruch, 'Gesetzliches Unrecht und Übergesetzliches Recht' (1946) 1 *SJZ* 105.

[30] On this, also see ch 4, section II.A.

(lex corrupta), can be exceptionally corrected by judges resorting to substantive ideas of natural justice that reflect the commitment of the GFR to human rights.[31]

Soon after the foundation of the GFR, it became clear that the new *Bundestag* was not willing to legislate to implement a relevant part of the programmatic provisions contained in the GG. In this context, a famous essay criticising the gender pay gap called for the 'direct application of fundamental rights' as a 'replacement solution' by courts.[32] The call found some support in a 1954 ruling of the BAG,[33] triggering anxiety among scholars concerned with its impact on the separation of powers principle and the individuality of private law.[34] The issue was finally settled in the landmark decision of the 1958 *Lüth* case,[35] opening the floodgates to substantive constitutional reasoning in private law.

In *Lüth*, the BVerfG held that the GG establishes an 'objective order of values' that carries its force into all areas of law (including private law), providing guidelines and impulse for legislative, administrative and judicial action. As a result, fundamental rights not only give protection to individuals against the state, but also operate horizontally against other individuals (*Lehre der Drittwirkung von Grundrechte*),[36] and impose a duty on the state to actively protect fundamental rights (*Schutzpflichten Lehre*).[37] In private law, for example, this lead the BVerfG[38] to derive the social protection of tenants from the right to private property contained in Art 14(1) GG,[39] arguing that this provision protects both the ownership of lessors and the right to possession of lessees.[40] The overall resulting picture has been described as one of 'materialisation' of private law, in which formalist ideas of justice and equality have been gradually replaced by substantive or distributive justice criteria that seek to achieve social change through private law,[41] typically by 'balancing' conflicting interests (*Ausgleichung*).[42]

This does not imply that the relevance of formalism in German private law should be easily discarded. In the prevailing view, the subjection of judges to

[31] Neuner (n 18) 39–41.

[32] Hans-Carl Nipperdey, 'Gleicher Lohn der Frau für Gleiche Leistung' [1950] *RdA* 121.

[33] BAGE 1, 185.

[34] Stefan Oeter, '"Drittwirkung" der Grundrechte und die Autonomie des Privatrechts: Ein Beitrag zu den Funktionell-Rechtlichen Dimensionen der Drittwirkungsdebatte' (1994) 119 *AöR* 529, 532–34.

[35] BVerfGE 7, 198.

[36] Neuner (n 18) 50; Schwab and Löhnig (n 27) 33–34; Grundmann, Micklitz and Renner (n 10) 132–33.

[37] Kumm (n 26) 350.

[38] BVerfGE 89, 1.

[39] Neuner (n 18) 51.

[40] Valesca Maria Molinari, *Die Tradition Staatlicher Interventionen in den Mietwohnungsmarkt* (Mohr Siebeck 2021) 83.

[41] Grundmann, Micklitz and Renner (n 10) 193, 196.

[42] eg BVerfGE 148, 267, 280 f. Also see section III.C.

law (in the sense of *lex*) cannot be degraded for 'small change'.[43] This idea is already present in the high standard imposed by the Radbruch formula: 'positive law shall be applied, even when its content is unjust or disproportionate, unless it contradicts justice in an unbearable manner'.[44] In line with this, the invalidity of a statute can – in principle – (only) be declared by the BVerfG (Art 100 GG), making resort to Art 20(3) GG (only) permissible as *ultima ratio*.[45] Hence, private law disputes are to be solved, in the first instance, through the BGB and should not easily be transformed into constitutional problems. The rationale for this is that, even if private law is not fully self-standing and autonomous, it still has its own individuality. This is reinforced by Art 1(3) GG holding that rights contained in the GG 'shall bind the legislature, the executive and the judiciary as directly applicable law', without referencing individuals. Hence, in the prevailing view, fundamental rights only have an *indirect* horizontal effect between private parties, which is typically channelled through the general clauses of the BGB.[46] However, whether this has really protected private law from dilution by constitutional law has been doubted,[47] leading some to argue that, in practice, the difference between *direct* and *indirect* horizontal efficacy is 'negligeable'.[48]

B. Form and Substance of the *Numerus Clausus*

The 'form and substance' distinction has an obvious intuitive appeal to characterise property rights as one of the building blocks of the institutional theory adopted by this book.[49] However, despite seeming clear in theory, the metaphorical nature of this distinction makes it hard to apply in a consistent manner across broader real-life scenarios. Even if limited to the Anglo-American conceptual framework, the same rule or doctrine can be formal from one perspective, but substantive from another. For starters, all rules have some essential minimal forms: to be such, rules must be at least minimally prescriptive, general, definite and complete.[50]

However, the real complexity results from the circumstance that the formality of rules can be assessed from variety of perspectives that tend to be continuous, rather than binary. The two core factors are the ones mentioned above when discussing the Anglo-American approach: first, rules are said to have a high

[43] Neuner (n 18) 42 (my translation).
[44] Radbruch (n 29) 107 (my translation).
[45] Neuner (n 18) 42.
[46] On horizontal effects in private law, ibid 47–50.
[47] Oeter (n 34) 534.
[48] Kumm (n 26) 532. Also see n 164 and accompanying text.
[49] See ch 1, sections III.B and IV.B.
[50] Robert Summers, 'How is Law Formal and Why it Matters' (1997) 82 Cornell L Rev 1165, 1166–67.

level of 'authoritative' formality when their validity to solve a dispute derives from their source rather than from their content; and, second, rules are considered to have a high level of 'mandatory' formality when they tend to exclude other possible reasons for a decision, this is, when they work as 'exclusionary reasons'.[51] In this view, the English and German versions of the *numerus clausus* are rather formal: courts cannot create new property forms because the law says so and judges – at least in principle – cannot consider other reasons to decide whether a right created by A and B should be treated as proprietary.[52] In contrast, the American version of this doctrine seems less formal, having been described as a judicial self-restraint principle based on policy arguments, not clearly encapsulated in a precise authoritative manner.[53]

However, the terminology of 'form and substance' is also used in other contexts, especially in relation to the content and interpretation of rules. 'Content formality' is associated with the level of arbitrariness of a rule. For example, the rule stating that motorists must drive on one side of the road is highly formal as to its content: which side does not really matter, the important thing is that there is a rule. From this perspective, the English and German versions of the *numerus clausus* are not really formal. As argued in chapter five, the internal content of the list of property rights in both jurisdictions is far from arbitrary. The doctrine did not develop to protect standardisation for its own sake (ie to protect *any* form of standardisation), but rather to ensure that property law retains a very precise substantive structure that ensures that people will have significant liberty to redeploy assets over time. The analysis of foundational English cases as *Keppell v Bailey*[54] and *Hill v Tupper*[55] and the historical project enshrined in the BGB exemplify this.[56] This is key for the broader argument put forward in this book: despite its formal nature, the *numerus clausus* exists to protect the substantive design of modern property law, that is, its 'substantive forms'.[57]

In turn, 'interpretative formality' relates to whether rules are construed relying on the literal meaning of words or the substantive reasons that underlie them.[58] As with content formality, the *numerus clausus* principle does not have an extremely high level of interpretive formality. For example, *Keppell* in England and the BayObLG case involving the refusal of registration of an atypical mortgage in Germany,[59] evidence that courts – at least on occasions – apply

[51] Atiyah and Summers (n 11) 12, 16. On 'exclusionary reasons' in general, Joseph Raz, *Practical Reason and Norms* (2nd edn, OUP 1999), especially 35–48.

[52] See ch 3, sections II and III and, generally, ch 5.

[53] See ch 5, section II.

[54] *Keppell v Bailey* (1834) 2 My & K 517.

[55] *Hill v Tupper* (1863) 2 H & C 121, 159 ER 51.

[56] See chs 5, 6 and 7.

[57] See ch 5, section IV.

[58] Atiyah and Summers (n 11) 13–15.

[59] BayObLG, NJW 1967, 1373, 1374.

the doctrine-making reference to its underlying substantive justification.[60] More important, cases as *Regency Villas Title Ltd v Diamond Resorts (Europe) Ltd*[61] in England and the '*Wagons case*'[62] in Germany show that courts do not apply the elements of individual property types with blind formalism, but rather with an eye on the changing nature of the outside world.[63]

Nonetheless, the formal nature of the English and German *numerus clausus* principle is not completely alike. Formalism has, at least, two different strands: 'doctrinalism' and 'conceptualism'. Both share an 'internal' view of the law, meaning that they see it as 'autonomous' and, therefore, capable of providing its own solutions to certain problems, without reference to external elements. However, these views also have important differences. Doctrinalism can be seen as part of the English empiricist philosophical tradition. It starts with cases and other legal materials and, from there, induces principles and taxonomies that seek to bring order to legal chaos. Hence, it is not dogmatic about substantive reasons but is only willing to consider them if they are 'part of the law', for example because courts *actually* rely on them. In contrast, conceptualism has been associated with continental rationalism. This approach starts with *a priori* inherent principles and taxonomies and seeks to fit the law in them. Because of that, conceptualists do not tolerate conceptual overlaps nor policy arguments as well as doctrinalists.[64]

From this point of view, the English version of the *numerus clausus* seems to lean towards doctrinalism, while the German version seems more conceptualist. As discussed in chapters three and five, English scholarship primarily infers this principle from nineteenth century case law and the LPA 1925, and then tries to explain it based on arguments that can be found or deduced from the relevant materials.[65] In line with this, English doctrine seems relatively comfortable making exceptions to fit rights that bind only successors but not trespassers (ie 'pure ABC rights'), as well as accounting for the role of policy arguments in justifying occasional deviations of the principle. In contrast, German doctrine starts with a reading of the *Motive* in light of Savigny's aprioristic and 'inherently correct' distinction between rights in things and rights against persons.[66] Based on this distinction, traditional doctrine concludes that property *has to be* autonomous, a point from which the *numerus clausus* principle is said to 'follow like a theorem'.[67] By the same token, German doctrine also has to make relevant,

[60] For details, see ch 5, sections III and IV.

[61] *Regency Villas Title Ltd v Diamond Resorts (Europe) Ltd* [2018] UKSC 57, [2017] EWCA Civ 238.

[62] BGH 18.7. 2014 – V ZR 151/13.

[63] See ch 7, section II and III respectively.

[64] Dan Priel, 'Two Forms of Formalism' in Andrew Robertson and James Goudkamp (eds), *Form and Substance in the Law of Obligations* (Hart 2019) 166–77.

[65] See ch 3, section III and ch 5, section III.B.

[66] Friedrich Carl von Savigny, *System des Heutigen Römischen Rechts*, vol 1 (Veit & Comp 1840) 331–45, 367–79. See ch 2, section II for details.

[67] See ch 5, section III.A.

and sometimes artificial, efforts to force 'pure ABC rights' into the canonical distinction between personal and property rights,[68] instead of resorting to pragmatic reasons that could better explain them.

In summary, the *numerus clausus* is formal from some perspectives, but substantive from others. On the one hand, the doctrine clearly enjoys a high level of formality as to its authoritative nature and exclusionary character. On the other, however, this formal nature is directly linked to the substantive content of the property rights of each system. As argued in chapter five, besides generic second-level reasons (eg 'closing the debate'), the doctrine exists to ensure that property law keeps a certain substantive design, namely one that protects individual autonomy over time. In short, the *numerus clausus* is about legal forms serving substantive contents. Furthermore, the formal nature of this doctrine does not imply that it is also applied in a 'formalistic' manner. In both England and Germany courts have assessed whether the rights created by private parties qualify as proprietary in light of social and economic changes and, occasionally, disapplied the principle for goal-reasons. The next two sections show how this combination of formalism and substantivism allows English and German property law to deal with new realities without undergoing visible structural transformation.

II. FUNCTIONAL TRANSFORMATION: 'REDEPLOYMENT' AND 'RELOCATION' OF MODULES

As shown in chapter five the ultimate justification of the *numerus clausus* principle remains contested, but in operative terms, the principle works by standardising property rights in manners that preserve the autonomy of third parties, including those with property rights in the same thing (ABC cases) or in another thing (ABX cases).[69] This liberty enables private parties to 'functionally transform'[70] the object of their property rights in light of changing circumstances. In other words, by limiting the effects that private dealings can have on third parties, the *numerus clausus* ensures that property law retains a 'modular structure'[71] that allows private parties to re-deploy existing property rights in the face of new realities. Chapters six and seven offer several examples of this, which not only provide evidence supporting the modular theory, but also highlight its close connection with the *numerus clausus* principle. The following subsection explains this link in more detail.

[68] See nn 136 and 137 and accompanying text.

[69] See chs 7 and 6, respectively.

[70] Borrowing from Karl Renner, *The Institutions of Private Law and Their Social Functions* (Agnes Schwarzschild tr, Routledge and Kegan Paul 1976). For details, see ch 1, section I. On how this concept is used in this book, see especially ch 6, section IV.

[71] Borrowing from Henry E Smith, 'Property as the Law of Things' (2012) 125 *Harv L Rev* 1691; Henry E Smith, 'Economics of Property Law' in Francesco Parisi (ed), *The Oxford Handbook of Law and Economics: Volume 2: Private Law and Commercial Law* (OUP 2017).

A. Successor and Trespassory Liability

The modular design of property law is not a result of chance, but the outcome of the push of a variety of economic and ideological forces during the nineteenth century. These gave the property laws of England and Germany structures that are inherently capable of dealing with the changes of the modern world. The key to understanding how the *numerus clausus* achieves this is in the realisation that property rights have two distinctive effects that should not be confused: trespassory (ABX patterns) and successor liability (ABC patterns).[72] In both Germany and England, the effect that the *numerus clausus* has on the creation of trespassory liability is close to absolute. Save for certain low-intensity duties that cannot really be explained as correlative to a proprietary interest,[73] private parties can generally not create new and additional duties upon strangers, unless authorised by the law. In this manner, the *numerus clausus* effectively creates a 'normative firewall' that ensures that dealings between A and B will not impose duties on X that will affect the modular structure of her property rights. Thereby, the *numerus clausus* facilitates the functional transformation of property rights by limiting the number of people towards whom strangers might become liable in tort while they exercise a Hohfeldian liberty over their own property. Good examples of this are those of the pub owner in *Hill* and the developer in *Hunter and others v Canary Wharf Ltd*,[74] both discussed in detail in chapter six, section II.

The effect that the *numerus clausus* has on successor liability is harder to assess. However, in most cases, its impact is apparent. Either because rights that have ABC effects are the same as rights triggering trespassory liability or because they mirror their content,[75] most rights creating duties 'running with the asset' are also subject to a content control which aims to preserve the modular structure of property law. As shown in chapter seven, the standardised content of ABC rights varies depending on whether the right provides for the 'cross exploitation of land' or the 'temporal slicing of ownership'. However, the ultimate rationality of their content-control is the same: ensuring, first, that successors in title (C) will retain a module of property that will grant them discretion enough to 'set the agenda' of the thing,[76] including the power to 'functionally transform it' and, second, that any limitations of such power will be offset by enduring policy benefits. In addition, because the standardisation of most ABC rights relies on semi open-ended terms, parties can fit new variants of the same right

[72] Using the terminology of James Penner, 'Duty and Liability in Respect of Funds' in John Lowry and Mistelis Loukas (eds), *Commercial Law: Perspectives and Practice* (LexisNexis Butterworths 2006) 215. For details, see ch 2, ch 6, section I and ch 7, section I.

[73] As the tort of inducing the breach of a contract. See ch 6, section I.

[74] *Hunter and others v Canary Wharf Ltd* [1997] AC 665, HL.

[75] eg see ch 7, section I on the doctrine of anticipation.

[76] Using terminology from Larissa Katz, 'Exclusion and Exclusivity in Property Law' (2008) 58 *U Toronto LJ* 275.

within the pre-existing conceptual structure, as long as judges are prepared to find that the policy reasons justifying them are sufficiently enduring. This is apparent in the 'accommodation test' of English easements and the problem of 'eternal servitudes' in German law, both discussed in chapter seven.[77]

The difficulty in assessing the impact of the *numerus clausus* on successor liability is largely explained by the existence in both England and Germany of a group of 'pure ABC' rights that are not subject to a strict control as to the content they might have. English doctrine is accustomed to treat such rights (especially beneficial rights under a trust), as part of property law; while German scholarship tends to see them as obligations with far-reaching third-party effect (eg the right of lessees of land).[78] However, their creation is not entirely free nor without restrictions, while their effects on successors (C) are not idiosyncratic. In these cases, modern property law has developed other doctrines, either to limit the ability of A and B to impose duties on successors in title[79] or to provide for means in which successors can easily take property free from such duties.[80] These cases show that the *numerus clausus* is not as stringent for successor liability as it is for trespassory liability, but that the effects of pure ABC rights on successors are still limited. In this manner, the doctrine provides private parties with a certain level of freedom to delineate rights with some third-party effects in contexts like wealth management and housing, while ensuring that these rights will not impose idiosyncratic duties on third parties that could affect the modular structure of their property rights: complexity is contained in the AB relation, while its impact on C is simple and always the same.

B. Spontaneous and Directed Functional Transformation

From a static perspective, the modular design protected by the *numerus clausus* primarily relies on private autonomy to functionally transform and relocate the modules of property in a spontaneous manner. It does so by ensuring that the current owners enjoy a broad Hohfeldian liberty to apply the relevant asset to new purposes they can freely choose based on their 'knowledge of the particular circumstances of time and place'.[81] Behind this lies an ideological view that recognises the existence of a vast body of unorganised and rapidly changing 'local knowledge' that can only be accessed by those who are immediately exposed to it and, therefore, must be free to make decisions based on it,[82] like

[77] See ch 7, sections II and III.

[78] See ch 2, section IV.C.

[79] For example, the limited nature of the duties that beneficial rights in a trust impose on successors in title holding as constructive trustees. See ch 7, section II.B.

[80] For example, overreaching in English law. See ch 7, section II.

[81] Using an expression from FA Hayek, 'The Use of Knowledge in Society' (1945) 35 *Am Econ R* 519, 521.

[82] This is, of course, the view of Hayek (n 81).

Mr Bailey finding new routes to supply his mill in *Keppell*, Mr Tupper converting his pub into a leisure attraction in *Hill*, or the developers building on the derelict Isle of Dogs in *Hunter*.[83]

However, the 'spontaneous' re-arrangement of the modules of property law by free individuals is not enough to ensure the smooth operation of a modular property system. That is why, as explained in chapter two, the private allocation of property rights is routinely supplemented by their forced relocation through expropriations, compulsory purchases and 'takings', which are ultimately decided by the state.[84] These 'directed' or 'planned' relocations of the modules of property are key to solving holdout problems facilitated by the broad Hohfeldian liberty enjoyed by owners of modular property rights, and the existence of this state power is an implicit assumption of the modular designs protected by the *numerus clausus*. Historically, these 'forced relocations' have been instrumental in allowing societies to adapt to new realities, as exemplified by the British and German transitions from agricultural to industrial economies, and the role such forced relocations still have in building infrastructure projects.[85]

However, it is worth noting that the forced relocation of property rights does not undermine the modular structure of the system nor its basic spontaneous re-arrangement mechanism. Expropriations normally only take place in well-defined circumstances (eg the public interest), are subject to strict procedures, and trigger the payment of compensations that tend to make their distributive effects neutral.[86] Furthermore, when they occur, at least in standard cases, the modular design is not affected, as the individual modules simply pass to new hands, retaining their basic structure. Alternatively, these mechanisms impose duties that replicate the patterns of existing property rights, typically servitudes.

III. STRUCTURAL TRANSFORMATION: 'RE-MODULARISATION', 'RE-SHAPING' AND 'SCAFFOLDING'

The functional transformation of property rights by autonomous agents acting in markets, supplemented by expropriations as means to solve holdout problems, does not have an unlimited capability to deal with new realities: sometimes the creation of new building blocks or the reform of the existing ones is needed. This happens in three distinctive manners: legislative re-modularisation of property law, regulatory re-shaping of property rights, and judicial 'legal scaffolding'.[87]

[83] See ch 6, section II and ch 7, section II.
[84] See ch 2, section IV.
[85] See ch 2, section IV.
[86] For details, see ch 2, section IV.
[87] The last term comes from Alan Watson, *Society and Legal Change* (Temple UP 2001) 87, 91, 122. For details, see section III.C.

Each plays a key role in how the state adapts property law to new realities, but none seems to affect the core of the *numerus clausus* principle.

A. Legislative Re-modularisation

Legislation allows an escape from the dilemma of having to choose between 'formal certainty' and 'substantive justice': good legislation can both keep law technical (formal) and provide solutions to substantive challenges.[88] Thus, as argued in chapter four, under the English and the German *numerus clausus* principle, the primary avenue for structural transformation of property law is the enactment of new property types by Parliament. Because this implies creating new modules through private law, it can be described as an internal and legislative 're-modularisation' that can introduce substantive change in property law in a manner entirely consistent with the formal nature of the *numerus clausus* principle.

The problem with this re-modularisation is that passing legislation is normally extremely time-consuming,[89] might require reaching complex compromises between stakeholders and is frequently highly dependent on party-politics. Thus, a common perception is that the enactment of new property rights only happens in rare cases, which reinforces the static aura of property law. However, as shown in chapter three,[90] the impact of legislative reform in property law should not be underestimated. For example, in England, the 1922–25 land reform (quietly but radically) re-modularised property rights in land,[91] while subsequent legislation introduced an array of reforms in fields such as the family home,[92] trusts of land,[93] and registration.[94] In recent times this includes the enactment of a fully new module of property in the form of the commonhold[95] that – despite only enjoying moderate success so far[96] – the Law Commission seeks to expand.[97] Similarly, in Germany, the original strong principle of the BGB, providing for the unity of land and building in one single module of property, was brought to an end by legislation creating new property modules, first by fully regulating the superficies right[98] and then by providing for separate ownership in flats.[99]

[88] Priel (n 64) 191–94.
[89] ibid.
[90] See ch 3, section II.B, section III.B and section IV.B.
[91] See ch 3, section III.B.
[92] Matrimonial Homes Act 1967.
[93] TOLATA 1996.
[94] LRA 2002.
[95] Commonhold and Leasehold Reform Act 2002.
[96] Lu Xu, 'Commonhold Developments in Practice' in Warren Barr (ed), *Modern Studies in Property Law*, vol 8 (Hart 2015).
[97] Law Commission, *Reinvigorating Commonhold: The Alternative to Leasehold Ownership* (Law Com No 394, 2020).
[98] ErbbauVO, now ErbbauRG.
[99] WEG.

A relevant question is why these reforms have not affected the static aura of property law. There are two answers for this. In some cases, as with the English commonhold, this can be explained by the inability of a reform to take hold in legal practice. In other, this might be explained by reforms not being seen as introducing a break with the past, thereby making change less conspicuous. As explained in chapter 7, section III, the German WEG is a good example of the later: flat ownership is deemed to be conceptually the same as generic ownership under the BGB.

This difference is very telling. The WEG and the commonhold reform sought to introduce a very similar module of property law in two countries that are quite similar when it comes to factors such as economic development, urbanisation, demographics and so on. There are many elements at play that might explain the different fortunes of these reforms.[100] One of them seems to involve the *style* of re-modulisation chosen in each case. Reforms that reproduce the pre-exiting modular structure of the relevant property system seem to work better, as shown by the success of the German flat ownership.[101] In contrast, reforms that depart from the pre-existing modular patterns, like the English commonhold, can struggle to become accepted in practice because they introduce types of rights that are unfamiliar to their purported users.[102] The implication is that reforms that build on preexisting 'substantive forms' seem to be easier to implement and thus, tend to be more successful in practice.

B. Regulatory Re-shaping

In contrast to legislative re-modularisation, 'regulatory re-shaping' of property is external to private law. As discussed in chapter two, at least since the dawn of the twentieth century, governments have enacted vast bodies of public law regulation that alter the building blocks of property rights 'from outside', normally by limiting the uses owners can make of their things,[103] but without granting specific individuals correlative claim-right.

Although it is clear that the impact of regulation in contemporary societies is massive, this phenomenon does not seem to have altered the static perception of property law. This may largely be because regulatory change of property rights is normally channelled through constitutional law doctrines that operate in parallel to private law, such as the American doctrine of regulatory takings, the development of a separate constitutional concept of ownership by the BVerfG, or the supremacy of the UK Parliament, but also by the fact that domestic private

[100] The point is expanded in ch 9, section I.C.

[101] See ch 7, section III.B.

[102] See (n 96) 332, 334–35, on the practical irrelevance of the common hold reform.

[103] For example, German regulations protecting the environment, animals and housing. See ch 2, section II.B.

law scholars have historically downplayed its impact on traditional property law concepts.[104]

Nonetheless, the impact of regulation on property law is visible at many levels. For example, in the context of Anglo-American property theory, it has left an enduring legacy in the form of the bundle of rights metaphor;[105] while in Germany, the acknowledgment of leases as a form of property under the GG and the constant growth in importance of rent controls seem to have substantively affected the contractual nature of leases, bringing them closer to property law.[106] However, because these phenomena are perceived as happening 'outside' private law, they do not seem to affect the basic modular structure of property law.

C. Legal Scaffolding

Finally, property law also evolves through 'legal scaffolding'.[107] This is a back-up mechanism in which a complex combination of existing legal categories is used to cure or moderate the divergence between law and social needs. This typically happens when institutional bodies with formally recognised law-making powers fail to introduce simpler rules that could close the gap.[108] Thus, if legislative re-modularisation is 'internal' to private law and regulatory re-shaping is 'external' to it, judicial legal scaffolding is better described as an 'anomalous' or 'remedial' re-modularisation of property law.

As shown in chapter three, when bodies holding the formal competence[109] to develop property law fail to do so, this function is occasionally assumed by judges. Arguably, this qualifies as a breach of the *numerus clausus*, but courts rarely – if ever – admit it.[110] Formalism often plays a central role in this, because scaffolding involves using legal technicalities (forms) to achieve substantive ends. The problem with this is that these 'fictions' hide the 'inner truth' (substance) behind a 'false appearance' (form),[111] making law, in the long run, more complex and detached from everyday life.[112] Thus, even if scaffolding can make law more responsive to specific demands, it does so at the cost of making the law generally more formalistic and cumbersome and, therefore, detached from lay people. In England, the evolution of Equity is a

[104] See ch 2, section IV.
[105] See ch 2, section II and section IV.
[106] See ch 7, section III.
[107] Borrowing a term from Alan Watson. See n 108 below.
[108] Watson (n 87) 87, 91, 122.
[109] Rules that distribute competences are also typically described as 'formal', see Summers (n 50) 1180.
[110] See ch 3.
[111] Burrows (n 7) 19, 22.
[112] Watson (n 87) 122.

good example. Although this body of law originally developed as a pragmatic reaction to correct unsatisfactory substantive outcomes produced by the rigid and formalist common law of the late Middle Ages, over time it became more formal, becoming as rigorous and unyielding as the common law.[113] However, at least in one view, the *particular* formal structure developed by modern Equity over the centuries holds the key to explaining its success in infusing flexibility to the law, without distorting it: Equity does not deny, disapply or modify the common law, but acts as a 'supplement' to it, creating 'equitable' rights that control how 'legal' rights are exercised.[114]

Because legal scaffolding relies on pre-existing legal forms, it is subject to inherent limits on the scale and timing of the changes it can introduce. In contemporary England this is well reflected in an opinion delivered by Lord Goff holding that, as a general rule, judges

> not only … must act within the confines of the doctrine of precedent, but that the change so made must be seen as a development, usually a very modest development, of existing principle and so can take its place as a congruent part of the common law as a whole. In this process, what Maitland has called the 'seamless web,' and I myself … have called the 'mosaic,' of the common law, is kept in a constant state of adaptation and repair, the doctrine of precedent, the 'cement of legal principle,' providing the necessary stability.[115]

Thus, when developing the law, common law judges are not free. They must move step by step, with each step normally being anticipated in previous case law, preventing judges from staring afresh and becoming mini-legislators with no democratic mandate.[116] As a result, as with Maitland's 'web' or Lord Goff's 'mosaic', legal scaffolding works by slowly reproducing the 'substantive forms' of pre-existing legal patterns.

This idea is also broadly consistent with the *indirect* horizontal efficacy of fundamental rights in German private law, at least in theory. According to this doctrine, the substantive irradiation of fundamental rights into disputes between individuals should not dissolve private law, but operate through its forms. As a consequence, the formal style of Conceptual Jurisprudence still plays an essential role in German legal thinking.[117] Despite the contemporary

[113] Sarah Worthington, *Equity* (2nd edn, OUP 2006) 8–9, 11–12; Jeffrey Hackney, *Understanding Equity and Trusts* (Fontana Press 1987) 15–20.

[114] Ben McFarlane, 'Form and Substance in Equity' in Andrew Robertson and James Goudkamp (eds), *Form and Substance in the Law of Obligations* (Hart 2019) 197; Ben McFarlane, 'The Persistence of Equity: Lessons from the Trust', *Equity Today: 150 Years of the Judicature Reforms* (Hart 2023) 7–8, 13–17.

[115] *Kleinwort Benson Ltd v Lincoln City Council* [1999] 2 AC 349, 378.

[116] Burrows (n 7) 26–27.

[117] Karl Larenz and Manfred Wolf, *Allgemeiner Teil des Bürgerlichen Rechts* (9th edn, Beck 2004) 73; Heinrich Honsell, 'Einleitung Zum BGB' in Dagmar Kaiser and Markus Stoffels (eds), *J. Staudingers Kommentar zum Bürgerlichen Gesetzbuch mit Einführungsgestetz und Nebengesetzen. Eckpfeiler des Zivilrechts* (6th edn, Sellier & de Gruyter 2018) 52. For example, standard textbooks

acknowledgment of the power of judges to 'extend law' based on rightness-reasons (like fundamental rights or the principle of good faith) and goal-reasons (eg the 'needs of legal affairs'), they still remain bounded by legislation.[118] Thus, even when intentionally establishing new legal principles that can then be generalised, German judges almost universally avoid describing themselves as creators of law.[119] As in England, German scaffolding based on human rights is supposed to work within the pre-existing categories of the legal system. In this vein, the BVerfG makes a conscious effort to control the impact of the GG in private law, recognising that the court

> only has a limited scope to review the constitutionality of private law disputes. Fact finding, interpretation and applications of the law are for ordinary courts. The constitutional court can only intervene when the holding from an ordinary court incurs in a fundamental mistake about the meaning and scope of the GG or when the outcomes of the decisions go against its order of values.[120]

However, unlike English Equity, the *indirect* application of human rights does not (yet) have a well-established doctrinal structure capable of channelling substantive reasoning into individual disputes in a fully predictable manner. Despite the clear consensus that the intervention of the BVerfG has a moderate scope, its decisions tend to only have vaguely recognisable structures.[121] The BVerfG's case law on termination of leases is a good example. Since the 1970s, the court issued several rulings on the constitutionality of statutory limitations imposing rent caps and requiring lessors to have legitimate reasons to give notice to end residential tenancy agreements.[122] The BVerfG upheld these limitations as a balance between the rights of owners and the social function of property, both contained in Art 14 GG. These decisions laid the ground for a line of cases that ended up holding that the owner's mere desire to move into her own flat or let it to a person of her choosing (ie personal use), is not *per se* a 'legitimate reason' to give notice on a lease (*ordentliche Kündigung*), as the 'mere desire' to live in one's own flat is not legally equivalent to *needing* it, as the law requires. The rationale for this is the following: the hallmark of the constitutionally protected right to private property is the free use and disposal of what one owns. This includes the right to give notice to tenants. However, the landlord cannot exercise this monopoly over residential space in manners that produce harmful consequences for society or the economy. Therefore, Parliament introduced a balancing test which makes the right of landlords to

present the 'subsumption' paradigm as the primary approach to legal application, eg Hans Brox and Wolf-Dietrich Walker, *Allgemeiner Teil des BGB* (36th edn, Vahlen 2012) 29–33.

[118] See Larenz and Wolf (n 117) 77–79, 88, 93–96, 221–222; Neuner (n 18) 33–34, 44–46. For details, see ch 4, section II.

[119] Uwe Kischel, *Comparative Law* (Andrew Hammel tr, OUP 2019) 373.

[120] BVerfGE 32, 311, 316 (my translation).

[121] Oeter (n 34) 531.

[122] eg BVerfGE 37, 132.

give notice dependent on their motivation.[123] From a practical perspective, the implication is that, although the substance of ownership includes the freedom to use the object of property oneself, the trial courts must also investigate the seriousness and reasonability of this personal use.[124]

In practice, the application of this maxim turns a balancing test that is said to be established by Parliament into broad judicial discretion to make case-by-case decisions based on substantive justice criteria. Indeed, the same BVerfG recognises that the 'scope of the horizontal efficacy of fundamental rights depends on the circumstances of the individual case'.[125] This is visible in the different outcome of two cases that were tried together before the BVerfG.[126] In both cases, the appellants argued that the application by the trial court of the rules that require landlords to have a 'legitimate interest' to terminate residential leases[127] had violated their constitutional right to private property. In one case, the BVerfG upheld the decision of the trial court to deny the landlord the right to terminate a lease of a very large flat because he now wanted to use it with his partner. The trial court argued that this reason was disproportionate in light of the large size of the flat and the relatively limited needs of the landlord and would, therefore, impose an excessive burden on the tenant. However, in the other case, the BVerfG reversed a holding denying an elderly lady the right to terminate a lease over a flat that she owned, located in the same building she lived in, and which she now required in order to house someone to take care of her. The BVerfG argued that such denial had breached her constitutional right to private property.[128] In both cases, the court implied that it was only applying a legislative decision, consisting in appropriately acknowledging the needs of landlord and tenant. However, it is hard to mask that these decisions are primarily underpinned by substantive considerations regarding the desirability of the outcomes of the cases at hand.[129] Thus, even if decisions such as these take the form of a balancing test established by legislation, the substantive outcome in a specific case is difficult to predict *ex ante*, due to the high dependence on judicial discretion.

Despite not being desirable, legal scaffolding is typically tolerated for lack of a better alternative.[130] In English law, equitable intervention is probably historically[131] and conceptually[132] the paradigm of a legal scaffolding that is

[123] BVerfGE 89, 1.

[124] On these development, Oeter (n 34) 554–55; Molinari (n 40) 101–08.

[125] BVerfGE 148, 267, 280 (my translation).

[126] BVerfGE 68, 36.

[127] Now contained in §§ 573 and ff BGB.

[128] For discussion, Christian Bumke and Andreas Voßkuhle, *Casebook Verfassungsrecht* (8th edn, Mohr Siebeck 2020) 298–300.

[129] See Honsell (n 117) 69–70.

[130] Watson (n 87) 89.

[131] See Worthington (n 113) 8–13; Hackney (n 113) 15–20.

[132] See Henry E Smith, 'Equity as Meta-Law' (2021) 130 *Yale LJ* 1050.

placed 'on top' of a pre-existing structure. In property law, the maturation of (initially purely personal) restrictive covenants into rights with ABC and ABX effects through the exercise of equitable jurisdictions is a good example. This also shows the addition of unnecessary complexity by scaffolding: from a functional perspective, restrictive covenants would nowadays be better conceptualised as legal rather than equitable property rights.[133]

German private law does not possess an institutionalised 'supplementary' legal system like Equity[134] to correct the excesses of a strict application of the law. Instead, it normally relies for this on certain open ended 'general clauses' contained in the BGB to introduce substantive reasons into legal discourse.[135] However, leaving lease law aside, German property law is not prone to these general clauses. As a result, legal scaffolding in this area tends to feature elaborate and arcane constructs, like the distinction between the 'internal' and 'external' effects of the *Treuhand*,[136] or artificial formulas, such as the one holding that the anticipation right of the buyer (*Antwartschaftsrecht*) is 'less than ownership, but still essentially the same' (*wesengleiches Minus*).[137]

D. Pure Substantivism

Legal scaffolding, understood as the careful and purposeful use, or even manipulation of legal forms to achieve substantive ends, must be distinguished from 'pure substantivism' or 'remedialism'; that is, cases where judges who dislike the outcome that a rule produces simply disregard it, arguing that applying it would be 'formalistic' or 'legalistic'. Such a trend, that bluntly puts substance over form, seems to be on the rise in English property law, as seen in recent cases like *Shell UK Ltd and others v Total UK Ltd and others*[138] and *Manchester Airport plc v Dutton and others*.[139] Similar concerns have also been raised by German scholars in connection to the doctrine of horizontal efficacy of fundamental rights, warning against a 'constitutional totalitarianism' that could dissolve the 'individuality of private law',[140] turning Germany into an

[133] See ch 3, section III.C and ch 6, section II.B.

[134] On Equity's supplemental role, Jessica Hudson, Ben McFarlane and Charles Mitchell, *Hayton, McFarlane and Mitchell on Equity and Trusts* (15th edn, Sweet & Maxwell 2022) 16.

[135] The, so called, 'escape to the open legal provisions' (*Flucht in die Generalklauseln*), see Honsell (n 117) 31.

[136] eg see Jan Wilhelm, *Sachenrecht* (5th edn, De Gruyter 2016) 12; Marina Wellenhofer, *Sachenrecht* (34th edn, Beck 2019) 17, 18; Fritz Baur, Jürgen Baur and Rolf Stürner, *Sachenrecht* (18th edn, Beck 2009) 787. For details, see ch 3, section II.C.

[137] BGHZ 28, 16 (my translation).

[138] *Shell UK Ltd and others v Total UK Ltd and others* [2010] EWCA Civ 180, [2011] QB 86, openly at [136] and[144], discussed in ch 6, section II.B.

[139] *Manchester Airport plc v Dutton and others* [2000] QB 1333, CA, discussed in ch 6, section II.B.

[140] See Thomas Simon, '"Grundrechtstotalitarismus" oder "Selbstbehauptung des Zivilrechts"' (2004) 204 *AcP* 264, 265 (my translation).

'oligarchical judicial state'.[141] These are worrying developments. As explained below, the simple disregard of legal forms to achieve immediate substantive outcomes poses an existential threat to the modular design of property law. In contrast to scaffolding, which hides and distorts the clean facade of property law to achieve an end, substantivism destroys its structure, leaving no certainty to build on in the future.

This does not imply that courts should be oblivious to the consequences of their decision, but rather that judges should use the 'substantive forms' of property law to achieve just and sensible ends, instead of disregarding them. For example, in *Dutton*, Laws LJ argued that not extending the protection of licensees in possession to those who are not yet in possession is based on a 'false assumption ["the form"]' and that the 'true principle ["the substance"] is that a licensee not in occupation may claim possession against a trespasser if that is a necessary remedy to … give effect to such … licence'.[142] That is an unnecessary destruction of legal forms to make a remedy available to the claimant. As discussed in chapter six,[143] the same outcome could have been met by arguments consistent with the 'substantive forms' of the *numerus clausus*: Manchester Airport (B) could have forced the National Trust (A) to seek possession against Dutton (X) to comply with A's contractual obligation to B.[144]

However, formalism also requires accepting that courts *will* and *should* not always be able to achieve the substantive outcomes they desire by manipulating legal forms. In *Shell*, for example, denying compensation to the claimant (B) was not 'legalistic',[145] as argued by the court, but conceptually and practically sound. B could have also chosen to be the legal owner of the damaged site, but for good reasons it did not. Thus, contrary to what was held by the court, Shell (B) was *not* the '*real*'[146] owner of the damaged property. For the reasons explored in chapter six,[147] B cannot have the benefits of a trust and at the same time have the rights of a legal owner.

Finally, cases as *Dutton* and *Shell* illuminate the limits of 'doctrinalist formalism'. The fact that courts *actually* rely on certain substantive reasons to disregard previous rules does not make those reasons *per se* part of the law. The law has and needs some level of 'conceptual' formalism to keep its shape. Otherwise, the edifice of property simply collapses, diluted in substance. That is why Equity had to develop formal rules and principles to be workable over time. German courts also correctly identified this, at least at a conceptual level, when

[141] Bernd Rüthers, 'Methodenrealismus in Jurisprudenz Und Justiz' (2006) 61 *JZ* 53, 60 (my translation).
[142] *Dutton* (n 139) 149–50.
[143] See ch 6, section II.B.
[144] Ben McFarlane, *The Structure of Property Law* (Hart 2008) 345, fn 22. Also see Oscar Han, 'Licensee versus Trespasser: Hill v Tupper Resuscitated' (2016) 6 *Prop L Rev* 87.
[145] *Shell* (n 138) [136].
[146] ibid [144].
[147] See ch 6, section II.B.

holding that fundamental rights should only be applied *indirectly* through the categories of private law. To what extent they achieve this is a different question that will be addressed in the next and final section of this chapter.

IV. PROPERTY'S NEED FOR FORMALISM

A. The Substance of Property Forms

Formalism has a bad reputation[148] and is often ridiculed in legal discourse.[149] That is why the perceived long historical trend from formal to substantive law[150] is frequently regarded as a positive one. However, these optimistic views forget that *modern* formalism developed for good reasons, downplaying the perils of moving towards more 'responsive' forms of law. Modern legal formalism is not akin to that of 'irrational' magical rituals of archaic Roman law or the strict writs of medieval English law, but is the result of a rational and conscious effort to control or tame the arbitrary exercise of power by isolating adjudication from political power.[151]

In property law, controlling discretion is essential. Property rights have an inherent ability to impose duties or liabilities on people who have not accepted nor been informed of them. Thus, for pragmatic reasons associated with certainty, as well as for moral reasons related to the protection of autonomy, the private creation of property rights must be controlled by law. The *numerus clausus* achieves this through a sound combination of formal and substantive elements. At its core, this doctrine is effectively a formal one: at least in England and Germany, it derives its normative force from its source, it normally works as an 'exclusionary reason' to deny proprietary effects to rights not contained in the list, and its content is essentially about distributing competencies and powers to create property rights.

However, the *numerus clausus* is not a *formalistic* doctrine. From the perspective of 'content formality', the legal forms it protects are not arbitrary. As argued in chapter five, the content of the rights contained in the English and German list of property rights responds to a substantive rationality that relies both on goal (policy) and rightness (principle-based) reasons. In this sense, the *forms* of property can be said to reflect a *substantive* design, somehow collapsing the rigid distinction between 'form and substance'. Furthermore, from an 'interpretative' standpoint, the *numerus clausus* doctrine is not applied in a formalistic manner, as courts often interpret the elements of property right

[148] Atiyah and Summers (n 11) 7.
[149] Priel (n 64) 186.
[150] Häcker (n 9) 36.
[151] On formalism as instrument to control power, Philippe Nonet and Philip Selznick, *Law and Society in Transition: Toward Responsive Law* (2nd edn, Transaction Publishers 2001) 53, 57.

with a certain regard to its substantive underpinning. Finally, in both England and Germany the contemporary formulation of the doctrine is somewhere in between doctrinalism and conceptualism. On the one hand, domestic doctrine recognises that judges have, on occasions, used legal scaffolding to enforce rights that are not part of the list as proprietary and tries to rationalise this. On the other hand, however, modern formulations of the *numerus clasus* principle do not tolerate all deviations: pure substantivism or 'remedialism' is not acceptable under this doctrine. Under the principle of *numerus clausus*, courts must use the 'substantive forms' of private law to accommodate change. This is not formalism for the sake of forms, but rather to protect the substance of the modular design of property law.

Once these formal and substantive elements are put together, the resulting picture is one in which the *numerus clausus* principle works as a formal doctrine that protects the substantive design of a system that has the inherent capability of accommodating new realities. From a static perspective, the bulk of the work is done by the functional transformation of the modules of property law by autonomous individuals acting in markets. In those exceptional cases in which individual modules become 'trapped' in situations that encourage speculative behaviours that hinder their spontaneous functional transformation, this basic mechanism is supplemented by the forced relocation of modules by the state. From a dynamic perspective, the system adapts to new realities through the legislative reform and creation of new property modules ('re-modularisation') and the regulation by public law of the existing ones ('re-shaping'). Exceptionally, when none of this works, judges use the forms of property to develop 'legal scaffoldings' that close gaps between the law and social needs, at the cost of adding complexity to the systems.

B. The Challenge of Substance

In practice, modular systems will not always be able to accommodate new realities. Functional transformation and legal scaffolding have inherent limits, while legislators and regulators may fail to re-modularise and re-shape property law in a timely manner. As a consequence, the autonomy of formal law comes at the cost having legal systems that can be relatively irresponsive to outcomes and, therefore, on occasions, not adequately address social needs.[152] This implies that formalism is subject to a structural dilemma, as even good rules sometimes produce bad outcomes.[153] Therefore, in practice, claimants will inevitably push judges to rely on substantive elements to make law more responsive to reality. This is why formalism has been said to carry the seed of its own demise.[154]

[152] ibid 70–72.
[153] Emily Sherwin, 'Formalism and Realism in Private Law' in Andrew S Gold and others (eds), *The Oxford Handbook of New Private Law* (OUP 2021) 468, 471.
[154] Nonet and Selznick (n 151) 70–72.

The emergence of an equitable jurisdiction in late medieval England and the rise of the doctrine of horizontal effects of fundamental rights in post war Germany are good examples of this evolutionary pressures.

However, movements towards substantivism also have costs. Having a more 'responsive law' involves sacrifiging other values in favour of achieving substantive purposes. This trend might make law more accessible in the short run, but in the long rung it also weakens the authority of its rules, enlarges the discretion of judges and makes legal institutions more vulnerable. These conditions create risks of regression to 'repressive law', this is, to the arbitrary exercise of power, not subject to form,[155] including the retroactive application of law to well-established situations that individuals might have legitimately relied upon.[156] Thus, if autonomous law is structurally exposed to erosion by substantive reasoning, it is essential that judges – at least – channel substantive arguments through pre-existing legal patterns.

Adherence to a certain ideological view on the role of judges and legislators is central to this. On the one hand, preserving the forms of private law requires a 'volitional commitment'. Agents must decide *ex ante* that they will not reassess rules when applying them, unless there is a *very good* reason to reconsider,[157] in which case these reasons must be channelled through doctrines that are consistent with the existing structures of the legal system. The development of English Equity into a formalised set of rules and principle over the centuries is a good example of this. That is also why the assertation by German courts that human rights can only bind individual rights *indirectly* is well-targeted, even if this doctrine still lacks a conceptually robust structure that makes its outcomes more predictable. On the other, formalism requires accepting that preserving an autonomous law requires calling on legislators to fix important problems, especially when they involve redistributive goals. Formalism can tolerate occasional substantive deviations, but only as long as these are limited and not too frequent.[158] Without this basic ideological adherence to the distribution of state-power over law, *a numerus clausus* of property rights will struggle to survive.

The question is what is 'too much' and 'too frequent' substantive judicial reasoning. If classic views as the one put forward by Summers and Atiyah are to be believed, there is little doubt that the pendulum swung further towards substantivism in America. In England, by contrast, the pendulum has been said to have settled for most of the twentieth century into a relatively stable mid-way position.[159] However, in recent years some scholars have denounced a worrying trend towards understanding whole bodies of rules as open-textured, not only

[155] ibid 116–17.
[156] On this, see ch 4, section III.B and section III.C.
[157] Sherwin (n 153) 473–74. On what this could mean for the *numerus clausus*, see ch 5, section IV.
[158] Priel (n 64) 187, 189, referring to private law in general.
[159] Häcker (n 9) 62.

at the margins, but even at their core,[160] while courts have also been criticised for too readily disregarding legal forms to provide remedies to what they see as deserving claims.[161] Notably, in England this trend has not relied in a relevant manner on human rights. Even after the entering into force of the HRA 1998, the impact of human rights on English property law remains fairly limited.[162]

In Germany, this trend has taken a different form. Due to the expansive nature of constitutionalism during the post-war years, fundamental rights now play a key role in introducing substantive reasoning into private law adjudication. However, this swing of the pendulum has not diluted the forms of property law. As shown in previous chapters, German property law still enjoys a healthy level of formalism, among other things, thanks to human rights being applied only *indirectly* in private law disputes. This has an important merit: it implies that substantive arguments introduced into private law adjudication are, at least, broadly 'legally formalised' as fundamental rights. Thus, under this doctrine, for example, courts cannot rely on substantive considerations that cannot be reconducted to the GG. However, this doctrine still lacks conceptual structure and the BVerfG has been said to *de facto* apply fundamental rights *directly* in private law disputes.[163] Not all see a problem in this, as there is also a visible push in German scholarship to understand private law as a form of 'applied constitutional law' that reduces all disputes to a process of balancing conflicting interest.[164]

The contemporary movement from form to substance represents a menace for the modular structure of property law, as it overhauls the three basic institutional building blocks that explain how a society deals with change: the structure of property rights, the role of the state and the ideology that underpins its operation. Instead of fixed property rights, underpinned by a classic liberal ideology, which can only be changed by legislators and shaped by regulators based on general policy goals, substantive trends promote a flexible list of property rights, which can be changed and shaped by courts looking at their immediate substantive effects on the case at hand, based on strongly intuitive ideas of justice.[165]

[160] eg ibid.

[161] For example, *Shell* and *Dutton*. See respectively, Robertson and Goudkamp (n 8) 5; William Swadling, 'Opening the Numerus Clausus' (2000) 116 *LQR* 354.

[162] See Ben McFarlane, Nicholas Hopkins and Sarah Nield, *Land Law: Text, Cases and Materials* (5th edn, OUP 2021) 147–48; Rachael Walsh, 'Stability and Predictability in English Property Law – the Impact of Article 8 of the European Convention on Human Rights Reassessed' (2015) 131 LQR 585, 600–03.

[163] Neuner (n 18) 51 mentioning the 'Stadium-prohibition decision' (Stadionverbot-Entscheidung), BVerfGE148, 267. Similarly, Bumke and Voßkuhle (n 128) 56.

[164] eg Kumm (n 26) 359.

[165] eg, in the context of continental Europe, Bram Akkermans, *Sustainable Property Law. Reckoning, Resilience, and Reform* (Eleven International Publishers 2022) 15, 20–22. In the context of the common law, Hanoch Dagan, *A Liberal Theory of Property Law* (CUP 2021) 110–12. For details, see ch 1, section II.B.

If this goes too far, the trend could be fatal for the current structure of English and German property law: it is simply not possible to have a closed list of property rights without a formal doctrine that provides an 'exclusionary reason' to decide what rights count as proprietary. Thus, if the *numerus clausus* serves valuable substantive goals and principles, formalism in property law cannot be pejoratively disregarded as 'mere' or 'blind' legalism nor be dissolved into an unstructured balancing of substantive interests. This does not imply that property law should not evolve in line with social needs, but acknowledges that the responsibility to adapt property law to new realities lies primarily with legislators and regulators, as only they enjoy the political legitimacy and technical competences to change the 'substantive forms' of property law.

9

The Future of the Numerus Clausus

THE FIRST CHAPTER of this book started with a quote from Benjamin Cardozo stating that the law must have a 'principle of growth'.[1] Over the following chapters, this monograph argued that, in property law, such a principle is found in a loose understanding of private autonomy, based on a collection of ideas from nineteenth century political and economic liberalism. The book has shown that, thanks to the principle of *numerus clausus*, this broad conception of private autonomy has – until now – allowed English and German property law to be 'ready for the morrow'.[2]

This has relevant implications for contemporary property theory. Contrary to views advanced by progressive theorists, it shows that the functioning of a property system animated by a principle of personal autonomy requires strict controls on the ability of private parties to impose duties and liabilities on others. A key implication is that reliance on autonomy as 'organisational principle' of property law has led real-life legal systems to adopt 'modular designs', like those proposed by information theorists. Thereby, this book adds a principle-based justifications to the efficiency arguments that support the *numerus clausus* and the modular theory of property law. In this combined view, the *numerus clausus* promotes both individual autonomy and allocative efficiency by ensuring that property law maintains a carefully designed internal structure that allows the 'functional transformation' of property rights over time, displacing most concerns of progressive theorists from private law to public law and politics.

Having an awareness of the central role that the *numerus clausus* principle plays in protecting private autonomy and how this enables modern property law to accommodate new realities is of key importance. Over the twentieth century this idea was almost lost in Anglo-American private law theory, under the heavy push of economic analysis of law; while in civilian systems, where the *numerus clausus* principle never lost visibility (but remained undertheorised), it has recently come under attack by scholars arguing for its relaxation and for expanding the list of property rights.

[1] Benjamin N Cardozo, *The Growth of the Law* (Yale UP 1924) 20.
[2] ibid, for the quote.

This does not imply that property law should not be reformed in light of new policy needs. The *numerus clausus* principle does not call for keeping property law static, but rather for its re-modularisation to occur via well-thought legislative interventions that are consistent with the internal structure of property law and ensure that any diminishing of its modularity will be outweighed by policy gains that will stand the test of time. These findings have some relevant implications for the future of the *numerus clausus*, and for property law more broadly. This final chapter briefly explores these repercussions, focusing on scholarship (section I) and legal reform (section II).

I. PROPERTY LAW SCHOLARSHIP

A. Rise of Comparative Property Law

From a methodological perspective, this book has shown that comparative research can be useful for both conceptual and doctrinal approaches to property law. This is *per se* a significant finding, as only 25 years ago, research in this field was scarce and frequently seen as incapable of producing relevant outcomes.[3] While it is true that since the turn of the millennia comparative property law has been on the rise,[4] conceptual cross-fertilisation in this field has been limited to doctrines that are very general in nature. By combining the pragmatic style of English law with the conceptualist approach of German doctrine to assess a theoretical problem, this monograph has shown that there is still much to gain in this field: comparative property law is still only at the beginning of its path.

In this book, probably the best example showing how much there is to gain from comparing specific aspects of national doctrine and borrowing theoretical developments from other traditions is the use of the distinction between trespassory and successor liability. In this monograph, the distinction has been used as an analytical device to approach the effects of the *numerus clausus* on the private delineation of property rights, but its conceptual power is not limited to this. The distinction, which in England has been recently applied to explain the nature of rights that are in the border between the law of property and the law of obligations, especially equitable property rights,[5] could also be usefully applied in civilian systems to rationalise obligations that have effects on successors in

[3] Sjef van Erp, 'Comparative Property Law' in Mathias Reimann and Reinhard Zimmermann (eds), *The Oxford Handbook of Comparative Law* (2nd edn, OUP 2019) 1032; Jan Smits, *The Making of European Private Law* (Intersentia 2002) 245; J Michael Milo, 'Property and Real Rights' in Jan M Smits (ed), *Elgar Encyclopedia of Comparative Law* (2nd edn, Edward Elgar 2012) 727.

[4] Michele Graziadei and Lionel Smith, 'Preface' in Michele Graziadei and Lionel Smith (eds), *Comparative Property Law: Global Perspectives* (Edward Elgar 2017) x; van Erp (n 3) 1034, 1036.

[5] See ch 2, section III.B.

title. For example, the English 'right against rights' theory might provide new angles to explain the successor liability of German leases, anticipation rights of buyers, and security ownership. In turn, the German idea 'anomalous obligations with far reaching third-part effects' might enlighten English views on the nature of equitable property rights.

B. Beyond English and German Land Law

The findings of this book also call for new research on the *numerus clausus*. As a consequence of having its main focus on land as an object of property, the conclusions of the book have a narrow scope. To what extent these findings are relevant for other forms of property, especially movable and intangible property, requires more research, including relevant inroads in insolvency, intellectual property[6] and corporate law.

Similarly, whether the conclusions of this book are valid for jurisdictions different from Germany and England also requires further investigation. From both a comparative and conceptual perspective this offers vast new research opportunities. Due to their importance in comparative law and their different property arrangements, America and France are the most obvious candidates for this. However, other jurisdictions might offer other interesting contrasts, including some that are said to follow a *numerus apertus* principle, like Spain and South Africa,[7] or jurisdictions that have Torrens registration systems, as in Australia.[8]

C. Legal Formants and Interdisciplinarity

The general thesis put forward in this book calls for additional research relating to the people and state bodies that set property law in motion. The most obvious gap relates to the 'functional transformation' of property rights: the building blocks of a modular property systems do not combine themselves alone. *Someone* has to combine them. These 'legal builders' are normally lawyers.

[6] This is research is already in motion, eg Poorna Mysoor, *Copyright as Personal Property* (OUP 2025, forthcoming) ch 1, s 6, demonstrating the impact of *numerus clausus* on the existing copyright regime and arguing that it should play a greater role.

[7] Bram Akkermans, 'The Numerus Clausus of Property Rights' in Michele Graziadei and Lionel Smith (eds), *Comparative Property Law: Global Perspectives* (Edward Elgar 2017) 102; Christian von Bar, 'The Numerus Clausus of Property Rights: A European Principle?' in Louise Gullifer and Stefan Vogenauer (eds), *English and European Perspectives on Contract and Commercial Law: Essays in Honour of Hugh Beale* (Hart 2014) 447; Hanoch Dagan, *A Liberal Theory of Property Law* (CUP 2021) 113.

[8] For example, see the Real Property Act (SA) 1858. On this, Brendan Edgeworth, 'The Numerus Clausus Principle in Contemporary Australian Property Law' (2006) 32 *Mosash U L Rev* 387.

As the practical uses of the building blocks of property law expand among these builders, practising lawyers can become a non-explicitly formulated 'legal formant' of their legal systems.[9] However, as these practices do not necessarily make it to courts, the role that the creativity of lawyers plays in putting the generative power of property law in motion remains underexplored. Even if some of the utilitarian theories discussed in chapter five, section II explicitly acknowledge that legal advice is essential in allowing private parties to combine the building blocks of property law, their vision is too fragmentary to explain *how* this works in practice, as they only see legal advice as a cost of their optimal standardisation matrix.[10] Therefore, even if correct, such an account does not tell us anything about how lawyers fulfil this role in practice, the impact this has on the development of property law nor the importance that the prevailing legal culture might have in this process.

The last point is very interesting from a comparative perspective, as lawyers from different legal systems are also said to have distinctive views regarding their role and that of the law. For example, German lawyers have traditionally been seen as especially loyal to the values embedded in their legal system, while English lawyers are often described as much more independent and committed to the interest of their clients.[11] This suggests that cultural elements can play an important role in explaining, for example, why flat ownership took off so rapidly in Germany, while the commonhold remains scarcely used in England. Exploring this aspect requires going beyond property theory and doctrine, and into socio-legal studies.

A second gap relates to the role of legislators and judges. This book has argued that, for good reasons, under the *numerus clausus* principle, the elimination and creation of new property types – that is, the 'structural reform' of property law – is for legislators. However, the book has also shown that when legislators fail to fulfil this role, judges occasionally deviate from the principle using 'legal scaffolding' to close gaps between law and social needs. Fully accounting for legal change in property law requires a theory that explains when and why legislators decide to re-modularise the property system and why sometimes they fall short in this role. By the same token, a more elaborate account of the factors explaining when and why judges are willing to intervene is also needed.

Accounting for these wider elements requires interdisciplinary methods and approaches that go beyond traditional black letter rule analysis. In this book, this has mainly been done by relying on comparative law and New Institutional

[9] On legal formants, Rodolfo Sacco, 'Legal Formants: A Dynamic Approach to Comparative Law (Installment II of II)' (1991) 39 *Am J Comp L* 343, 384–85. For example, see ch 1, section II.C.

[10] Thomas W Merrill and Henry E Smith, 'Optimal Standardization in the Law of Property: The Numerus Clausus Principle' (2000) 110 *Yale LJ* 1, 35, 39–41.

[11] Roger Cotterrell, *The Sociology of Law: An Introduction* (2nd edn, OUP 1992) 180–81, 191–94.

Economics, but there are many other options that could be explored, from empirical legal studies to urban studies.

II. POLICY MAKING AND LEGAL REFORM

The primary finding of this book is that property law systems subject to a *numerus clausus* principle are capable of accommodating social and economic change without undergoing frequent structural transformation and that the principle itself plays a key role in this. This has several implications for policy making and legal reform.

A. Keeping the Principle

A first implication is that the many views arguing for the derogation or relaxation of the *numerus clausus* principle[12] should be assessed with caution. The English judges and German scholars of the nineteenth century introduced this principle for a good reason: protecting the autonomy of third parties. As argued in chapter five, from both a utilitarian and a principle-based perspective, this reason is still valid today. Furthermore, as shown in chapters six and seven, it also plays a key role in preserving the ability of private law to deal with legal change, without the need of undergoing constant structural reform.

A key point here, is that contrary to arguments put forward by some law and economics and progressive scholars,[13] registration can simply not take over the function of the *numerus clausus*. On the one hand, registration is not capable of internalising the costs associated with splitting property rights, because the costs of reversing this fragmentation are not connected with the higher price that rational owners will charge for splitting the bundle in the first place.[14] On the other hand, from a rights-based perspective, allowing people to bind others simply by giving notice, seems to run directly against the respect of individual autonomy that underpins progressive property views.

B. Expanding and Regulating the List

A second implication is that, if the *numerus clausus* principle aims to contain the creation of successor and trespassory liability and this is a valuable function, attempts of reform providing for new property rights should also be approached with care. At the present, this is especially true for common law jurisdictions,

[12] See ch 1, section II.B.
[13] See ch 5, section II.
[14] See ch 5, section II.

where some scholars are actively calling to expand the list of property rights as a means to enhance party autonomy.[15]

Over the last decades, a number of these jurisdictions have introduced[16] or considered introducing[17] new property rights running with the land that expand the scope and intensity of the duties private dealings can impose on third parties. However, the outcome of these reforms has not always been met with positive comments. Indeed, some have even been said to be a cautionary tale against introducing new property rights without considering their impact on the rest of the property system.[18] Thus, since reversing changes in property law is extremely difficult,[19] reforms introducing new property rights should probably be subject to a high threshold.[20] This suggests that the frequently criticised 'technocratic conservatism' of property law[21] should be seen in a more charitable light.

A third implication, closely connected to the prior, relates to the impact of regulation on the modular structure of property law. The rise of the 'regulatory state' over the twentieth century shows that property law can tolerate a good deal of regulation and still be able to deliver on its promise of promoting personal liberty and economic efficiency.[22] However, this has limits. As shown by the negative impact that rent regulation had on the housing stock of the GDR,[23] excessive curtailing of the owner's power to functionally transform the individual modules of property can heavily affect their application to new worthy uses. Bearing this in mind is relevant in a time in which many policies to ease the housing crisis rely on limiting what owner can do with their property,[24] instead of increasing the supply of dwelling space.[25] In a similar line, measures

[15] eg Dagan (n 7) 7, 104–05.

[16] eg 'Covenants in Gross' introduced in New Zealand by the Amendments to the Property Law Act 2007 contained within the Land Transfer Act 2007.

[17] For England, see Law Commission, *Easements, Covenants and Profits à Prendre* (Law Com No 186, 2008) and *Making Land Work: Easements, Covenants and Profits à Prendre*' (Law Com No 327, 2011).

[18] Ben France-Hudson, 'The Recognition of Covenants in Gross in New Zealand: A Dangerous Advancement?' in Ben McFarlane and Sinéad Agnew (eds), *Modern Studies in Property Law*, vol 10 (Hart 2019) 205.

[19] See ch 1, section II.B.

[20] See Ben McFarlane, 'The Numerus Clausus Principle and Covenants Relating to Land' in Susan Bright (ed), *Modern Studies in Property Law*, vol 6 (Hart 2011) 326–27; Pamela O'Connor, 'Careful What You Wish for: Positive Freehold Covenants' (2011) 3 *Conv* 191.

[21] van Erp (n 3) 1037.

[22] See ch 2, section II.B, section III.C and section IV.C and ch 8, section III.B.

[23] See ch 3, section II.B.

[24] As with the ZwVbG, discussed in ch 2, section II.B.

[25] For example, an empirical study on the 2015 German Rent Control Act (*Gesetz zu Mietpreisbegrenzungen und neuen Regeln für Maklergebühren)*, mentioned in ch 7, section III.B, concluded that its effects faded after a few years and that, in the long run, it ended up decreasing the quality of housing. Philipp Breidenbach, Lea Eilers and Jan Fries, 'Temporal Dynamics of Rent Regulations – The Case of the German Rent Control' (2022) 92 *Regional Sciences and Urban Econ* 103737.

as the proposed 'socialisation' of flats in Berlin[26] might risk being counterproductive in the long run, as they disincentive supplying new housing space.

C. The Role of Politics

The prior should not be understood as an argument in favour of *statu quo*, but as a call of confidence in politics to reform property law via legislation and regulation. Although this book has not intended to provide a plan for policy action, it still offers an insight into some elements that can make reforms in this field successful. One of them is that legislation that reproduces the modular structure of the relevant property system tends to work better. Probably the best example of this is the contrast between the success of the German flat ownership[27] and the relative irrelevance of the English commonhold.[28]

This call of confidence in politics must be accompanied by a 'volitional commitment'[29] of judges not to reassess the structure of property law in individual cases, unless there is a *very good* reason for this,[30] which must be channelled through preexisting legal patterns of the system.[31] However, this is not enough. A smooth functioning of property law also requires that political systems respond to social change in a timely and adequate fashion. The more that legislators and regulators fail to act when required, the greater the pressure on judges to disregard the forms of property law. In the best case scenario, this can lead to legal scaffolding, which makes the management of the whole property system unnecessarily complex and detached from everyday life. In the worst case, lack of adequate legislative reform can push courts willing to achieve much needed substantive outcomes to openly disregard the forms of property law and collapse its structure. Even if we accept that property law is a 'sleeping beauty' that needs to be awakened,[32] this must be done by the right person with the right kiss.

[26] See ch 2, section II.B.
[27] See ch 7, section III.
[28] See Lu Xu, 'Commonhold Developments in Practice' in Warren Barr (ed), *Modern Studies in Property Law*, vol 8 (Hart 2015) 332, 334–35.
[29] The term comes from Emily Sherwin, 'Formalism and Realism in Private Law' in Andrew S Gold and others (eds), *The Oxford Handbook of New Private Law* (OUP 2021) 473–74.
[30] On these reasons, see ch 5, section IV.
[31] See ch 8, section IV.
[32] See Introduction.

Bibliography

Abelshauser W, *Deutsche Wirtschaftsgeschichte Seit 1945* (Beck 2004).

A'Hearn B, 'The British Industrial Revolution in a European Mirror' in Roderick Floud, Jane Humphries and Paul Johnson (eds), *The Cambridge Economic History of Modern Britain*, vol I 1700–1870 (CUP 2014).

Akkermans B, *The Principle of Numerus Clausus in European Property Law* (Intersentia 2008).

——, 'The Numerus Clausus of Property Rights' in Michele Graziadei and Lionel Smith (eds), *Comparative Property Law: Global Perspectives* (Edward Elgar 2017).

——, *Sustainable Property Law. Reckoning, Resilience, and Reform* (Eleven International Publishers 2022).

Alexander G and others, 'A Statement of Progressive Property' (2009) 94 *Cornell L Rev* 743.

Allen T, *Property and The Human Rights Act 1998* (Hart 2005).

——, 'The Right to Property' in Tom Ginsburg and Rosalind Dixon (eds), *Comparative Constitutional Law* (Edward Elgar 2012).

Amann H, 'Grunddienstbarkeiten im Wandel der Zeit und von Verjährung Bedroht – Zugleich Anmerkungen zu den Urteilen Des BGH v. 18. 7. 2014 – V ZR 151/13 Und v. 22. 10. 2010 – V ZR 43/10' [2015] DNotz 164.

Anderson S, 'The 1925 Property Legislation: Setting Context' in Susan Bright and John Dewar (eds), *Land Law. Themes and Perspectives* (OUP 1998).

Arruñada B, 'Property as Sequential Exchange: The Forgotten Limits of Private Contract' (2017) 4 *J Inst Econ* 753.

Atiyah PS, *The Rise and Fall of Freedom of Contract* (Clarendon Press 2003).

—— and Summers RS, *Form and Substance in Anglo-American Law* (Clarendon Press 1987).

Atkinson M and Baber C, *The Growth and Decline of the South Wales Iron Industry 1760–1880* (University of Wales Press 1987).

Auer M, *Der Privatrechtliche Diskurs der Moderne* (Mohr Siebeck 2014).

Badura P, 'Eigentum' in Ernst Benda, Werner Maihofer and Hans-Jochen Vogel (eds), *Handbuch des Verfassungsrecht der Bundesrepublik Deutschland* (2nd edn, De Gruyter 1994).

Baker J, *Introduction to English Legal History* (5th edn, OUP 2019).

Banner S, 'Transitions between Property Regimes: The Evolution of Property Rights' (2002) 31 J *Legal Stud* 359.

Bar C von, 'The Numerus Clausus of Property Rights: A European Principle?' in Louise Gullifer and Stefan Vogenauer (eds), *English and European Perspectives on Contract and Commercial Law: Essays in Honour of Hugh Beale* (Hart 2014).

——, *The Foundations of Property Law* (OUP 2023).

Barker K, 'Form and Substance: Three Observations of the State of the Debate' in Andrew Robertson and James Goudkamp (eds), *Form and Substance in the Law of Obligations* (Hart 2019).

Bärmann J, 'Zur Theorie des Wohnungseigentumsrechts' (1989) 1989 *NJW* 1057.

Barnett RE, *The Structure of Liberty: Justice and the Rule of Law* (OUP 2000).

Baron J, 'The Contested Commitments of Property' (2010) 61 *Hastings LJ* 917.

Barriere F, 'The Security Fiducie in French Law' in Lionel Smith (ed), *The Worlds of the Trust* (CUP 2013).

Baur F, Baur J and Stürner R, *Sachenrecht* (18th edn, Beck 2009).

Bell J, 'Sources of Law' in Andrew Burrows (ed), *English Private Law* (3rd edn, OUP 2013). Bentham J, *The Collected Works of Jeremy Bentham: An Introduction to the Principles of Morals and Legislation* (JH Burns and HLA Hart eds, OUP 1998).

Bernhardt C, *Bauplatz Groß-Berlin. Wohnungsmärkte, Terraingewerbe und Kommunalpolitik im Städtewachstum Der Hochindustrialisierung (1871–1918)* (De Gruyter 1998).

Bevan C, 'The Doctrine of Benefit and Burden: Reforming the Law of Covenants and the Numerus Clausus "Problem"' (2018) 77 *CLJ* 72.

Birks P, 'Five Keys to Land Law' in Susan Bright and John Dewar (eds), *Land Law. Themes and Perspectives* (OUP 1998).

——, 'Personal Property: Proprietary Rights and Remedies' (2000) 11 *King's LJ* 1.

Blackstone W, *Commentaries on the Laws of England. Book I: Of the Rights of Persons* (Wilfrid Prest ed, OUP 2016).

——, *Commentaries on the Laws of England. Book II: Of the Rights of Things* (Wilfrid Prest ed, OUP 2016).

Blandy S, Bright S and Nield S, 'The Dynamics of Enduring Property Relationships in Land' (2018) 81 *MLR* 85.

Breidenbach P, Eilers L and Fries J, 'Temporal Dynamics of Rent Regulations – The Case of the German Rent Control' (2022) 92 *Regional Sciences and Urban Econ* 103737.

Bridge S, Cooke E and Dixon M, *Megarry & Wade: The Law of Real Property* (8th edn, Sweet & Maxwell 2019).

Bright S, 'Uncertainty in Leases – Is It a Vice?' (1993) 13 *Legal Stud* 38.

——, 'Of Estates and Interest: A Tale of Ownership and Property Rights' in Susan Bright and John Dewar (eds), *Land Law. Themes and Perspectives* (OUP 1998).

——, *Landlord and Tenant Law in Context* (Hart 2007).

Brink D, 'Mill's Moral and Political Philosophy' in Edward N Zalta (ed), *Stanford Encyclopedia of Philosophy* (Winter 2018).

Brophy AL, 'Doing Things with Legal History: Historical Analysis in Property Law' in Markus D Dubber and Christopher Tomlins (eds), *The Oxford Handbook of Legal History* (OUP 2018).

Brophy J, 'The End of the Economic Old Order: The Great Transition, 1750–1860' in Helmut Walser Smith (ed), *The Oxford Handbook of Modern German History* (OUP 2011).

Brox H and Walker W-D, *Allgemeiner Teil des BGB* (36th edn, Vahlen 2012).

Buchheim C, 'Die Währungsreform 1948 in Westdeutschland' (1988) 36 *Vierteljh Zeitgesch* 189.

Bumke C and Voßkuhle A, *German Constitutional Law. Introduction, Cases, and Principles* (Andrew Hammel tr, OUP 2019).

——, *Casebook Verfassungsrecht* (8th edn, Mohr Siebeck 2020).

Burrows A, 'Between Form and Substance' in Andrew Robertson and James Goudkamp (eds), *Form and Substance: Fictions and Judicial Power* (Hart 2019).

Caenegem RC van, *An Historical Introduction to Private Law* (CUP 1992).

Calabresi G and Melamed AD, 'Property Rules, Liability Rules, and Inalienability: One View of the Cathedral' (1972) 85 *Harv L Rev* 1089.

Calnan R, *Taking Security* (4th edn, LexisNexis 2018).

Cane P, 'Rights in Private Law' in Donal Nolan and Andrew Robertson (eds), *Rights and Private Law* (Hart 2011).

——, *Key Ideas in Tort Law* (Hart 2017).

Cardozo BN, *The Growth of the Law* (Yale UP 1924).

Casson M, *The World's First Railway System: Enterprise, Competition, and Regulation on the Railway Network in Victorian Britain* (OUP 2009).

Catala P and Weir JA, 'Delict and Torts: A Study in Parallel – Part IV' (1964–5) 39 *Tul L Rev* 701.

Chambers D, 'The City and the Corporate Economy since 1870', *The Cambridge Economic History of Modern Britain*, vol II 1870 to the Present (CUP 2014).

Chang Y, *Property Law: Comparative, Empirical and Economic Analyses* (CUP 2023).

—— and Smith HE, 'An Economic Analysis of Civil versus Common Law Property' (2012) 88 *Notre Dame L Rev* 1.
—— and Smith HE, 'Structure and Style in Comparative Property Law' in Theodore Eisenberg and Giovanni B Ramello (eds), *Comparative Law and Economics* (Edward Elgar 2016).
Coase R, 'The Problem of Social Cost' (1960) 3 *J Law and Econ* 1.
Cooke E, 'To Restate or Not to Restate? Old Wine, New Wineskins, Old Covenants, New Ideas' [2009] *Conv* 448.
——, *Land Law* (2nd edn, OUP 2012).
Cooter R and Ulen T, *Law & Economics* (6th edn, Pearson 2012).
Cornish W and others, *Law and Society in England 1750–1950* (2nd edn, Hart 2019).
Cotterrell R, *The Sociology of Law: An Introduction* (2nd edn, OUP 1992).
Cowan D, Fox O'Mahony L and Cobb N, *Great Debates in Land Law* (3rd edn, Hart 2023).
Dagan H, *A Liberal Theory of Property Law* (CUP 2021).
—— and Samet I, 'Express Trust: The Dark Horse of the Liberal Property Regime', *Philosophical Foundations of the Law of Express Trusts* (OUP 2023).
Davies PS, *Accessory Liability* (Hart 2015).
Deane P, *The First Industrial Revolution* (2nd edn, CUP 1980).
Demsetz H, 'Toward a Theory of Property Rights' (1967) 57 *Am Econ Rev* 347.
Depoorter B and Parisi F, 'Fragmentation of Property Rights: A Functional Interpretation of the Law of Servitudes' (2003) 3 *Global Jurist* i.
Di Robilant A, 'Property and Democratic Deliberation: The "Numerus Clausus" Principle and Democratic Experimentalism in Property Law' (2014) 62 *Am J Comp L* 367.
——, *The Making of Modern Property Law. Reinventing Roman Law in Europe and Its Peripheries* (CUP 2023).
Dicey AV, 'The Paradox of the Land Law' (1905) 21 *LQR* 221.
Dixon M, 'Proprietary and Non-Proprietary Rights in Modern Land Law' in Louise Tee (ed), *Land Law: Issues, Debates, Policy* (Willan Publishing 2002).
——, 'A Doctrinal Approach to Property Law Scholarship: Who Cares and Why?' in Susan Bright and Sarah Blandy (eds), *Researching Property Law* (Palgrave 2016).
——, *Modern Land Law* (12th edn, Routledge 2021).
Dorfman A, 'Property and Collective Undertaking: The Principle of Numerus Clausus' (2011) 61 *U Toronto LJ* 467.
Douglas S, *Liability for Wrongful Interferences with Chattels* (Hart 2011).
—— and McFarlane B, 'Defining Property Rights' in James Penner and Henry Smith (eds), *Philosophical Foundations of Property Law* (OUP 2013).
Downward P, Hallmann K and Rasciute S, 'Exploring the Interrelationship between Sport, Health and Social Outcomes in the UK: Implications for Health Policy' (2017) 28 *Eur J Public Health* 99.
Dulckeit G, *Die Verdinglichung Obligatorischer Rechte* (Mohr 1951).
Dworkin R, *Taking Rights Seriously* (Bloomsbury 2013).
Edelman J, 'Two Fundamental Questions for the Law of Trusts' (2013) 129 *LQR* 66.
Edgeworth B, 'The Numerus Clausus Principle in Contemporary Australian Property Law' (2006) 32 *Mosash U L Rev* 387.
Eichler H, *Institutionen des Sachenrechts*, vol 1 (Duncker & Humblot 1954).
Eisenberg M, *The Nature of the Common Law* (Harvard UP 1988).
Ellickson RC, 'Two Cheers for the Bundle-of-Sticks Metaphor, Three Cheers for Merrill and Smith' (2011) 8 *Econ Journal Watch* 215.
Emerich Y, *Droit Commun des Biens: Perspective Transsystémique* (Éditions Yvon Blais 2017).
Emmerich V, 'Miete' in Dagmar Kaiser and Markus Stoffels (eds), *J. Staudingers Kommentar zum Bürgerlichen Gesetzbuch mit Einführungsgestetz und Nebengesetzen. Eckpfeiler Des Zivilrechts* (6th edn, Sellier & de Gruyter 2018).
Epstein RA, 'Possession as the Root of Title' (1979) 13 *Ga L Rev* 1221.
——, 'Notice and Freedom of Contract in the Law of Servitudes' (1981) 55 S *Cal L Rev* 1353.

——, *Takings: Private Property and the Power of Eminent Domain* (Harvard UP 1985).
——, 'Why Restrain Alienation?' (1985) 85 *Colum L Rev* 970.
——, 'Past and Future: The Temporal Dimension in the Law of Property' (1986) 64 *WashU LQ* 667.
——, 'A Clear View of The Cathedral: The Dominance of Property Rules' (1997) 106 *Yale LJ* 2091.
——, 'The Plasticity of Property: Legal Transitions between Property Regimes for Different Resources' in Ernst Nordtveit (ed), *The Changing Role of Property Law. Rights, Values and Concepts* (Edward Elgar 2023).
Erp S van, 'A Numerus Quasi-Clausus of Property Rights as a Constitutive Element of a Future European Property Law' (2003) 7 *Electronic J Comp Law*.
——, 'From "Classical" to Modern European Property Law?' in National and Kapodistrain University of Athens (ed), *Essays in Honour of Konstantinos D. Kerameus – Festschrift für Konstantinos D. Kerameus*, vol I (Sakkoulas and Bruylant 2009) 1519.
——, 'Comparative Property Law' in Mathias Reimann and Reinhard Zimmermann (eds), *The Oxford Handbook of Comparative Law* (2nd edn, OUP 2019).
—— and Akkermans B (eds), *Cases, Materials and Text on Property Law* (Hart 2012).
Ewing KD, 'Economic Rights' in Michel Rosenfeld and András Sajó (eds), *The Oxford Handbook of Comparative Constitutional Law* (OUP 2012).
Expertenkommission zum Volksentscheid Vergesellschaftung großer Wohnungs- unternehmen, '*Abschlussbericht*' (June 2023).
Faust F, 'Comparative Law and Economic Analysis of Law' in Mathias Reimann and Reinhard Zimmermann (eds), *The Oxford Handbook of Comparative Law* (2nd edn, OUP 2019).
Fikentscher W and Heinemann A, *Schuldrecht: Allegemeiner und Besonderer Teil* (11th edn, De Gruyter 2017).
Flanders J, *Consuming Passions: Leisure and Pleasure in Victorian Britain* (Harper 2006).
Fleischer H, 'Der Numerus Clausus der Sachenrechte im Spiegel der RechtsÖkonomie' in Thomas Eger and others (eds), *Internationalisierung des Rechts und seine ökonomische Analyse. Festschrift für Hans-Bernd Schäfer zum 65. Geburtstag* (Gabler Verlag 2008).
Foster N and Sule S, *German Legal System and Law* (4th edn, OUP 2010).
Fox O'Mahony L and Roark M, *Squatting and the State. Resilient Property in an Age of Crisis* (CUP 2022).
France-Hudson B, 'The Recognition of Covenants in Gross in New Zealand: A Dangerous Advancement?' in Ben McFarlane and Sinéad Agnew (eds), *Modern Studies in Property Law*, vol 10 (Hart 2019).
French S, 'Highlights of the New Restatement (Third) of Property: Servitudes' (2000) 35 *Real Prop Prob & Tr J* 225.
Gaier R, 'Einleitung zum Sachenrecht' in Franz Jürgen Säcker and others (eds), *Münchner Kommentar zum BGB* (7th edn, Beck 2017).
Gardner S, '"Persistent Rights" Appraised' in Nicholas Hopkins (ed), *Modern Studies in Property Law*, vol 7 (Hart 2013).
—— and MacKenzie E, *An Introduction to Land Law* (4th edn, Hart 2015).
Getzler J, *A History of Water Rights at Common Law* (OUP 2006).
Gierke O, *Die Soziale Aufgabe des Privatrechts* (Springer 1899).
Glendon MA, Carozza P and Picker C, *Comparative Legal Traditions: Text, Materials and Cases on Western Law* (3rd edn, West Academic Press 2006).
Glenn HP, *Legal Traditions of the World* (5th edn, OUP 2014).
Glover G, *Gale on Easements* (12th edn, Sweet & Maxwell 1932).
Gold AS, 'Internal and External Perspectives: On the New Private Law Methodology' in Andrew S Gold and others (eds), *The Oxford Handbook of The New Private Law* (OUP 2021).
—— and Smith HE, 'Sizing up Private Law' (2020) 70 *U Toronto LJ* 489.
Goldberg JCP, 'Introduction: Pragmatism and Private Law' (2012) 125 *Harv L Rev* 1640.
Gordley J, *Foundations of Private Law* (OUP 2006).

Goymour A and Hickey R, 'The Continuing Relevance of Relativity of Title Under the Land Registration Act 2002' in Amy Goymour, Stephen Watterson and Martin Dixon (eds), *New Perspectives on Land Registration: Contemporary Problems and Solutions* (Hart 2018).

Gray K, 'Property in Thin Air' (1991) 50 *CLJ* 252.

Gray C (ed), 'Justifications', *The Philosophy of Law: An Encyclopedia* (Garland Publishing 1999) 469.

Graziadei M, 'The Structure of Property Ownership and the Common Law/Civil Law Divide' in Michele Graziadei and Lionel Smith (eds), *Comparative Property Law: Global Perspectives* (Edward Elgar 2017).

—— and Smith L (eds), *Comparative Property Law: Global Perspectives* (Edward Elgar 2017).

—— and Smith, 'Preface' in Michele Graziadei and Lionel Smith (eds), *Comparative Property Law: Global Perspectives* (Edward Elgar 2017).

Grechenig K and Gelter M, 'The Transatlantic Divergence in Legal Thought: American Law and Economics vs. German Doctrinalism' (2008) 1 *Hastings Int'l & Comp L Rev* 295.

Grey TC, 'The Disintegration of Property' (1980) 22 *Nomos* 69.

Grundmann S, *Der Treuhandvertrag: Insbesondere die Werbende Treuhand* (Beck 1997).

——, 'Trust and Treuhand at the End of the 20th Century – Key Problems and Shift of Interests' (1999) 47 *Am J Comp L* 401.

Grundmann S, Micklitz H-W and Renner M, *New Private Law* (CUP 2021).

Grüneber C, 'Einleitung', *Palandt. Bürgerlicher Gesetzbuch mit Nebengesetzten* (80th edn, Beck 2021).

Grziwotz H, 'Gesetz über das Wohnungseigentum und das Dauerwohnrecht (Wohungseigentu-mgestz)' in Harm Peter Westernmann, Barbara Grunewald and Georg Maier-Reimer (eds), *Erman Bürgerliches Gesetzbuch* (15th edn, Otto Schmidt 2017).

Häcker B, '"Substance Over Form": Has the Pendulum Swung Too Far?' in Andrew Robertson and James Goudkamp (eds), *Form and Substance in the Law of Obligations* (Hart 2019).

Hackney J, *Understanding Equity and Trusts* (Fontana Press 1987).

Hage J, 'Legal Reasoning' in Jan M Smits (ed), *Elgar Encyclopedia of Comparative Law* (2nd edn, Edward Elgar 2012).

Hager J, 'Das Recht der Unerlaubten Handlungen' in Dagmar Kaiser and Markus Stoffels (eds), *J. Staudingers Kommentar zum Bürgerlichen Gesetzbuch mit Einführungsgestetz und Nebengesetzen. Eckpfeiler Des Zivilrechts* (6th edn, Sellier & de Gruyter 2018).

Han O, 'Licensee versus Trespasser: Hill v Tupper Resuscitated' (2016) 6 *Prop L Rev* 87.

Hansmann H and Kraakman R, 'Property, Contract, and Verification: The Numerus Clausus Problem and the Divisibility of Rights' (2002) 31 *J Legal Stud* 373.

Hansmann H and Mattei U, 'The Function of Trust Law: A Comparative Legal and Economic Analysis' (1998) 73 *NYU L Rev* 434.

Harpum C, 'The Law Commission and the Reform of Land Law' in Susan Bright and John Dewar (eds), *Land Law. Themes and Perspectives* (OUP 1998).

Harris JW, 'Legal Doctrine and Interests in Land' in John Eekelaar and John Bell (eds), *Oxford Essays in Jurisprudence. Third Series* (Clarendon 1987).

——, *Property and Justice* (OUP 1996).

Harris R, 'The History and Historical Stance of Law and Economics' in Markus D Dubber and Christopher Tomlins (eds), *The Oxford Handbook of Legal History* (OUP 2018).

Hart HLA, 'American Jurisprudence through English Eyes: The Nightmare and the Nomble Dream', *Essays in Jurisprudence and Philosophy* (OUP 1983).

——, *The Concept of Law* (3rd edn, OUP 2012).

Hawes J, *The Shortest History of Germany* (Old Street 2018).

Hayek FA, 'The Use of Knowledge in Society' (1945) 35 *Am Econ R* 519.

Heck P von, *Grundriss Des Sachenrechts* (Mohr 1930).

Hegel GWF, *Grundlinien Der Philosophie Des Rechts* (Meiner 2009).

Heller M, 'The Tragedy of the Anticommons: Property in the Transition from Marx to Markets' (1998) 111 *Harv L Rev* 621.

——, 'The Boundaries of Private Property' (1999) 108 *Yale LJ* 1163.

Herresthal C, 'Das Recht der Kreditsicherung' in Dagmar Kaiser and Markus Stoffels (eds), *J. Staudingers Kommentar zum Bürgerlichen Gesetzbuch mit Einführungsgestetz und Nebengesetzen. Eckpfeiler Des Zivilrechts* (6th edn, Sellier & de Gruyter 2018).

Herrler S and Wiecke H, 'Sachenrecht', *Palandt. Bürgerlicher Gesetzbuch mit Nebengesetzten* (80th edn, Beck 2021).

Hobsbawm E, *Industry and Empire* (3rd rev edn, Penguin 1999).

Hodge J, *Railways and Industry in the Western Valley* (Pen & Sword 2016).

Hohfeld WN, 'Some Fundamental Legal Conceptions as Applied in Judicial Reasoning' (1913) 23 *Yale LJ* 16.

——, 'Fundamental Legal Conceptions as Applied in Judicial Reasoning' (1917) 26 *Yale LJ* 710.

Honoré AM, 'Rights of Exclusion and Immunities Against Divesting' (1959) 34 *Tul L Rev* 453.

——, 'Ownership' in AG Guest (ed), *Oxford Essays on Jurisprudence* (Clarendon Press 1961).

Honsell H, 'Einleitung zum BGB' in Dagmar Kaiser and Markus Stoffels (eds), *J. Staudingers Kommentar zum Bürgerlichen Gesetzbuch mit Einführungsgestetz und Nebengesetzen. Eckpfeiler des Zivilrechts* (6th edn, Sellier & de Gruyter 2018).

Hösch U, *Eigentum und Freiheit. Ein Beitrag zur Inhaltlichen Bestimmung der Gewahrleistung des Eigentums Durch Art. 14 Abs. 1 Satz 1 GG* (Mohr Siebeck 2000).

Hübner H and Riegner J, *Sachenrecht* (Translatia 1948).

Hudson J, McFarlane B and Mitchell C, *Hayton, McFarlane and Mitchell on Equity and Truts* (15th edn, Sweet & Maxwell 2022).

Ibbetson D, *A Historical Introduction to the Law of Obligations* (OUP 2001).

Jhering R von, *Scherz und Ernst in der Jurisprudenz* (Breitkopf und Härtel 1884).

Jones B, 'Garner v. Gerrish and the Renter's Life Estate: Teaching A New Concept of "Home"' (2010) 2 *Faulkner L Rev* 1.

Kahn-Freund O, 'Introduction' in Karl Renner, *The Institutions of Private Law and their Social Functions* (Routledge & Kegan Paul Ltd 1949).

Käppner J, 'Wohnungsnot in der Kaiserzeit – Berliner Häuserkampf' *Süddeutsche Zeitung* (Munich, 10 May 2019).

Katz L, 'Exclusion and Exclusivity in Property Law' (2008) 58 *U Toronto LJ* 275.

——, 'The Regulative Function of Property Rights' (2011) 8 *Econ Journal Watch*.

——, 'Property's Sovereignty' (2017) 18 *Theo Inq L* 299.

——, 'Corporate Shares as Shares' in Ben McFarlane and Sinéad Agnew (eds), *Modern Studies in Property Law*, vol 10 (Hart 2019).

Kelly D, *Slapper and Kelly's English Legal System* (19th edn, Routledge 2020).

Kelsen H, *Reine Rechtslehre. Studienausgabe der 1. Auflage 1934* (Matthias Jestaedt ed, Mohr Siebeck 2008.

Kischel U, *Comparative Law* (Andrew Hammel tr, OUP 2019).

Klinck F, 'Sachenrecht' in Dagmar Kaiser and Markus Stoffels (eds), *J. Staudingers Kommentar zum Bürgerlichen Gesetzbuch mit Einführungsgestetz und Nebengesetzen. Eckpfeiler Des Zivilrechts* (6th edn, Sellier & de Gruyter 2018).

Kloth A, 'Der Kleine Unbekannte – Art. 15 GG: Die Sozialisierungsermächtigung des Grundgesetzes im Lichte der Berliner Enteignungsinitiative' (2022) 2 *BRZ* 86.

Knowles D, *Hegel and the Philosophy of Right* (Routledge 2002).

Kofner S, *Wohnungsmarkt und Wohnungswirtschaft* (Oldenburg Verlag 2004).

Kötz H, *Trust und Treuhand. Eine Rechtsvergleichende Darstellung des Anglo-Amerikanischen Trust und Funktionsverwandter Institute des Deutschen Rechts* (Vandenhoeck & Ruprecht 1963).

Kumm M, 'Who Is Afraid of the Total Constitution? Constitutional Rights as Principles and the Constitutionalization of Private Law' (2006) 4 *German LR* 341.

Larenz K, *Methodenlehre der Rechtswissenschaft* (6th edn, Springer 1991).

—— and Canaris C-W, *Methodenslehre der Rechtswissenschaft* (3rd edn, Springer 1996).
—— and Wolf M, *Allgemeiner Teil des Bürgerlichen Rechts* (9th edn, Beck 2004).
Law Commission, *Transfer of Land: Trusts of Land* (Law Com No 181, 1989).
——, *Easements, Covenants and Profits à Prendre* (Law Com No 186. 2008).
——, *Making Land Work: Easements, Covenants and Profits à Prendre* (Law Com No 327, 2011).
——, *Updating the Land Registration Act 2002* (Law Com No 380, 2018).
——, *Reinvigorating Commonhold: The Alternative to Leasehold Ownership* (Law Com No 394, 2020).
Lawson A, 'Easements' in Louise Tee (ed), *Land Law: Issues, Debates, Policy* (Willan 2002).
Lawson FH and Rudden B, *The Law of Property* (3rd edn, OUP 2002).
Lee B and Smith HE, 'The Nature of Coasean Property' (2012) 59 *Intl Rev of Economics* 145.
Lee M, 'Hunter v Canary Wharf Ltd (1997)' in Charles Mitchell and Paul Mitchell (eds), *Landmark Cases in the Law of Tort* (Hart 2010).
Lehavi A, 'Land Law in the Age of Globalization and Land Grabbing' in Michele Graziadei and Lionel Smith (eds), *Comparative Property Law: Global Perspectives* (Edward Elgar 2017).
Libchaber R, 'La Recodification du Droit des Biens', *Le Code civil 1804–2004. Livre du Bicentenaire* (Dalloz and Litec 2004).
Locke J, 'Second Treatise of Government', *Second Treatise of Government and A Letter Concerning Toleration* (OUP 2016).
Lorenz S, 'Grundwissen – Zivilrecht: Deliktsrecht – Haftung Aus § 823 I BGB' [2019] JuS 852.
Low KFK, 'Certainty of Terms and Leases: Curiouser and Curiouser' (2012) 75 *MLR* 401.
Lucy W, 'Adjudication' in Jules L Coleman, Kenneth Einar Himma and Scott J Shapiro (eds), *The Oxford Handbook of Jurisprudence and Philosophy of Law* (OUP 2004).
Luther P, 'Easements and Exclusive Possession' (1996) 16 *Legal Stud* 51.
Maitland FW, *Equity: A Course of Lectures* (AH Chaytor and WJ Whittaker eds, 2 rev, CUP 1936).
Manchester AH, *A Modern Legal History of England and Wales, 1750–1950* (Butterworth 1980).
Markensis B, Bell J and Janssen A (eds), *Markesinis's German Law of Torts: A Comparative Treatise* (5th edn, Hart 2019).
Mattei U, 'Efficiency in Legal Transplants: An Essay in Comparative Law and Economics' (1994) 14 *Int Rev Law and Econ* 3.
——, *Comparative Law and Economics* (U of Michigan Press 1997).
——, *Basic Principles of Property Law: A Comparative Legal and Economic Introduction* (Greenwood 2000).
Matthews P, 'The Compatibility of the Trust with the Civil Law Notion of Property' in Lionel Smith (ed), *The Worlds of the Trust* (CUP 2013).
Mayer J, 'Dienstbarkeiten' in Wolfgang Wiegand (ed), *J. von Staudingers Kommentar zum Bürgerlichen Gesetzbuch mit Einführungsgesetz und Nebengesetzen. Buch 3. Sachen Recht. EbbVo; §§ 1018–1112* (Sellier & de Gruyter 2002).
McBride NJ, 'Vindicatio: The Missing Remedy?' (2016) 28 *Sing Ac LJ* 1052.
——, *Key Ideas in Trust Law* (Hart 2023).
McClean A, 'The Nature of an Easement' (1966) 5 *W L Rev* 32.
McFarlane B, 'Equity, Obligations and Third Parties' (2008) *Sing J Legal Stud* 308.
——, *The Structure of Property Law* (Hart 2008.
——, 'The Numerus Clausus Principle and Covenants Relating to Land' in Susan Bright (ed), *Modern Studies in Property Law*, vol 6 (Hart 2011).
——, 'Tulk v Moxhay (1848)' in Charles Mitchell and Paul Mitchell (eds), *Landmark Cases in Equity* (Hart 2012).
——, 'Keppell v Bailey (1834); Hill v Tupper (1863): The Numerus Clausus and the Common Law' in Nigel Gravells (ed), *Landmark Cases in Land Law* (Hart 2013).
——, 'The Trust and Its Civilian Analogues' in Lionel Smith (ed), *The Worlds of the Trust* (CUP 2013).

——, 'Form and Substance in Equity' in Andrew Robertson and James Goudkamp (eds), *Form and Substance in the Law of Obligations* (Hart 2019).
——, 'Equity' in Andrew S Gold and others (eds), *The Oxford Handbook of New Private Law* (OUP 2021).
——, 'Property: Duties, Diversity and Limits' (2022) 1 *King's LJ* 23.
——, 'The Persistence of Equity: Lessons from the Trust', *Equity Today: 150 Years of the Judicature Reforms* (Hart 2023).
——, 'Trusts, Property, and Rights' in Simone Degeling, Jessica Hudson and Irit Samet (eds), *Philosophical Foundations of the Law of Express Trusts* (OUP 2023).
—— and Douglas S, 'Property, Analogy and Variety' (2022) 42 *OJLS* 161.
——, Hopkins N and Nield S, *Land Law. Text, Cases and Materials* (5th edn, OUP 2021).
—— and Stevens R, 'The Nature of Equitable Property' (2010) 4 *J Eq* 1.
Merrill TW, 'Introduction: The Demsetz Thesis and the Evolution of Property Rights' (2002) 31 *J Legal Stud* 331.
—— and Smith HE, 'Optimal Standardization in the Law of Property: The Numerus Clausus Principle' (2000) 110 *Yale LJ* 1.
—— and Smith HE, 'The Property/Contract Interface' (2001) 101 *Colum L Rev* 773.
—— and Smith HE, 'What Happened to Property Law in Economics?' (2001) 111 *Yale LJ* 357.
—— and Smith HE, *Property: Principles and Policies* (Foundation Press 2007).
—— and Smith HE, 'Making Coasean Property More Coasean' (2011) 54 *J Law and Econ* 77.
Merry M, 'Landmark Cases in Land Law (Review)' (2013) 5 *Conv* 455.
Michaels R, 'Im Westen nichts Neues? 100 Jahre Pariser Kongreß für Rechtsvergleichung – Gedanken anläßlich einer Jubiläumskonferenz in New Orleans' (2002) 66 *Rabels Z* 97.
——, 'The Functional Method of Comparative Law' in Mathias Reimann and Reinhard Zimmermann (eds), *The Oxford Handbook of Comparative Law* (2nd edn, OUP 2019).
Mill JS, 'Utilitarianism' in JM Robson (ed), *The Collected Works of John Stuart Mill. Essays on Ethics, Religion and Society*, vol X (University of Toronto Press; Routledge & Kegan 1969).
——, 'On Liberty' in JM Robson (ed), *The Collected Works of John Stuart Mill. Essays on Ethics, Religion and Society*, vol XVIII (University of Toronto Press; Routledge & Kegan 1977).
Milo JM, 'Property and Real Rights' in Jan M Smits (ed), *Elgar Encyclopedia of Comparative Law* (2nd edn, Edward Elgar 2012).
Mitchell P, 'Patterns of Legal Change' (2012) 65 *Current Legal Problems* 177.
Molinari VM, *Die Tradition Staatlicher Interventionen in den Mietwohnungsmarkt* (Mohr Siebeck 2021).
Motive zu dem Entwurfe eines bürgerlichen Gesetzbuches für das deutsche Reich (J Guttentag 1888).
Murphy JG and Coleman JL, *Philosophy of Law. An Introduction to Jurisprudence* (Rev ed, Westview Press 1990).
Mysoor P, *Copyright as Personal Property* (OUP 2025, forthcoming).
Neuner J, *Allgemeiner Teil Des Bürgerlichen Rechts* (13th edn, Beck 2023).
Nipperdey H-C, 'Gleicher Lohn der Frau für Gleiche Leistung' [1950] RdA 121.
Nolan D, 'The Essence of Private Nuisance' in Ben McFarlane and Sinéad Agnew (eds), *Modern Studies in Property Law*, vol 10 (Hart 2019).
Nonet P and Selznick P, *Law and Society in Transition: Toward Responsive Law* (2nd edn, Transaction Publishers 2001).
Nordtveit E, 'The Changing Role of Property Rights: An Introduction' in Ernst Nordtveit (ed), *The Changing Role of Property Law. Rights, Values and Concepts* (Edward Elgar 2023).
North DC, *Structure and Change in Economic History* (WWNorton 1981).
—— and Weingast BR, 'Constitutions and Commitment: The Evolution of Institutions Governing Public Choice in Seventeenth-Century England' (1989) 49 *J Econ History* 803.
O'Connor P, 'Careful What You Wish for: Positive Freehold Covenants' (2011) 3 *Conv* 191.
Oeter S, '"Drittwirkung"" der Grundrechte und die Autonomie des Privatrechts: Ein Beitrag zu den Funktionell-Rechtlichen Dimensionen der Drittwirkungsdebatte' (1994) 119 *AöR* 529.

Overton M, *Agricultural Revolution in England: The Transformation of the Agrarian Economy* (CUP 1996).
Parisi F, 'Entropy in Property' (2002) 50 *Am J Comp L* 595.
——, 'Freedom of Contract and the Laws of Entropy' (2003) 10 *Sup Ct Econ Rev* 65.
Parkinson P, 'Reconceptualising the Express Trust' (2002) 61 *CLJ* 657.
Partington M, *Introduction to the English Legal System: 2018–19* (OUP 2018).
Pascoe S, 'Re-Evaluating Recreational Easements- New Norms for the Twenty-First Century?' in Ben McFarlane and Sinéad Agnew (eds), *Modern Studies in Property Law*, vol 10 (Hart 2019).
Patton D, 'Anus Mirabilis: 1989 and German Unification' in Helmut Walser Smith (ed), *The Oxford Handbook of Modern German History* (OUP 2011).
Peifer K-N, *Schuldrecht: Gesetzliche Schuldverältnissse* (5th edn, Nomos 2016).
Penner JE, 'Duty and Liability in Respect of Funds' in John Lowry and Mistelis Loukas (eds), *Commercial Law: Perspectives and Practice* (LexisNexis Butterworths 2006).
——, 'The Bundle of Rights Picture of Property' (1996) 43 *UCLA L Rev* 711.
——, *The Idea of Property in Law* (OUP 1997).
——, *Property Rights: A Re-Examination* (OUP 2020).
——, 'Property' in *The Oxford Handbook of New Private Law* (OUP 2021).
Peukert A, *Güterzuordnung als Rechtsprinzip* (Mohr Siebeck 2008).
Polanyi K, *The Great Transformation* (2nd edn, Beacon 2001).
Posner RA, *Law and Legal Theory in England and America* (OUP 1996).
——, 'The Future of the Law and Economics Movement in Europe' (1997) 17 *Int Rev Law and Econ* 3.
——, *Economic Analysis of Law* (7th edn, Aspen 2007).
Praduroux S, 'Objects of Property: Old and New' in Michele Graziadei and Lionel Smith (eds), *Comparative Property Law: Global Perspectives* (Edward Elgar 2017).
Priel D, 'Two Forms of Formalism' in Andrew Robertson and James Goudkamp (eds), *Form and Substance in the Law of Obligations* (Hart 2019).
Proudhon P-J, *What Is Property?: An Inquiry into The Principle of Right and of Government* (U of Virginia Library; NetLibrary 1996).
Quack F, *Münchener Kommentar zum Bürgerlichen Gesetzbuch. Sachenrecht*, vol 6 (3rd edn, Friedrich Quack ed, Beck 1997).
Racinska I and Vahtrus S, 'The Use of Conservation Easements in the European Union' (NABU Bundesverband 2018).
Radbruch G, 'Gesetzliches Unrecht und Übergesetzliches Recht' (1946) 1 *SJZ* 105.
Räfle S, *Erbbaurechtsverordnung* (De Gruyter 1986).
Rapp M, 'Ebrbaurecht' in Wolfgang Wiegand (ed), *J. von Staudingers Kommentar zum Bürgerlichen Gesetzbuch mit Einführungsgesetz und Nebengesetzen. Buch 3. Sachen Recht. EbbVo; §§ 1018–1112* (2002).
——, 'Einleitung zum Wohnungseigentumgesetz' in Wolf-Rüdiger Bub and others (eds), *J. von Staudingers Kommentar zum Bürgerlichen Gesetzbuch mit Einführungsgesetz und Nebengesetzen.* (13th edn, 2005).
Raz J, *The Authority of Law: Essays on Law and Morality* (Clarendon Press 1979).
——, *Practical Reason and Norms* (2nd edn, OUP 1999).
Reid, Lord, 'The Judge as Law Maker' (1972) 12 *JALT (New Series)* 22.
Reimann M, 'The Progress and Failure of Comparative Law in the Second Half of the Twentieth Century' (2002) 50 *Am J Comp L* 671.
Renner K, *The Institutions of Private Law and their Social Functions* (Agnes Schwarzschild tr, Routledge and Kegan Paul 1976).
Richman B, 'New Institutional Economics' in Andrew S Gold and others (eds), *The Oxford Handbook of New Private Law* (OUP 2021).
Ripstein A, 'Property and Sovereignty: How to Tell the Difference' (2017) 18 *Theo Inq L* 243.

Ritter J, 'Person und Eigentum' in Ludwig Siep (ed), *G. W. F. Hegel – Grundlinien der Philosophie des Rechts* (3rd edn, De Gruyter 2014).

Robbie J, 'Moving Beyond Boundaries in the Pursuit of Sustainable Property Law' in Bram Akkermans and Gijs van Dijck (eds), *Sustainability and Private Law* (Eleven International Publishers 2019).

Robertson A and Goudkamp J, 'Between Form and Substance' in Andrew Robertson and James Goudkamp (eds), *Form and Substance in the Law of Obligations* (Hart 2019).

Rosenberg R, 'Fixing a Broken Common Law – Has the Property Law of Easements and Covenants Been Reformed by a Restatement?' (2016) 44 *Florida State U L Rev*.

Rostill L, *Possession, Relative Title, and Ownership in English Law* (OUP 2021).

Rowan M, *Slow Burn City* (Picador 2017).

Rubin PH (ed), *The Evolution of Efficient Common Law* (Edward Elgar 2007).

Rudden B, 'Economic Theory v. Property Law: The Numerus Clausus Problem' in John Eekelaar and John Bell (eds), *Oxford Essays in Jurisprudence. Third Series* (Clarendon 1987).

Rüthers B, 'Methodenrealismus in Jurisprudenz und Justiz' (2006) 61 *JZ* 53.

Sacco R, 'Legal Formants: A Dynamic Approach to Comparative Law (Installment I of II)' (1991) 39 *Am J Comp L* 1.

——, 'Legal Formants: A Dynamic Approach to Comparative Law (Installment II of II)' (1991) 39 *Am J Comp L* 343.

Sage NW, 'Original Acquisition and Unilateralism: Kant, Hegel, and Corrective Justice' (2012) 25 *CJLJ* 119.

Samuel G, 'Common Law' in Jan M Smits (ed), *Elgar Encyclopedia of Comparative Law* (2nd edn, Edward Elgar 2012).

——, *An Introduction to Comparative Law Theory and Method* (Hart 2014).

Samuelson PA and Nordhaus WD, *Economics* (19th edn, McGraw-Hill 2010).

Savigny FC von, *Vom Beruf Unserer Zeit für Gesetzgebung und Rechtswissenschaft* (Mohr und Zimmer, 1814).

——, *System des Heutigen Römischen Rechts*, vol 1 (Veit & Comp 1840).

Schäfer H-B and Ott K, *The Economic Analysis of Civil Law* (2nd edn, Elgar 2022).

Schefczyk M, 'John Stuart Mill: Ethics' in James Fieser and Bradley Dowden (eds), *The Internet Encyclopedia of Philosophy*.

Schmoeckel M, 'Omnia Sunt Regis: Vom Allgemeinen Eigentum des Königes zur Enteignung des Bürger. Ein Überblick zur Geschichte der Enteignung bis zum 18. Jahrhundert', *Die Enteignung. Historische, vergleichende und politische Perspectiven auf ein Rechtsinstitut* (Springer 2017).

Schubert W, 'Die Diskussion über eine Reform des Rechts der Mobiliarsicherheiten in der Späten Kaiserzeit und in der Weimarer Zeit' (1990) 107 *ZRG Germ Abt* 132.

Schwab D and Löhnig M, *Einführung in das Zivilrecht* (20th edn, CF Müller 2016).

Seiler HH, 'Einleitung zum Sachenrecht' in Elmar Bund and others (eds), *J. von Staudingers Kommentar zum Bürgerlichen Gesetzbuch mit Einführungsgesetz und Nebengesetzen* (Sellier & de Gruyter 2007).

Sherwin E, 'Formalism and Realism in Private Law' in Andrew S Gold and others (eds), *The Oxford Handbook of New Private Law* (OUP 2021).

Shiravini F, 'Entwicklung des Enteignungsrechts vom Frühen 19. Jahrhundert bis Zur Weimarer Reichsverfassung', *Die Enteignung. Historische, vergleichende und politische Perspectiven auf ein Rechtsinstitut* (Springer 2017).

Siems M, *Comparative Law* (2nd edn, CUP 2018).

Simon T, '"Grundrechtstotalitarismus" oder "Selbstbehauptung des Zivilrechts"' (2004) 204 *AcP* 264.

Singer JW, 'Democratic Estates: Property Law in a Free and Democratic Society' (2009) 94 Cornell L Rev 1009.

Smith HE, 'Property as the Law of Things' (2012) 125 Harv L Rev 1691.

——, 'Introduction' in Kenneth Ayotte and Henry E Smith (eds), *Research Handbook on the Economics of Property Law* (Edward Elgar 2012).
——, 'Emergent Property' in James Penner and Henry Smith (eds), *Philosophical Foundations of Property Law* (OUP 2013).
——, 'Economics of Property Law' in Francesco Parisi (ed), *The Oxford Handbook of Law and Economics: Volume 2: Private Law and Commercial Law* (OUP 2017).
——, 'Equity as Meta-Law' (2021) 130 *Yale LJ* 1050.
Smith L, 'Constructive Fiduciaries?' in Peter Birks (ed), *Privacy and Loyalty* (OUP 1997).
——, 'Trust and Patrimony' (2008) 38 *Rev Gen Dr* 379.
Smits J, *The Making of European Private Law* (Intersentia 2002).
Spamann H, 'Civil v. Common Law: The Emperor Has No Clothes' (2024) 24–11 Harvard Public Law Working Paper.
Sparkes P, 'Certainty of Property: Numerus Clausus or the Rule with No Name?' (2012) 20 *Euro Rev Priv L* 769.
Sprau H, 'Unerlaubte Handlungen', *Palandt. Bürgerlicher Gesetzbuch mit Nebengesetzten* (80th edn, Beck 2021).
Stigler GJ, *The Theory of Price* (3rd ed, Macmillan NY; Collier-Macmillan 1966).
Struycken T, *De Numerus Clausus in Het Goederenrecht* (Kluwer 2007).
Stürner R, 'Sachenrechtsbereinigung Zwischen Restitution, Bestandsschutz und Rechtssicherheit' (1993) 48 *JZ* 1074.
——, 'Dienstbarkeit Heute' (1994) 194 *AcP* 265.
Summers R, 'Two Types of Substantive Reasons: The Core of a Theory of Common-Law Justification' (1978) 63 *Cornell L Rev* 707.
——, 'How is Law Formal and Why it Matters' (1997) 82 *Cornell L Rev* 1165.
Swadling W, 'Opening the Numerus Clausus' (2000) 116 *LQR* 354.
——, 'Property: General Principles' in Andrew Burrows (ed), *English Private Law* (3th edition, OUP 2013).
——, 'In Defence of Formalism' in Andrew Robertson and James Goudkamp (eds), *Form and Substance in the Law of Obligations* (Hart 2019).
Tebbit M, *The Philosophy of Law. An Introduction* (2nd edn, Routledge 2005).
Televantos A, *Capitalism before Corporations: The Morality of Business Associations and the Roots of Commercial Equity and Law* (OUP 2021).
'The West India Docks: Historical Development', *Survey of London: Volume 43 and 44, Poplar, Blackwall and the Isle of Dogs* (Hermione Hobhouse 1994).
Torp C, 'The Great Transformation: German Economy and Society, 1850–1914' in Helmut Walser Smith (ed), *The Oxford Handbook of Modern German History* (OUP 2011).
Underhill A, 'Property' (1932) 51 *LQR* 221.
Urmson JO, 'The Interpretation of the Moral Philosophy of J. S. Mill' (1953) 3 *Phil Q* 33.
Valsan R, 'Rights against Rights and Real Obligations' in Lionel Smith (ed), *The Worlds of the Trust* (CUP 2013).
Vargas Weil E, 'Map and Territory in Comparative Law & Economics' (2022) 11 *Global J Comp L* 1.
——, 'The Numerus Clausus and the Governance of Property Law: A Comparative Approach to German, English and American Legal Reasoning' (2024) 11 *EJCL & G* 330.
Vernon J, *Modern Britain: 1750 to the Present* (CUP 2017).
Virgo G, *The Principles of Equity and Trusts* (5th edn, OUP 2023).
Vogenauer S, 'Sources of Law and Legal Method in Comparative Law' in Mathias Reimann and Reinhard Zimmermann (eds), *The Oxford Handbook of Comparative Law* (2nd edn, OUP 2019).
Wacks R, *Law: A Very Short Introduction* (2nd edn, OUP 2015).
Wagner G, 'Comparative Tort Law' in Mathias Reimann and Reinhard Zimmermann (eds), *The Oxford Handbook of Comparative Law* (2nd edn, OUP 2019).

Wagner-von Papp F, 'Comparative Law & Economics and the Egg-Laying Wool-Milk Sow' (2014) 9 *J Comp L* 137.
Waldron J, *The Right to Private Property* (OUP 1988).
Walsh R, 'Stability and Predictability in English Property Law – the Impact of Article 8 of the European Convention on Human Rights Reassessed' (2015) 131 *LQR* 585.
——, *Property Rights and Social Justice. Progressive Property in Action* (CUP 2021).
Walt A van der and Walsh R, 'Comparative Constitutional Property Law' in Michele Graziadei and Lionel Smith (eds), *Comparative Property Law: Global Perspectives* (Edward Elgar 2017).
Wank R, *Die Auslegung von Gesetzen* (6th edn, Vahlen 2015).
Ward R, Wragg A and Walker RJ, *Walker & Walker's English Legal System* (10th edn, OUP 2008).
Watson A, *Legal Transplants: An Approach to Comparative Law* (2nd ed., University of Georgia Press 1993).
——, 'From Legal Transplants to Legal Formants' (1995) 43 *Am J Comp L* 469.
——, *Society and Legal Change* (Temple UP 2001).
Webb C and Akkouh T, *Trusts Law* (5th edn, Palgrave 2017).
Weichlein S, 'Nation State, Conflict Resolution, and Culture War' in Helmut Walser Smith (ed), *The Oxford Handbook of Modern German History* (OUP 2011).
Weidenkaff W, 'Einzelene Schuldverhältnisse. Titel 5. Mietvertrag, Pachtvertrag', *Palandt. Bürgerlicher Gesetzbuch mit Nebengesetzten* (80th edn, Beck 2021).
Weinrib EJ, *The Idea of Private Law* (rev edn, OUP 2012).
——, 'Ownership, Use, and Exclusivity: The Kantian Approach' (2018) 31 *Ratio Juris* 123.
Weir T, *Economic Torts* (OUP 1997).
——, 'Pushing the Envelope of Proprietary Interests: The Nadir of the Numerus Clausus Principle?' (2015) 39 *MULR* 651.
Wellenhofer M, *Sachenrecht* (34th edn, Beck 2019).
Whittaker S and Zimmermann R, 'Good Faith in European Contract Law: Surveying the Legal Land Scape' in Reinhard Zimmermann and Simon Whittaker (eds), *Good Faith in European Contract Law* (CUP 2000).
Wieacker F, *A History of Private Law in Europe with Particular Reference to Germany* (Tony Weir tr, Clarendon 1995).
——, *Privatrechtsgeschichte der Neuzeit unter besonderer Berücksichtigung der deutschen Entwicklung* (3rd edn, Vandenhoeck & Ruprecht 2016).
Wiecke H, 'Gesetz über das Wohnungseigentum und das Dauerwohnrecht', *Palandt. Bürgerlicher Gesetzbuch mit Nebengesetzten* (80th edn, Beck 2021).
Wiegand W, 'Numerus Clausus der Dingliche Rechte. Zur Entstehung und Bedeutung eines Zentralen Zivilrechtlichen Dogmas' in Gerhard Köbler (ed), *Karl Kroeschell zum 60. Geburtstag dargelegt von Freunden, Schülern und Kollegen*, vol 60 (Verlag Peter Lang 1987).
——, 'Die Entwicklung des Sachenrechts im Verhältnis zum Schuldrecht' (1990) 1/2 *AcP* 112.
——, 'Funktion und Systematische Stellung des Sachenrechts im BGB' in Michael Martinek and Patrick L Sellier (eds), *J. von Staudingers Kommentar zum Bürgerlichen Gesetzbuch mit Eiführungsgesetz und Nebengesetzen. 100 Jahre BGB – 100 Jahre Staudinger* (Sellier & de Gruyter 1999).
Wieser E, 'Der Schadensersatzanspruch des Besitzers Aaus § 823 BGB' [1970] *Juristische Schulung* 557.
Wilhelm J, *Sachenrecht* (5th edn, De Gruyter 2016).
Williams I, 'The Certainty of Term Requirement in Leases: Nothing Lasts Forever' (2015) 74 *CLJ* 592.
Wilson W and Barton C, 'Leasehold and Commonhold Reform' (House of Commons Library 2021) 8047.
Wolf M, 'Beständigkeit und Wandel im Sachenrecht' [1987] *NJW* 2647.
Worthington S, *Equity* (2nd edn, OUP 2006).

——, 'Revolution and Evolution in Private Law' in Sarah Worthington, Andrew Robertson and Graham Virgo (eds), *Revolution and Evolution in Private Law* (Hart 2018).

Xu L, 'Commonhold Developments in Practice' in Warren Barr (ed), *Modern Studies in Property Law*, vol 8 (Hart 2015).

Zimmermann R, 'Savigny's Legacy': Legal History, Comparative Law, and the Emergence of European Legal Science' (1996) 112 LQR 576.

——, *The Law of Obligations: Roman Foundations of the Civilian Tradition* (OUP 1996).

——, *The New German Law of Obligations: Historical and Comparative Perspectives* (OUP 2005).

Zipursky BC, 'Philosophy of Private Law' in Jules L Coleman, Kenneth Einar Himma and Scott J Shapiro (eds), *The Oxford Handbook of Jurisprudence and Philosophy of Law* (OUP 2004).

Zweigert K and Kötz H, *An Introduction to Comparative Law* (Tony Weir tr, 3rd edn, OUP 1998).

Index

www.ingramcontent.com/pod-product-compliance
Ingram Content Group UK Ltd.
Pitfield, Milton Keynes, MK11 3LW, UK
UKHW020242290926
15470UKWH00002B/688